International Partnership in Russia

International Partnership in Russia

Conclusions from the Oil and Gas Industry

James Henderson

Alastair Ferguson

First published 2014 by
PALGRAVE MACMILLAN

Palgrave Macmillan in the UK is an imprint of Macmillan Publishers Limited, registered in England, company number 785998, of Houndmills, Basingstoke, Hampshire RG21 6XS.

Palgrave Macmillan in the US is a division of St Martin's Press LLC, 175 Fifth Avenue, New York, NY 10010.

Palgrave Macmillan is the global academic imprint of the above companies and has companies and representatives throughout the world.

Palgrave® and Macmillan® are registered trademarks in the United States, the United Kingdom, Europe and other countries

ISBN: 978-1-137-35226-2

This book is printed on paper suitable for recycling and made from fully managed and sustained forest sources. Logging, pulping and manufacturing processes are expected to conform to the environmental regulations of the country of origin.

A catalogue record for this book is available from the British Library.

A catalog record for this book is available from the Library of Congress.

To my wife Liz and to my two children Abby and Alex, with much love and thanks for their support over the decade that it has taken to complete the work

J.H.

To Mashenka and Igor for your love, support and inspiration

A.F.

Contents

List of Figures

List of Tables

Acknowledgements

The authors would like to express their thanks to a number of people who have contributed their help and encouragement to the process of completing this book.

James Henderson:

Firstly I would like to thank my supervisor, Professor Slavo Radosevic from SSEES, whose practical assistance and advice were invaluable and whose patience and understanding were much appreciated during the completion of the doctoral thesis at London University which has formed the foundation for this book. I would also like to thank Alena Ledeneva and Tomas Mickiewicz for their helpful comments and suggestions at various stages during the process. A special mention should also go to Professor Philip Hanson and Professor Klaus Nielsen who examined my final thesis and gave me many useful comments on how to turn my work into a book.

My sincere gratitude also goes to various colleagues who have provided assistance and also allowed me the time away from work to pursue my academic research. At Wood Mackenzie Consultants in Edinburgh I would particularly like to thank Tim Lambert, Steve Halliday, Simon Frame and Paul Gregory for their support. I would also like to thank all my colleagues at Lambert Energy Advisory, and in particular Philip Lambert, Onursal Soyer, Olga Mordvinova and Alexander Landia, both for their contributions to my thoughts on various issues and also for their forbearance when I was focused more on academic rather than commercial endeavours.

Professor Jonathan Stern of the Oxford Institute for Energy Studies has also provided me with useful advice during various stages of my research, and I thank him for his help. In Moscow, Roland Nash, Steve Allen, Al Breach and Rory MacFarquhar also provided significant input, while my many conversations with fellow doctoral student Yuko Iji also provided many useful insights that contributed to my analysis.

A special word of thanks must also go to my co-author, Alastair Ferguson. His input has helped to turn a rather dry PhD thesis into a more living and practical analysis of the issues facing foreign investors in Russia. Furthermore, his insights have proved invaluable in reaching our definitive conclusions and his personal experiences have added a real-world perspective to a previously more theoretical analysis.

Finally I would also like to thank my wife Liz for her occasional editing and her constant support and encouragement, particularly when it all seemed too much of a struggle, and my children Abigail and Alex for stopping me from taking it all too seriously.

Alastair Ferguson:

The experience of working in Russia over the last ten years has been invaluable to me and provided me with some real insight into the Russian soul. Russia can be a curious mixture of fascination and frustration but it has a way of changing and shaping the way you think. I would therefore like to acknowledge the support from my ex-colleagues and many individuals at TNK-BP, BP and other Russian companies that I have had the pleasure to interact and engage with. In particular, the Russian staff in Moscow and the regions who helped me understand the complexity and ambiguity in the Russian business and political environment and how the Russian system really works. They helped me get under the skin of Russia and at the same time I established some lifelong friendships.

I would like to thank my Russian and international friends in Moscow and Irkutsk, who have also helped to shape my thinking and provided insight into the Russian reality. They have challenged my conventional ideas and provided valuable guidance and support. I would also like to thank the managing partners at Xenon Capital Partners where I have the opportunity to continue to expand my Russian knowledge and to my fellow Directors at JKX Oil and Gas where I get the opportunity to put into practice what I have learned.

I remain a strong believer in the potential of Russia and in constructive engagement with Russian partners with the proviso that you need to know how to engage and how to position and protect yourself.

Joint Acknowledgements

The authors would both like to acknowledge the help of John Lough, Kris Sliger and Peter Charow, who have provided invaluable assistance in the editing of the book, as they read some or all of the chapters and made comments on them. We are most grateful for their contributions which have significantly enhanced the quality of the analysis and conclusions. We would also thank Professor Yelena Kalyuzhnova at Reading University for her support in reading an initial draft and her encouragement in the process of finding a publisher.

We have also appreciated the assistance of the staff at Palgrave Macmillan, in particular the Senior Commissioning Editor Taiba Batool and Editorial

Assistant Ania Wronski for their hard work and support through the publication process. We are also very grateful to our copy editor Shirley Tan for her hard work and patience during the preparation of the book.

We would also like to thank all of the industry executives, investment bankers, consultants, government officials and journalists who gave up their time to talk to us as we conducted the research for the book. They remain anonymous as many of them wished their comments to remain off the record, but we thank them all for their kind contributions without which the analysis would have been impossible.

The input of everyone mentioned above has been invaluable and they have our grateful thanks, but of course any errors remain the responsibility of the authors alone.

Note on Transliteration

Throughout the text, the authors use the system of Russian transliteration developed by United States Library of Congress. However, exceptions are made in some cases of names commonly rendered differently in English (e.g. Yeltsin rather than El'tsin). When citing English language sources, the transliteration from the original source is preserved.

List of Abbreviations

AAR	Alfa Access Renova
ADR	American Depository Receipt
AMI	Area of Mutual Interest
bcm	Billion cubic metres
boe	barrels of oil equivalent
boepd	barrels of oil equivalent per day
bpd	Barrels per day
CFPC	Change in Foreign Partner Control
CIS	Commonwealth of Independent States
DP	Domestic Partner
EBRD	European Bank for Reconstruction and Development
ESPO	East Siberia Pacific Ocean
FDI	Foreign Direct Investment
FIG	Financial Industrial Group
FP	Foreign Partner
FSU	Former Soviet Union
GDP	Gross Domestic Product
HSE	Health, Safety and the Environment
IAS	International Accounting Standards
IEA	International Energy Agency
IJV	International joint venture
IMF	International Monetary Fund
IOC	International oil company
IPO	Initial Public Offering
JSC	Joint Stock Company
JV	Joint Venture
KGB	"Komitet gosudarstvennoy bezopasnosti" (National Security Agency of the Soviet Union)
KMO	Kaiser-Meyer-Olkin score
KMOC	Khanty-Mansiisk Oil Company
M&A	Mergers and Acquisitions
MET	Mineral Extraction Tax
MNC	Multinational corporation
MNE	Multinational enterprise
MoU	Memorandum of Understanding
MSA	Measure of Sampling Adequacy
NOC	National Oil Company

NPV	Net Present Value
NRDT	Natural Resource Depletion Tax
OECD	Organisation of Economic Co-operation and Development
OLI	Ownership, Location, Internalisation (Dunning's eclectic paradigm)
OLS	Ordinary Least Squares (regression)
OPEC	Organisation of Petroleum Exporting Countries
PPM	Planning and Performance Management
PR	Public Relations
PSA	Production Sharing Agreement
ROC	Russian Oil Company
SOE	State-Owned Enterprise
Tcf	Trillion cubic feet
US GAAP	US Generally Accepted Accounting Principles
USSR	Union of Soviet Socialist Republics
VIOC	Vertically Integrated Oil Company
WSR	Wilcoxson Signed Rank

Conversion Factors

	Equals	
1 tonne oil	7.3	barrels of oil equivalent
1 tonne condensate	8.0	barrels of oil equivalent
1 bcm gas	6.6	million barrels of oil equivalent
1 bcm gas	35.3	billion cubic feet of gas
1 bcm gas	0.9	million tonnes of oil equivalent

Source: BP Statistical Review 2012

Preface

> I cannot forecast to you the action of Russia. It is a riddle wrapped in a mystery inside an enigma; but perhaps there is a key. That key is Russian national interest.
>
> Winston Churchill, October 1939

The most well-known part of Winston Churchill's famous quote about the difficulty of understanding Russia ("it is a riddle wrapped in a mystery inside an enigma") is often cited as evidence that the country is impenetrable as a place to work and live for most foreigners. This book concerns the history of foreign involvement in the Russian and Soviet oil and gas industries, and there have certainly been enough examples of sub-optimal outcomes for international investors over that time to suggest that the enigma continues. Indeed the history of foreign company participation in the Russian oil and gas industry has often been one of unfulfilled potential. In the earliest years of the industry companies such as Royal Dutch Shell and Nobel Oil founded their dynasties on the back of oilfield developments in the Caucasus region, only to be stripped of their investments in the 1917 revolution. During the Soviet era foreign contractors were occasionally welcomed when the need for new technology became urgent, but essentially domestic players dominated the industry until the start of the 1990s, when the collapse of the USSR catalysed a sharp decline in what had then become the Russian oil and gas industry.

This collapse, caused by a lack of funds for investment in increasingly mature and dilapidated fields and infrastructure, offered the potential for significant co-operation between Russian and international oil companies in a region containing 10% of the world's proved oil and gas reserves.[1] Foreign oil companies had the capability to provide technology, management expertise and capital, while the domestic players had access to reserves as well as an understanding of how to operate within the emerging Russian institutional and business environment. The potential contribution of foreign companies was recognized by the political elite at an early stage, with President Yeltsin welcoming companies such as Shell, Exxon and Total into the first (and ultimately only) Production Sharing Agreements (PSAs) granted in Russia. However, the subsequent privatization of the Russian oil industry, and the fight for cheap assets that this catalysed among domestic entrepreneurs, undermined the investment opportunities for international oil companies

---

[1]Data from BP Statistical Review of World Energy, 2013

(IOCs), as they were often regarded as competitors for assets rather than potential partners in their development.

The arrival of President Putin in 2000 brought an end to an era of somewhat anarchic politics and domination by the business elite known as the "oligarchs", and initially suggested that more stable times would herald increased foreign investment. The formation of Russia's largest international joint venture, TNK-BP, in 2003, prompted a resurgence in IOC interest, but enthusiasm was then dented by the bankruptcy of Yukos, and the consequent rise of Russia's national oil company Rosneft introduced a period of state consolidation of the energy sector that once again precluded significant foreign involvement. However, the natural progression of the Russian oil industry from the exploitation of Soviet era assets, which has continued to produce wealth for the country and its oil entrepreneurs for the past 20 years, towards the development of more remote and challenging new fields has created a new opportunity for foreign oil companies. Suddenly their technical experience and financing capability are relevant to Russia again, as is their long experience of managing large oil and gas developments in the global arena, especially offshore. Joint ventures between Rosneft and Exxon, Statoil and ENI have focused on Arctic development and unconventional oil assets where domestic companies have little previous experience, while BP's position as a 19.75% shareholder in Russia's national oil company is a further example of the evolving foreign involvement in the country's oil sector.

However, at this time of increasing confidence that IOCs can have a long-term role in Russia's oil sector, we believe that it is appropriate to review the volatile history of foreign investment in the industry during the post-Soviet era. We have seen enthusiasm before, especially in the 1990s, but the outcome then was rarely positive for the IOCs involved. It might be argued that Russia has changed dramatically since those somewhat chaotic days, but we would assert that the differences are rather superficial and that the weak institutional structures which were in place then, and which were dominated by key business entrepreneurs, are still in place and remain weak today, being controlled by a different but equally influential elite group. As a result we would argue that there is much to be learnt from an analysis of the partnerships between foreign and domestic oil companies in Russia over the past two decades, from which we aim to draw conclusions not only about historical relationships but also about the potential for future positive engagement. To return to the Churchill quote, we believe that, although Russia is clearly a complex place to do business, one key to greater success is to work hard to understand the competitive advantages that have been used to bolster the interests of the country and its entrepreneurs over the past 20 years and to establish a strategy for balancing them with appropriate international contributions to create a more mutually beneficial partnership for the future.

In Chapter 1 we chart the history of the Russian oil industry since the 19th century, focusing on foreign company involvement. After a brief description of the Tsarist and Communist eras, when the might of the Soviet oil industry was constructed, we focus mainly on the post-Soviet era when initial collapse was followed by dramatic recovery as new production techniques were introduced to rehabilitate old fields, firstly through partnership with IOCs and then by domestic oil companies alone using equipment provided by oilfield contractors. We trace the turbulent history of foreign investment in the industry, from the early joint ventures, through the first equity investments to the current partnerships with Russia's national champions, Rosneft and Gazprom. We describe how the competitive landscape has changed and also how the dynamic business environment in Russia has affected the ability of foreign companies to bargain on equal terms with their domestic counterparts.

In Chapter 2 we provide a theoretical background for the discussion of partnership in a weak institutional environment. We briefly discuss some general theories of foreign investment, in particular in the oil and gas industry, before discussing the academic literature on joint ventures and establishing that learning and a competition for knowledge are at the heart of most partnerships. We then review the theories of state capture and establish how, in an environment in which institutions are inherently weak, local knowledge is a core competence for domestic entrepreneurs. We discuss how this core competence can be used and exploited in an asymmetric business environment to bargain with foreign partners in joint venture negotiations, and to balance the contributions of management, technology and finance brought by IOCs. However, we also establish that this balance can be lost if the foreigners, whose skills are relatively easy to transfer, do not make the effort to acquire local knowledge in return. Importantly we also argue that this is as relevant today, in the Putin/Medvedev era, as it was in the 1990s, showing that the institutional situation has not changed significantly despite the claims of current politicians that the power of the state has been restored.

In Chapter 3 we present a series of case studies of joint entities from the period 1990–2003 in order to allow the experiences of specific investors, both foreign and domestic, to create a platform for further discussion. We outline the history of each joint entity, based on documentary evidence, quotes from participants and interviews with the central players, before examining the key issue of how the relationship between the foreign and domestic partners developed. We aim to show how each party viewed the contributions of its partner, how these contributions became bargaining strengths over time and what actions (from a foreign partner perspective) contributed to the success or failure of the joint entity. In particular we focus on the issue of how the domestic partner's competitive advantage of local knowledge played a vital role not only in the formation of the joint entities but also as a continuing source of bargaining strength that most foreign investors found hard to counter.

In Chapter 4 we build on this subjective and personal evidence by presenting an objective survey of foreign participants in joint entities in the Russian oil and gas sector. We outline the results of a survey that included 33 respondents from international joint ventures and review some initial conclusions on the main characteristics of the partnerships before proceeding to a more detailed statistical analysis of the results, with the goal of establishing what the significant drivers of foreign partner success might be. Using a combination of statistical techniques we determine that one key predictor of greater foreign partner success is the willingness and ability of a foreign partner to participate in issues involving the use of local knowledge.

Chapter 5 brings our analysis up to date, as it is based on interviews with both foreign and domestic participants in the oil and gas sector in Russia over the past decade. We seek to show that the views of partners in international joint ventures have not altered much, with many describing the situation in 2013 as reminiscent of the 1990s. We highlight the importance of key individuals to the decision-making process, with the result that strong relationships and access to specific members of the political and business elite remain vital to any company or joint venture wishing to prosper. A number of interviewees offer their thoughts on how to optimize the balance in partnerships in such an environment, introducing the ideas of mutual learning, exchange of assets and long-term commitment as vital to success.

Chapter 6 then focuses on the experiences of one of the authors, Alastair Ferguson, as he describes his experiences both at TNK-BP and in other ventures in Russia. While not hiding from the fact that Russia is a very difficult place to operate as a foreigner, he emphasizes that with the appropriate cultural sensitivity, robustness of character, commitment to detailed analysis and willingness to adapt to a tough business environment it is certainly possible to engage successfully with a domestic partner in a profitable joint venture. Indeed TNK-BP offers the clearest example of a venture that certainly had its fair share of instability and partner disputes but nevertheless resulted in a very lucrative outcome for all the major partners, and even allowed BP to retain a significant position in the Russian oil industry.

Chapter 7 offers our conclusions and builds on the view that, although business life and the creation of partnerships in Russia involve very different experiences than most OECD-based businessmen normally encounter, it is nevertheless possible to operate successfully if you are prepared to adopt a rigorous and systematic approach to the potential problems. This approach involves not only acquiring local knowledge but most importantly applying it by becoming more involved in issues concerned with the domestic business environment, in other words being proactive in the process of knowledge transfer. As a means of pursuing this positive strategy, we offer in particular the concept of an engagement model that combines both protective and proactive measures that we believe can help to maintain the relevance of foreign companies in a weak institutional environment such as Russia. We believe that there is a need to fully understand the reality of the environment in which they are operating, using rigorous analysis and a wide network of relationships to create as full a picture as possible of the situation. Through this process it will become clear that, although there are challenging issues to be addressed, they are by no means insurmountable, and that the opportunities available in Russia can more than compensate for the effort needed to access them. We also believe that foreign companies can optimize their chances of success by being prepared to continuously renew their knowledge base and their contributions to any joint venture, by offering reciprocity both of assets outside Russia and also of mutual learning inside the country, and by ensuring that the resources they offer, in particular the staff they contribute, are of a high quality and are adaptable to the domestic environment.

As a final introductory note we would add that both of us have experienced the full range of positive and negative emotions involved in Russian business over the past 20 years, having worked in the country and analysed the energy economy there, and yet remain very positive about the potential for successful partnership between foreign and domestic players. We are firm believers in the need for constructive engagement with Russia but also in the need to develop a sustainable model. It is easy to categorize Russia as a flawed environment and to dismiss it as too difficult to deal with, but the expanding number of foreign companies now beginning to re-enter the Russian oil and gas sector suggests that the opportunities remain both interesting and very tempting. We believe that with the right mental, cultural and operational approach, foreign companies can be successful if they adopt a systematic process of engaging with the full range of key individuals, politicians, industry experts and domestic employees who will be at the heart of their business. Although this engagement can often be uncomfortable, in a working environment that is tough and confrontational, it can also provide huge mutual benefits to all the partners and stakeholders involved. Indeed, it can provide valuable experience for companies to use across their global operations. Russia is not unique in having a weak institutional environment where local knowledge is vital. There are many countries in a similar situation, and we hope that the lessons drawn from the examples in this book can provide useful insights which can assist in the formation of partnerships in many other countries where the governance of commercial transactions is more reliant on individual decision-makers than traditional institutional mechanisms.

1
The Turbulent History of Foreign Involvement in the Russian Oil and Gas Industry

Introduction

The history of the Russian oil industry dates back to the middle of the 19th century when oil was dug from pits near Baku, but the country's emergence by 1900 as a major global oil producer had much to do with the involvement of foreign investors. Indeed the development of one of the world's major oil companies, Shell, was based on its work in establishing production in southern Russia and a transport network to move its oil to the developing global market. In this chapter, we chart this early period of Russian oil history, which ended with the departure of foreign investors following the 1917 revolution, before describing the subsequent development of the Soviet oil industry. This occurred largely without foreign involvement, as first the oil fields in European Russia were brought on-stream in the 1930s and 40s and then the giant resources of West Siberia were explored and developed from the 1960s onwards. Russian oilmen remain rightly proud to this day of the achievements of their Soviet predecessors as they not only found and produced oil in vast quantities in the harshest of conditions but also constructed the massive infrastructure of rigs, pipelines and supply routes that still service the industry today.

However, as we describe in the second half of the chapter, the inadequacies of the Soviet command system, combined with a declining oil price in the late 1980s, led to increasingly desperate attempts to maintain oil production at the high levels of 10–11 million bpd that had been reached by that stage. When the collapse of the Soviet Union arrived in 1991 the consequent fall in oil production epitomized the decline in the then Russian economy, and we describe not only this fall but also how initially at least foreign companies were welcomed for the potential assistance they brought to arrest it. However, the emergence of wealthy and influential domestic entrepreneurs in the sector created a conflict of interest that caused significant turbulence for foreign companies, who were already struggling with the opaque legal and regulatory framework in the country. Although their help was wanted they were also viewed as potential competitors for cheap assets, and during the period of mass privatization in Russia during the late 1990s this led to ownership and governance issues which we describe in some detail.

The arrival of Vladimir Putin as Prime Minister and then President in 1999 has heralded a period during which the Russian state has re-asserted its position in the oil industry via its state-controlled companies Rosneft and Gazprom. This process in itself created initial uncertainty for all participants in the sector, but by 2003, despite the concern caused by the destruction of Yukos, foreign oil companies had started to return to Russia, led by BP and its investment in its huge partnership at TNK-BP. The subsequent decade has by no means been smooth sailing for foreign investors but has seen them gradually re-discover their position in the Russian oil industry, increasingly focused on partnership with the state companies or those closely related to them. As a result many of the major IOCs are now involved in partnerships that will help to develop the next stage of the Russian oil industry, developing offshore fields and unconventional resources to replace the gradual decline in the traditional oil-producing regions. This new set of partnerships means that foreign companies may be set to play as important a role in the future of Russian oil production as they did in its initial development 150 years ago, and this chapter aims to provide the historical context for a subsequent discussion of how this can occur in a manner that is beneficial for the Russian state and domestic and foreign investors alike.

The Russian oil and gas industry in a global context

By an accident of geography and geology Russia contains the largest hydrocarbon resource base in the world and is the largest global producer of oil and gas combined. According to the BP Statistical Review published in 2012 the country contains 88 billion barrels of oil reserves and 45 trillion cubic metres of gas, while producing a combined total of approximately 20 million barrels of oil equivalent (boe) per day. On a graph of global hydrocarbon producers only Saudi Arabia, Venezuela and Iran come close to Russia, and its huge undiscovered resource base marks it out as a country not just of current importance but also of future growth for the oil and gas industry. In a recent survey, for example, the USGS[1] estimated that two thirds of the world's total Arctic resources, amounting to more than 250 billion boe, are located in Russian waters, and regions such as East and West Siberia, the Black Sea and the Caspian Sea are believed to contain a further 150 billion boe.[2]

It should therefore be no surprise that the world's major oil companies are interested to seek investment opportunities amid this vast resource base, espe-

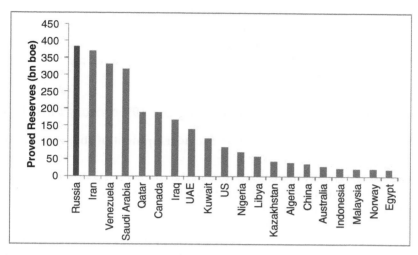

Figure 1.1 Top 20 countries by proved hydrocarbon reserves (2012)
Source: Graph created by author from data in BP Statistical Review of World Energy 2012

cially at a time when many of the world's other large hydrocarbon producing areas are not always open to foreign involvement. Access to the huge reserves located in the Middle East is in many cases closed to outsiders or at least very difficult to achieve for domestic or geo-political reasons, while other prolific oil and gas regions such as Latin America, Africa and Asia carry their own political and economic risks. North America has re-emerged as an expanding hydrocarbon opportunity thanks to its shale oil and gas reserves, but nevertheless the huge resources located in post-Soviet Russia have demanded the attention of the global oil industry for the past 23 years, even if not everyone has decided that the potential rewards are worth the risk.

However, this situation is not unique to the 20th or 21st centuries, as in the 19th century Russia also offered an alternative investment location for oil companies excluded from the opportunities in the world's largest oil producer at the time, the US. As we will discuss in the next section, the turbulence of the late Tsarist period offered huge opportunity for foreign players and even helped to create one of the world's major oil companies, but also brought other investors to their knees as domestic politics wreaked havoc with the commercial landscape. The Soviet era then brought 70 years of exclusion for foreign companies as the USSR developed its giant fields and their attendant infrastructure alone, but low oil prices and economic decline in the 1990s finally brought the industry close to collapse. Since 1991 opportunities for foreign investment in the now Russian oil and gas industry have again emerged, but once again turbulence and volatility have been key features of the commercial environment. We therefore chart the history of the post-Soviet industry as a whole, before describing the changing role of foreign investors and the fate that befell them in the ever-changing world of Russian domestic politics, vested interests and changing commercial priorities.

The Russian oil and gas industry from the 19th century until 1930

Foreign investment was the key to the development of the early Russian oil industry

The history of the oil industry in Russia, the involvement of foreigners in it and the impact this has had on the global energy economy really dates back to the second half of the 19th century. At that stage 82 hand-dug pits were producing miniscule amounts of oil around Baku next to the Caspian Sea, and further development seemed unlikely thanks to the remoteness of the region and the incompetence of the Tsar's administration. As a result, it was not until competitive private enterprise was allowed in the 1870s that the first oil wells were drilled and output began to increase rapidly.

The key catalyst for entrepreneurial activity in the region was the introduction of an efficient public auction system for exploration and production leases in 1873, which extended the lease term beyond the previous four years and encouraged more serious investment. The result was that oil production expanded 15-fold over the next decade.[3] The arrival of Robert Nobel to Baku in March 1873 was a further catalyst for growth in Russian oil production. A Swede whose father had emigrated to Russia in the early 19th century, Nobel became entranced with the opportunities that he saw for Russian oil, and having secured imperial blessing he set about acquiring oil assets and modernizing the industry. Learning from the experience of America, which had a 20-to 30-year head start on Russia, he improved drilling and refining technology, brought in more efficient business practices and consolidated his business into a major industrial concern.[4] Most importantly he also improved the domestic transport system, building the first oil pipeline system in Russia and the first oil tanker in the world, which he used to move oil across the Caspian Sea and on to the major markets of Moscow and St. Petersburg.[5] As a result the first significant Russian oil company was born, albeit that the Nobel Brothers Petroleum Producing Company was owned by foreigners.

The sharp increase in Russian oil production, combined with the introduction of hefty import tariffs, also created the first major clash in the global oil market. In the early 1870s the American oil industry had targeted Russia as a major potential export market, and by 1884 imports from the United States had reached 4,400 tonnes, three times the level of indigenous Russian production. By 1896, however, this had dwindled to an insignificant 22 tonnes, as

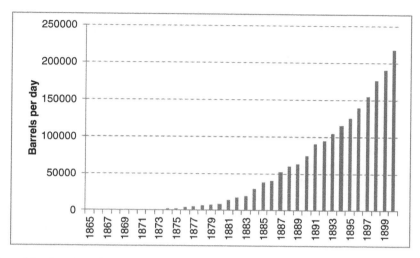

Figure 1.2   Russian oil production, 1865–1900
Source: Graph created by author from data collected from Alekperov, V. (2011) "Oil of Russia" and Yergin, D. (1990) "The Prize"

the Russians not only had sufficient crude oil to supply their home market but also to seek to compete in the European export market.[6]

Despite the Nobel family's success in saturating the domestic crude oil market, the limitations of domestic demand and the cost of transporting oil within Russia meant that any profit maximization strategy must involve exports. With the Nobel family dominating the domestic market, other Russian producers were also forced to look for alternatives, and following the defeat of the Turks by the Russian army at Batum in 1878, the possibility of an export route to Europe through the Black Sea became a reality. Two Russian producers named Bunge and Palashkovsky began to build a railroad from Baku over the Caucasus mountains to Batum. Running short of funds due to a fall in the oil price they turned to the Nobel family for assistance, but having been refused they found a new backer, the Rothschild family, who had been looking for an alternative crude oil supply for their Fiume refinery on the Adriatic coast in order to reduce their dependence on oil supplies from Standard Oil in the US.[7] The railroad was completed in 1883–1884, and Russian oil exports then expanded rapidly. Indeed by the end of the century Russia had become the world's largest oil producer and exporter,[8] initiating the first major struggle for domination of the global oil market.

Despite an initial attempt by Standard Oil to react to this new competition by cutting oil prices, Russian crude oil became firmly established in the European and Asian markets, with the latter being a particular region of competitive strength.[9] Indeed the Shell Oil Company, now Royal Dutch Shell, was founded on its owner Marcus Samuel's entrepreneurial insight that the export of Russian kerosene to the East could be facilitated by the use of the Suez Canal and the building of storage depots throughout the Asian continent.

However, in a foretaste of events later in the 20th century, the rapid expansion of Russia's oil industry was to lay the foundations for its first period of stagnation. So productive were many of the wells drilled in the Caucasus in the late 19th century that little thought was given to production planning, improving technology or conservation. By 1900 3,000 wells had been drilled in the Baku region alone,[10] but Russian output then peaked in 1901 at just under 12 million tonnes (240 thousand bpd), at which point it was contributing 7% of the country's export earnings.[11] However, this level of output was not achieved again for almost three decades. The continued use of primitive production methods and a failure to import more modern techniques from the West was one major factor in the stagnation of the early 20th century, with the primitive and dangerous sump production method used in the 1860s still being employed by some producers in 1913.[12] However, corporate rivalry, commercial scheming, a changing fiscal regime and domestic political unrest also contributed to unease among producers and a reluctance to invest in output growth. In particular competition for global market share led to the oil entrepreneurs cutting world prices for kerosene at a time when the Tsarist authorities were attempting to increase their share of oil revenues by changing the concession system.[13] This clearly undermined the economics of investment in the oil industry at a time when the political risks were being increased by a series of wildcat strikes initiated by amongst others a young Joseph Stalin. These reached a climax in 1905 with the first revolution against the Tsarist regime, leading to a 3 million tonne drop in oil output that year alone. Although the situation improved enough over the next few years for Royal Dutch Shell (as it had become) to feel confident enough to buy out the Rothschild family oil interests in 1911, Russian output did not recover significantly prior to the 1917 revolution. Again, in a harbinger of future disputes, blame for this continued stagnation was placed by some at the door of the "oil magnates", who were accused of encouraging under-investment in order to protect their own monopoly positions.[14] Whatever the underlying cause, by 1913 Russia's share of world exports had fallen from a peak of 31% to only 9% and by the time of the revolution in 1917 output had fallen to below the level it had been at the turn of the century.

The advent of the Bolshevik revolution in 1917 brought a further collapse in output, with production in 1918 being less than half the level seen just one year before. Interestingly, though, despite the formal announcement of the nationalization of the country's oil fields on 6 June 1918, foreign oil company involvement in Russia/the Soviet Union did not come to an immediate halt.

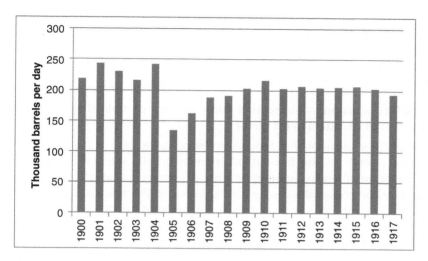

Figure 1.3   Russian oil production, 1900–1917
Source: Graph created by author from data collected from Alekperov, V. (2011) "Oil of Russia" and Yergin, D. (1990) "The Prize"

Initially the Turks, and then the British, seized Baku, with the latter attempting to form an independent state of Azerbaijan.[15] With this effective denationalization of the region's oil assets, Standard Oil attempted to exploit the situation and strengthen its position in an area where it had been competitively weak by buying up concessions and acquiring the stock of Nobel Oil. However, by 1920 the British had been evicted from Baku and Standard's investment was worthless.

Despite this further setback, the relationship between foreign capital and Russian oil was not completely terminated. The Bolsheviks discovered that the combination of a sudden loss of western oil expertise and a western oil company boycott of Russian oil exports was enough to undermine production yet further, and it fell to 3.78 million tonnes in 1921. However, the embargo against Russian exports was as weak as the resolve to completely exclude foreigners from Russian oil assets. As Shell began to purchase Russian crude oil again in 1923, Lenin authorized the use of foreign help to boost production under the New Economic Plan. An American company, Barnsdall Corporation, had actually been operating in the Soviet Union since 1921,[16] and it not only brought in more advanced technology to restore production but also encouraged other foreign investors, including British Petroleum (later renamed BP). The result was an impressive rebound in output to a historical high of more than 13 million tonnes by 1929 thanks both to domestic investment and foreign technical assistance in the exploration, production and refining businesses.[17] However, the recovery in output led to a reversal of

Soviet policy, and almost all new agreements with foreign oil companies had been cancelled by 1930. Apart from a few contracts with companies such as Badger, Universal Oil and Lummus to rebuild refineries,[18] the history of direct foreign involvement in the Russian/Soviet oil industry came to an end until almost the end of the Soviet era in the late 1980s.

Initial conclusion – There is a long history of volatility for foreign investors in the Russian oil sector

Overall, it is apparent that foreign investment was one of the key catalysts for the growth of the Russian oil industry in the late 19th century. The introduction of new technology and business practices saw the emergence of integrated oil companies run by the Nobel and Rothschild families that could rival the current industry monolith, Standard Oil of the US. As it became clear that output from Russia could provide a balance to previous US dominance, the first global competition for oil markets emerged and companies such as Royal Dutch Shell used the purchase of Russian oil assets to diversify their international portfolios in competition with Standard Oil. Indeed by the end of the 19th century, Russia had become the world's largest oil producer and exporter. However, a combination of technological lethargy, political turbulence, corporate rivalry and the Russian government's fiscal demands brought about stagnation in the Russian oil industry in the early years of the 20th century that culminated in the ousting of foreigners after the 1917 revolution. The subsequent production collapse was reversed in the 1920s with foreign help, but foreigners were again effectively excluded from direct involvement in the industry from 1930 onwards.

The Soviet era from 1930 to 1990: Development of the Volga-Urals and West Siberia regions

Despite the lack of foreign involvement, overall production from the Soviet Union continued to climb as Stalin's government used growing hydrocarbon output to fuel the country's industrial revolution. From a level of 18 million tonnes (360 thousand bpd) in 1930 total production reached more than 33 million tonnes (660 thousand bpd) in 1939, located almost entirely in the original Baku area and the newly developed fields in and around Grozny in the north Caucasus region. However, the advent of World War Two (or the Great Patriotic War as it is known in Russia), combined with the increasing maturity of exiting fields in the USSR, meant that by 1945 output had fallen back to 21 million tonnes (422 thousand bpd), leaving the Soviet Union in need of a new source of oil production and revenues.[19]

This new source was provided by the discovery of a huge hydrocarbon province in the Volga-Urals region, and as a result the history of the modern

Russian oil industry really begins with the development of the extensive reserves in this area after 1945. Oil had first been discovered in the Volga-Urals in 1929, and production from the area was only 2 million tonnes per annum (40 thousand bpd) by the time the Great Patriotic War commenced in 1941, but output grew so rapidly in the post-war years that overall production from the Soviet Union reached a new high of 36.5 million tonnes (730 thousand bpd) in 1949. Production from the Volga-Urals region continued to climb until the 1970s as huge fields, such as Romashkino in Tatarstan, were discovered. However, after two decades of growth from the area all the major discoveries had been made and reserves, and therefore production, became increasingly difficult to replace. Gustafson (1989) notes[20] that this trend was exacerbated by a sharp slump in exploration drilling in the late 1960s, while Goldman (1980) observes that attempts to halt the slide in production at many fields were unsuccessful.[21] The use of secondary recovery techniques such as water injection often brought only short-term benefits, if they worked at all, and the increasing share of water being brought to the surface sharply increased the unit costs of oil output.

As production from Volga-Urals began to stagnate in the early 1970s, geologists in the recently discovered West Siberia region then came under increasing pressure to deliver the growth that was needed to sustain oil output.[22] Following the discovery of the super-giant Samotlor field in 1968[23] output from the region increased dramatically and by 1977 the Tyumen region, where Samotlor is located, had increased its annual production seven-fold to 210 million tonnes (4.2 million bpd). As Gustafson describes it: "Samotlor is one of the wonders of the oil world....Its crucial role can be judged by the fact that the Nizhnevartovsk Oil Association, within which Samotlor is located, supplied 89.6 million tonnes of the total 116.6 million tonnes of the net increase in West Siberian output during 1971–75, or 77 percent."[24]

However, the outstanding performance of West Siberia in compensating for the downturn in output from the Volga-Urals region was to create its own problems, as Soviet planners assumed that success would be easy to replicate. Unfortunately, this overconfidence was to sow the seeds of the first Soviet oil crisis even as West Siberian production was reaching its initial peak. Essentially the problem was four-fold. Firstly, exploration funding had been focused on attempts to bolster output in older producing regions rather than in West Siberia, with the result that the Russian oil industry did not replace its asset base fast enough. The almost inevitable consequence was that existing assets were pushed too hard in a desperate attempt to meet production targets. The 120–125 million tonne target for West Siberia in 1975 was achieved with relative ease, with final output being over 140 million tonnes, but the very aggressive 300–310 million tonne target for 1980 was only just met (the final output being just under 304 million tonnes).[25] Indeed by the end of the 1970s

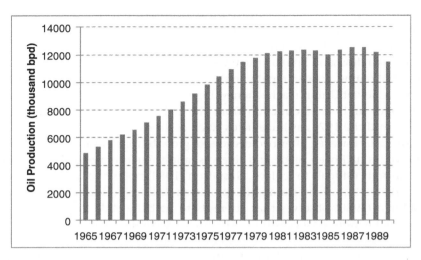

Figure 1.4 Oil production from the Soviet Union, 1965–1990
Source: Graph created by author from data in BP Statistical Review of World Energy 2012

the Soviet authorities had already begun to respond to the urgent requests of the oil industry for more funding, but the roots of this first crisis were to haunt the Soviet and then the Russian oil industry for the next two decades.

Secondly the entrenched bureaucracy in the central administration, many of whom had begun their careers in the older producing regions, preferred to attempt to sustain output in those regions rather than accelerate it in the new heartland of West Siberia. Thirdly, and perhaps more crucially, technology was starting to let the Soviet oil industry down in a significant manner for the first time. As one example Marshall Goldman (1980)[26] quotes an American manufacturer as stating that his drill bits could carve out 6–8.5 metres per day compared to one metre for a Soviet bit, and that his drill bits could last five to 20 times longer than a Soviet bit. It is therefore not surprising that Soviet drilling teams were struggling to keep up with ever more demanding targets throughout the 1970s and 1980s. A fourth legacy of the Soviet system that undermined all parts of the economy during the latter part of the Soviet era and continued to plague the oil industry well into the 1990s was the perverse incentive system. This effectively encouraged a focus on investing to meet short-term goals rather than planning for longer-term optimization of assets and meant that the only response to a stagnation of oil production was a huge increase in investment. This was precisely the response of the Brezhnev government in 1977, when a massive increase in development drilling was combined with a significant shift of emphasis towards Western Siberia. However, the attainment of short-term production goals came at the cost of reduced efficiency, meaning that as soon as spending slowed, the fundamental problems of the industry re-appeared – short-sighted production practices, excessive reliance on a small number of older fields, low drilling productivity and neglected well repair and maintenance.[27] Essentially the Soviet authorities lost sight of the need for investment in the efficient long-term development of their hydrocarbon resources, instead spending huge sums on short-term projects in a desperate drive to sustain immediate revenues. As a result, although oil production did reach a peak of 625 million tonnes (12.5 million bpd) in 1987/88 (BP, 2009),[28] the seeds for its sharp decline had already been laid and resulted in the collapse that occurred as the Soviet Union came to an end in the early 1990s.

The seeds of the Russian oil collapse in the 1990s were sown in the Soviet era

Thane Gustafson, in his recent history of the Russian oil industry "Wheel of Fortune" (Gustafson, 2012) provides a clear insight into the problems faced by the Soviet oil industry at the end of the 1980s. As he clearly shows, despite the heroic efforts of an industry operating under the harshest of conditions "some of the very things that had made [the Soviet oil industry] great also made it fragile. Many of its practices – adaptations to the constraints of the centrally planned system – aged the fields prematurely. By the end of the 1980s, the Soviet oil industry was struggling."[29] Examples of this struggle included the inefficient use of waterflooding, an oil reservoir management technique that involves pumping water into oil fields to "sweep" out the oil but which, if executed inefficiently, can lead to excessive water, rather than oil, production. Unfortunately this was the case in the Soviet Union, as a lack of modern modelling systems and excessive political pressure to increase output led to excessive drilling of water injection wells, with the result that by 1991 the share of water in each barrel of liquids produced had reached an astonishing average of 80%.[30] Further evidence that the efficiency of many Soviet operating techniques was clearly below international standards was provided by the fact that average well output had fallen by more than 30% in only five years to reach 11.5 tonnes per well in 1990, while the number of wells that remained idle due to a lack of maintenance work had quadrupled in the period 1986 to 1991 and accounted for almost 10% of the total well stock. Essentially the Soviet oil industry had to apply out-of-date techniques ever more rapidly and at ever greater expense to a portfolio of fields that by the end of the 1980s had reached maturity and was on the point of going into natural decline.

President Mikhail Gorbachev summarized the impending crisis in the oil industry in a speech in 1987, stating that "the striving to restrain the fall of growth rates led to making inordinate expenditures to expand the fuels and energy sector, to bringing new natural resources into production at forced rates, and to using them irrationally".[31] As Gustafson explains, markets and economics had no place in the Soviet world of administratively set production targets, with the result that "the true costs of developing and producing Soviet oil, being largely invisible, were systematically discounted".[32] However, reality could not be ignored for much longer due to a combination of three factors that ultimately culminated in the disintegration not only of the Soviet oil industry but also of the Soviet Union itself. Firstly, "the Soviet oil industry was running up against an inexorable fact of nature: the rate of discovery of large new oil fields was slowing down...[with the result that] Soviet oilmen were developing ever-smaller and more costly fields".[33] Secondly, just as costs of production were rising, the oil price went into decline, falling from an average of almost $37 per barrel in 1980 to below $15 per barrel in 1988.[34] This led to a more than halving of rents from the oil industry from $270 billion per year in 1980/81 to less than $100 billion in 1986 and beyond,[35] with disastrous consequences for the entire Soviet economy.

The third factor which undermined the Soviet oil industry was President Gorbachev's drive to restructure the command economy, known as "perestroika". Despite having the noblest of intentions, namely to introduce gradually the forces of market economics onto the Soviet system and to reduce the overbearing influence of state bureaucracy, in fact the weakening of central government authority that it caused led to chaos in the oil industry and across the economy as a whole when it was combined with the fall in oil prices described above. Funding for oil industry expenditure fell sharply (by 47% between 1985 and 1989) while demands for increasing production remained in place, leading to a stand-off between the oil men and their government bosses. Ultimately the heads of individual production associations began to rebel and either cut production or demanded their own export quotas in order to generate cash to spend on maintaining their facilities. Furthermore senior oil figures such as Vagit Alekperov, now head of LUKOIL but then the head of the Kogalym production association (the "K" in LUKOIL), began to form the plans for independent oil companies that were to emerge in the post-Soviet era.

Interestingly, one of the other consequences of "perestroika" was the involvement of foreign companies in the Soviet oil industry for the first time since the 1920s. In 1988 the government authorized oil-producing companies to form joint ventures (JVs) with foreign oil-service companies in order to attract the technology that was increasingly needed to maintain Soviet oil production.[36] Any extra oil produced by the new JVs over the planned targets could be exported, with the proceeds being kept in separate hard currency accounts overseas, which opened a world of new opportunity for the Soviet oil industry and its leaders. Companies such as Canadian Fracmaster were introduced to Russian production companies such as Yugankneftegaz, who formed a highly successful JV called Yuganskfracmaster in 1989 to perform fracking work on a number of Yugansk fields, and in particular the giant Mamontovo field on the south side of the Ob River in West Siberia.[37] With well productivity improved from an average of 15 barrels per day to almost 130 barrels per day, and in some cases to a maximum level of 500 barrels per day, this initial JV and others like it demonstrated the potential that could be gained from the application of international technology to Soviet legacy oil fields.

However, the introduction of joint ventures and the consequent opportunities for generating hard currency outside Russia also encouraged those with access to oil production to exploit the weakening governance system as the Soviet Union collapsed. The use of schemes to transfer revenues away from legal entities to private ventures, the re-allocation of assets to new ventures owned by well-connected individuals, the exploitation of access to preferential export allocations and the use of legal entities to disguise the laundering of illegal revenues[38] were all prevalent at this time and heralded their wide use in Russia during the 1990s. As a result, even before the Soviet Union ended foreign companies were already being exposed to the vagaries of a weak state environment and the opportunities available to those who had local knowledge and knew how to use it. As we will discuss in Chapters 3 and 4, it tended to be the case that, although the foreigners could gain some initial benefits, sustaining a profitable position for the long term was to prove much more problematic.

The oil industry after the collapse of the USSR

Disintegration and initial restructuring

The weakening of the Soviet state was initiated by Gorbachev, who in 1988 started to reduce the staff at many of the government ministries and also shut down the economic departments of the Communist Party that had been responsible for co-ordinating industrial activity across the Soviet Union.[39] During the Soviet era the oil industry had been controlled by a horizontal structure of ministries, with no single co-ordinating central authority. Hydrocarbon extraction was controlled by Minnefteprom, refineries by Minneftekhimprom, distribution of oil products by Gosnab and exports by Soyuzneft Export (a division of the Ministry of Foreign Trade). Exploration and exploitation came under three ministries (Geology, Minnefteprom and Mingazprom). In addition there were Ministries of Oil Equipment Building and Gas Equipment Building.[40] Importantly, though, during the 1980s a Bureau for Fuel and Energy was created to co-ordinate policy, and production associations were formed, which brought together regional exploration, extraction and transport assets. Refineries, however, remained independent and continued to report to Minneftekhimprom. Already, then, "one might conceive of the industrial structure being made up of a heterogeneous set of units each with its own economic (and political) interests – all with different outlooks and agendas".[41]

When the ministries of the USSR were finally liquidated in 1991, a single Ministry of Fuel and Energy of the Russian Federation (Mintop) was formed, which had a legal and regulatory role but no direct control over production activities. As such the production associations and independent refineries became key actors, taking over the administrative roles formally controlled by the state bureaucracy. Initially Rosneftegaz was formed in 1991 and was designated to oversee the sector, through a voluntary agreement between 47 regional production associations. However, having had their first taste of autonomy under the Gorbachev regime, a number of the leaders of the component parts of Rosneftegaz started to seek their economic independence, with Vagit Alekperov, the general director of Kogalymneftegaz and First Deputy Oil Minister, leading the way.[42] He persuaded two other general directors to bring their production associations into a new entity called LUKOIL, modelled on the structure of a western integrated oil company. Presidential Decree No. 1403 of the 17th of November 1992 then took this model as a way of creating order in the industry, re-organizing all enterprises involved in oil production, oil refining and product marketing into joint stock companies (JSCs).[43] The Decree also created the first three vertically integrated oil companies (VIOCs), LUKOIL, Yukos and Surgutneftegas, and established the state enterprise Rosneft to replace Rosneftegaz. Rosneft was to manage in trust for a period of three years the majority of shares of those oil organizations that were not members of the three original VIOCs. The VIOCs had two tiers, holding companies and operating subsidiaries, with the holding companies having controlling stakes (51% of the voting shares, equivalent to 38% of the total share capital including non-voting preference shares) in the exploration and production, refining, distribution and support subsidiaries.[44]

In May 1994 the Russian government, responding to the pressure being created by non-payments in the economy as a whole, decided to strengthen the position of the oil-producing companies under its control by combining them with downstream companies where cash was being generated more easily, and therefore ordinance No. 452 created a further four VIOCs (Sidanco, Slavneft, Eastern Oil Company (VNK) and Onaco).[45] This was followed in April 1995 by the creation of the eighth and ninth VIOCs, Rosneft and TNK (Tyumen Oil Company),[46] which included the remaining upstream and downstream companies that had not been included in the other VIOCs. Rosneft's transformation into a VIOC reversed the government's original intention to dissolve it after three years, but it was soon also reduced in size as in August 1995, after active lobbying from the regional authorities in West Siberia, two of its subsidiaries (Noyabrskneftegaz and the Omsk refinery) were taken to create a tenth VIOC, Sibneft.

In the context of the future development of the industry it is important to note that the combinations of subsidiaries that were formed into the original VIOCs were based not so much on economic and commercial logic as on "personal connections and power plays".[47] Individual relationships between specific general directors and between general directors and the state played a key role in the allocation of assets, with the result that the geographical spread of subsidiaries was often very broad and some VIOCs were less integrated than others. This process of asset allocation also continued to a lesser extent among smaller regional companies with a greater emphasis on consolidating regional assets within one entity rather than necessarily emphasizing vertical integration. In addition other private firms involved in trading and exporting also sprang into existence.[48]

Privatization and ownership structures

Presidential decree No. 1403 (November 1992) not only laid out the proposed structure of the Russian oil industry but also the general provisions of its privatization. The overall structure of the share capital of each subsidiary company (production, refining or marketing) was that it should comprise 75% voting ordinary shares and 25% non-voting preference shares. As a result ownership of 51% of the ordinary shares (38% of the total share capital) would give voting control over the company.

Initially the government retained 38% of the total share capital in each subsidiary (entirely in ordinary shares to give voting control), with the remainder distributed 10% on advantageous terms to employees, 5% to management, 22% for voucher auctions and 25% as preference shares given free to employees. As regards the Holding Companies, they were given the government's 38% stake in each subsidiary they controlled, but the government then took a 51% stake in the Holding Companies (45% for LUKOIL, Yukos and Surgutneftegaz) for a minimum of three years in order to retain control over the industry. The remaining Holding Company shares were to be distributed 30% via voucher auctions, 15% at cash auctions open to all investors including foreigners and 5% to employees and management. The limit on foreign ownership in the Holding Companies was initially set at 15%. For all companies involved in transportation, 51% of the shares were owned by Transneft or Transnefteprodukt, with the balance of 49% remaining federal property, and as such the entire sector remained effectively state-owned.

Although the original privatization plan envisaged a fairly broad dispersion of oil company shares among management, employees, investors (both foreign and local) and the state, the reality evolved somewhat differently. In effect various schemes were used to maintain as much concentrated

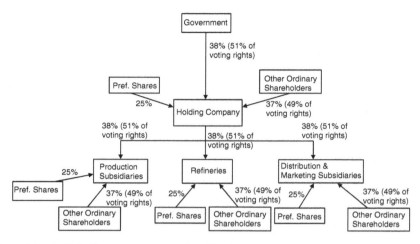

Figure 1.5   Initial oil company ownership structure

management ownership and control as possible by manipulating the auction processes and by exerting pressure on employees to sell shares to entities that would then be under the control of management. The most controversial alleged manipulation was the "loans for shares" scheme first advocated by Vladimir Potanin in March 1995, which clearly demonstrated the power of local knowledge and influence to enable both the purchase of cheap assets and the exclusion of foreign competition. Considerable debate has taken place concerning the exact rationale for the scheme, but it is perhaps best summarized by Duncan Allen[49] who noted that the Russian government, having seen its privatization process close to abject failure by the summer of 1995 and faced by an urgent need to raise revenues for the federal budget, accepted an opportunity to raise financing when it was offered. As Allen puts it: "The Russian State was weak in a number of ways, including its vulnerability to corruption, its shortcomings as an administrator, its insatiable appetite for budgetary revenues and the absence of consensus among and within the organs of power. In 1995 these weaknesses enabled the banks to manipulate officials and politicians to stunning effect."[50] A further motivation for the Russian banks was the fact that talks between the Russian authorities and western financial institutions concerning the sale of state assets on the stock exchange had reached an advanced stage in 1994. In response the Russian banks, faced with their inability to compete in terms of resources or experience in equity market transactions or corporate restructuring, may also have launched "loans for shares" as "a strategic offensive...in their struggle with foreign investors for Russian property".[51] Further evidence of this was the fact that foreigners were excluded from the auctions, which not only reduced competition but also decreased the revenues that the State could expect to receive. As such we can perhaps see the first attempt by the Russian business elite to interrupt the potential bargain that might have been expected to take place between the State and foreign business over the re-development of the country's natural resource assets.

Potanin proposed that a consortium of banks would lend money to the Russian government to cover some of the privatization revenues anticipated in the 1995 budget, with the loans underpinned by the collateral of shares in State enterprises. If the loans were not repaid in time the shares would become the property of the banks.[52] This idea was adapted to involve first a competitive tender process to provide the loans and then a further tender process for the sale of the shares by the banks should the loans default. In the event of government default on the loans the creditors would then have the right to sell the assets, again at a public auction, with the realized funds being used to repay the debts (and with any surplus being repaid to the government).[53]

Of the 17 companies that were eventually approved to participate in the "loans for shares" auctions five were from the oil sector – LUKOIL, Surgutneftegaz, Sidanco, Yukos and the newly created Sibneft. However, the impact on each company was rather different, with significant consequences for company strategy and potential interaction with foreign investors over the next five years. At LUKOIL and Surgutneftegaz the incumbent management were able to consolidate their positions through controlling the auction processes to ensure that only they could fulfill the investment requirements. Meanwhile at Yukos, Sidanco and Sibneft the incumbent management teams lost control of their companies to new financial investors, who used their influence and contacts with the Russian authorities to subvert the auction process. As a result, Interros (Sidanco), Menatep (Yukos) and FNK (Sibneft) became significant players in the Russian oil industry. As the Economist commented: "Rarely can privatisations have been more private; the government has been obliged to dispose of shareholdings in even more opaque ways to the few domestic investors both willing and able to put up the money."[54]

However, as Gustafson (2012) highlights, the "loans for shares" scheme was not the only route to control over large blocks of shares in Russian oil companies.[55] The state continued to offer packages in share sales and investment tenders, although those groups that had already gained a significant level of ownership of an oil company were always likely to be the winning bidder for any new blocks of shares. Indeed, in many instances they were almost guaranteed to be the only real bidder, as no investor wanted to find themselves as a minority shareholder with limited protection under Russian law.

As such, during the years 1994 to 1997 a significant transfer of ownership took place in the leading Russian oil companies, with the dominant theme being the transfer of control from the state to powerful insiders or to well-connected financial-industrial groups. The changing shareholdings of the state and the subsequent majority owners are exemplified in the table below, which also demonstrates that similar, if less dramatic, privatization processes were also taking place at some of the smaller oil companies too. After 1997 the privatization process largely came to a halt for two years, mainly as a result of the financial crisis of August 1998 which destroyed both domestic and international investor confidence. As a result, the Russian state continued to maintain a significant interest in companies such as Rosneft, Slavneft and Norsi Oil, although it had given up its interest in many of the other major oil companies.

The first government sale of oil assets following the 1998 crisis did not occur until late 1999, when AAR purchased the remaining 49.8% stake in TNK that it did not already own for the tiny sum of $90 million (equivalent to 1 cent per barrel of reserves) (Poussenkova, 2004) providing a prime example of the benefits available to well-connected insiders. In the following summer of 2000, a tender for the sale of an 85% stake in Onaco was held, with TNK winning the auction with a higher than expected bid of US$1.08 billion for a company with 2.2 billion barrels of oil reserves and 150,000 bpd of production, and then having to pay a further US$825 million to buy out a minority share owned by Sibneft and thus take full control of the company. In the same year the state's remaining 36.8% stake in Eastern Oil (VNK [Vostochny Nefte Kompanyie]) was also auctioned, although it was sold to Yukos for only US$0.4 million over the starting price of US$225 million,

Table 1.1   State shareholding of Russia's major VIOCs (%)

	1993	1994	1995	1996	1997	1998	1999	2000
LUKOIL	90.8	80.0	54.9	33.1	26.6	26.6	16.9	14.1
Yukos	100.0	100.0	48.0	0.1	0.1	0.1	0.1	0.1
Sidanko	n.a.	100.0	85.0	51.0	0.0	0.0	0.0	0.0
Surgutneftegaz	100.0	40.1	40.1	40.1	0.8	0.8	0.8	0.8
Tyumen Oil Co.	n.a.	n.a.	100.0	100.0	51.0	49.8	49.8	0.0
Eastern Oil Co.	n.a.	100.0	85.0	85.0	36.8	36.8	36.8	36.8
East Siberian Oil Co.	n.a.	100.0	85.0	38.0	1.0	1.0	1.0	1.0
Orenburg Oil Co.	n.a.	100.0	85.0	85.0	85.0	85.0	85.0	0.0
Rosneft	100.0	100.0	100.0	100.0	100.0	100.0	100.0	100.0
Slavneft	n.a.	83.0	83.0	79.0	75.0	75.0	75.0	75.0
Norsi-Oil	n.a.	n.a.	85.5	85.4	85.4	85.4	85.4	85.4
Sibur	n.a.	n.a.	85.0	85.0	85.0	14.8	14.8	0.0
Sibneft	n.a.	n.a.	100.0	51.0	0.0	0.0	0.0	0.0
KomiTEK	n.a.	100.0	100.0	92.0	1.1	1.1	1.1	1.1

Source: Table reproduced from IEA Russia Energy Survey 2002, available free at www.iea.org

increasing the latter's interest to over 90%. The final state asset put up for auction was the government's 74.95% stake in Slavneft, and although the auction was heralded as the most competitive in Russian privatization history, the contest again came down to just two players, Sibneft and TNK, who at the final moment decided to co-operate with the intention of running the company as a joint venture. The result was that a pre-agreed bid of US$1.86 billion was made, well below the anticipated price in a competitive auction. As such, although the prices paid at auction for Russian oil assets had increased and reflected a truer valuation of the underlying resources, the existing financial-industrial groups continued to dominate the process and on occasion manipulate the outcome by reducing competition.

Importantly, though, one company remained firmly in state hands, despite repeated attempts to sell it, as Rosneft continued to be 100% owned by the Russian government. Although its asset base had shrunk dramatically over the ten years of the post-Soviet era, and it had been close to extinction on at least two occasions (in 1996 when it almost lost its last major producing subsidiary Purneftegaz and in 1997/98 when attempts to sell it off in the privatization process were finally scuppered by the 1998 economic crisis),[56] by 2000 it remained as a fully state-owned company. Although it did not seem likely at the time, the arrival of Vladimir Putin as president and the subsequent plan to re-assert state control over the Russian economy would soon see a resurgent Rosneft re-asserting its place as the dominant force in the Russian oil sector and as the country's National Oil Company.

The consolidation of the VIOCs and their subsidiaries

To return to the 1990s, though, the privatization process was only one element of the transfer of ownership of the oil companies into private hands. As described above, the structure of the individual VIOCs had been arranged such that the producing, refining and marketing subsidiaries were not fully controlled by the holding companies above them. As a result, the new owners of the VIOCs had to go through a further process of industry re-organization which had a significant impact on the role of the major players in the Russian oil industry, including foreign investors. The second process incorporated the consolidation of the cashflows and ownership of the subsidiary companies into their respective holding companies and it affected each of the VIOCs differently, depending upon how much control they had managed to establish early in the privatization process. For example, LUKOIL had essentially consolidated full control over its operating companies in the mid-1990s, as senior management had controlled the subsidiaries already and managed to ensure that the privatization process did not spread ownership too widely. In contrast Yukos, Sibneft, TNK, Surgutneftegas and Sidanco went through a process of swapping shares in the holding companies for shares in the subsidiary companies between 1997 and 2002. The means by which they optimized the value of this process to the benefit of holding company shareholders was rather controversial,[57] although the strategic rationale was driven by business logic.

Essentially, because of the two-tier industry structure, designed to allow the government to manage the oil sector through its control of the holding companies, there was a significant separation between ownership/senior management and the core assets of the businesses. The fundamental business operations and the initial cash generation were carried out at the level of the subsidiaries, and although the holding companies had voting control over the subsidiaries within their own structure, this did not necessarily mean that they had effective operating and financial control. In some instances the general directors of production associations or refineries would simply ignore the instructions received from the holding company, with one particularly rebellious example being Viktor Paliy, the general director of TNK subsidiary Nizhnevartovskneftegaz. Despite the fact that the Alfa Group owned 51% of the shares of his company, Paliy plainly ran his business with no regard for the interests of his major shareholder, and indeed was described as running "a guerrilla war" against the company's owners.[58]

In response to similar problems the owners of the VIOCs sought to exert their control over their subsidiaries in a staged process. Initially they looked to increase their board representation, then to centralize cashflows at the holding company level and then finally to remove the subsidiaries as individual entities altogether. The consequences of these moves had the greatest negative impact on minority investors (including a large number of foreign investors) in the subsidiary companies, who often found their interests diluted or the assets of the companies that they owned being stripped. The impact on foreign direct investment was sometimes practical (a shifting of assets or a breaking of agreements) but was also psychological, as the problems affecting minority financial investors exposed the inadequacies of the legal and corporate systems and revealed the potential ease with which value could be stripped from any investment. One of the most controversial examples involved US investor Kenneth Dart and his substantial investments in a number of subsidiaries of Yukos, which were heavily diluted when Yukos CEO Mikhail Khodorkovsky arranged for preferential share issues by those subsidiaries to Yukos itself and to the exclusion of other shareholders.[59] These share issues would have allowed Yukos to consolidate the subsidiary companies into the holding company structure at prices that would have been very beneficial to the owners of the holding company but to the detriment of the minority shareholders in the subsidiaries themselves. Legal disputes dragged on through 1999 and 2000, and were eventually resolved in a compromise that allowed minority investors to gain some value from the process while Yukos took full control of its subsidiaries.[60]

Similar consolidation processes were taking place at the other Russian oil majors, with more or less similar consequences for minority shareholders in the subsidiary companies, with the overall result that by the end of 2002 all the major Russian VIOCs had achieved full control over their subsidiaries, and in most cases the VIOCs themselves were controlled directly or indirectly by the majority shareholders and/or the management of the company. However, the fact that the transformation of the Russian oil industry from a state-dominated sector to a largely private sector had taken a decade to complete, due to the length of the privatization process and the need for a further consolidation of individual VIOCs, meant that the industrial leaders had been largely distracted from the core job of maintaining production levels. When this distraction with corporate affairs was combined with an economy that was encumbered with a huge non-payment problem (Gaddy and Ickes, 2002), a falling oil price[61] and a legacy of Soviet fields that required massive investment just to sustain levels of output, it is perhaps no surprise that during this period Russian oil production collapsed to levels not seen since the early 1970s. Figure 1.6 shows the extent of the fall in production, from over 10 million bpd in 1990 to approximately 6 million bpd in the years 1995 to 1999, although it is interesting to note that the decline was halted at the time when the privatization process began in earnest (1995) and also that the rebound from the 1999 low began as the consolidation of some of the new VIOCs started to be completed in 2000.

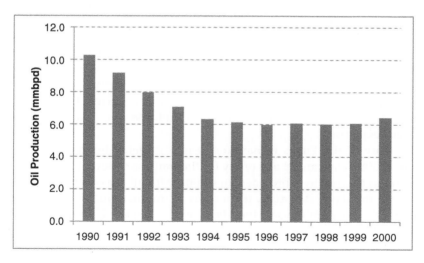

Figure 1.6 The collapse of Russian oil production, 1990–2000
Source: Graph created by author from data collected from "Almanac of Russian Petroleum 2000" published by Energy Intelligence Group and from www.energyintel.com

Rehabilitation and renewal from 2000

The turnaround in Russian oil production in 2000 was catalysed by three main factors, namely a rebound in the oil price from a low of US$9 per barrel in December 1998[62] to more than US$28 per barrel in June 2000, the devaluation of the rouble following the 1998 financial crisis (which dramatically reduced the cost base of the Russian oil companies in dollar terms),[63] and the renewed focus of the VIOCs on improving their operational performance. While the first two factors are clearly external forces over which the companies themselves had no control, the third factor marked a fundamental change in the strategic outlook of the oil company owners once they had managed to bring their subsidiaries under full control. As described in detail by Gustafson (2012) the combination of these themes brought about "the Russian oil miracle",[64] which saw the introduction of international working practices and technology transform the performance of the Soviet legacy oilfields, in particular in West Siberia.

As suggested by some theorists of reform in transition economies, in particular Shleifer and Treisman (2000), privatization had created a new class of owners in the Russian oil industry who were now incentivized to maximize the returns on their investments.[65] There was a clear split over the exact definition of maximizing returns, with companies run by former Soviet oilmen (such as LUKOIL and Surgutneftegaz) interpreting it as the optimal long-term exploitation of reserves while those run by the new breed of financial oligarchs focused more on maximizing production and short-term financial returns. It was this latter group, led initially by Yukos, which sparked the turnaround in Russian oil production via the formation of alliances with international service companies. Indeed the landmark agreement which really marks the start of the transformation process, was the strategic alliance struck between Yukos and Schlumberger in October 1998, under which Schlumberger would not only provide the technical services to help recover output from Yukos' declining fields but would also offer management and financial expertise.[66]

The story of the Yukos turnaround is told in detail by Economides and D'Aleo (2008), and can act as a proxy for the transformation of the Russian oil industry as a whole as it provided an example for all the other companies in the sector to follow. Essentially it concerns an international service company, one of its former employees (Joe Mach) who joined Yukos with a remit to manage the implementation of new production techniques and the Yukos CEO Mikhail Khodorkovsky, who as an enlightened entrepreneur was keen to move away from traditional Soviet practices in the search for improved operational performance. Between them they identified that the initial problems were actually rather simple to solve, involving not the traditional drilling of extra wells to increase production but rather a focus on a smaller number of wells that could be improved with some simple changes, including the use of better pumps placed deeper in the wells. Through a process of prioritizing which wells would benefit most from enhancement, Mach was able to focus investment and create maximum short-term value, before moving on to introduce other production enhancement techniques such as fracking (the cracking of hydrocarbon reservoirs by injecting fluids at high pressure to increase the flow of oil or gas) and improved reservoir management (in particular by adjusting the amount and location of waterflooding wells). As a result of these activities, which were rolled out across all of Yukos' production subsidiaries by a team of specially trained Russian staff, the company's oil output jumped from 44.7 million tonnes (900 thousand bpd) in 1999 to 80.7 million tonnes (1.6 million bpd) in 2003, at which point it had become Russia's largest oil-producing company.[67]

As other Russian oil companies saw the success being generated by Yukos, and the impact it was having on both its profitability and its market value (which grew from only $320 million in 1999 to over $30 billion in 2003), they started to copy the techniques that it had employed. The first to react were those companies with similar owners (namely financial oligarchs keen to generate short-term returns), and Sibneft became the second success story of the oil recovery miracle as its owners created alliances with Schlumberger and Halliburton to carry out field rehabilitation work akin to that done at Yukos.[68] TNK, owned by the oligarch group known as AAR, were slightly slower to progress due to their lengthy battle with BP over the ownership of Sidanco, which we will discuss further later, but by 2003 they had also joined the race to increase production having consolidated their assets under the TNK-BP banner. Even LUKOIL and Surgutneftegaz, with their more traditional methods, were persuaded that the introduction of international technology could benefit their assets, although they chose to do it using in-house technicians and engineers rather than forming alliances with western service companies.[69] Nevertheless, the growth in output at all these companies around the turn of the 20th/21st century was remarkable, with Figure 1.7 showing that overall Russian oil production rose from 6 million bpd in 1999 to 8.4 million bpd by 2003, an increase of 43% in only four years.

The resurgence of Russian state influence in the oil sector

One noticeable omission from the list of companies with sharply increased production during the period 1999–2003 is Rosneft, the last remaining state-owned company in the sector by 2003. Its output remained flat at around 250 thousand bpd from 1999–2002 and increased to 300 thousand bpd in 2003 thanks only to an acquisition (of Northern Oil) rather than any fundamental change in its operating procedures. However, this acquisition, small although

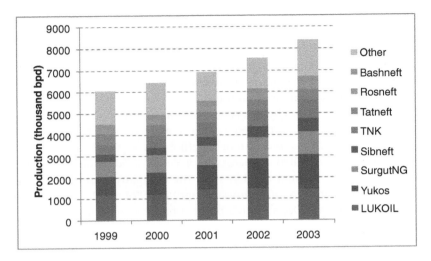

Figure 1.7   Russian oil production, 1999–2003
Source: Graph created by author from data collected from "Nefte Compass" published by
Energy Intelligence Group and from www.energyintel.com

it was, marked another turning point in the development of the Russian oil
industry as it heralded not only the start of Rosneft's return to a leading role
but also laid the seeds for the demise of Yukos.

In order to understand the rise of Rosneft as a resurgent National Oil
Company, however, we need to return briefly to 2000 and the election of
Vladimir Putin as President of Russia. Putin had effectively been chosen by the
former President, Boris Yeltsin, as his successor when he had been made Prime
Minister in September 1999, and had also been endorsed, perhaps even
selected, by the financial oligarchs who were part of the so-called Yeltsin
"family". However, when he came to power it became clear quite quickly that
his view of the path for Russia's development was rather different than the
free-for-all capitalism that had been seen in the 1990s. As Marshall Goldman
(2008) describes, Putin came to power with a view that state leadership in the
economy was required to correct the market failures which had allowed
private enterprise to run rampant in the first decade of the post-Soviet era,
and his preferred method for achieving this leadership was through the
vehicle of national champions.[70] Evidence of this strategy is provided by a
series of articles published by Putin and his close associates in St. Petersburg in
the late 1990s, as well as two doctrinal theses published at the same time, one
by Putin himself and one by his close ally and the current CEO of Rosneft Igor
Sechin. Within this body of literature is a call for "state capitalism" in which
the State and private companies are partners in catalysing and sustaining the

recovery of the Russian economy, but with the State in the lead role via direct intervention in industrial activity in key sectors.[71]

Although in the oil sector the state-owned oil pipeline company Transneft had provided an element of state control throughout the post-Soviet period, effectively managing oil company access to domestic and, more importantly, export markets for crude oil and oil products, Putin clearly also wanted to establish dominance over the upstream and refining sectors where the real money was being made. As a result, on coming to power, he quickly made his intentions clear as he began to reassert the State's authority on a number of companies in the hydrocarbon industry, in tandem with moves to increase its influence in the media and banking sectors.[72] He also called the leading private entrepreneurs together for a meeting in July 2000 in which he outlined the role which they could play in this new political and economic environment. They could keep their existing assets and continue to profit from them as long as they paid adequate taxes in full and kept out of politics (Tompson, 2005).[73] For the next two years an uneasy truce held in the oil sector, as the oligarchs consolidated their businesses and began the process of regeneration described above, but in 2003 it became clear, via the Rosneft acquisition of Northern Oil (Severnaya Neft in Russian), that the State was set to assert its role in the industry. At a subsequent meeting between Putin and the oligarchs in February 2003 frustration at this move was expressed by Yukos CEO Mikhail Khodorkovsky, who openly accused Rosneft of using corruption to acquire Northern Oil and also accused the Ministry of Energy of being "the most corrupt ministry in the country".[74]

These public accusations, combined with Yukos' relatively blatant attempts to influence political life in Russia (especially through its lobbying efforts in the Duma), turned Putin and the force of the Russian state against Mikhail Khodorkovsky, culminating in his arrest in October 2003 and his subsequent imprisonment. The relevance to our analysis of the Russian oil industry is that the fall of Yukos catalysed the rise of Rosneft, which managed to acquire many of the Yukos' assets that were sold off in bankruptcy proceedings in the years 2004–2007 in order to pay Yukos' historic tax bills and the fines associated with previous non-payment. In the process Rosneft also managed to remain an independent entity, despite the fact that in 2004 it was almost merged with Gazprom, by demonstrating its worth both as a vehicle for consolidating oil assets under state control and also as a counter-balance to the growing presence of Gazprom across Russia's energy economy.

Increasing state control over the oil sector did not stop with Rosneft's purchase of the majority of Yukos' assets, however. In 2005 Gazprom was compensated for its failure to merge with Rosneft by being allowed to acquire Sibneft, the oil company owned by Roman Abramovich's Millhouse Capital group, paying just over $13 billion for a 73% stake before buying a further 3%

in the market to take its share over the vital 75% mark.[75,76] Gazprom then purchased a further 20% of Sibneft for \$4.2 billion from ENI in 2009 (who had acquired it on Gazprom's behalf at an auction of Yukos' assets in 2007),[77] after which it also assumed control of a 50% stake in Slavneft which Sibneft had bought in partnership with TNK in 2002.[78] As a result Gazprom has become a significant player in the oil sector, with Sibneft, subsequently re-named as Gazprom Neft, now contributing 1.1 million bpd of production to add to Gazprom's own liquids output of approximately 300 thousand bpd.

The most recent move in the strategy to re-establish state control over the oil sector has been the completion of Rosneft's acquisition of TNK-BP in 2013. The purchase, for \$56 billion in cash and shares paid to AAR and BP, has seen Rosneft's oil production rise to over 4 million barrels per day, or 40% of Russia's total output, and has brought not only TNK-BP but the remaining 50% of Slavneft under state control. Gazprom Neft and Rosneft also hold 50% interests each in Tomskneft, a former Yukos subsidiary located in the eastern part of West Siberia, and when this is added to the total of state-controlled oil assets it is now clear that half of Russian oil production is back in government hands. Indeed, Figure 1.8 demonstrates very starkly how dramatic the shift has been from state control in 1995 to private ownership in 2004 (prior to the Yukos bankruptcy) and now back to state ownership of 50% of production in 2013.

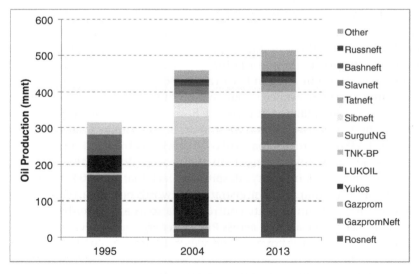

Figure 1.8 Changes in state ownership of Russian oil production, 1993–2013
Source: Graph created by author from data collected from "Nefte Compass" published by Energy Intelligence Group and from www.energyintel.com

However, it is also important to recognize that this return to state ownership was not just the result of an altruistic belief in the benefits of state intervention into a market that was perceived to be failing. It is also likely, as has been identified by a number of authors, that it was the result of a desire by an alternative set of "entrepreneurs", using state authority, to obtain their share of the wealth that had been, as they saw it, handed to the oligarchs in the 1990s.[79] The arrival of Putin to the presidency in 2000 and the initiation of his plan to re-assert the control of the State over the "commanding heights" of the economy, including the oil and gas sector, offered the opportunity for this desire to be turned into reality while also allowing Putin to create competitive tension between the competing clans that make up his power base. The appointment of a St. Petersburg colleague Alexei Miller to become CEO of Gazprom in 2001, the election of Igor Sechin to become chairman of Rosneft in 2004 while also holding a senior political position and the appointment of Nikolay Tokarev, a former colleague of Putin in East Germany and in various government roles, as President of Transneft in 2007 are three senior examples of this balancing act. Goldman (2008), also describes the practice of what he terms "double dipping" by which "former colleagues are appointed not only to the most senior positions in government but also to senior and lucrative posts in the business world" and he goes on to detail a number of vehicles through which members of the security services are able to profit from business opportunities.[80] He also outlines the numerous examples of members of the families of senior officials being appointed to important posts in state corporations, and this theme of the use of patronage between the state and business is also explored by Tompson (2005), who claims that: "In general, Russian state-owned companies are run for the benefit of insiders and their patrons in the state administration."[81] The prominence of the security services in particular in the world of business "in private and state-owned companies", is re-iterated by Schneider (2012), while Inozemtsev (2009) claims that no other country in the world has so many members of the government serving on the boards of major corporations. A further twist to the tale of vested interests in Russian business, and in particular in the oil and gas sector, is highlighted by Pirani (2010) who identifies that "a significant trend in the 2000s has been the success in private business of some of Putin's associates". He names Gennady Timchenko, the head of oil trading company Gunvor and now also a major shareholder in the gas company Novatek, as one particular example in the oil and gas sector, while he also notes the success of Bank Rossiya in acquiring assets in the gas sector while under the control of a number of men with close relationships with Putin.[82]

As a result the re-assertion of state control over the oil and gas industry since 2000 would therefore appear to have two key drivers. The first is catalysed by political strategy and the belief that the state needed to step in to exert some control over a market place that was perceived to have provided sub-optimal results for the Russian economy during the 1990s. The second is somewhat less altruistic, and has involved the re-allocation of rents from the winners of the 1990s (the oligarchs) to the losers (the government bureaucrats and the siloviki who arrived in power with Putin).[83] Nevertheless the two were complimentary, as the President could use goals implied by the former to provide positions for his associates in state companies that would allow them to achieve the latter, while also providing himself with the levers to exert control over the competing forces within his political supporters and over the most important commercial organizations operating in the Russian economy.

The challenge of maintaining production growth from 2005

Figure 1.8 shows that oil production in Russia has continued to grow since 2004, when Yukos came under attack, until 2013, when the state had reclaimed ownership of 50% of the country's oil output. However, a more detailed look at the Putin era since 2000 reveals two contrasting periods, from 2000–2004, when production grew at an annual average rate of 9.2%, and from 2005–2012 when it grew at a much lower rate of 1.3%. Given the mixed political and personal reasons for the re-assertion of state control in Russia's oil and gas sector and the broad evidence across the global industry that state-run oil companies are often less efficient that their privately-owned peers,[84] it

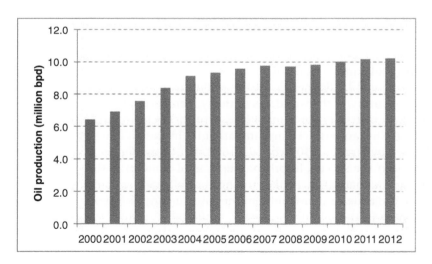

Figure 1.9 Russian oil production, 2000–2012
Source: Graph created by author from data provided by Ministry of Energy of Russian Federation at www.minenergo.gov.ru

might be tempting to blame this slow-down in growth on the rise of the influence of Rosneft, GazpromNeft and to an extent Gazprom in the sector. However, in the period 2006–2012 output from these three State companies increased by 3.7% per annum compared to 1.1% per annum for the industry as a whole. While this performance may be explained to an extent by the acquisition of privately-owned assets that continued to perform well under state ownership (Yukos by Rosneft and Sibneft by Gazprom), it would nevertheless be unfair to conclude that increased state ownership is the only driver of the slowdown in Russian oil production growth.

In fact, as has been documented by many oil companies, analysts and academic commentators,[85] the key factor behind the deceleration in growth has been the imminent end of the era of the "brownfield miracle" in Russia and the transition to the development of greenfield sites both onshore and offshore. In essence the Soviet legacy fields in West Siberia, that went into decline so sharply in the 1990s and were resuscitated so profitably in the first decade of the 2000s, are now finally succumbing to the laws of nature and are in decline again, this time for good. The situation was summed up in a stark fashion by the CEO of Surgutneftegaz Vladimir Bogdanov in a briefing to then President Medvedev who was on a visit to Khanty Mansiisk in 2010. "60% of our reserves have already been produced", he stated "...73% of our oil comes from low grade reserves. 90% of what we produce is water".[86] Given that 90% of Russia's production comes from three regions that were first exploited in the Soviet era (West Siberia, the Volga-Urals and North Caucasus) and where Bogdanov now sees natural decline as inevitable, the real surprise is that Russia has managed to sustain the increase in production since 2005, once the initial brownfield recovery phase was over.

However, as Gustafson (2012), Kostanian (2012), Kononczuk (2012) and others have pointed out, although the effort to stabilize production from Russia's older fields has been immense, the country's oil industry is now moving into a phase where new regions and new reservoirs will have to be developed if the targets set in the Energy Strategy (published in 2009) are to be met.[87] The Strategy sees overall production being maintained at around 10.5 million bpd, but even in 2009 acknowledged the shifting trends in the geography of this output. For example, the amount of drilling in East Siberia is expected to be double that in West Siberia by 2020, and the levels of seismic exploration activity on Russia's continental shelf are expected to match that in West Siberia by the same date. As such, a fundamental shift is underway that will see more remote regions of the country become increasingly important areas for investment and ultimately output over the next decade. Production in East Siberia and the Far East of Russia, for example, is expected to account for 20% of the country's total oil production by 2030, up from only 3% in 2008.[88]

Russia's offshore regions could also play a huge role in replacing output from the current core production areas, although this potential is only likely to be realized in the much longer term. Estimates of potential resources in Russia's Arctic Seas alone are as high as 250 million boe, accounting for two thirds of the total global resources in the Arctic region,[89] while the Black Sea, the Caspian Sea and the seas offshore Eastern Russia could hold a further 50–100 billion boe.[90] Another potentially important new source of production could come from unconventional onshore fields, where significant resources of heavier and more difficult to recover oil have been identified. In particular the Bazhenov formation has been identified as a reservoir that could offer large reserves, and Gazprom Neft, which is already involved in two projects to exploit this alternative resource, has estimated that up to 65 billion barrels of oil could be located across West Siberia in this layer.[91] Rosneft has also begun to take active steps to assess its licences for Bazhenov oil, and estimates that its acreage alone could contain up to 9 billion barrels of oil with the potential to produce more than 300 thousand bpd.[92] However, both Gazprom Neft and Rosneft examples highlight four key issues for Russia's future oil production as the industry moves into more difficult regions – the need to use new technology that has not been available in Russia before, the high up-front investment cost in exploration and potential field development, the need for tax breaks to create a commercial environment that will incentivize investment in high-risk projects and finally the increasing role of foreign companies in these new oil regions.

From a technological standpoint, the issue is simply that Russian companies are now starting to explore geographical regions and geological horizons where they have little or no experience, but where the global oil industry has already been operating in similar environments for many years. Russia's first offshore production only started off Sakhalin Island, in the Far East of the country, in 1999 (from the Sakhalin 2 project) and since then only two other offshore fields have produced either oil or gas in Russia (Sakhalin 1 in the Far East and Yuri Korchagin in the Caspian Sea). By comparison the global offshore industry stretches from the traditional basins of the North Sea to the deep water offshore Brazil and as far north as the Arctic waters off Canada and the US, meaning that it can offer a wealth of experience and industry tools to the Russian oil companies. The same is true of unconventional oil and gas development, where the experiences in the US in particular can provide a wealth of operational data as well as tried and tested methods such as horizontal drilling and fracking that can be applied to similar resources in Russia.

Exploiting international learning can help Russia to avoid "re-inventing the wheel" when it comes to the development of its new resources, but the costs will nevertheless be high, especially in regions such as offshore on the Russian continental shelf where the environment is often harsh and lacks existing infrastructure. Rosneft estimates that the cost of developing its initial offshore projects in the Kara, Barents and Black Seas could be as high as $500 billion over the next 20 years, while the cost of gasfields to be developed by Gazprom will be no less expensive. The Shtokman field in the Barents Sea, for example, has a current cost estimate of $20–40 billion just to complete the first phase of a potential four phase project.[93] New onshore regions such as East Siberia will also be expensive to develop, mainly because of the lack of infrastructure in the region. The movement of exploration and development equipment into remote territories with few roads and even fewer railways will be a costly venture, while the sale of any hydrocarbons that are found will be made more difficult by the limited amount of current pipeline infrastructure. Although Transneft, the state pipeline operator, is expanding a new trunk pipeline system to the Far East (the ESPO or East Siberia Pacific Ocean pipeline) the construction of spur pipelines to individual fields will increase the costs and potentially inhibit the economics of specific assets.

Even the relatively low-cost development of unconventional reserves could prove too expensive unless the third issue, the current tax regime for oilfields, is addressed by the Russian government in the near future. Historically the Russian upstream oil tax system has been based on the need for ease of calculation and collection and has been focused on fields that were either already in production in the Soviet era or were cheap to develop as they had been discovered and were close to existing infrastructure. As a result the main features of the oil tax system have been a royalty (known as Mineral Extraction Tax or Natural Resource Depletion Tax – MET or NRDT) and an export tax, both of which are related to the prevailing level of oil prices. Companies also then pay a corporate tax and various local or regional taxes. Importantly, though, the MET and export taxes are based on revenues not profits, and although this simplifies the system for the tax authorities and reduces the opportunities for tax avoidance schemes, it also undermines the incentives to invest as it makes no allowance for costs or the rate of return of any specific project. Indeed, the marginal rate of tax under the current regime if the oil price exceeds $25 per barrel amounts to well over 80% of revenues, while the average overall upstream tax burden for oil companies in 2012 amounted to just under 60% of gross revenues.[94]

This high rate of taxation has encouraged companies to enhance the production at the easiest low-cost fields, in other words the ones that are already in production and require less expenditure to sustain or increase output, but has failed to provide a stimulus for new field development aimed at maintaining Russia's long-term production profile. In the meantime the state budget has become increasingly reliant on the oil sector, which accounts for approximately 50% of total budget revenues,[95] meaning that the Russian government is facing a difficult dilemma. On the one hand it needs to maintain a high level of oil taxation to sustain its income for social and other budget spending, but on the other it faces the prospect that if it does not start to provide fiscal incentives (i.e. lower taxes) to encourage new exploration and field developments then its major source of revenue will start to go into decline. As Kononczuk (2012, p. 44) notes "the tax system performs [not] only the fiscal function of supplying revenues to the budget, which is increasingly dependent on the oil sector, [but] at the same time fails to stimulate production and act as a mechanism for setting the trends of its development".

Initially the Russian government's response to this dilemma had been to make ad hoc changes to the tax system as and when the industry had complained loudly enough. In 2007, for example, the MET rate for very mature fields (with greater than 80% depletion) was reduced, and was removed completely for some fields in East Siberia for the first ten to 15 years of their producing life. This exemption spread to other new regions in 2009, including the Polar Shelf, the Caspian and the Sea of Azov, although this had only a limited effect on field development plans as the tax change was viewed as unstable (no-one knew if it would be revoked as fast as it had been implemented) and also because MET actually makes up quite a small proportion of the overall tax burden on the sector.

A more significant change was introduced in 2009/10 when 22 fields in East Siberia were exempted from the much more significant export tax for the first 25 million tonnes of production or until the fields had generated a 15% rate of return.[96] However, even this had a rather unpredicted consequence, as it encouraged the initial development of fields up to the tax exemption limits (i.e. production of 25 million tonnes of oil), before companies then reduced investments and did not fully exploit field production potential, preferring to develop other fields that could qualify for the tax breaks. A more general reduction in the top rate of export tax from 65% to 60% was then introduced in 2011 (compensated by higher taxes on oil products), but the oil industry has argued for some time that the only way to avoid a rather ad hoc development strategy based on random tax level adjustments is a total reform of the tax policy across the sector, basing taxes on the profitability of individual fields and also companies as a whole, rather than imposing taxes on revenues and providing random exemptions that offer no long-term stability.

In 2012 the first sign that the Russian government was prepared to act in response to these proposals came with the introduction of a new tax regime for the offshore regions, targeted in particular at the joint ventures being formed by Rosneft to develop resources in the Arctic (see next section for a full description of these JVs). Essentially this new tax regime is a profit-based scheme with a reduced royalty and a profit tax that allows rates of return in the range of 16–22% to be made depending on the geography of the licences and the implied difficulty of field development.[97] This new focus on rates of return as the basis for a tax system can now provide increased security for oil companies making long-term high risk commitments to Russia, while the increased focus on taxing profits will allow the investing companies to recover their costs faster, thus further reducing the risks.

However, despite this change there has been little indication that this form of tax system will be rolled out across the Russian oil sector as a whole. The clear concern of the Ministry of Finance is that any new profit-based system could reduce short-term revenues and also be open to longer-term abuse, if companies revert to the profit-minimization tactics employed in the 1990s. Meanwhile the ability of the Tax Authorities to administer a more complicated profit-based system, implying multiple calculations and negotiations, must also be a doubt given the limited resources available to them. Introducing such a system in a new region such as the offshore, with no short-term revenue consequences and limited company involvement, is achievable, but a broader application would seem unlikely in the near term. Negotiations between the oil industry and the relevant government ministries are ongoing, and decisions on new tax rates for unconventional oil, new greenfield developments, difficult to recover oil deposits and tight oil are expected to be given final approval at the end of 2013. However, it seems likely that, although the overall rates of royalty and export tax may be adjusted a full overhaul of the tax system is unlikely in the near term.

Within the context of the shifting focus of the Russian oil industry away from the traditional producing regions towards new greenfield areas, with the implications for the use of new technology, the high capital costs and the need for a new tax system, the role of international companies is also likely to become much more important. Many of the technologies that will be needed on the Russian continental shelf or in the new more difficult onshore reservoirs that contain the country's future oil growth prospects have been used in the international arena before. Partnership with IOCs can therefore not only bring knowledge of these technologies, but equally importantly an understanding of how they can be applied most efficiently. Furthermore, the management of huge offshore projects is also a skill that Russian companies will undoubtedly learn over time, but where initially the experience of international companies can speed the learning process. The high costs of these projects can also be shared with IOCs, who can provide an additional source of financing capability as well as an opportunity for risk mitigation. Finally, the need to attract new investors into greenfield oil developments can also act as a catalyst for negotiations on the tax system, and indeed this has already been the case concerning the new offshore regime. With these issues in mind, the arrival of ExxonMobil, ENI and Statoil into joint ventures with Rosneft during 2012 has potentially marked a new era of foreign company involvement in the Russian oil sector. However, before discussing the future for IOCs in

Russia, it is important to discuss the history of foreign involvement in the sector to date and to discuss what lessons can be learnt from their experiences.

The role of foreign investors in the post-Soviet oil industry

Fluctuating involvement during five periods of post-Soviet development

Any participation by foreign companies in the development of key domestic resources in a host country is best described relative to the needs of that host country and the roles and ambitions of the domestic actors involved, in particular when the resources being discussed are as strategic as oil and gas. Russia is no different in this regard, and from the very inception of the country's hydrocarbon industry in the 19th century the role of foreign companies has fluctuated according to the political and commercial dynamics in the country. Throughout the period, though, one constant has been in place, namely that Russia's vast oil and gas resources have been of consistent interest to foreign companies looking to enhance their position in the global energy economy.

The first major foreign participant in the Russian oil industry, Royal Dutch Shell, partnered with and then bought out the Nobel family's oil interests in order to counter the influence of Standard Oil in the global market place and to find a source of reserves that could match those in the US and provide oil and products for the growing Asian and European markets. In return for access to new resources Nobel Oil and Royal Dutch Shell brought to Russia the (then) modern concept of drilling for oil, as opposed to the hand-dug pits which had been in use until the 1870s, as well as funds for investment, access to new markets to sell the increasing production and ultimately taxes paid to the Tsar's treasury as profits were made. Russia's oil production, spurred by this foreign investment, more than tripled between 1885 and 1915 to reach approximately 500 thousand bpd,[98] before the role of international companies was undermined by the 1917 revolution, which of course introduced a radically different domestic approach to management of the new Soviet economy.

As described in the previous section, following initial stagnation of the oil industry in the 1920s, the Soviet era saw a dramatic growth in oil output as the North Caucasus, Volga-Urals and ultimately the West Siberian regions were explored and developed. The significant achievements of the Soviet oil industry included not only the development of fields that would produce more than 12 million bpd by the end of the 1980s (of which more than 11 million bpd came from Russia), but also the construction of a huge network of transportation infrastructure and a massive refining complex to supply the Soviet industrial and military machine with oil products for use across the economy. This was all accomplished, of course, with minimal foreign assistance other than the occasional exchange of ideas and the provision of equipment (at a cost) from international service companies, with both the Soviet Union and its western "Cold War" adversaries keen to minimize contact for their own political gains.

The increasing pressures being faced by the Soviet oil industry to sustain production in the late 1980s combined with the reforms being introduced by Soviet leader Mikhail Gorbachev saw the exclusion of foreign participation start to ease from 1987, when the Soviet government authorized the first joint ventures with foreign companies in order to attract capital and technology into the country. Access to the oil sector remained severely limited at first, due to its strategic nature, but by the end of the Soviet Union in 1991 over 100 oil JVs were under negotiation as the desperate needs of the industry became increasingly obvious, with US and Canadian companies at the forefront of the international bandwagon.[99]

The involvement of foreign companies in the post-Soviet oil industry can then be traced through five periods of fluctuating fortunes within the Russian political and business environment. Although it is not possible to be absolutely definitive with either the timing or the specific types of foreign investment, as there is certainly some overlap between the divides we will describe, it is nevertheless possible to identify some significant shifts in the attitudes of both domestic and foreign investors, and also the Russian government, towards FDI in the oil and gas sectors over the past 20-plus years. The first period can be timed from the end of the Soviet Union in 1991 through to the low of Russian oil production in 1996–1999, when the key priority was how to stem the sharp decline in output and eventually to return it to growth. The second period, which overlaps to an extent, covers the privatization of the Russian oil industry, the bulk of which occurred from 1994 to 2000 as the major oil companies were formed and then sold off in auctions of various types.

The third period, again overlapping with its predecessor, captures the subsequent consolidation of the newly privatized entities and their establishment as ongoing vertically integrated concerns. It is difficult to be precise on the timing of this period, but it can perhaps be defined as reaching from the shareholder wars at Yukos in 1998 through to the commencement of bankruptcy proceedings against the company in 2004. The fourth period can then be approximately timed from 2005 to 2012, during which time the major theme was the increasing control of the Russian state in the Russian oil sector, with the expansion of Rosneft and the acquisition of Sibneft by Gazprom. The fifth period is then from 2012 forward, which has seen a shift in strategy, in particular by Rosneft as the established Russian NOC, towards more international co-operation as the need to expand the geography and the complexity of the country's oil production increases.

Joint ventures as the preferred investment model following the Soviet collapse

During the first period of the post-Soviet oil industry, the Ministry of Fuel and Energy, in recognition of the impending production crisis, adopted its "Programme to Stabilise Operations in the Oil and Gas Industry in 1992–5 and until 2000" that envisaged a rebound in production beginning in 1995. However, it was painfully clear that Russia's own oil companies did not have the resources to meet the challenge of spending the US$50–75 billion[100] that would need to be invested by the end of the decade to achieve any form of recovery, and as a result the need for international investment in the sector was obvious.[101] Initially, as Russia first opened its oil industry to private investment, there were three main ways for foreign players to get involved, all of which were variations on the joint venture model. The simplest, and least risky, was a well workover contract, by which an international company was contracted to carry out refurbishment work on wells that had fallen idle due to lack of maintenance and investment. The international company was then paid from the proceeds of the increased oil production, which was exported for dollars, while all title to the oil produced remained with the Russian side. This form of contract was particularly encouraged by the Russian government in 1992, when it was clear that immediate work was needed to stem the decline in Russia's oil output. Exemptions from export tax were granted for oil sold to pay western contractors, and special export quotas were provided to ensure that the necessary amounts of oil could be sold abroad.

An alternative was to form a joint venture with a Russian partner in order to gain access to existing hydrocarbon reserves and production. Under these schemes entire fields were essentially leased by joint venture companies and then rehabilitated, again with the incremental production being used to credit the JV partners. Finally, the third form of joint venture involved obtaining the license to a brand new field that could be developed from scratch. This form of JV had the clear benefit of avoiding the need to deal with fields that had been affected by Soviet development techniques, but also involved higher risk as the amounts of capital needing to be invested prior to production were much greater.

Overall, though, the combination of these three forms of joint venture was to become the dominant vehicle for FDI in the Russian oil and gas sector in the first half of the 1990s, and as early as 1993 about 75 joint ventures had already been officially registered, including 66 that were producing hydrocarbons. Sixty different foreign entities from 17 different countries were represented in these ventures, of which more than one third were US or Canadian companies. Most of the ventures were located in three regions of Russia; the Komi Republic, the Khanty-Mansiysk Autonomous District and the Volga-Urals region.[102]

Joint ventures continued to be formed and dissolved throughout the period 1992–1996, and in August of the latter year the US Energy Intelligence Agency identified 106 ventures either in operation, with contracts signed or with some other formal agreement reached.[103] Production data concerning joint ventures is somewhat confusing because of the number of other minor Russian companies that were also producing small quantities of oil at the time. However, Gustafson (2012) estimates that joint venture output peaked in 1996 at 22 million tonnes (440 thousand bpd), accounting for 7% of the total for Russia, while exports reached their highest level in 1998 at 12.6 million tonnes (252 thousand bpd), 11% of Russia's total crude oil exports.[104]

These figures reflect the fact that the boom in the creation of joint ventures ended around 1996, and in the latter half of the 1990s several large- and medium-sized companies that had established ventures – notably Gulf Canada and Deminex – left Russia. Over time this list of leavers grew to include British Gas, BHP, Pennzoil, Bula Resources, Calgary Overseas and Phibro Energy as the investment climate worsened.[105] Particular difficulties included a significant tightening of the tax regime and a cancellation of all previous concessions granted to small enterprises with regards to tax, customs and export regulations. Perhaps the most important of these was the removal of 100% export rights, as it not only seriously undermined the economics of many of the projects but also demonstrated for the first time the lobbying power of the major Russian oil companies in reaction to competition for access to the limited oil export capacity. In essence, it had started to become clear that the advantages brought by international partners in the joint ventures established in the early 1990s were outweighed by the disadvantages. New technology and capital had helped to improve the productivity and economics of a number of assets, but came at the price of increasing competition for licenses and for access to limited pipeline capacity.

The debate over Production Sharing Agreements

Nothing describes the inherent competition between foreign and domestic investors in the Russian oil industry throughout the post-Soviet period better than the debate over the introduction of PSAs that took place over a decade from the early 1990s. As described by the International Energy Agency (2002) PSAs are used in many oil-producing countries outside the OECD as a means of providing foreign investors with a stable legal and tax framework for specific projects in an environment where the general legislative situation remains unstable. The PSA creates a division of profits between the investor and the state through the allocation of cost oil and profit oil throughout the life of a field, enabling the investor to recover his investment and make an agreed rate of return while also allowing the state to take an increasing share of profits (once costs have been paid off).[106] As a result, PSAs seemed to offer an ideal solution for Russia in the early 1990s, when the uncertainties of the fiscal and legal regimes did not provide a solid platform for the significant levels of FDI that were needed, and as a consequence the balance between the contribution of foreign investors and their potential return did not appear to be acceptable.

Before discussing the implications of the PSA debate in more detail, it is worth pausing for a moment to consider what foreign investors believed they were contributing and also what barriers they faced in making those contributions, as the issues will be very relevant to our continuing analysis. Specifically, the international oil companies brought three key contributions – technical know-how, access to capital and business management skills – which have consistently formed the basis for their negotiations with the Russian state and Russian domestic players throughout the post-Soviet period. From a technical standpoint, foreign oil companies had been using the techniques required to initiate a recovery in Russian oil output in similar fields in Alaska and Canada for many years, in particular through the use of 3D seismic, directional and horizontal drilling and the use of advanced well enhancement and recovery techniques. As one example of the bargaining strength this clearly gave the IOCs, a key driver for the merger of TNK's and BP's Russian assets was the Russian partners desire to access BP's technical skills. German Khan, a senior manager at AAR, the Russian shareholder in the joint venture, identified that the joint venture with BP would mean "better reservoir management as well as the establishment of integrated professional teams for specific technical purposes", bringing "approaches [that] have never been used in Russia before".[107]

However, the higher initial cost of this new technology was a clear barrier for the Russian oil industry in the early post-Soviet years. As a result the potential for international oil companies to bring much needed capital for investment was a big incentive to encourage FDI in the early to mid-1990s. At the very least the presence of an IOC in a project could provide the extra credibility needed to win over the financial institutions cautious about lending to the Russian VIOCs. At best it could mean the carrying of a Russian partner through the initial investment stages of a project development in return for a share of cashflows once the field had started to produce hydrocarbons.

Thirdly, IOCs brought many years of experience in managing large oilfields and project developments. Although this might not have seemed relevant to a country with a long oil industry history, in fact the command structure of the Soviet Union had created an environment in which instructions concerning all major issues were handed down from Ministries or technical institutes, meaning that the operating units that formed the major Russian oil companies had little experience of either managing projects or optimizing the organizational structure of their companies. Even in the early 1990s, when the priority appeared to be rapid oilfield recovery rather than corporate organiza-tion, the benefits of an international mentality were noted by Russian oilmen, who commented on personal incentives that each foreign specialist appeared to have to operate in the most efficient and cost effective manner.[108] As time progressed, the broader benefits of international management techniques were also appreciated by Russian businessmen such as German Khan, who explained that: "Entering into a partnership with BP seemed the best means of getting access to world-class international energy experience and to accelerate the behaviours and processes we had already recognized as vital to the company's [TNK's] future ... such as greater transparency, enhanced corporate governance, improved management processes, longer-term strategic thinking, HSE[109], etc."[110]

Key problems for foreign investors

However, the ability of foreign companies to apply these skills in a profitable manner in Russia during the 1990s (and arguably to the current day) was being undermined by some key "above ground" risks. As described by the International Energy Agency (2002) in making the case for PSAs they can be briefly summarized as:[111]

a) *The absence of a stable and competitive fiscal framework* – in particular, the levels and structure of taxation on the oil sector were an issue throughout the post-Soviet era, often acting as a major disincentive to invest. During the 1990s the key problem was a vicious cycle of high tax burden accom-panied by tax evasion on a massive scale, which was endemic to the Russian economy during the 1990s.[112] The total number of taxes on the oil sector collected at a Federal, regional and local level reached almost 100 in some areas during the 1990s, with the overall system being based exces-sively on revenues and volumes rather than on profits, and being subject to frequent changes.[113] As a result companies were particularly vulnerable at times of low oil prices, with the oil extraction industry running at an aggre-gate loss during the 1990s because of the combination of low prices and a tax rate that amounted to over 100% of the operating margin for much of the period. As one official of the Ministry put it at the time, "While most Russian producers are not even breaking even, the finance ministry regards the oil sector as a primary source of budget revenue."[114]

Over the past decade the situation has improved to an extent, mainly thanks to the fact that taxes on the oil sector are now linked to oil prices, meaning that a sliding scale has been introduced that allows profits to be made. However, although one major problem from the 1990s, namely non-payment of taxes, has been solved, the current tax laws continue to be revenue rather than profit-based, and therefore provide little incentive for new investment, as companies have no guarantee that they will be able to recover their costs and make an adequate rate of return. The debate on this issue is continuing, and as discussed earlier some adjustments have been made in new regions such as the offshore, but the Russian oil tax system remains a key issue for foreign investors in the industry.

b) *The legal system and property rights* – uncertainty over both the meaning of laws and their implementation has been at the heart of foreign investor concerns over investing in Russia. The key issues can be summarized through an analysis of the Law on Underground Mineral Resources, which was introduced as a temporary umbrella law in February 1992 to define who owned and who could produce Russia's natural resources. The idea was that it would be supplemented by more specific mineral laws, but due to numerous delays and debates among vested interest groups it has remained one of the key pieces of legislation for the sector throughout the past 20 years. Its main initial inadequacy as a piece of legislation was that it failed to identify which level of government owned the country's resources,[115] setting up a process of joint jurisdiction between the federal and regional governments that caused numerous disputes. Described as the "two-key" process, it caused significant problems for all investors, but particularly for foreigners who were trying to understand how to balance the requirements of laws that often appeared to conflict with each other. Substantial amendments were finally introduced in January 2000 which clarified a number of issues concerning the rights of licence owners, but importantly the issue of license transfer remains unclear even now.

The centralization of power under President Putin from 2000 has significantly reduced the power of the regional authorities, but new complications have emerged as multiple federal agencies are now competing to have influence over the oil sector. For example, when the Ministry of Natural Resources proposed changes to the 1992 Law to introduce more competition for licences in 2004, it was opposed not only by the state companies Rosneft and Gazprom, but also by regional authorities, who were fearful of losing yet more influence, and by the Ministry of Economy.[116] Disputes with the Ministry of Energy and the Ministry of Finance are also commonplace, while regional authorities continue to have a significant say on specific issues concerning land use, the environment and licences for specific activities. As a result, the potential confusion and complexity, whether deliberately manufactured or accidental, remains.

A further level of difficulty for foreign investors has also been caused by the inclusion of an amendment on strategic reserves, which restricts control of oilfields with reserves larger than 70 million tonnes (511 million barrels) and gas fields over 50 bcm (1.8 tcf) to companies with more than 51% Russian ownership.[117] When this rule is combined with the additional issue that exploration licenses are separate from production and development licenses, a perverse set of incentives is created for investment in the sector. Private companies are reluctant to explore extensively for large new fields under exploration licenses for fear that, if "strategic" discoveries are made, the production and development license will not be awarded to them but to a state company. However, the reduced level of exploration activity which results from this fear can trigger an investigation by the Ministry and lead to the potential removal of the exploration licence.

c) *Export rights and access to the transport system* – an issue that was especially relevant during the late 1990s as oil production began to recover but capacity on the export system was restricted. Access to export markets in the 1990s was of particular relevance to oil companies not only because of the disparity between domestic and international prices (which consistently saw domestic prices at 50% or less of world prices)[118] but also because of the problems of non-payment in Russia.[119] At first, many joint ventures were offered the incentive of 100% export rights in order to encourage their initial capital investment. As a result of this incentive, the average export share for joint ventures was 84.6% of their total production in 1992.[120] However, as pressure on the export system from domestic producers increased during the 1990s, export privileges for joint ventures were gradually reduced, leading to a fall in the average share of production exported to 46% in 1993 and to 37% in 2000. This became a particular issue when Russian oil production increased sharply from 1998, as capacity utilization in the state-owned pipeline system increased from 78% to 88% between 1999 and 2003, and the need for contacts, influence and local knowledge became a vital factor in maintaining access to the most important oil export market.

Significant investments in new pipelines by Transneft, the state-owned oil trunk pipeline company, over the past decade have reduced the pressure on the export system, although explicit and implicit restrictions do remain in place that effectively limit the share of production that can be exported in order to ensure that the local market is supplied. However, the fact that domestic crude oil and oil product prices are now close, and in some instances above, international levels, means that the issue of export restrictions is not as relevant today as it was when PSAs were being discussed in the 1990s.

d) *General levels of transparency and corruption* – including a lack of clarity in dealings with the state and domestic companies, as well as the fear of being caught up in corrupt practices due to the lack of a stable legal environment. Lack of transparency ranged from the accounting standards being used by Russian companies to the identity of shareholders and other stakeholders in various entities throughout the oil sector, which caused uncertainty for foreign investors in establishing reliable contracts and deal valuations. Corruption meanwhile has been and continues to be endemic in the Russian commercial environment. As noted by the World Bank, "in countries where national wealth is highly concentrated in a few productive assets, there are significant risks that powerful interests will seek to gain control over them and invest some portion of their windfall gains to capture state institutions in an effort to sustain and strengthen their positions".[121] This was clearly the case in Russia during the 1990s, where the wealth generated in the oil and gas sector encouraged state officials and the oil elite to form corruption networks in order to sequester profits, with an increasing number of state bodies trying to get involved in the sector in order to share the rewards (McPherson, 1996).[122] These networks, and the state capture they involved, were aimed at achieving three key objectives, namely to keep control over the oil industry and ensure favourable market conditions, to increase profits through illegal activities, especially smuggling, and to launder illegal profits and invest them for personal profit, avoiding tax if possible.[123] In addition state officials and the oil elite also attempted to avoid unnecessary competition for rents in the sector, and so any new player was viewed with suspicion. This was particularly the case when that player was a foreigner with vested interests outside Russia that might conflict with its dealings inside the country. As such, the evolution of "state capture", whereby local actors could use their influence and contacts to encourage state institutions to make decisions in their favour,[124] acted as a significant barrier to entry for foreign investors in the natural resource sector.

Interestingly, even in the 2000s as the major Russian players attempted to move their companies towards a more international business ethic as they prepared for entry into the global market, the continued perception that any strategic investor in Russia needs to partner with an influential local has emphasized the ongoing need to deal with the local business environment, including corrupt practices. Indeed Russia ranked 45th out of 54 countries in the Corruption Perception Index published by Transparency International in 1996 (i.e. in the bottom 20%) and in 2012 it ranked in 133rd place out of 176 countries (still in the bottom 25%), underlining the continuing problem even today.

Given these business issues, it is not surprising that many foreign investors decided to delay their investment decisions in Russia until a more stable legal and tax regime had been introduced that could give them clarity on specific issues for their own field developments via an individual PSA agreement. However, increasingly opposed to them were Russian domestic players who were not only becoming skeptical about the real benefits being brought by foreigners but were also increasingly concerned about foreign competition in the oil sector. As Gustafson (2012) points out, the joint ventures that had operated in the early 1990s had not brought as much new technology and cash as had been hoped and by the late 1990s many Russians were convinced that "[with] the same type of equipment...we would be able to compete with our colleagues from the United States".[125] Given this belief, however, what they did not need to do was to make it easier for foreign companies to gain control of domestic assets, and as a result opposition for the PSA regime that could make this easier began to emerge.

In fact three PSA agreements pre-dated any official legislation on the subject in Russia, having been signed in 1993/94 with an Exxon-Rosneft partnership at Sakhalin 1, a Shell consortium at Sakhalin-2 (both located in the Far East of Russia) and a Total group at Kharyaga in north-west Russia. However, these "grand-fathered" PSAs, signed on favourable terms due to the strong bargaining position of the foreign investors at a time of desperation in the Russian oil industry, themselves contributed to the overall perception of PSAs as being "privileges granted to foreign investors" (Landes, 2003a).[126] As a result, when a more general PSA law was introduced to the Russian Duma in 1995 it was passed only with much difficulty, but the enabling legislation that would have put it into practice was consistently blocked and delayed.[127] The most aggressive opponents of the legislation were Russian oil companies that appeared to have wanted to restrict access to opportunities for any form of competition in the domestic oil sector. Initially the legislation had helped to do this by restricting the use of PSAs to a maximum of 30% of the country's oil resource base, which would effectively have capped the number of PSAs at the original 28 approved by the Duma between 1995 and 1998. By 2000, though, as Russian output climbed sharply, it became clear that even allowing these fields to go ahead would undermine the potential for domestic players to continue to expand both output and export sales. Aggressive lobbying in the Duma, in particular by Yukos,[128] ultimately encouraged a further change of the government's position and brought about a series of amendments that effectively ended the prospects for further PSAs. Indeed the success of the Russian oil lobby is evidenced by the fact that, apart from the three original and unique deals signed in 1993/94 not a single PSA with a foreign investor was signed after the initial passing of the general law in 1995.[129]

Equity investment as an alternative for IOCs in Russia

The fierce opposition to the PSA proposals was driven not only by a desire to minimize competition for specific fields and for access to pipeline infrastructure and export quotas but also because a much bigger prize, involving the sale of entire companies, was available in the mid-to-late 1990s. As described in the previous section, the privatization of the Russian oil industry began as early as 1993 with the initial sale of some shares in LUKOIL, but the momentum really accelerated in 1995/1996 with the shares-for-loans auctions and the subsequent sale of other more peripheral state-owned oil assets. Indeed the process of privatization continued all the way through until 2002, when the sales of 37% of Eastern Oil, 75% of Slavneft and a small rump of shares in LUKOIL brought the significant sales of state equity in the country's oil companies to a close (Landes, 2003c).[130] Arguably the entire privatization process was an exercise in the use of influence and vested interest that allowed key entrepreneurs to gain access to valuable assets at low prices, and the absence of international companies at the privatization auctions certainly helped to reduce competition and keep the prices down. As a result, Russia saw the emergence across its economy of the Financial Industrial Groups (FIGs) that wielded so much influence during the late 1990s and early 2000s.

Indeed by 2002 the IEA noted the trend in Russia towards "a concentration of economic activity in large financial industrial groups, many of which enjoyed special relations with government institutions".[131] Although these groups were not all related to the oil industry, it is clear from Table 1.2 that oil companies played a significant role in at least five of the major groups, of which three (Menatep, Millhouse Capital and Alfa Group) were owned by financial entrepreneurs who had little experience in the industry. This ownership structure was to become relevant for potential foreign investors, but only after the next stage of the privatization process had been completed, namely the consolidation of the newly acquired assets under firm central control. The new owners of Russian oil companies understood that they had to change the ownership and governance structures of their businesses in order to take firmer control over the financial flows within their organizations, and this led to some of the battles described earlier as the shares of subsidiary companies were acquired often under controversial terms. However, the second reason for consolidating ownership was to create an entity in which a part of the equity could be sold to foreign investors, either in an IPO or as a strategic sale (or both). In this way the new owners could not only hope to make some initial return on their investment by "cashing out" some of their shares but could also attempt to bring in some of the international management skills that they recognized would be required to turn their collection of oil assets into truly integrated and world-class companies.

As a result, investment in the equity of oil companies became the new option for IOCs looking to invest in Russia. The availability of equity in individual companies related not only to the timing of their consolidation but also to the motivations of the Russian owners, as all of the companies proceeded to consolidate their corporate structures at different rates. Interestingly, the first to make shares available to foreigners was not one of the oligarch-owned entities but LUKOIL, that had become a coherent enough

Table 1.2   Russia's largest industrial groups in 2001

Shareholder Group	Key Assets	Aggregate 2001 Revenues ($bn)	Revenues as % of fully privatized companies
LUKOIL	LUKOIL Includes Sidanco by 2001	13.6	24.5%
Menatep	Yukos	9.8	17.7%
Alfa Group	TNK Golden Telecom, Akrikhin	5.5	9.9%
Surgutneftegaz	Surgutneftegaz	5.5	9.9%
Millhouse Capital	Sibneft, GAZ, Pavlovo Bus	4.7	8.4%
Interros	Norilsk Nickel	3.6	6.5%
Avtovaz	Avtovaz	3.1	5.7%
Severstal	Severstal, UAZ	2.0	3.7%
Total for "Eight"		**47.8**	**86.3%**

Source: Data compiled and estimated from multiple company sources

entity even as early as 1995 to offer a 7.99% share that was purchased by US oil company ARCO,[132] initially in the form of convertible bonds. In tandem with this purchase the two companies also formed a joint venture, LUKARCO, that was intended to invest in assets both inside and outside Russia (Gorst, 2007).[133] It achieved this with investments in Kazakhstan and Azerbaijan but ultimately failed to provide ARCO with access to Russian assets or LUKOIL with access to broader international assets due to continuous disagreements over valuation, a theme that would be prevalent among many JVs involving the interaction between Russian and overseas assets. Furthermore, ARCO's 7.99% stake was specifically determined to be below the level at which ARCO could gain an automatic seat on the LUKOIL Board, underlining the fact that the new relationship was not seen as a true strategic partnership but more as a financial investment with possible added benefits. In the end, the BP acquisition of ARCO in 2000[134] put an end to what had already become an ultimately disappointing first foray into equity investment by the IOCs in Russia, and BP sold its new LUKOIL stake in January 2001.[135]

BP's disposal of its LUKOIL shares did not indicate a reluctance to invest in Russian companies, however, as it had already made a landmark purchase of a 10% stake in Sidanco, bought from the Interros Group owned by Vladimir Potanin for $571 million in late 1997.[136] The investment allowed BP to place directors on the Sidanco Board and to have significant influence throughout the company, where its secondees offered advice on and management of financial, operational and technical issues. However, the risks inherent in such an equity stake within a weak institutional environment were laid bare following the financial crisis of 1998, when BP's key partner, Potanin, became more focused on the survival of his other assets (in particular his core mining company Norilsk Nickel) than on Sidanco and the company, already in a precarious financial state, was left at the mercy of a corporate predator and Russia's unique bankruptcy laws.

Initially the downturn in both the Russian economy and the oil price in 1998 led to a conflict between Sidanco and the regional authorities over unpaid taxes, with the regional authorities reacting to the tax shortfall by bringing bankruptcy proceedings against a number of Sidanco subsidiaries. These proceedings were then exploited by Sidanco's rivals using the legal rights given to creditors under a combination of Russia's 1998 Federal Law on Bankruptcy, the 1999 Law on Insolvency of Credit Organisations and the Law on Restructuring Credit Organisations. Essentially these laws allowed creditors with even a small amount of debt outstanding to call for a company to be placed under bankruptcy proceedings, at which point a court could appoint independent external management to run the company during the bankruptcy process. However, as the IEA pointed out, "Inconsistent actions by liquidators and courts indicate that the bankruptcy mechanism remains subject to lobbying pressure and political influences."[137]

The clearest example of the problems caused by the bankruptcy law was seen in the attempts by TNK to acquire some of Sidanco's assets in 1999. In essence TNK was able to force, quite legally, a number of Sidanco subsidiaries into bankruptcy through refusing repayment of debts they were owed,[138] and to arrange the appointment of a friendly administrator who put the subsidiaries' assets up for sale and managed the auctions to ensure that it (TNK) won.[139] As BP and Sidanco's shareholders attempted to regain control of their assets it proved impossible in practice to enforce any court orders and persuade TNK management to return effective control. A final resolution was only reached in August 2001, when Sidanco shareholders other than BP agreed to sell their stake to TNK,[140] Sidanco's assets were returned and BP increased its stake in the company to 25%, heralding the ultimate formation of TNK-BP two years later. However, the process had demonstrated that judgements, particularly in regional courts, could be heavily influenced by vested interests to strip any company of its prize assets,[141] with the result that even the largest foreign investor could be left exposed to the vagaries of the Russian legal system and the exploitation of legal loopholes by aggressive domestic players.

BP's experiences with Sidanco had a significant effect on the perceptions of other foreign investors during the late 1990s and early 2000s.[142] As described by one commentator at the time, "BP has faced repeated and seemingly intractable difficulties. Potential foreign investors are closely watching its fortunes in Russia, and do not seem in a hurry to commit themselves given what they have seen, especially this year."[143] In the light of this attention, and inflamed comments such as "successful marriages do not begin with rape"[144] and "you don't talk to someone who's just stolen your wallet"[145] from those close to the negotiations between TNK and BP it is not surprising that a hiatus in significant foreign investment occurred between 1998 and 2003. During this period Elf opened discussions with Sibneft about purchasing a strategic equity stake,[146] but retreated under pressure from its international shareholders who were concerned about the impact of the investment risks in Russia on the French company's share price.[147] Meanwhile Shell's strategic alliance with Gazprom, announced with great fanfare in 1997 the day before BP's investment in Sidanco, also failed to produce any positive results, due to a combination of the impact of the financial crisis, an inability to agree the terms for specific investments and Gazprom's dismay at Shell's continuing interest in gas from the Caspian region, which it regarded as a direct threat to its own gas business (Stern, 2005).[148]

The hiatus was broken, perhaps not surprisingly, by the resolution of the dispute over Sidanco between BP and TNK and the ultimate merger of the Russian assets of the two companies into TNK-BP in 2003. BP contributed its 25% interest in Sidanco as well as its stake in Rusia Petroleum, a gas company in Irkutsk, plus $6.2 billion while AAR, the owners of TNK, contributed all their oil assets, including TNK and the rest of Sidanco, to form Russia's third largest oil company. The deal emphasized not only that Russia's most experienced foreign investor felt that it was still possible to do business in the country but also that Russian investors saw the benefits of IOC involvement again, as they started to focus on the potential for creating and extracting value from their companies' stock market capitalization rather than just on the consolidation of financial flows. This was a theme that was also starting to be adopted by companies such as Yukos and Sibneft, but with a rather different ultimate outcome.

The nearly sale of Yukos

The consolidation phase at Yukos moved towards its conclusion in 1999 as it reached agreements, not always amicably, with the shareholders in its subsidiaries to buy them out in return for shares in the central holding company. However, Menatep, the vehicle through which Mikhail Khodorkovsky owned Yukos, decided not to adopt the Interros strategy of an immediate sale of shares to an IOC but instead sought to increase its value first, with the intention of multiplying the value of its ultimate exit strategy. As described by Landes (2003c) it went about this in two ways. Firstly it responded to the negative shareholder reaction caused by its controversial consolidation techniques by launching an internationally traded ADR programme and improving its transparency and corporate governance, including the appointment of independent directors and the introduction of US GAAP financial reporting. Secondly, as described earlier, it pioneered the use of foreign service contractors to rehabilitate its oilfields and catalysed a remarkable turnaround in production. The impact of these events on potential foreign investment in the Russian oil sector was significant. In particular, the arrival of the international oil service companies and their willingness to operate in a risky environment removed one of the main competitive strengths of the international oil companies. The Russian VIOCs could access the latest technology and expertise via contractors rather than strategic investors, and they saw the output from their fields and the value of their companies jump as a result. When combined with the uncertainties caused by the BP-Sidanco debate, this factor further contributed to the lack of foreign investment in the period 1998–2003.

By 2003, though, Yukos had achieved its initial goal of increasing its market value, from a low of below $1 billion in 1998 to over $30 billion in 2003.[149] The time had come to generate some value for the major shareholders from this growth through the sale of a significant stake to a foreign company, and as reported in September 2003 two companies in particular, Chevron and ExxonMobil, were competing for a 25% interest in the company for a possible price of $11 billion.[150] However, as documented in detail by Gustafson (2012)[151] the negotiations took place under the cloud of increasing resentment and suspicion of Khodorkovsky from the Russian authorities, who were particularly concerned about his lobbying activities in the Duma and his interference in foreign policy issues such as Russia's relationships with China and the US. Ultimately Chevron fell out of the negotiations after its final offer was refused by Yukos, who at the time was also negotiating a merger with its fellow Russian company Sibneft, and this left Exxon as the final potential buyer of as much as 40% of the company. President Putin himself confirmed that negotiations were at an advanced stage in October 2003,[152] but at the same time regulators in Moscow were raiding Yukos offices searching for evidence of the tax evasion charges that would ultimately bring down the company. Indeed, within days of Putin's acknowledgement of discussions between Yukos and Exxon, Khodorkovsky had been arrested at an airfield in Novosibirsk[153] and any realistic prospect of an investment by Exxon had ended. It is unclear whether the prospect of a major US company taking a stake in Russia's largest company had been any form of catalyst behind the demise of Yukos, but what is certain is that no major international oil company was offered another significant opportunity to invest in the Russian oil sector until the corporate landscape had altered very dramatically.

Although Exxon continued to be mentioned as a possible buyer of Yukos in 2004,[154] while Chevron, Shell and Total were supposedly competing to buy into Sibneft,[155] which had ended its merger arrangement with Yukos after the arrest of Khodorkovsky, it soon became obvious that the Russian Administration would not be prepared to sanction the deals.[156] As the cases against Yukos proceeded, and the company's subsidiaries were ultimately sold off in bankruptcy auctions, the Russian oil sector entered its fourth phase of the post-Soviet era, namely the return of the State as a major resource owner. Rosneft was the main beneficiary of this process, dramatically increasing in size as it acquired Yuganskneftegaz, Samaraneftegaz and other Yukos companies in the upstream and downstream sectors. Gazprom meanwhile acquired Sibneft, which had been encouraged not to sell a stake to a foreign investor, and renamed it GazpromNeft.

LUKOIL and ConocoPhillips

However, just before the period of re-assertion of state control really took hold, which can probably be timed from the auction of Yuganskneftegaz (Yukos' biggest upstream subsidiary) in December 2004, one final private sector sale took place. In September 2004 ConocoPhillips, the US major, purchased a 7.6% stake in LUKOIL from the Russian government for almost $2 billion, and committed to increase its interest to 20% over the next two years.[157] In addition to the equity interest, LUKOIL and ConocoPhillips also formed a joint venture called Naryanmarnefetgas for the development of fields in the Timan Pechora region of north-west Russia, with Conoco taking a 30% interest. The acquisition had clearly been approved by the Kremlin, with many commentators seeing it as a sign that the Russian authorities wanted to signal "business as usual" despite the issues surrounding Yukos, but in more practical terms it was based on the relationship between the two company CEOs and their desire for reciprocal investment in and outside Russia. However, despite promises of strong co-operation between Vagit Alekperov and Jim Mulva[158] the relationship between the companies failed to develop as planned. Despite an initial investment in Iraq opportunities for further joint international investment were not forthcoming, much to LUKOIL's disappointment. In Russia the Timan Pechora JV started well but then ran into geological and production problems which saw both reserves and oil output downgraded by more than 50%. In addition the relationship between the companies, which initially had promised to cover wide-ranging technical and strategic co-operation never really went further than the friendship between the two leaders. In the end even this was not enough to keep the alliance together once it became clear, according to Mulva, that "the Russian government was handing over large deposits to Gazprom and Rosneft, while the business development outlook for private oil companies, let alone those with foreign ownership, was grim".[159]

Effectively, from 2005 it became increasingly apparent that any foreign investor wishing to play a significant role in the oil and gas sector would need to partner with one of the main state-owned companies. This is not to say that small deals did not occur "under the radar". Marathon bought 100% of

West Siberian company KMOC in 2003 and ultimately sold it to LUKOIL in 2006. ONGC, the Indian state oil company, purchased 100% of Imperial Oil, another small producer in 2007. However, anything of a significant nature would now have to involve a company with close connections to the Kremlin.

The challenge of partnering with Gazprom

One company that had a head start in this regard was Wintershall, who had formed a partnership to market Russian gas in Germany with Gazprom as early as 1990, and in 2003 formed its first upstream joint venture in Russia. The Achimgaz JV, in which Wintershall took a 50% stake, was formed to develop the deep gas condensate reserves in licences below the giant Urengoy gas field, and was supplemented by the acquisition of a 35% interest in the South Russkoye field in West Siberia in 2007. In return Wintershall was one of the first international companies that was able to offer acceptable international reciprocity in the form of upstream assets (in Libya) but more importantly a 50% stake in the WINGAS marketing operation in Germany. The companies' partnership to sell gas in Germany and across Europe provided Gazprom with much sought-after access to downstream markets, which it has now extended through the purchase, in 2012, of the remaining 50% of WINGAS in return for giving Wintershall access to extra licenses in West Siberia via the Achimgaz JV.[160] As will be discussed in a later chapter, this element of reciprocity, as well as the joint learning that has taken place as the two companies developed their understanding of deep gas condensate developments, have formed the basis of one of the strongest international partnerships in Russia.

The success of Wintershall in Russia is rather in contrast with its German utility competitor E.ON, which has had a more fraught relationship with Gazprom over the past decade. Initially Ruhrgas, the major German gas importer until its acquisition by E.ON in 2002, had developed Germany's long-term gas relationship with Gazprom and Russia that culminated in the purchase of 6.5% of Gazprom equity between 1996 and 1997, which was widely seen as a move to assist the Russian government in raising funds during difficult economic times and to cement the long-term relationship between the companies. However, Wintershall's offer of reciprocal asset ownership in 2003 allowed it to overtake E.ON as Gazprom's favoured Russian partner, and although E.ON did finally gain some upstream assets in Russia (a 25% stake in the South Russkoye field in 2007), it sold half its shares in Gazprom to acquire this asset and the remaining half in 2010 as it ended its close ties with the company. This apparent deterioration in affairs may well have reflected the difficult contractual negotiations going on at the time, which culminated in E.ON going to arbitration to settle a price dispute in

2011,[161] a case that was only settled in late 2012 and inevitably caused a cooling of relations between the companies.[162]

Dealing with Russia's state-owned gas company has proved difficult for other foreign companies too, in particular as the Russian state has re-asserted its authority over the domestic energy economy. One example of the potentially volatile nature of a relationship with Gazprom is provided by the history of Shell in Russia since the early 1990s. Having initially formed a consortium with Japanese partners to take a 100% interest in the Sakhalin 2 project in the Far East of Russia in 1994, Shell attempted to broaden its exposure to Russia by forming a strategic alliance with Gazprom in 1997 (Kryukov and Moe, 1999). The alliance was planned to include equity investment by Shell into Gazprom shares via a convertible bond and also a wide-ranging exchange of assets in Russia and overseas. However, the 1998 financial crisis dampened Shell's enthusiasm for the convertible bond while negotiations over assets in Russia were undermined by Shell's continued interest in gas in Central Asia, which was regarded by Russia as a threat to its business. As a result discussions over Shell's possible involvement in the giant Zapolyarnoye field in West Siberia were stalled for many years,[163] but eventually in July 2005 an agreement was reached that would have seen Shell gain its long sought-after stake in return for Gazprom entering the Sakhalin 2 project. However, only weeks after the agreement had been signed Shell announced a significant increase in its cost estimates for the Sakhalin project, and although this is unlikely to have been much of a surprise to Gazprom it appeared to trigger a complete change in the negotiations between the companies. A co-ordinated attack on the Sakhalin 2 project was orchestrated by the Ministry of Natural Resources (focused on breaches of environmental rules[164]) with the result that Shell and the other Sakhalin 2 partners were ultimately forced to cede control (in the form of a 51% stake for Gazprom) in return for effective repayment of past costs.[165] Since then relations between Shell and Gazprom do appear to have recovered to the extent that the companies discussed a protocol on international co-operation in 2012,[166] but it is interesting to note that Shell has made no further definitive progress in its Russian business expansion plans since the 2005/06 Sakhalin 2 debate.

Other European companies have also had fluctuating relations with Gazprom over the past decade that have demonstrated not only how difficult it can be to deal with a state company but also how important it is for foreign investors to understand the shifting levels of influence and power within domestic politics. For example, in 2007 ENI (with its Italian partner Enel) offered to help Gazprom during the Yukos auction process as the Russian gas company was concerned about possible law-suits concerning the Yukos bankruptcy process.[167] The Italians bid just under $6 billion for an asset package that included 20% of Gazprom oil subsidiary GazpromNeft as well as 100% of a gas company called Severenergia, which owned a license to develop a gas condensate field in West Siberia. Having won the auction ENI offered Gazprom an option to buy the GazpromNeft shares and also 51% of Severenergia, which was duly exercised in 2009.[168] However, instead of finding itself a partner of Gazprom at Severenergia, as it had expected, ENI discovered that within a year Gazprom's share would be sold to a partnership between GazpromNeft and Novatek, the largest independent Russian gas company.[169] Although this was by no means a disaster for the company, it nevertheless was an odd turn of events for the Italian major that thought that it was developing a strong reciprocal relationship with Gazprom, which also included access to international assets in Libya.

Statoil, the Norwegian national oil company, and Total, the French major oil company, have also had a difficult relationship with Gazprom since their 2007 decision to form a joint company to develop the Shtokman field in the Barents Sea. While Gazprom, with a 51% stake, has been the operator of the project, Statoil (24%) and Total (25%) have contributed much of the technical work thanks to their long experience of offshore developments. However, significant changes in the global gas market, in particular in the US where Shtokman LNG was targeted to be sold, and continuing debate about the development concept and cost of the field led to Statoil giving up its interest in the development company in 2012[170] and the project being postponed, most likely until beyond 2020.[171] Although the ultimate decision to delay the project appears to have been reached fairly amicably, and Total remains a partner in the development company, it is nevertheless interesting to see how all the European companies have reacted in terms of their partnership aspirations during 2012 and 2013.

Total has opted to invest in the shares and a major asset belonging to one of Gazprom's emerging domestic gas competitors, Novatek. In 2011 the French company agreed to purchase 12% of the company, and increased this to 15% in 2012, while it has also taken a 20% interest in the Yamal LNG project in northern Siberia.[172] The choice of both equity stake and project are informative, as Novatek's principle shareholder, Gennady Timchenko, is widely believed to be a member of President Putin's inner circle and an influential investor in the energy sector,[173] while the Yamal LNG project would appear to be in direct competition with Shtokman but has received significant state support in the form of tax exemptions and the construction of regional infrastructure, and may even catalyse the end of Gazprom's monopoly on gas exports from Russia.[174] As such, Total's choice appears to have been to diversify its gas partner options in Russia, and to increase its links with a rapidly emerging force in the domestic, and possibly international, gas markets.

Rosneft as the new magnet for foreign partnership

Statoil and ENI have also opted to diversify their partner relations, but have chosen the oil sector rather than the gas sector as their means to this end, where they have mirrored the strategy chosen most significantly by ExxonMobil to form joint ventures to develop domestic and international assets with Russia's largest, and state-owned, oil company Rosneft. In the development of these joint ventures, that were formed in 2012, we are perhaps now seeing the emergence of the fifth stage in the development of the Russian oil and gas industry, with the return of international partnership to encourage transfer of technology and investment dollars but under the direct control of state companies rather than the private sector.

ExxonMobil has been involved in the Russian oil and gas sector since the early 1990s, but has remained largely on the periphery both in terms of the geography of its investment (the Sakhalin 1 project offshore the Far East of Russia) and in terms of the extent of its financial commitment. However, importantly it has been in a partnership with one of Rosneft's subsidiaries, Sakhalinmorneftegas, since the start of the Sakhalin 1 project, successfully managed a major project through the multiple administrative and operational hurdles prevalent in Russia and demonstrated that it can deliver a multi-billion dollar project into production on a timely and efficient basis. First oil production started in 2005, and the multi-phase development of the project's three fields will continue through the current decade. Disputes over the sale of gas have led ExxonMobil and Rosneft to now consider the option of an LNG export plant, again creating potential competition with Gazprom, but overall the success of the project and the burgeoning relationship between the partners led to the announcement of a major exploration deal between ExxonMobil and Rosneft in 2011.

In August of that year the two companies announced a strategic co-operation agreement that would see joint ventures formed to explore three huge licenses in the South Kara Sea in the Russian Arctic and one license in the Black Sea, to develop tight oil resources in West Siberia and to offer Rosneft the opportunity to participate in international assets in the US and Canada.[175] In February 2013 this agreement was expanded further to include seven more license areas in the Chukchi, Laptev and Kara Seas, again in the Russian Arctic, with Rosneft gaining access to a natural gas project in Alaska.[176] The strategic relevance of these deals for both companies is very significant, and demonstrates a potential path of foreign investor partnerships in Russia.

ExxonMobil has gained access to an enormous swathe of acreage in a number of prospective new regions in Russia. The estimated resources in the Kara Sea licenses alone total 36 billion boe[177] (of which ExxonMobil would have a 33.3% share) while the more recently awarded blocks in the Chukchi,

Laptev and Kara Seas could hold up to 150 billion boe.[178] Of course the exploration for and development of any reserves that are actually discovered will be a lengthy and expensive process, especially given the remote geography and harsh environmental conditions involved, but the long-term potential of the acreage is undeniable. The shorter-term potential of the deals could be enhanced by the potential development of Rosneft's tight oil resources onshore, where 8.8 billion barrels of oil is estimated to have the potential to produce up to 300 thousand bpd by 2020.[179] In addition the Black Sea acreage also offers significant potential reserves in a relatively easier and more accessible environment. Importantly for ExxonMobil, though, the joint ventures offer the company the opportunity to bring some real value to Russia in the form of technology (for offshore and tight oil), financial support (the South Kara Sea developments alone could cost up to $50 billion) and risk mitigation (ExxonMobil will fund the initial exploration phase for all the joint ventures). In the process it will also give it the opportunity to create a unique joint learning experience between its employees and those of Rosneft as the two companies seek to develop Russia into a world leader in Arctic oil development.

From Rosneft's perspective, its lack of offshore and tight oil experience meant that international partnership was desirable, and perhaps even necessary, if these new regions were to be developed in a timely and effective manner. The ExxonMobil model also offers it risk-free exposure to the exploration phase as well as financial risk mitigation at the time when developments are undertaken. Importantly the deals also offer access to international assets where the company can gain direct experience of the types of developments that are becoming more crucial in Russia. Rosneft has gained access to 20 licenses offshore in the Gulf of Mexico as well as to unconventional oil and gas developments in the US and Canada which will have direct relevance to the emerging unconventional opportunities in Russia. Furthermore the opportunity for technology transfer will be further enhanced by the development of an Arctic Research and Design Centre for Offshore Projects, which will allow the joint ventures to make a lasting impression on the development of Russia's oil sector. As a result there is a strong element of reciprocity in the agreements between ExxonMobil and Rosneft, underlining that Russia is not only trying to access the advanced technology to develop its own resources but is also keen to develop international partnerships overseas in order to expand its presence in the global energy economy.

ENI and Statoil have followed similar models to ExxonMobil in developing their new joint ventures with Rosneft. ENI has taken a 33% interest in two licenses in the Barents Sea plus a similar stake in a block offshore in the Black Sea.[180] Statoil has one license in the Barents Sea to the north of those where ENI is a partner plus three blocks in the Sea of Okhotsk in the Far East of Russia and an interest in some onshore tight oil acreage in West Siberia and

Stavropol.[181] The agreement with Statoil bears close similarities with the ExxonMobil deal, as it offers Rosneft international reciprocity (in the form of access to the 22nd licensing round in Norway) as well as IOC involvement in a new technology centre in Russia, this time focused on environmental protection. For Statoil, the opportunity to access new resources both onshore and offshore is clear, and it has also been able to take advantage of the warmer geo-political relations between Norway and Russia since the end of the border dispute between the two countries in the Barents Sea in 2012. The opportunity for a broader development of oil and gas reserves in the region, with the exploitation of synergies between the hydrocarbon industries in both countries, clearly offers both Rosneft and Statoil significant opportunities for further partnership in future. The ENI-Rosneft partnership follows a similar, but as yet less well-developed, route, with the Italian company financing the exploration costs in its three blocks, providing technical expertise and promising international assets, although nothing specific has yet been identified. Nevertheless, as Rosneft has firmly stated at the announcement of all three deals "[these new joint ventures are] further proof that Rosneft is committed to doing business with world-class majors that have offshore production expertise, cutting-edge technologies and are ready to invest in long-term hi-tech projects in Russia. I strongly believe that our partnership will help boost the two companies' resource base and capitalization."[182]

BP's route from oligarch to NOC partnership

The move towards international partnership with Russia's NOCs, and in particular Rosneft, is further underlined by the decision of the largest foreign investor in Russia, BP, to adopt the same strategy following a decade or more of co-operation with private companies and entrepreneurs in Russia. Indeed, the history of BP's investment in Russia provides in one example a microcosm of the experiences of international companies over the past two decades and demonstrates the changing reality of partnership in a country where the shifting power of institutions and influence of individuals has been difficult for foreign companies to interpret and understand.

As discussed above, BP and TNK brought four years of dispute over the assets and ownership of Sidanco to a close in 2003 by agreeing to merge their Russian assets into a joint venture named TNK-BP, in which BP took a 50% interest and the AAR[183] consortium took the remaining half. Interestingly and uniquely this 50:50 partnership was the only example of a major joint venture in which the foreign partner had equal control,[184] and although the structure was criticized by President Putin as being a recipe for continuing disputes[185] it was arguably this structure which kept the company together for the decade of its existence. Indeed BP CEO John Browne commented in his book "Beyond Business" (2010): "I tried to push for 51 percent but both Putin and Fridman told me we could not have it. I knew if we had 49 percent we would have no power whatsoever. So in the end the only option was going for a 50-50 deal."[186] Nevertheless, Putin was certainly prescient about the likelihood of disputes between the partners as the turbulent history of the joint venture company amply demonstrated, especially as BP, in common with its international peers in Russia, began to realize that the future lay in partnership with state companies.

Initially the story at TNK-BP was similar to those seen at Yukos and Sibneft in the early 2000s, as rehabilitation of Soviet era fields using modern international development techniques resulted in significant increases in production and recoverable reserves. A presentation by the company's Chief Operating Officer Tim Summers in 2006 highlighted the dramatic improvements that had been made in the first three years of the partnership, with output up by 30%, 2.5 billion boe of new reserves added and a reserve replacement ratio of 132%.[187] However, inevitably the benefits derived from the brownfield re-development slowed and by 2010 a similar presentation to investors showed that production growth had fallen to 1–2% per annum and highlighted that greenfields and the search for opportunities in new regions of Russia would be the drivers for growth in future.[188]

However, this combination of factors became a source of frustration for both partners at TNK-BP. AAR began to express disappointment that the large number of secondees brought in at high cost from BP could not continue to produce the results seen in the first years of the partnership.[189] Meanwhile it had become clear to BP, in common with its international peers in Russia, that growth opportunities were far more likely to be offered to the partners of state-owned rather than private companies, and with this in mind they began to seek to broaden their sphere of activities. Although it was no doubt BP's desire to keep its intentions secret, in 2007 and 2008 it was being widely reported in the domestic and international press that a deal to swap assets was being negotiated with Gazprom, and AAR perceived this as a threat to their own interests in Russia.[190] Nevertheless, BP and TNK-BP together signed a Memorandum of Understanding with Gazprom in June 2007, implying that all the TNK-BP partners were supportive of a deal,[191] but then by March of the following year it appeared that open conflict had broken out between them. A series of attacks on TNK-BP appeared to be aimed at disconcerting the foreign employees and shareholders, including the arrest of an employee by the FSB, the withdrawal of expat visas, an investigation by the Environmental Agency and the start of an investigation by the Tax Authorities.[192] By May the Russian partners were calling for the resignation of TNK-BP CEO Bob Dudley, a former BP executive, and by June he had left Russia fearing the threat of legal action being taken against him.[193] However, despite this high level of friction, which ultimately forced Dudley to resign, AAR and BP managed to find a resolution that allowed the Russian partners to take more control of TNK-BP while BP secured its rights through the appointment of independent directors and an agreement on governance and dividend issues.

Nevertheless, the dispute appeared to have convinced BP that the future of the TNK-BP partnership was limited, and its search for an NOC partner in Russia continued. By 2010 negotiations with the increasingly powerful Rosneft were underway, but they were kept no more secret than the discussions with Gazprom in 2007/08.[194] The Deep Water Horizon disaster in the Gulf of Mexico in April 2010 put the agreement on hold for a while, but by January 2011 both parties were ready to announce a deal that involved a share swap and a joint venture to explore three Arctic licenses in the South Kara Sea.[195] However, once again AAR responded to the perceived threat to their position, took BP to court arguing that it was in breach of the TNK-BP share-holder agreement and managed to get a temporary injunction placed on the deal. Ultimately this temporary delay turned into a permanent collapse when Rosneft decided to pursue its Arctic exploration plans with ExxonMobil, and BP was left to look for an alternative exit strategy from TNK-BP.[196]

Despite this setback BP remained convinced that its future lay with a Russian state company rather than with a private company, and especially not with partners who had acted so aggressively (albeit legally) over the previous four years. In a proactive move clearly designed to catalyse a response BP announced in June 2012 that it was seeking buyers for its 50% interest in TNK-BP,[197] and by October of the same year had negotiated an agreement with Rosneft to sell its interest in return for 12.84% of Rosneft shares plus $17.1 billion in cash, $5 billion of which would be re-invested into more Rosneft shares to take BP's total stake to 19.75%. Importantly this time AAR were included in BP's transaction plans and also sold their shares in TNK-BP to Rosneft for a cash sum of $28 billion, allowing Rosneft to consolidate 100% of TNK-BP into its balance sheet.

As a result, in spite of the turbulence of its relationship with AAR, that has often masked the operational and financial successes at TNK-BP, it is pertinent to note that BP has turned an approximate initial investment of $8 billion in 2003 into an 18.5% stake in Russia's largest oil producer (worth approximately $16 billion) plus $12 billion in cash in 2013,[198] having received around $19 billion in dividends in the intervening decade. BP will also be able to book its share of Rosneft's 29 billion boe of proved reserves and 4.7 million boepd of production following the transaction. This means that BP is still by far the largest foreign investor in the Russian oil and gas sector, and although it remains to be seen whether its large interest in Rosneft and the two board seats to which it is now entitled will give it significant influence at the company or access to industrial assets, it nevertheless has finally found a route to partnership with Russia's state oil company and the potential for growth that this could imply.

Conclusions

Foreign oil companies have been involved in the development of the Russian oil industry since its earliest days in the 19th century, but their participation has nearly always involved volatility and uncertainty as they have struggled to balance a desire to reap the rewards of Russia's abundant hydrocarbon resources with the risks inherent in investing in a complex commercial and political environment. Initially Russian oil was the catalyst behind the development of international institutions such as the Rothschild's banking empire and the Royal Dutch Shell oil company, but the Russian revolution led to many of their early investments being left worthless. During the ensuing Soviet period foreign activity was limited to technical advice or state-sponsored assistance, until the economic and political reforms initiated by President Gorbachev in the mid-1980s and the subsequent ending of the era of socialism in Russia and the FSU offered the hope that the prospects for the industry could be boosted through an exposure to foreign technology, management skills and capital. International joint ventures were introduced as a vehicle to encourage investment to catalyse the recovery of the Russian oil industry, and at one stage in 1994 a senior US administration official implied that US companies alone were preparing to invest US$20–25 billion in the Russian oil and gas industry,[199] while other estimates for potential foreign investment in the sector ranged as high as US$70 billion.[200]

However, despite the enormous requirements for investment in the oil and gas sector, total cumulative FDI in the upstream oil sector had only reached about US$4 billion by the end of 2000, and even this total was only achieved thanks to the relative success of three key projects.[201] Indeed in the five-year period 1997–2001 FDI in the oil sector was actually outstripped by foreign investment in the food processing sector, which attracted US$3.2 billion during the period compared to US$2.6 billion for the "oil extraction sector".[202] Indeed as Nash summarized the situation in 2002: "there have only ever been a handful of significant foreign investments in the Russian oil and gas sector".[203] The reasons for the lack of activity centered around the conflicting interests of the international and domestic actors involved in the Russian oil and gas sector at that time. International investors were looking for a secure legal and financial framework within which they could gain some certainty that any investments made would have some chance of generating an adequate return. In trying to achieve this they explored various investment routes, including joint ventures around specific assets, corporate-style structures, equity investment in existing companies and combinations of all three. However, most of their attempts foundered because domestic entrepreneurs were focused on buying assets cheaply in the privatization process, consolidating their assets under firm control and establishing their position within the industry without the threat of competition from wealthier and more experienced foreign players. This contrast was definitively exposed in the dispute between BP and TNK over the assets of Sidanco, and the controversy this caused was enough to put off most foreign investors until its resolution in 2003.

Following the formation of TNK-BP the future for FDI in the Russian oil sector appeared much brighter, but the conflict between the Russian Administration and Yukos, followed by the rise of the Russian state oil and gas companies as major actors in the oil sector, undermined the plans of most IOCs. For a number of years the political environment did not encourage foreign participation as the state attempted to regain control of its strategic industries, and it is only now that Rosneft has established itself as the major player in the oil sector, with Gazprom in a similar position in the gas sector, that international partnership is again being considered, but in a much more controlled environment. The renewal of interest in partnering with foreign companies is also being inspired by the decline of Russia's old Soviet era assets and the need to explore and develop new regions outside the comfort zone of the country's existing oil companies. As a result the IOC contributions of technology, management experience and financing have become relevant again in regions such as the Arctic, the Russian offshore, East Siberia and the new reservoirs where unconventional oil and gas resources can now be developed. Furthermore, the increasing tendency of foreign companies to offer reciprocal international assets as part of any deal to gain access to resources in Russia is also encouraging a greater enthusiasm on the Russian side, as they can gain greater experience of foreign industry practices as well as a diversification of their asset base.

In light of this new enthusiasm for foreign partnership, the remaining chapters of this book will explore what lessons can be learnt from the history of the past 20 years and will ask if they are relevant today, highlighting future risks for the IOCs who are now returning to Russia. The following chapter will seek to explain, in theoretical terms, the motivations of both international, but in particular domestic, actors in environments such as Russia, and will place the discussion about the experiences of foreigners in the Russian oil and gas industry in an overall context. Chapters 3 and 5 will then describe the real experiences and thoughts of a number of foreign investors over the past two decades to provide some practical examples from which initial conclusions can be drawn. Chapter 5 will then draw from these experiences and from other analytical work carried out by the authors to offer some statistical findings on the drivers of foreign partner success or failure in an environment such as Russia. Chapter 6 will then pull together the findings through the considered thoughts of one of the co-authors, Alastair Ferguson, whose lengthy experience both at TNK-BP but also as an advisor to numerous foreign companies operating in Russia leaves him uniquely positioned to draw some initial conclusions. Chapter 7 will then offer overall conclusions on the main issues facing foreign investors in the Russian oil industry as well as some practical thoughts on the best way to think about partnership in Russia in order to minimize risks and optimize investment opportunities.

2
A Review of Academic Theory on Joint Ventures, Partnership and the Importance of Local Knowledge

Introduction and synopsis

Having described the historical context of foreign investment in the Russian oil and gas industry it is now important to outline the key theoretical foundations for a discussion of why this investment may, or may not, have been successful in the post-Soviet era. This chapter presents a thorough review of the academic literature concerning this topic. However, although the authors believe that such a review is valuable in providing a context for the book as a whole, they also appreciate that a lengthy chapter covering academic theory may not be of interest to all readers. As a result, we first provide a brief synopsis of the chapter as a whole, which can act as an introduction for those who wish to read the chapter in full but can also provide a short summary of the main arguments to those who might wish to move on more rapidly to the case studies in Chapter 3.

In the first section of the chapter we introduce a traditional model that can be used to describe the interaction between foreign investors and host governments in the oil and gas sector. Dunning's eclectic paradigm, which is also known as the OLI paradigm, describes the natural locational (L) advantage of a host government, which is reinforced both by the pre-determined geographical location of oil and gas reserves and by their non-renewable nature, meaning that IOCs not only have little choice about where to invest but also that what little choice there is will be continuously reduced as any hydrocarbon reserves are produced. However, the capital and technological intensity of natural resource extraction can provide IOCs with balancing ownership (O) advantages. They bring the technical skills required to find and produce oil and gas, the management skills needed to optimize the efficiency and profitability of the process and the financing skills required to raise the large sums of investment capital needed to pay for vast industrial projects. Unfortunately, these IOC advantages are eroded over time because of the importance of the host country's locational advantage, and as a result IOCs need to generate internalization (I) advantages that will allow them to retain as much of the benefit of their ownership advantages as possible. In a business environment of strong institutions and a reliable legal and judicial system they could hope to do this by negotiating firm and binding contracts for access to exploration and production licences and also by controlling access to their core skills through a 100%-owned subsidiary. Any challenge to their position could then be met both by a legal response and also by a viable threat of withdrawing skills that the host country needs to develop its natural resources. However, in a weak state environment where the influence of a domestic partner is vital, the IOCs' ability to internalize its ownership advantages is undermined by their need to involve a third party in the investment process.

Within this context we then explore the emergence of the domestic investor as a key third actor in the bargaining process, using the literature on state capture and the formation and development of business groups to emphasize the importance of "local knowledge" as a core competence of domestic entrepreneurs. We define local knowledge as an understanding of the informal processes that allow an economy and a political system to operate in a weak institutional environment, with entrepreneurs using a network of local contacts and influence to optimize business outcomes. We argue that this key skill was used not only to gain competitive advantage in the domestic market, primarily through the formation of large Financial Industrial Groups, but also as a key bargaining tool with foreign investors. We also argue that the weak state environment that existed during the Yeltsin era of the 1990s has not, in reality, changed very much during the Putin era of the 2000s. Despite Putin's claims to have strengthened the Russian state, we assert that in reality the institutions of state have in fact been hollowed out and used as a front for the continuation of the informal practices seen in the 1990s, but under a different guise. As a result, any conclusions drawn from examples in the 1990s are still applicable today.

Having acknowledged that the domestic partner is an important actor in a weak state environment, we then move on discuss how he exploits his strengths in the bargaining process with foreign investors. In a review of the literature on bargaining and joint ventures we highlight the dynamic nature of bargains struck between foreign investors and the state, with the relative bargaining strengths of the two parties changing over time. The introduction of a domestic partner adds a further dynamic, and although his skills are initially complimentary to those of the foreign partner, essentially allowing them to function in a weak state environment, over time a learning process takes place which shifts the balance of bargaining power. Essentially a "competition to learn" takes place, and we argue that in this competition it is relatively easy for domestic investors to acquire the "knowledge" brought by their foreign partners, as it involves technical and management skills that can be learned through experience and training or acquired. On the other hand, it is much more difficult for the opposite learning process to take place, as domestic investor skills are much more deeply embedded into a social network, or "sistema", which is hard for a foreign investor to penetrate. It is this imbalance of learning possibility and potential for information asymmetry which, we argue, can lead to the instability of many JVs and ultimately to problems in particular for the foreign participant.

In conclusion we attempt to redefine the bargaining process in a weak state environment as a tri-partite negotiation between three different types of investors, namely the state, the foreign investor and the domestic investor. We place this three-way negotiation in the context of Dunning's eclectic paradigm to show how the domestic investor is effectively incentivized to interrupt the standard negotiation between the state and the foreign investor and is also motivated to maintain the imbalance in the bargaining environment in order to maximize his own advantage. We therefore assert that in a weak state environment Dunning's framework needs to be adjusted to take account of this new feature, and reach an initial conclusion that one strategic response for a foreign investor is to attempt to gain as much local knowledge as he can through a combined process of learning and participation in relevant business areas in order to reduce the bargaining power of any domestic partner.

Finally, we also identify an alternative partnership strategy as the use of a corporate model, which is essentially defined as an entity with a corporate governance structure in which all the participants are incentivized to work for the entity as a whole rather than for their individual benefit. The literature on Business Groups demonstrates that the formation of such a structure, which is focussed on the growth prospects for multiple assets over an extended time period rather than on the exploitation of a single asset (as in many joint ventures), can provide the basis for a more collaborative rather than competitive environment. We acknowledge that this variant is more of a progression from the initial JV model rather than a replacement of it, but it nevertheless provides an additional partnership option as we move on to Chapter 3 to discuss a number of case studies of joint entities formed in the oil and gas industry in Russia during the 1990s.

The eclectic paradigm as a framework for discussing FDI

By their very nature hydrocarbon resources are finite and their location has been pre-determined by natural forces. As such, general theories of FDI which seek to establish either the determinants of FDI or the alternative modes of entry into foreign countries, and focus on the outcome of the FDI decision in which the foreign investor has a number of different choices, are only of limited relevance to discussions of FDI in the oil and gas industry. For an oil and gas company the choices to be made are much more limited, because if it wants to survive and grow, in general it has no choice but to invest beyond its domestic borders (unless it is fortunate to be located in a country with an excess of hydrocarbons). Furthermore its choice of where to invest has also been significantly reduced by the random geological forces that have created and trapped hydrocarbons only in certain countries over the past tens of millions of years. Finally, an oil company also has a very limited choice of entry mode. It cannot export oil to an oil-producing country and has nothing to license, because essentially if it wants to produce oil in any country it has to invest in assets there through a wholly or partially-owned subsidiary.

Nevertheless, a discussion of foreign investment in the oil and gas industry can still be framed in general theory, in particular through the use of Dunning's eclectic paradigm.[1] In his seminal work, Dunning states that firms will decide to invest overseas if:

1. They possess **O**wnership advantages which can give them market power, such as ownership of products, production processes or skill-sets that provide a competitive advantage
2. There is a **L**ocation advantage in locating their plant in a foreign country rather than domestically
3. They can gain an advantage from **I**nternalizing their international activities through subsidiary companies rather than carrying them out through market activity via third party contractors or suppliers

In an oil and gas industry context, foreign investors generally bring the ownership advantages of management skills and experience, technological expertise and availability of capital. Locational advantage is generated by the pre-determined geography of oil and gas reserves, and essentially means that international oil companies have limited choices in where they invest, providing a bargaining strength to the countries and their governments which have the oil and gas reserves within their geographic borders. Internalization advantages can then be generated through the application of the foreign partner skills to the oil and gas assets, with the benefits being reaped by both the foreign partner and the state. Throughout the following discussion we will use this OLI paradigm to help describe the situation in the oil industry, and will then highlight how, in an environment of state capture, the key to optimizing the internalization advantages is the use of local knowledge, which is where a domestic partner becomes an essential part of the process.

However, before moving on we should first explain in more detail the theoretical context behind Dunning's O, L and I advantages. The first hint of ownership and internalization as motivations for FDI were provided by Hymer (1976)[2] (and his supervisor Kindelberger),[3] who identified control as a key element of direct investment and asserted that the main motivations for FDI and the control of business abroad are collusion and the weakening of competition in expectation of higher profits as well as the fuller exploitation of a company's abilities and advantages. As such they touched for the first time on the key issue of the ownership advantages that companies can seek to exploit if there is demand for products or services outside of their domestic economic environment and also discussed the need to control, or internalize, these advantages in order to maximize the benefit to the foreign investor.

Building on this theme Navaretti and Venables (2004)[4] found that the drivers of companies' FDI choices are largely based upon how each company's assets can be characterized. They divide assets into "firm-level" activities and "plant-level" activities, with the former being largely intangible (scientific know-how, management skills, patents, brand reputation) and the latter relating to the economies of scale or cost that can be generated within an individual plant owned by the company. Citing a number of theories on the determinants of FDI, in particular James Markusen's "knowledge capital model",[5] Navaretti and Venables show that firms which have a higher proportion of firm-level economies of scale relative to plant-level economies are more likely to invest overseas. In other words, they demonstrate that companies with core skills that can be applied across a broad industrial geography containing similar assets are likely to move overseas using horizontal integration, as in this way they can expand internationally by replicating their production processes in different countries. The upstream oil industry is a clear example of this process in action, with IOCs using similar skills to exploit oil and gas resources across the world.

The oil industry also provides a good example of vertical integration of course, as oil companies also have "plant-level activities" (refineries) that encourage international activity because it is cheaper to locate the plant in overseas markets than to bear the high cost of transporting the products to the end-users, and a number of academics have interpreted this as a key driver of FDI.[6,7,8] However, although the oil and gas industry does provide examples of both forms of FDI, in the context of our analysis the dominant form of integration is horizontal because of the pre-determined geographic location of oil and gas resources, which plays a large part in determining where IOCs make their international investments and which has certainly been the key driver behind their interest in Russia. The IOCs can then apply their Ownership advantages, to use the Dunning terminology, or core skills across a broad sweep of their international activities.

In terms of Locational advantage in the oil and gas industry, it is clear that the geology and geography of global hydrocarbon resources is a key driver of international activity in the sector. However, this obvious catalyst can be enhanced by a number of other dynamics that are discussed in more general FDI literature. For example Navaretti and Venables also highlight the importance of cost reduction as part of any international strategy, with resource-based industries being a prime example as companies need to find the lowest cost reserves both in terms of production cost and transport cost, given the fixed geographical location of the world's hydrocarbon resources.[9] An interesting further development of this argument in an oil industry context is that it is vital for companies to access resources not just because they are low cost, but also because oil is a diminishing resource and failure to invest in new fields would leave a company heavily reliant on competitors for its source of supply. This argument is developed further in the FDI theories of Frederick Knickerbocker,[10] whose theories suggest a constant game of move and counter-move is taking place as companies try to enhance their position with aggressive tactics while others counter with defensive moves. Russia provides a good example of a country that can offer significant oil and gas resources in a world of diminishing opportunity for global IOCs, and as such competition for access to these resources has been high, with almost all of the major IOCs now taking competing positions. Domestic Russian players, and the Russian State, have clearly understood the locational advantage which this competition has provided, and have exploited the situation to their advantage. They first grabbed as many assets for themselves as possible, while attempting to limit competition from foreign investors, and then used their domestic advantages (ownership of assets and knowledge of how to operate in Russia) as a strong bargaining chip when foreigners came seeking a share of a scarce resource.

Another key element of locational advantage in the oil and gas industry is the difference in tax and trade policies between resource-rich countries. Various studies[11,12] have shown that while some countries may offer various incentives to encourage foreign investment (with Ireland's development as the Celtic Tiger during the late 1990s being a prime example), others have taken a more cautious approach to the entry of MNEs,[13] with restrictive trade policies being used to limit foreign exploitation of valuable resources. The strategic nature of oil and gas reserves is often cited by countries as they justify the allocation of production licences between domestic and foreign players, and indeed in Russia the state has provided a strict definition of fields that are classed as "strategic" and where levels of foreign investment are limited.[14] These limits on foreign control over core resources echo early Marxist theories of FDI by authors such as Rosa Luxemburg (1913)[15] while later neo-Marxist writers from the 1960s, 1970s and 1980s continued to emphasize the dominance of big corporations and the risk this caused to undeveloped countries. In particular Frobel, Heinricks and Kreye[16] (1980) develop the overall theme of the creation of "world market factories", with MNEs choosing and changing sites according to levels of cost and infrastructure without reference to the impact on the host countries. As a reaction to this potential threat, countries and governments need to re-assert their locational advantage, and the Russian Law on Investment in Strategic Assets is a clear demonstration of a state's desire to limit what is regarded by many in Russia as the imperialistic tendencies of the world's major oil companies.

A further reason to exploit this locational advantage is captured by the literature on "dependencia", identified by Sunkel[17] as "the process by which foreign firms and the interaction of international markets have fostered development in some countries while leading to underdevelopment in others". In the context of the oil industry this dependency can be technological, where the foreign investor attempts to keep any technical skills to itself in order to keep its partner in a subordinate role, or can be more general, as governments feel increasingly reliant on foreign producers to generate export revenues and pay taxes. In Russia, for example, oil and gas revenues have accounted for up to two thirds of the country's export earnings and the sector contributes around 50% of budget revenues, making foreign involvement in the sector a very sensitive issue. As a result, the Russian state has limited foreign ownership of resources and has also insisted on significant transfer of technology as part of any joint venture agreements.[18] As will be discussed later, this sharing of foreign company knowledge is in stark contrast to the secrecy surrounding the "local knowledge" used as a bargaining strength by domestic partners. As a result, it is a further example of how a host country's locational advantage can be used to alter the balance of any bargaining in favour of the domestic players.

In conclusion, then, the State's role can be seen as being based on its inherent locational advantage of owning valuable oil and gas resources within the country it governs and its desire to prevent the profits from the exploitation of these resources from being dominated by the foreign companies whose help is needed to develop them. As such, a good relationship with the State is vital for any foreign investor who wishes to be allocated access to develop oil and gas reserves in any country. In a strong institutional environment, this relationship can be based on a firm legal and commercial foundation, but as we will discuss later, in a weak state environment involving state capture, the local knowledge of a domestic partner becomes a necessity.

Having established that firms move internationally in order to exploit firm-level or plant-level economies of scale, or in a more general sense to exploit their Ownership advantages, and that Locational advantages also play a key role in determining where FDI takes place, we now need to address the question of Internalization advantages and how they can be generated. In terms of Dunning's eclectic paradigm, a company needs to decide whether it can benefit from internalizing its operational advantages or rely on dealings in the market place. The decision is essentially based on the trade-off between the direct cost of internalizing and the problem of contractual incompleteness in the market place, and in general theory is viewed as the choice between operating a 100% subsidiary in a foreign country or relying on third party suppliers or contractors.

The drivers behind the decision-making process have been debated by numerous authors,[19,20,21] who identified three key benefits of internalization. Firstly, firms may prefer to keep activities internal in order to avoid the hold-up problem, which can occur when it is not possible to write contracts covering all possible contingencies between a firm and its suppliers. In this situation firms may prefer to carry out activities themselves, even if it costs more than using a third party, in order to avoid the risk of being held to ransom over a vital contract re-negotiation. Secondly, firms may decide on internalization if they do not want to dissipate their firm-specific assets, especially their knowledge capital, or if they feel that it would be too expensive to transfer this knowledge to a third party. Caves (1971)[22] and Buckley and Casson (1976)[23] develop the concept that "the exploitation of knowledge is logically an international operation"[24] which firms will tend to exploit, if they can, by keeping the knowledge "in-house" and then using it in countries where they can adapt it to the local labour skills and customer base. A third key benefit of internalization is to reduce agency costs. These are the costs that are associated with monitoring and motivating employees and managers, and arise because of a lack of perfect observation. For example, local third party agents could manipulate information about local markets to extract surplus benefits for themselves to the detriment of an international company, and in this case use of a subsidiary company would be preferred. Navaretti and Venables note that this problem is particularly acute in international activities where the potential for informational asymmetries is greater, and hence where the opportunity for third parties to manipulate information is higher.[25]

In summary, it appears that firms which have significant firm-level ownership advantages are most likely to move overseas in order to generate economies of scale by spreading the benefits of their largely intangible skills across a broader geographic range of production sites. As they internationalize they are likely to prefer internalization as a methodology in order to protect their firm-level knowledge assets and also to avoid the costs of having to transfer these assets to a third party. However, governments and domestic players in the countries where the FDI takes place are likely to use their locational advantages to ensure that all the benefits of this process do not accrue to the foreign company but are shared with the host economy.

Dunning's eclectic paradigm can therefore provide a foundation for examining the determinants of FDI decisions made by oil companies seeking to invest in the Russian oil and gas sector. In general IOCs each have ownership advantages that can be characterized as firm-level assets, with the most important of these being the knowledge assets identified by Markusen (2002) in his "knowledge capital model".[26] They have technical and management skills that can be applied across multiple oil and gas fields, and are therefore naturally inclined to operate across the globe, wherever these fields are located. Their natural form of FDI will be horizontal due to the nature of their firm-level knowledge assets and because of the pre-determined location of oil and gas reserves, but IOCs are also involved in vertical integration in their downstream businesses, where plant-level economies of scale can be generated. In a Russian context, the technical and management advantages brought by the IOCs have been widely acknowledged and used as an initial source of significant bargaining strength, as has their access to capital at times of low oil prices.

In an oil industry context, the locational advantage very clearly lies with countries where oil resources reside. When this locational advantage is added to the fact that oil is a diminishing resource, the bargaining strength of any country (and its government) which controls access to these resources is very clear. IOCs need to gain the right to explore for, develop and produce oil reserves if they are to survive and grow, and countries that have the good fortune to be resource-rich have become increasingly adept at exploiting this need and the competition between the IOCs in an oligopolistic oil industry. Russia's decision to declare its energy assets to be strategic and to restrict foreign access to them has demonstrated its intentions in this regard, making the Russian state a key player in any negotiation and emphasizing the strength of its locational bargaining power.

The key question then is how can any IOC optimize the benefits of internalization as they operate internationally? In a theoretical world of robust institutions and a perfect legal system, they would negotiate with a state for legal access to oil resources before applying their firm-level skills to those resources via a wholly-owned subsidiary in order to protect their knowledge assets and maximize the returns for themselves (and for the state via tax payments). However, in the case of Russia its locational advantage and the imperfect nature of its legal and commercial systems have inhibited the realization of this goal. Access to oil resources has been effectively restricted to partnerships with state-owned or Russian domestic partners, in particular by the country's "Law on Strategic Reserves" which has limited IOC access to large fields. Technology transfer has been a key element in all transactions, reducing the ability to internalize. And most importantly, the environment of state capture in Russia, which will be discussed later, has meant that IOCs have been operating in a setting of asymmetric information where they have had to rely on partners with local knowledge and influence. This has further reduced their ability to internalize their own operational advantages and subsequently weakened their bargaining position.

The uniqueness of FDI in the natural resources sectors

A number of specific theories concerning foreign investment in natural resource sectors have been developed which have highlighted the unique nature of the industry, with McKern (1993)[27] being one of the specific authors to identify the key elements that differentiate the debate concerning hydrocarbons from the more traditional discussions of foreign investment that tend to focus on manufacturing or service industries. Despite these unique features, however, I will argue below that theories on FDI by natural resource companies can still be related to the Dunning eclectic paradigm framework, albeit with the important difference that locational advantage has a higher priority than is the case in more general FDI theories.

According to McKern the key features of an analysis of natural resource industries are:

1. The immutability of geography, particularly with non-renewable resources, means that the location of those resources is fortuitous and asymmetric with both markets and with the ability to extract those resources efficiently. In the context of the eclectic paradigm this clearly provides locational advantage to the host country, which is magnified by the fact that oil is a depleting resource. Not only must IOCs invest in specific countries where oil is located, but they must also do it on a timely basis before all resources have either been allocated or run out.
2. The sector is also capital intensive, with significant scale economies, creating a potentially large entry barrier. This provides an ownership advantage to major IOCs, especially in times of low oil prices, as they are generally able to provide access to capital via global financial markets.
3. Processing of minerals and hydrocarbons requires significant energy resources, encouraging local processing. This also creates a locational advantage, although not always in the countries that own the resources. In the case of the oil industry, the refining of crude oil into useable products is best carried out close to end-user markets, as the cost of transporting crude oil is generally lower than the cost of transporting products, creating an incentive for vertical integration by IOCs.
4. Capital intensity, technological necessity and oligopoly create an incentive for horizontal and vertical integration. Essentially, IOCs are incentivized to internalize their international operations because in an industry dominated by a few powerful players they are keen to protect their firm-level assets and to prevent, where possible, their competitors from gaining access to

resources. Furthermore, because of the levels of capital required to develop oil and gas resources, IOCs are keen to establish control over their investments either through horizontal integration (subsidiaries owning oilfields in different countries) or through vertical integration (subsidiaries owning downstream assets such as refineries and marketing companies in countries where there is greatest demand for oil products). Russia is generally seen as part of the horizontal integration process for most IOCs, as they are keen to gain access to the country's huge upstream resources.

5. Cartelization has also been a driver in the petroleum industry. The majors have preserved some of their oligopoly through their overall experience of managing the entire oil value chain of industrial processes including upstream exploration and production, oil processing, distribution and marketing. As a result the IOCs have managed to create a cartel of sorts not only due to their control of downstream assets, where oil products are marketed and sold, but also due to their embedded experience of 100 years of management of oil industry processes. This experience has given them an ownership advantage, especially in negotiation with host countries with little or no experience of international oil industry practices, and has also incentivized the IOCs to internalize their international operations in order to preserve and exploit their knowledge asset of "management experience".

A particularly vital factor, as also noted by Hughes (1975),[28] is the "once-and-for-all" character of hydrocarbon extraction. It is this factor that influences both the IOCs in their decisions on where to invest, and also the governments of the host country as they negotiate for the development of a resource that has extra value simply because of its irreplaceability. When this characteristic is added to the fact that hydrocarbons, if not in short supply, are at least becoming scarcer in terms of where private companies can hope to invest, then it is clear that the locational advantage for host countries provides a very powerful bargaining strength in their negotiations with IOCs. However, as noted in point 5 above, IOCs are also vital to the host countries, especially where those countries lack international experience or technology, or are short of capital. As Penrose (1968)[29] noted, IOCs in the oil and gas industry can generate bargaining power from their role as managerial bureaucracies with extensive oil industry experience. Therefore, although they have no growth prospects without access to the oil resources located in specific "geographically fortunate" countries, those countries often struggle to develop those resources without the involvement of the IOCs. As a result, both sides bring significant bargaining strength to any negotiation.

In his seminal work "Sovereignty at Bay" on MNCs in the petroleum industry Vernon (1971)[30] addressed many elements of this bargaining process. He argued that the key elements for foreign participation in any industry are the scale of undertaking required for effective performance, the complexity of the technology associated with the activity and the importance of captive overseas markets as an outlet for the raw material. In the case of the early oil industry, for example, by the 1870s it had become concentrated on large-scale enterprises that were selling the majority of their output overseas, thus predisposing them to international investment. Initially US companies, who dominated the early development of the oil industry, expanded by buying up marketing outlets, but as other sources of oil supply became more prevalent it was clear that this strategy would not work for long as it was too easy to replicate or circumvent. The only option was to invest in international sources of crude supply. Self-sufficiency through horizontal and vertical integration then became the key goal, from production through refining and transportation to marketing,[31] with IOCs seeking to optimize their ownership and internalization advantages by investing via overseas subsidiaries.

In an echo of Penrose's argument on vertical integration, Vernon also noted that scale economies, driven by high fixed costs, tended to lead to an oligopolistic structure and that vertical integration by some leads to a tendency for all competitors to follow suit to protect themselves. Vertical integration then led to a greater focus on costs and the maintenance of prices, as the cost of crude oil could no longer just be passed onto consumers if a competitor had secured a cheaper source of supply. This drove companies to explore and develop oil in all the areas where their competitors operated, to ensure that they were exposed to similar low-cost sources of supply. As a result it is clear that IOCs in the oil industry are driven to invest overseas using both horizontal and vertical integration, the former in the upstream business in order to access low-cost competitive resources in the countries where they are located and the latter to minimize costs throughout the production, transport, processing and marketing value chain.

The "obsolescing bargain"

Vernon's other important contribution was to highlight the fluid nature of the negotiating process between the host government and the international investor and the inherent risks this caused for the latter. As noted above, the bargaining strength provided by the locational advantage of hydrocarbon assets situated in a host country is matched by an IOC's ability to finance and manage the development of those assets. However, Vernon identified that the bargaining positions of the participants in the negotiations over mineral licences change over time, in what he termed the "obsolescing bargain".[32] Initially the challenges and risks of exploration, development, marketing and financing seem overwhelming to an inexperienced host government, and IOCs that can spread their risk and cost seem to be in a much better position to exploit the resources. However, once the exploration phase is over any failed projects are forgotten and the successes suddenly appear like a much lower-risk bonanza, where the returns being generated by the IOC no longer seem commensurate with the risk. Political forces may then want to establish greater control over the foreign investor and the returns he is generating by re-opening negotiations or asserting some control over local operations or infrastructure. In essence, as the risks of hydrocarbon development decrease, the host government is likely to want to increase its share of the economic outcome.

In conclusion, although specific theories of FDI in the natural resource industries focus on the uniqueness of the sector, they also confirm the relevance of Dunning's OLI paradigm in describing the interaction of corporate and government activity. The locational advantage of the host government is reinforced both by the pre-determined geographical location of oil and gas reserves and by their non-renewable nature, meaning not only that IOCs have little choice about where to invest but also that what limited choice they have will continuously decrease as global reserves are produced.

The capital and technological intensity of natural resource extraction provides the IOCs with their ownership advantages. They bring the technical skills required to find and produce oil and gas, the management skills needed to optimize the efficiency and profitability of the process and the financing skills required to raise the large sums of investment capital needed to pay for vast industrial projects. However, as noted by Vernon in his analysis of the obsolescing bargain, these IOC advantages are eroded over time because of the importance of the host country's locational advantage.

In order to offset the effects of the obsolescing bargain IOCs therefore need to generate internalization advantages that will allow them to retain as much of the benefit of their ownership advantages as possible. In a business environment of strong institutions and reliable legal and judicial system they could hope to do this by negotiating firm and binding contracts for access to exploration and production licences and also by controlling access to their core skills through a 100%-owned subsidiary. Any challenge to their position could then be met both by a legal response and also by a viable threat of withdrawing skills that the host country needs to develop its natural resources. However, as will be discussed in the following sections, in a weak state environment where the influence of a domestic partner is vital, the IOCs' ability to internalize its ownership advantages is undermined by their need to involve a third party in the investment process.

Weak state environments and the importance of local knowledge

State capture and state influence in a weak state environment

As has been identified above, the state is a key player in any bargain struck with foreign investors. Indeed, in the traditional literature on the minerals industries in developing countries it has been seen as the only other player in a bipartite bargaining process (Vernon, 1971[33]; McKern, 1977[34]). However, we will argue that in a weak state environment the bargaining process is tripartite, with the domestic investor having an equally important role. This raises the key issue of the definition of a weak state environment, and the further question of whether Russia has been an example of such an environment throughout some or all of the post-Soviet period.

In their paper on "The New Comparative Economics" Djankov et al (2003)[35] examine the trade-off between excessive state control and the potential for disorder in an excessively liberalized market given different societal differences across developing countries, and they highlight the propensity for sharp swings in institutional structure and the risk of "overshoot" in one direction or another. In the case of Russia they point out that the collapse of communism represented a sharp decline in dictatorship, with the decline of the communist party as a political force leading to the undermining of the mechanisms for keeping control of social, economic and political order. As a result Russia overshot in its liberalization process, leaving the nascent public institutions to be subverted by the powerful as "...the oligarchs who came to strongly influence the government preferred institutional disorder as a strategy for maximising their rents".[36] This view is supported by the analysis of Hellman et al (2000)[37] who begin their examination of state capture in transition economies by stating that: "Fear of the leviathan state [in the Soviet era] has been replaced by a new concern about the powerful oligarchs, who manipulate politicians, shape institutions and control the media to advance and protect their own empires at the expense of the social interest."

The analysis in Hellman et al's (2000)[38] paper relies on the 1999 BEEPS survey conducted by the World Bank and the EBRD,[39] which examines the impact of administrative corruption, "state capture" and influence on the transition economies. In administrative corruption the rents from the discretionary capacity of the state to regulate the activities of firms go to corrupt public officials (similar to the grabbing hand view of the state). In state capture the ability of firms to encode private advantages in the rules of the game generate rents that are shared by the firms and the public officials. In both cases, though, individuals and entrepreneurs can exploit the weakness of state institutions to their own benefit because of the inherent weakness of the institutional system – essentially a weak state environment.

Hellman's key findings, with relevance to Russia and its oil and gas sector, are that the most advanced reformers, and interestingly the least advanced, have the lowest levels of state capture. Most of the state capture countries can be classified as partial reformers, where advances have been made in liberalization and privatization with much less progress in concomitant institutional reforms to support the proper legal and regulatory framework. It is no surprise, then, that Russia rated second equal in the Capture Economy Index, with a score of 32 relative to Moldova (37), Ukraine (32) and the average (20). They also found that larger firms with greater command over resources are more likely to have influence and be involved in state capture, whereas administrative corruption has the greatest impact on small firms. State capture also seems to be a strategy in industries which suffer from insecure property and contract rights, with larger firms in particular (such as the oil and gas companies) using their influence and contacts to erect barriers to entry. Finally, they also point out that in high capture economies captor firms have managed to increase their security in an environment where the overall level of security has been falling. State officials have no incentive to improve the overall position because this would reduce their own ability to extract rent and thus captor firms beget more captor firms as they attempt to improve their position in a worsening overall environment.

A further conclusion is that the benefits of state capture for the captor companies also encourage them to keep the process alive. Additional evidence for this is provided by Sonin (2002),[40] who points out that the oligarchs invest in relational capital to secure their own property rights, and that "once a private protection system is maintained, it can be used to contest many types of rents at the same time". As the oligarchs have well-diversified businesses they can easily exploit this potential synergy, giving them more incentives to invest in private protection. This situation can be self-perpetuating, especially where natural rents (as opposed to one-off rents in privatization for example) are high (e.g. in the Russian oil and gas sector). In addition, as Hellman (1998)[41] points out, an additional impact is that "the winners might have an implicit veto power in the decisions over separate components of reforms, especially those that affect their existing rent streams". Again, the powerful have an incentive and the ability to maintain the system in their own interest.

Interestingly, too, it should be noted that corruption is by no means limited to the federal levels of government, as a paper by Slinko et al (2003)[42] demonstrates. The authors studied regional legislation in Russia in order to discover laws that treat economic agents unequally, and found evidence of institutional subversion in every one of the 73 regions that they examined in the period 1992–2000. In the face of this corruption at a federal and regional level potential foreign investors have some stark choices to make. As Smarzynska and Wei (2000)[43] state "corruption makes dealing with government officials, for example, to obtain local licences and permits, less transparent and more costly, particularly for foreign investors. In this case, having a local partner lowers the transaction cost". They show that corruption and the formation of joint ventures with a local partner are positively and significantly correlated, which is clearly reflected in the initial surge of joint venture formation in the Russian oil and gas sector in the immediate post-Soviet era. Furthermore, the continued acceptance amongst most foreign oil companies of the need for a domestic partner when working in Russia is evidence of the success of domestic companies and government officials in maintaining their bargaining power by sustaining the value of local knowledge.

An initial conclusion is that analysis of Russia in the 1990s reveals a country where interest groups were consistently able to exploit the relative youth and consequent weakness of institutions that had just started to emerge in the post-Soviet era.[44] Henisz and Zelner (2003)[45] described the new institutions designed to provide post-privatization property rights as "emergent" as opposed to "established" institutions, and argued that they were particularly susceptible to change in their early stages under pressure from well-organized interest groups. Within this weak institutional context the authors empha-sized that the "web of implicit contracts among political actors, interest groups and foreign investors substitutes for the bilateral dependency between investors and government".[46] As a result a local partner can be regarded as vital to help to unravel this web of weak new formal institutions and older informal institutions, although interestingly the authors also note that the choice of a joint venture model can also be risky as the local partner may also be well placed to undermine the economic interests and legitimacy of any foreign partner.

A number of commentators, though, have argued that the Russia of the 21st century, in the Putin era, is a very different environment to the chaos of the 1990s and that the strength of the Russian state has been rekindled by the new President.[47] He and his team could be regarded as having restored order to Russia after the quasi-anarchy of the 1990s, and in Putin's own words as having achieved "the restoration of the guiding and regulating role of the state".[48] Furthermore, images of Putin consistently portray the image of a man, and by inference a country, that is returning to its former position as a global superpower and a "strong state" that the Russian people appear to value.[49] If this is true, then arguments based on Russia as a weak state environ-ment, based on evidence from a previous era, would clearly carry little weight as the basis for advising foreign investors in the present day.

Interestingly, though, an increasing body of literature has emerged over the past few years presenting a robust argument that, although Russia under Putin looks very different from Russia under Yeltsin, the strength of the state can still be called into significant question. As Marie Mendras (2012), in her aptly named recent book "Russian Politics: The Paradox of a Weak State", sum-marizes the debate: "What kind of state and what kind of strength are we talking about? The State as an institutional construction and embodiment of public life is weak and dysfunctional. Power and resources are concentrated in the hands of individuals and networks that are not accountable to society."[50]

Indeed, it would appear that the very strength claimed by Putin and his associates (widely referred to as the *siloviki*) provides the clearest evidence of the weakness of the state institutions which they control. As Aslund (2007)[51] states, Putin has in fact managed a "systematic centralisation of authoritarian power in his own hands and a far-reaching de-institutionalisation [of the political system]". Despite having to give up the Presidency in 2008, he still managed, as Prime Minister, to establish himself as the ultimate arbiter in the political system, and "divided the elite in fierce competition to make sure that all need his arbitration".[52] He then, of course, managed the further transition of his role back to the Presidency in 2012, again emphasizing his own strength but the inherent weakness of the Russian electoral system. However, in centralizing political power and putting himself in an apparently immovable position, Putin has also created inherent weakness in the system due to the fact that its reliance on a few individuals could ultimately cause its downfall – essentially "the system is too centralised to handle crises" and despite attempts to control all information one day "some disaster may become too embarrassing [to avoid political unrest]".

Ledeneva (2006)[53] pursues a similar theme of individual or group strength at the expense of state institutions in her discussion of collective responsibility (*krugovaia poruka*) under Putin. She describes how on his election Putin merely replaced former President Yeltsin's clientele with his own, and then continued to use the informal leverage established by his personnel policy to reinforce his own individual power over that of the institutions where he had appointed his trusted colleagues. Further, Ledeneva also describes how Putin made use of this implicit control of state institutions to assert his authority over business and commerce in Russia, again using informal rules rather than formal legislation. The prime example of this is the informal agreement between the state and big business which was put in place by President Putin in June 2000, when he imposed an unwritten rule that the oligarchs could continue to run their business empires if they kept out of politics.[54] The very informality of this unwritten agreement, and the lack of a strong institutional system to impose any legislation on the issue was exactly what gave Putin and his team power and made life so uncertain for the oligarchs. Putin demonstrated that powerful individuals within the state machinery can exploit the weakness of the state by creating informal leverage over actors in all spheres of social, business and commercial life.

Ledeneva reinforces the point about the weakness of the state versus the power of individuals and groups within the political system in her paper "From Russia with Blat" (2009),[55] where she describes informality and informal practices as being at the heart of Russia's governance system, known as "sistema". Quoting Shevtsova (2003)[56] she defines "sistema" as "a specific type of governance structure [where]...the heart of the system was the all-powerful leader, above the law and a law unto himself, concentrating in his hands all powers, without a balancing accountability, and limiting all other institutions to auxiliary, administrative functions". Within the "sistema" networks of power are established through the recruitment of members based on loyalty and their appointment to senior institutional positions, with rewards and punishments for good or bad performance being distributed on an extra-legal basis. In this way the networks of power can be hidden behind formal offices of the state while the informal "sistema" continues to perpetuate itself.

Sakwa (2010) underlines the reference to two layers of power in his description of a "dual state model" in which he contrasts the constitutional state with the administrative regime below it. He takes the election process in Russia as a clear example of how this dual system works, as on the one hand the elections are held according to the appropriate legal framework (i.e. according to the constitutional requirements) while on the other a "parallel para-constitutional system" operates in which the administrative regime seeks to impose its own will and to influence the outcome in favour of specific parties (Sakwa, 2010). Essentially he argues that the institutional weakness of the Yeltsin era, in which powerful entrepreneurs were able to exert huge influence over the political and economic systems, has now been replaced by a different form of "institutional nihilism" in which the Putin regime has established a series of parallel institutions that have undermined the formal system.

The existence of the formal institutions is nevertheless vital to the current political system, as it provides the basis for the control exerted by the political elite. As Mendras describes the situation, Russian society is "hyper-legalistic", being overrun by laws and rules in both a political and commercial environment. The main issue, however, is that these laws and rules are applied in an ad hoc or arbitrary fashion, and as a result it is the ability to influence the interpretation and implementation of them that provides power to the elite. As such "the ultimate arbiter of right and wrong is the holder of the supreme office", and so if any individual or commercial concern wants or needs to circumvent the rules they need to keep on his good side. To quote Mendras again: "the power of individuals within this corporatist statism is based on the weakness of the institutions that could control them. The only rule imposed is total loyalty to Putin. Corruption has flourished because within this system money and gift exchange are the currency of business and power."[57]

Andrew Jack (2004) also emphasizes the use of the role of law as a political tool via the general manipulation of the legal system,[58] but he also raises the themes of secrecy, lack of transparency and inconsistency as additional features of the weak state environment that are deliberately cultivated in order to ensure that a general air of uncertainty is maintained. He highlights Putin's capacity to invent policy on the spot, and come up with surprising decisions, as being deliberate ploys to sustain the view that only he and his inner circle fully understand how decisions are being made, thereby further undermining the formal institutions that are nominally responsible for government and judicial proceedings.[59]

A good summary of the current situation in Russia, and the current weakness of state institutions, is provided by Hanson and Teague (2013) in their analysis of what might encourage economic reform in Russia. They begin by describing the existing weakness of both political and economic institutions in Russia, highlighting in particular World Bank statistics that show Russia ranking 112th out of 185 countries in an "Ease of Doing Business Survey" and 40th out of 49 upper-middle income countries.[60] They conclude that "What these scores and indicators reflect, in the economic life of Russia, is widespread extraction of bribes from companies and individuals, with corrupt officials and businesses closely associated with them as the beneficiaries; and the use by established firms of political connections, whether at national, regional or local level, to keep out or damage rivals by getting officials to deny operating licences or deploy tax demands and environmental and safety regulations to harm those rivals."[61] Furthermore, the political elites who benefit from the advantages created by this weak institutional environment are not incentivized to alter the status quo, even if as patriots they can see that it is undermining the Russian economy as a whole. The continued weakness of political institutions, such as those which permit political competition, media independence and free and fair elections, allow the elite to remain in power. Meanwhile the continuing weakness of economic institutions (which concern the rule of law, an independent judiciary, and greater transparency, predictability and stability in the economic sphere) allows them to use their political influence to make significant fortunes.

Interestingly, the weakness of state institutions, or at least corruption – the main consequence of the weakness – is also constantly acknowledged by the political elite themselves. In an interview with Moskovskie Novosti in March 2012 Alexei Kudrin, former Finance Minister and current head of the expert group the Committee for Civil Initiatives, highlighted the biggest problems for the Russian economy as the lack of effective working institutions, with the implication that the economy is subject to "manual control" (or direct intervention from above).[62] Meanwhile current Prime Minister, and former President, Dmitry Medvedev has consistently admitted that corruption is a major issue in Russia, most recently in an interview with CNN,[63] while the current President, Vladimir Putin, has also been forthright about the issues facing institutions in Russia. In a pre-election speech in 2012 he identified that one of the main problems in Russian society "is rooted in a lack of transparency in the work of state representatives from customs and tax services and their accountability to society. This is also true of the judicial and law enforcement systems. Calling things by their names, this amounts to system-wide corruption" (Kinossian, 2012).[64]

However, despite this acknowledgement of the weakness of state institutions, and regular threats by high ranking officials to stamp down on offenders, it would appear that little has really changed or is likely to change in the foreseeable future. Mendras (2012) paints a situation in which "the fluidity and adaptability in interpretation and implementation of the law give the Russian leaders precious advantages which they are not prepared to give up", while Hanson and Teague (2013) argue that many of the political elite are opposed to change as it would not benefit them personally. Although many of the senior ranking officials may argue against corruption because "as patriots they have grounds for deploring the status quo", when it comes to turning words into action they fail because "as self-interested individuals they have reasons to cling to it [the status quo]".[65] The system essentially operates as a result of the patron-client relationships and networks that are inherent to it, and to disturb these would not only risk undermining the power base of the elite but could also reduce their own earning potential and expose them to criminal charges in a more transparent and independent legal system. As bluntly stated by Tompson (2007) "it is not clear that the players involved have any incentive to correct the deficiencies. Too many of them have good reasons not to want good corporate governance."[66]

One final important point, however, is that Russia is clearly not alone in operating in a weak state environment. Although it ranks 112 in the World Bank survey, behind for example Colombia (45), Albania (85) and Namibia (87), it is ahead of Argentina (124), Brazil (130) and Ukraine (137) and 70 other countries in the 185 country study. Indeed, in his book "The Political Economy of Putin's Russia" Pekka Sutela (2012) suggested that although "Russia is not a textbook market economy...it is in many respects a normal country in the statistically descriptive sense of the word."[67] As Hanson and Teague conclude, "most of the world's population live in countries where the rule of law and the protection of property rights are weak, where corruption is widespread and where political connections at least partly block the freedoms of market entry and exit". As a result, to identify Russia as a weak institutional environment is not to vilify the country as a unique example of poor governance, but rather to highlight that it can be a very useful example of how such a political and economic environment operates and to offer conclusions for foreign investors that can be applicable in many other countries.

Conclusions on a weak state environment

Overall, then, it is vital to consider the state's influence on any bargain struck with foreign investors. However, corruption of and within the federal and regional authorities, as well as the emergence of powerful domestic investors using state capture and influence as core strategies, have significantly complicated the bargaining process. Furthermore, the apparent strength of state institutions can mask the fact that real power in fact lies with a few key individuals and their informal "sistema" of power networks which exploit the weakness of state institutions to exert influence over all areas of society. As such, Russia can be described as having a weak state environment even though various individuals, both entrepreneurs and politicians, continue to exploit the perceived strength of their positions within the state apparatus.

Within the weak state environment of Russia during the 1990s entrepreneurs (often known as the oligarchs) flourished, as has always been the case when bribes can be used to extract benefits from government officials and influence can be used to undermine the credibility of emerging institutions that might limit the rent-seeking opportunities of the powerful few. The core competence of these entrepreneurs was their "local knowledge" of how to operate in the uncertain investment environment, which, as Smarzynska and Wei (2000) have pointed out, made them important partners for foreign investors. In the Putin era since 2000 the relationship between business and the state has changed, but the influence of powerful individuals either at the head of commercial concerns or within government bodies has if anything become even more important as the institutions of power have continued to be "hollowed out".[68] However, the core competence of the individuals concerned has remained the same, namely their local knowledge, which can be used as a bargaining strength within the asymmetric environment created by the weakness of state institutions. However, given that all international joint ventures are, by definition, carried out between foreign and domestic companies, or firms (either private or state-owned), it is important to place the concept of local knowledge within a corporate context and to describe how it can become a competitive advantage.

Local knowledge and the resource-based theory of the firm

Ronald Coase (1937)[69] identified that although in theory all production activities could occur in the market place alone, many in fact occur within organizations, or firms. He concluded that this happens because there are costs associated with activity in markets, which he defined as transaction costs, and that firms exist because they can, by their nature, reduce these transaction costs. Williamson (1985)[70] further developed this transaction cost theory of the firm to define the firm as a mechanism, or governance structure, for organizing and managing the exchange process when transactional difficulties make it impossible to conceive complete contracts. Essentially, firms exist because they can reduce costs by combining individual activities efficiently, improve co-operation between individual actors and facilitate exchange in a complex and uncertain world. As summarized by Perman and Scouller (1999)[71] "firms develop whenever the costs of transactions through markets exceed the costs of organising and co-ordinating production within firms". The incentive for any entrepreneur, therefore, is to bring together a group of workers within a firm whenever he can see that this can provide a competitive advantage compared to the cost of the production of an individual good in the market place.

However, as Perman and Scouller also point out, the relative cost of market- and firm-based transactions is changing all the time, and when this is combined with the fact that numerous companies are competing to provide similar services wherever there is a profit to be made, it is clear that it is difficult for any firm to sustain competitive advantage. Nevertheless, it is also apparent that many firms do create sustainable advantage and use methods other than the simple exercise of market power. The Resource-based Theory of the Firm has therefore been developed as an attempt to explain how the differences in the nature and performance of heterogeneous firms occur, and to search for the roots of this heterogeneity.

Prahalad and Hamel (1990)[72] initiated the capabilities approach to explain firm performance when they argued that a key source of competitive advantage is the ability to consolidate a set of skills into core competencies. These are defined as the collective learning of an organization and provide the "soil from which a firm's products are nourished and sustained". They also argue that one key feature of core competencies is that they are difficult for competitors to identify precisely, which makes them difficult to imitate. Stalk et al (1992)[73] saw these competencies as the foundation on which a firm could "compete on capabilities", and John Kay (1993)[74] then developed the theory further by exploring the nature and significance of "distinctive capabilities", which he defined as architecture, innovation and reputation. Innovation is defined as the ability of a firm to develop new products or to lower costs of existing products, and reputation as the ability of a firm to convey information about its products to consumers, but architecture is seen as the most important capability because it allows a firm to create and store organizational knowledge. It is this third capability that allows a firm to protect its innovations and its relationships with customers and makes it more difficult for competitors to replicate capabilities.

The importance of architecture is that it puts other capabilities in a context where they are more valuable to one firm than another. Building on the work of Kay (1993)[75] and Peteraf (1993),[76] Perman and Scouller[77] observe that the sustainability of capabilities depends upon a number of factors, namely their tradability, their replicability, their transparency and their substitutability. Tradability refers to the ease with which a competitor could just buy the skill from a rival firm, for example by hiring a key employee, while replicability refs to the ease with which a capability could just be copied. Transparency refers to the ease with which a rival can identify what it is that makes a firm successful, while substitutability refers to its ability to create a suitable alternative if it cannot buy or copy an identified capability. In order to protect their capabilities firms therefore need to develop "isolating mechanisms" that can act as natural barriers against competitive activity. The creation of a successful firm architecture is one of these barriers, and others include lack of transparency, long-term relationship management and development of asymmetries in a specific business environment.

In the context of a weak state environment such as Russia, a number of authors have suggested that local skills have a key role to play as a core competence or capability. Kock and Guillen (2001)[78] introduce the idea that local skills such as contacts with government, with powerful entities in the market and perhaps with foreign firms are capabilities in themselves. They see a need for local firms to reduce the challenge from technologically advanced firms, which they can achieve by creating market asymmetries via the dimension of poor property rights. Local knowledge then becomes a natural barrier to entry which foreigners can only open with the help of a domestic partner. This need for local knowledge can be further encouraged through official protectionism of infant industries or through widespread corruption (Guillen, 2000),[79] which helps domestic players because if there is discrimination against foreigners, then foreign companies need the help of local entrepreneurs to enter the market. As such the ability to utilize contacts to set up and maintain businesses linking national resources with foreign organizational and technological capabilities is in itself a capability/competence. It is knowledge unique to a local entrepreneur, subject to causal ambiguity, difficult to imitate, and subject to path-dependent learning.[80] In addition, as contacts are expensive to create but less costly to apply over a series of investment opportunities, there is a clear scope for economies of scale by using this "local knowledge" capability within the architecture of a firm.

A definition of local knowledge

However, before moving on to discuss how entrepreneurs developed this strategy further via the creation of business groups, it is necessary to provide some criteria to define the "local knowledge" which has been identified as their key strength. In her book "How Russia Really Works"[81] Alena Ledeneva describes the informal practices that shaped post-Soviet business and politics and defines these practices as the "know-how of post-Soviet Russia...that are implicitly endorsed by the state and are divisive in their implications, serving and sustaining insiders at the expense of outsiders".[82] Using this know-how competent players can manage and manipulate the system to their own advantage as they use personal networks to exploit the inadequacies of the market mechanisms and political institutions prevalent in the first decade of Russia's independence.

Ledeneva's analysis of informal practices in the political sphere focuses on the dark arts of Black PR, on the use of Kompromat and on the prevalence of Krugovaia Poruka, or the ties of Joint Responsibility, as methods of influencing outcomes and establishing extra-legal control over situations to benefit specific individuals. For foreign investors in Russia's oil industry the concept of Krugovaia Poruka would have been the most opaque, being based on an understanding that individuals, as part of a bigger system, are encouraged to seek protection and repay favours in a process of mutual dependency based on long-term relationships, and that governance is according to flexible ethical standards rather than strict rule of law.[83] It is perhaps here that we can see the first foundations of local knowledge in the long-established ties between mutually dependent businessmen and politicians, with the most significant conclusion that "no equality in the face of the law can be observed".[84]

In a business context this had huge implications for an outsider, such as a foreign investor, wishing to do business in Russia. Knowledge of how to manipulate the system in terms of non-cash transactions, interpretation of conflicting regional and federal laws, avoidance of penal tax rules and influence of all-powerful central officials was essential for any businessman hoping to survive in Russia, but was only available to a domestic player steeped in the traditions handed down and adapted from the Soviet system. Ledeneva describes the situation concerning taxes using the following response from an interview: "In these conditions, it's pointless to pay too much attention to which rate of tax should be paid on profits because the whole country lives by different laws. The country does not pay taxes on profit. Rather, the country distributes the profit. People decide themselves how much they will pay and on which grounds. Lots of opportunities are provided by 'imaginative accounting'. So first we decide how much we want to pay and then adjust the books accordingly."[85]

As for the oil industry, another example demonstrates the extensive barter schemes that needed to be understood in order to make a commercial operation function: "A Ural equipment enterprise supplies its product to a Chernogorneft oil reservoir. Instead of paying for it directly, the latter makes a shift-a-debt deal, by which another company, say Sidanco, becomes a payee. Sidanco does not pay the Ural enterprise either; it supplies oil products to a refinery company, which, following the chain, supplies diesel fuel to an automobile plant in Novgorod. The Novgorod plant pays with cars, which are accepted by Uralenergo and the local telephone station as payment for the Ural enterprise's debt."[86]

Clearly then there are practical operational practices which a foreign investor, or indeed any outsider, would need assistance to understand and interpret. As identified by Makino and Delios (1996)[87] the need for this local knowledge was one of the key drivers for foreign investors to seek joint ventures with local partners, but beyond this basic ability to conduct business a further element of local knowledge was the ability to decipher the schemes and legal loop-holes often used to establish competitive advantage. Ledeneva describes the practices of *dvoinaia bukhgalteriia*, or double accounting, which "enable economic agents to protect their property and business operations from the exigencies of market reforms, from the arbitrary judgements of tax inspectors, corrupt authorities and the deformed institutional framework in general".[88] However, although this financial manipulation was described by many businessmen as a necessity, the implicit lack of transparency it entailed provided another barrier to foreign investors and necessitated their partnering with domestic players who had the local knowledge to see through the smokescreen.

Finally Ledeneva describes the work of "Post-Soviet Tolkachi", whose function in the Soviet era had been to manipulate the planning system to ensure that production targets were met. As Nielsen et al (1995) describe, they had operated in the period of late communism when "branch corporations, or trusts, were capable of finding the weakest links in the regulation chains and 'capturing' parts of the central State bureaucracy".[89] At that time all the communist countries had "developed into more or less unconstrained bargaining regimes"[90] and the Tolkachi were now using the skills developed in the Soviet era to help private businesses survive within the chaotic post-Soviet market system. The new "tolkachi", who are usually former high-ranking KGB officials, perform functions such as "security" (physical protection), "informational support" (anything from market research to gathering of kompromat), "dispute settlement and contract enforcement" (e.g. debt recovery) and "negotiation with the state authorities" (dealing with legal, tax and political PR issues).[91]

In the description of these "tolkachi" we perhaps see the fullest extent of the practical "local knowledge" that is required to prosper in a weak state environment such as Russia, and the key features correspond closely with those identified in our statistical analysis in Chapter 4. The tolkachi use their influence across the entire political and commercial arena to manipulate situations in favour of their own organization, as they interact with state organizations to help laws get passed or favourable decisions taken, undermine competitors' businesses using threats based on kompromat, financial or legal pressure, or physical violence, and protect their own associates via their network of contacts. These contacts range from the tax authorities to the legal courts, from state financial institutions to the security services and from ex-KGB colleagues to high-ranking government officials, and all are based on historical bonds that are constantly being refreshed and reinforced. As such they represent a clear business capability, in as much as they are not easily replicable or substitutable and represent a core competitive advantage for a domestic investor with these skills. As a result no foreign investor could hope to access or understand the impact of many domestic Russian business issues without the assistance of a domestic partner with this local knowledge.

This description of the key constituents of local knowledge would seem to conform with the view of Black et al (2002)[92] that successful oligarchs/entrepreneurs in Russia were "crooks, who transferred their skimming talents to the enterprises they acquired, and used their wealth to further corrupt the government and block reforms". However, Braguinsky (2007)[93] explores the role of the oligarchs in more detail in order to establish the key elements of their skill-set that allowed them to prosper during the 1990s and into the Putin era beyond 2000.

In his survey of more than 2,000 entrepreneurs who operated in Russia from 1989 to 2003, Braguinsky identifies two main blocks of oligarchs, namely "old oligarchs" with direct links to the Soviet system and "new oligarchs" who emerged under the Yeltsin regime and had no connection with the "Soviet Mafia". However, his first interesting finding is that, despite their difference in background, both groups ended up playing by the same rules, with the new oligarchs unwilling or unable to "change the rules and the reward structure of the socio-economic game established by the Soviet Mafia". This game involved the exploitation of influence within state organizations and the use of bribes for state officials to ensure personal economic gain in a weak state environment.

Further investigation of the key drivers of success and failure of both types of entrepreneurs identified the unfortunate trait of anti-Semitism as one key element in the rise and fall of a number of oligarchs, but it also established that the more general key to success was the establishment of a "special" relationship with the state. Braguinsky demonstrates this through empirical evidence that those entrepreneurs who supported President Yeltsin in his re-election campaign in 1995/1996 were the main beneficiaries of the asset re-allocation that took place at that time, which "is to be expected in an oligarchic system where economic and political powers are closely intermingled". He further demonstrates that as the Yeltsin-regime became the Putin-regime, political turbulence disturbed the fortunes of many of the entrepreneurs who had invested so much effort in their political connections during the 1990s. However, his overall conclusion is that, in a similar manner to the theories on state capture, the core skill of an entrepreneur in Russia during the 1990s, and indeed any entrepreneur in a similar weak state environment, was his ability to accept that the nascent institutions of the new democracy were inefficient and to exploit this situation through contacts and influence with the senior-ranking politicians and officials who could help one to benefit from the asymmetries created in the business environment. As Braguinsky rather depressingly states, the hopes for a new economic and political environment in post-Soviet Russia based on the emergence of the new oligarchic class have failed to materialize into significant change, as "the process of institutional transformation has demonstrated once again that it is impervious to rapid changes".

This conclusion would seem to be borne out from the evidence of the Putin era to date, which has seen the entire political system become "a constellation of clans, networks and corporations that ensure the movement and exercise and power".[94] Indeed, many of the characteristics of the local knowledge used by the "oligarchs" in the 1990s remain prevalent in 2013. As described by Mendras "the oligarchic phenomenon has developed within the very heart of the state apparatus".[95] As a result Russia has emerged as a country that Kononenko and Moshes (2011) define as a network state in which there exists "a sort of symbiosis between informal groups and formal institutions...in which elite groups foster their own special interests by infiltrating institutions, in effect merging with the state".[96]

Within this system Putin has placed himself at the top of a "power vertical" where he can act as the ultimate arbiter on all matters of importance, and as outlined by Pirani (2010) the President's links with private business mean that good contacts are required to be a successful businessman in Russia. However, for a foreigner this is complicated by the fact that "secrecy, manipulation and arbitrary decision-making" (Jack, 2004) are at the heart of the political and commercial environment, with "opacity, corruption and rent-seeking by insiders" inhibiting the ability of all but the most well-connected from advancing their interests. As highlighted by Tompson (2007) a further issue associated with this is increased state control in the corporate world, with the oil sector being a prime example of where the state prefers "a reliance on direct control and coercion rather than contract, regulation and taxation".[97] The risks for foreign investors inherent in this situation are highlighted by Goldman (2010), who states that "without an independent court of appeal to adjudicate [on] complaints and insist on due process, Gazprom or other state surrogates seem to feel no hesitation in launching campaigns of harassment that force the foreign companies involved to yield"[98] and adds that "there is little prospect that foreign companies will be able to count on the rule of law to protect their property".[99]

As a result of this shift towards the increasing importance of state companies, foreign investors "happily buy these stocks because they are reassured that companies with excellent Kremlin contacts can purchase valuable

Russian assets cheaply" and will also be protected from the vicissitudes of the Russian business environment (Aslund, 2007). However, in a country where "the enforcement of property rights is also a major barrier...with violations common and the business community often opting for informal resolution of conflicts rather than using formal institutions" (Aidis and Estrin, 2006) it is clear that local knowledge remains a vital component for business success, especially as the Putin offer to foreign participants in Russia appears to be "take what we give you, but do not expect any institutional guarantees over it" (Mendras, 2012).[100]

Conclusions on local knowledge

Local knowledge, then, is based on an understanding of the informal processes that allow an economy and a political system to operate in a weak state environment. In a practical sense it involves knowing how to complete transactions in a non-monetary economy using barter and understanding that the legal system is based as much on informal contacts and mutual responsibility as on the implementation of specific laws. It means knowing how to protect oneself or one's company from predatory officials or competitors who are prepared to exploit the weak institutional environment, and also being prepared to respond in a manner that might be deemed unethical or even illegal in other environments. Most importantly, though, it means establishing connections with senior politicians and government officials in order to have some influence with them at times of key importance for your business.

The importance of business groups and the application of local knowledge

In the bargaining process between domestic investors and foreign investors, it would therefore appear that the key bargaining strength held by domestic investors is their knowledge of the local market and how to operate within it. This may take the form of providing market access for goods and services provided by a joint venture, or it may be connected to a firm or individual's ability to use contacts and influence to facilitate the acquisition of assets, preferential treatment from the authorities or the undermining of competitors. As noted above, domestic entrepreneurs have used these talents in Russia to establish business empires in the weak state environment that has characterized the first two decades of Russia's post-Soviet existence, and in particular their skills catalysed the formation of the Financial Industrial Groups (FIGs) that continue to play such a large part in Russia's economy. It is therefore appropriate to review the literature on business groups in order to underline the impact of local knowledge in Russia and its potential relevance to foreign investors.

Granovetter (1995)[101] defines business groups as "a collection of firms bound together in some formal and/or informal ways". As described by

Guillen (2000)[102] the three traditional explanations for the emergence of business groups in emerging economies are market failure, social structure and state activity. Market failure causes the formation of business groups as entrepreneurs seek to use internalization as a means to solve issues of obtaining capital, labour, raw materials or technology in emerging markets (Ghemawat and Khanna, 1998).[103] An example might be the failure of capital markets, when business groups need to retain profits and redistribute them internally for the best economic use. This leads to Tarun and Krishna Palepu's view that "the greater the market imperfections, the greater the importance of business groups in an economy".[104] They provide evidence that business groups can fill the institutional void in product, capital and labour markets and can also supply regulations and enforce contracts, while in a Russian context this view is further supported by Prokop (1995).[105] She argued that in developing countries such as Russia where information flows are thin and financial markets do not perform their proper resource-allocation function, business groups are a natural response. As Starodubrovskaya (1995)[106] put it, financial industrial groups are "islands of stabilisation" in a chaotic world.

Alternatively, social structure has been proposed as another rationale, as in a society where relationships are predominantly vertical (e.g. based on a patrimonial concept of authority) business groups will tend to form around a patrimonial household, with all new activities integrated as subordinate units in order to maintain control. As there is little co-operation between patrimonial entrepreneurs, "the more vertical the pattern of relationships in a society, the greater the importance of business groups in its economy".[107]

Thirdly state activity is cited as a cause of business group formation, as authoritarian states, where there is little pressure from social demands or different class or group interests, can often encourage the growth of business groups in order to control the number of entrepreneurs operating within the economy. In particular this can happen when the state falls prey to special interests or does not have control over the financial system, as the state encourages business groups in order to gain political support.

Market failure and state activity can certainly be seen as factors in the development of the FIGs in Russia. The market chaos that accompanied the fall of the Soviet Union and the failure to establish secure institutions would certainly have encouraged the formation of business groups to solve the problems inherent in a semi-developed market place. In addition, Boris Yeltsin's presidential decree number 2096 of December 1993 "On the Creation of Financial Industrial Groups in the Russian Federation"[108] hints at the desire of the state to see a concentration of investment in the hands of a limited number of competent entrepreneurs. However, these factors do not fully describe the catalysts behind the formation of the FIGs in Russia, and indeed Guillen recognizes this himself when he asks how entrepreneurs build the capabilities to allow them to diversify into unrelated areas and also compete with foreign MNCs.

His initial answer is that their main skill is the ability to combine foreign and domestic resources in a situation where political and economic conditions allow, in other words when preferential treatment and certain limits to competition are prevalent. He argues, therefore, that in asymmetric situations a few entrepreneurs and firms with sufficient local knowledge can develop the capability of combining the requisite foreign and domestic resources for repeated industry entry. However, the asymmetries have to be maintained to make long-term survival possible, because the value of any local knowledge is based on its ability to solve problems in the domestic business environment.

In their analysis of the development of Russia's business groups Boone and Rodionov (2001)[109] agree that the initial formation of these corporate conglomerates involved extensive use of local knowledge. Essentially the break-up of the Soviet Union led to the destruction of the previous system of property controls, and when it was not immediately replaced politicians and enterprise directors realized that huge opportunities for rent-seeking existed amid the anarchy that followed. Contacts with government officials and public servants were necessary in order to exploit these, as preferential treatment was essential in the building of a large business concern (Freinkman, 1995).[110] This became particularly important during and after the privatization process of the mid- to late-1990s, when the opportunity to amass ownership of vast tracts of the Russian economy became available. As described by Black et al (2002)[111] many advisors in Russia believed that "dirty" privatization was better than no privatization at all, while shock therapy demanded a process that was fast and effectively just signalled that assets were being put up for grabs.[112] Companies such as Sibneft were created and sold at the whim of powerful players close to the Kremlin,[113] while overall a small number of influential businessmen were able to gain control of a huge share of Russia's privatized companies. Boone and Rodionov (2002)[114] conducted a survey of 64 medium and large Russian companies and estimated that overall a mere eight groups controlled 86% of the revenues of the country's privatized companies. Essentially the privatization process had resulted in a significant concentration of Russian industry within a very few FIGs. This view was further confirmed by a World Bank study in 2004 which identified that "horizontal integration has increased substantially...[and] is often associated with the expansion of financial-industrial groups...[which bring] a threat of market dominance and monopolization".[115]

Boone and Rodionov chart the progress of the FIGs in three stages. Stage 1 could be described as the wide-ranging use of contacts and influence for the purchase, consolidation or outright theft of assets, with the overall mantra of "buy now, think later"[116] being driven by the conviction that everything was cheap and could be sold on for a huge profit. This might be called the "Grabbing Hand" stage, and its key requirements were contacts with government officials and the managers of assets, protection from foreign competition and a weak property rights environment within which to operate.

Stage 2 can be equated with the consolidation of the ownership of businesses within the FIGs, the establishment of management control (particularly over cashflows) and the initial attempts at managing a true portfolio of businesses. Boone and Rodionov equate this period of ownership consolidation with the first attempts at corporate turnarounds and the initial introduction of corporate governance rules. Furthermore, as the entrepreneurs look to run the businesses in a more commercial fashion, management skills and appropriate technology become greater necessities, encouraging the first introduction of foreign skill-sets. However, they also note that the consolidation of subsidiary companies often involved fairly brutal business tactics and further use of influence over government and judicial officials, and as such local knowledge was still a key factor. In this "Consolidating Control" phase the involvement of foreign strategic players depended upon the needs of the specific industries and companies, but in the oil industry at least foreign participation was still seen both as unwanted competition for assets that remained cheap and also as an unnecessary hindrance if the foreign partners insisted on the application of international corporate governance rules during the consolidation process.

Finally Stage 3 is classified as the realization of the value of the assets grabbed and consolidated in Stages 1 and 2, and might be termed the "Cashing In" phase. Potential profit-generating strategies include the running of various firms for profit, the floatation of businesses on the stock market or the sale of strategic stakes to foreign firms. At this point the domestic players became interested in establishing a more conventional investment environment, not only to protect their own assets but also to encourage foreigners to purchase any assets which they might put up for sale. Interestingly, then, the value of local knowledge is diminished in Stage 3 and is replaced by competencies more normally associated with foreign investors and market participants.

In Table 2.1 below I summarize the three stages of development identified by Boone and Rodionov and also incorporate some of the ideas from Guillen to describe the objectives of the entrepreneur at each stage, the core competencies that he needs to be successful, the business model that is most appropriate and the ideal business environment. Progress through the three stages sees both a change in the need for local knowledge as a core competency as well as a shift in the business model, with local knowledge becoming less relevant as a more focused corporate model emerges. At the same time the relevance of foreign investor skills and competencies increases, and the ideal business environment adjusts to encourage their involvement.

Table 2.1   Stages in the development of Financial Industrial Groups (FIGs)

Phase	Description	Objectives	Core Competencies	Business Model	Ideal Business Environment
1	Grabbing Hand	Access cheap assets	Local knowledge and influence	Collection of diverse investments	Weak state, with state capture and corruption
2	Consolidating Control	Gain control over subsidiaries cheaply, and start corporate re-organization	Local knowledge, plus initial corporate management skills and technology where appropriate	Business Group with control over major subsidiary firms	Weak state, but with emerging institutions
3	Cashing In	Creation of a more rational and focused business to promote value realization	Management skills, technology, investor relations and corporate finance skills	Focused corporate model with good governance structure	Strong institutional environment to provide foreign investor confidence

The involvement of foreign participation and investment is most likely in Stages 2 and 3, although as we have seen in Russia foreign firms did also get involved in business activities during Stage 1. However, I believe that a number of conclusions about potential foreign investment at each stage can be drawn. Firstly, local knowledge is a core skill for any entrepreneur in phases one and two of the business-building process. The accumulation of assets and their re-organization into a manageable corporate structure requires high levels of influence at numerous layers of government, both federal and regional, as well as an ability to manipulate court decisions and exploit the weak institutional environment. However, the second conclusion is that there is recognition of the need for the skills brought by foreign investors, particularly in the organization of complicated business structures in Stage 2 and in the development of more focused business models in Stage 3. Thirdly, there is also a realization that the business model can change, and that there are benefits to be derived from a more corporate model with improved governance rules and more transparent ownership incentives.

Once again, though, it is important to establish whether the current situation in Russia in 2013 bears comparison with the period when FIGs thrived in the 1990s and early 2000s. Are the same business tactics in use during the Putin era as were prevalent under Yeltsin, and therefore is it correct to think of local knowledge being used in the same way, in particular as a bargaining tool with foreign investors?

In previous sections we have argued that, although the differences between the Yeltsin and Putin eras may appear superficially significant, in fact many of the underlying characteristics are the same. Emerging weak institutions were exploited by entrepreneurs using a strategy of state capture during the 1990s, while during the 2000s hollowed out institutions have been used as a "carcass" that influential networks need as an operating environment. In both cases real power is vested in the hands of a few, who use the opacity, lack of transparency and corruption inherent in the system as a whole to sustain their political and commercial standing. Within this environment a system of "state corporatism" has emerged, within which state companies are populated with members of the "unofficial oligarchy" and their clients to give the "impression of a Putin family corporation...with a high degree of family and personal relations amongst the leaders of top state departments and large corporations" (Mommsen, 2012). Tompson (2007) describes the state-owned companies that are starting to dominate as being "run for the benefit of insiders and their patrons in the state administration" and that they provide "attractive sources of funding for informal political or policy initiatives" as well as the more obvious profits in the formal commercial environment. However, it is the "informality of the process of the accommodation of oligarchic interests through personal connections" and the "overall lack of transparency that makes it very difficult to identify the main players within this complex structure of interests" (Mommsen, 2012) that highlight the similarities with the FIGs prevalent in the 1990s.

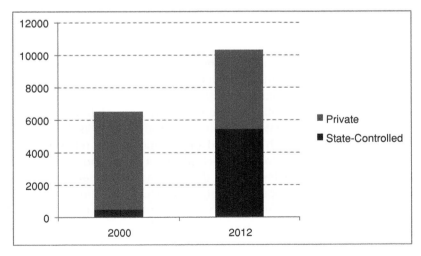

Figure 2.1   State control of oil production 2000 versus 2012 (million tpa)
Source: Graph created by author from multiple company sources

Furthermore, the particular consolidation of state control in the oil and gas sector further emphasizes the concentration of power and influence in the hands of a very few key individuals, as was the case with the oligarchs in the 1990s. Following the acquisition of TNK-BP by Rosneft in 2013, the state now controls more than half of Russia's oil production via its ownership of Rosneft, TNK-BP, GazpromNeft and Slavneft and continues to dominate the gas sector through its control of the country's largest producer Gazprom. The graph above (Figure 2.1) shows the dramatic change in this position since 2000, but once again it should be emphasized that although this presents a picture that is superficially different in terms of outward structure, in effect what has happened is that oligarchic corporatism has been replaced by state corporatism, one team of business leaders has been replaced by another, one set of companies has risen while others have declined, but the business practices have remained remarkably similar with local knowledge continuing to be the critical success factor.

Conclusions on the importance of local knowledge and the relevance of theories of business group formation

While the transaction cost theory of the firm suggests that firms are formed to provide a lower cost alternative to the production of goods that might otherwise have been produced using market transactions, the resource-based theory of the firm asserts that core competences or capabilities are the true foundation of value creation for a firm. These capabilities can be seen as the collective organizational learning of a firm, and their value is enhanced if they can be isolated within one corporate structure and not replicated, purchased or substituted by competing firms. The corporate architecture of a firm therefore plays a vital role in creating the barriers that can allow firms to retain and sustain their key capabilities as competitive strengths.

Taking this resource-based view as a foundation, Kock and Guillen (2001)[117] propose that in a weak state environment local knowledge is one such core competence for domestic entrepreneurs. They describe the ability to understand how to operate in asymmetric market conditions and to use local contacts and influence to optimize business outcomes as a skill idiosyncratic to individual entrepreneurs that is difficult to replicate as long as the weak institutional conditions on which it is based are maintained and refreshed.

Ledeneva (2006)[118] develops the definition of local knowledge further, describing it as an understanding of the informal processes that allow an economy and a political system to operate in a weak state environment. In a practical sense it involves knowing how to complete transactions in a non-monetary economy using barter and understanding that the legal system is based as much on informal contacts and mutual responsibility as on the implementation of specific laws. It means knowing how to protect oneself or one's company from predatory officials or competitors who are prepared to exploit the weak institutional environment, and also being prepared to respond in a manner that might be deemed unethical or even illegal in other environments. Most importantly, though, it means establishing connections with senior politicians and government officials in order to have some influence with them at times of key importance for your business. Makin and Delios (1996)[119] confirm this view and see the importance of local knowledge as the key reason why many foreign investors seek to form joint ventures with domestic partners as they make their initial moves into countries with a weak state environment.

The literature on business groups provides a clear example of how local knowledge is used by entrepreneurs in a weak state environment, whether they be private-sector "oligarchs" or state-appointed officials acting in an entrepreneurial way in a state-controlled company. It identifies the use of local knowledge in an asymmetric situation as a core competence that became the foundation for the formation and development of the widely diversified business groups seen in Russia. It also concludes that these asymmetries need to be maintained in order to ensure the survival of the business groups, suggesting that entrepreneurs will actively undermine attempts to create a more stable environment.

Boone and Rodionov (2001)[120] have taken this analysis a step further and provided a basis for explaining the development of business groups in Russia. In the initial "Grabbing Hand" stage entrepreneurs use their local knowledge to access as many assets as they can as cheaply as possible, and are keen to exclude all competition (including foreigners) from the process. At this first stage their businesses are essentially a series of investments in joint ventures with other investors where the key bargaining strength is local knowledge. In the second "Consolidating Control" stage the entrepreneurs look to increase their control over their investments by increasing their equity share in the individual ventures and consolidating ownership under one holding company. In this consolidation phase shares in individual ventures are exchanged for shares in the holding company, and while local knowledge remains important to ensure that this is done on the most favourable terms, the importance of other business skills such as management, organization and technology starts to increase as the process of corporate re-organization begins.

In the final "Cashing In" stage the goal of the entrepreneur is to maximize the value from his investment either by running it for profit or preparing it for sale on a stock market or to a strategic investor. At this stage a new investment model has effectively been created in order to incentivize all the shareholders in the holding company to work for the benefit of the group as a whole. This is particularly important to encourage the participation of foreign investors either as buyers of shares (so that the domestic entrepreneur can cash out and take some profit) or as co-investors in an ongoing concern. At this stage the value of local knowledge as a specific asset of the entrepreneur is diminished not only because he is now incentivized to demonstrate that he will be using this competence for the benefit of all shareholders but also because he is incentivized to encourage a stronger institutional environment, where local knowledge is less relevant, in order to boost foreign investor confidence.

A further possible conclusion from this analysis is that the state consolidation of the Putin era occurred in order to interrupt the "Cashing In" phase which some of the Yeltsin era oligarchs were set to engage in. As a result, the new "state-sponsored" oligarchs could be seen as having gone through their own "grabbing" phase in the early 2000s, followed by a consolidation phase as state-owned companies were put together as larger corporate entities. The key question during the third term of the Putin presidency is whether we will enter a "Cashing In" phase during which foreign investors can operate in a more secure governance environment or whether the asymmetric business environment will continue. The deals between Rosneft and a number of IOCs to explore offshore waters and unconventional oil reserves in Russia, as well as the decision to allow BP to become a 20% shareholder in Russia's NOC, hint that we may be approaching this third phase, but the broader evidence of the business environment as a whole (as provided by the World Bank Ease of Business Survey discussed earlier) suggests that the use of local knowledge as a powerful commercial tool is likely to remain a competitive advantage for some time yet.

Bargaining theory and joint ventures

Bargaining in an oil industry context

The literature on FDI in the oil industry points to management skills, technology and provision of capital as the core competencies and ownership advantages brought to any investment opportunity by foreign players, while the host country brings its oil resources as the locational advantage. Meanwhile the literature on state capture identifies local knowledge as the core competency of the domestic partner. In order to understand how a foreign partner can be successful within this environment it is necessary to understand how these advantages become bargaining strengths and how the balance of the bargaining positions changes within the context of joint venture formation and operation.

Initially bargains struck over concessions in the oil industry were viewed entirely as fixed bi-partite arrangements, with an agreement being struck between the host government and the international oil company. As Moran[121] points out, initially the bargaining is heavily weighted in favour of the investor, but once the investment is made and the operation is a success, the atmosphere changes and the terms that were negotiated in the face of big uncertainty no longer seem to reflect reality. With the reduction in uncertainty the balance of power shifts towards the host government, until the time when a major new corporate commitment is to be made. As the commitment to invest approaches, the bargaining strength of the investor increases, but once it has been made the balance starts to swing back towards the government again. However, as Smith and Wells (1975)[122] subsequently observed, this chain of events is only to be expected if one builds on Vernon's initial "obsolescing bargain" theory.

Smith and Wells[123] further highlight the issues from a government perspective. Primarily, the number of options available to a government, in terms of companies willing to invest, will determine its relative bargaining strength in specific industries (with one option always being to develop the resources by itself). Issues such as the level of capital investment needed, the technical and management skills required, access to markets, and the specific goals of the potential investors are also key considerations. The host government also needs to consider its own strengths and weaknesses in terms of the geography and quality of its resource base, the geological risks, the political risks (as perceived by an outside investor) and its own experience in negotiating in a specific industry.

McKern (1977)[124] re-emphasized that the strength of the foreign investors' position is based on technological complexity, the degree of concentration of the global industry and the investors' own financial and managerial strengths. In contrast the host country's strengths depend upon the uniqueness of its deposits, their size and accessibility, the investment climate and its experience in negotiating and implementing projects. He also noted that if the foreign investor belongs to an oligopolistic industry where there is a high degree of vertical integration, then there is a strong drive to secure supplies of material for an integrated worldwide production system.

Later writers such as Hennart (1986)[125] highlighted the issue of strategic bargaining in natural resource industries. In an oligopolistic situation (such as the tin or the petroleum industries) one player can be "held up" by another because there is nowhere else to turn for the required resources. Long-term contracts are one answer, but it is not always possible to foresee all the potential circumstances, thus making it expensive or impossible to mitigate against all risks, and so a combination of horizontal and vertical integration becomes a more economic alternative. In essence as the degree of uncertainty increases it becomes less feasible to create a suitable contract, and internalization of activities via the use of international subsidiaries therefore becomes a much more robust long-term arrangement. This is a particularly relevant observation in the case of foreign investment in the Russian oil and gas sector, as the international oil majors have come under increasing pressure to replace their reserves and so avoid strategic bargaining by gaining control of oil and gas resources via the formation of international subsidiaries that can invest in and control the development of oil and gas resources where they are located. Russia is one of the few remaining countries that can provide opportunities big enough to allow the IOCs to achieve this goal, thus giving the country and the domestic owners of oil resources a significant bargaining strength.

Thomas Walde (1991)[126] further examined the factors that are likely to attract or deter private, particularly foreign, investment in a country's natural resource industries (in other words to improve the bargaining position of the host country). He notes the obvious point that the geology and geography of resource deposits is of vital importance, and adds that the nature of the geological endowment determines the type of investor as big prospects attract big companies (as in the case of Russia). However, the investment climate is the other key determinant of initial investor interest in a country or prospect, as companies often shy away from geologically attractive sites in unstable countries. Conversely, legislation can improve the risk/reward calculations, and can persuade investors to take a higher geological risk. As a result he highlights the legislative and regulatory frameworks and the institutional framework as being the most important ways of assessing the investment climate for foreign investors, identifying the main issues as security of property rights, tax regulation and potential domestic obligations. In terms of the institutional framework, the minimization of bureaucracy and the clarification of the roles of different agencies are the key success criteria.

All these issues are vital in the discussion of Russia, as they reach to the heart of the debate over the key deterrents to foreign investment in the oil and gas sector and also lie behind the key bargaining strengths of the domestic investors who came to partner with the IOCs. The literature on state capture has demonstrated that the uncertain business environment benefited the domestic oil investors, who with the help of a weak state have encouraged the investment environment to remain asymmetric in order to maximize the value of their own "local knowledge" and to avoid foreign competition. It was also to the advantage of many of the bureaucrats operating within the system to maintain the status quo in order to maximize their own rent-seeking opportunities.

Bargaining power, ownership and control

A more general analysis of bargaining power in developing countries was carried out by Lecraw in 1984,[127] when he examined both the different characteristics that can influence relative bargaining power and also the importance of control in the success of any venture between an international investor and a local partner. He identified that within Dunning's OLI framework it is a company's ownership advantages (mainly intangible assets such as technical and management skills) that give it bargaining power over a host country, and it is incentivized to internalize these advantages by using subsidiary companies to enter a host country in order to avoid the dissipation of its core bargaining strengths and maximize their value. Conversely it is the locational advantages that give the host country its bargaining power over the MNC, allied with its ability to find competing MNCs to invest in its assets or alternatively to go it alone without FDI at all.

Lecraw's analysis builds on the work published by Fagre and Wells in 1982,[128] when they found a link between the bargaining power of an MNC and its equity ownership of any new foreign venture. They established that intangible resources such as technology, product differentiation, management experience and access to foreign markets are key ownership advantages for hierarchies such as an MNC which increases its bargaining position relative to a host government, allowing it to negotiate a higher equity share in any joint venture formed. Lecraw, however, notes the analysis of Killing (1980),[129] Schaan (1982)[130] and Beamish and Lane (1982),[131] all of whom conclude that the relationship between equity ownership and success is U-shaped, meaning that partners are more successful in JVs if they have very high or very low equity stakes rather than owning a venture equally. In other words, someone needs to be in control of a joint venture if it is to be successful and so it may be better for an MNC to accept a lower equity stake as long as it can control the other critical success variables of the venture.[132]

However, from a Russian oil industry perspective the most relevant observation is that effective control is a more important success factor for a venture, irrespective of equity ownership, as suggested in general theory by Cowling and Sugden (1987).[133] We intend to demonstrate that control was indeed exercised outside the boundaries of each partner's equity stake in a venture, in particular when a Russian partner could use his "local knowledge" as either a bargaining strength or as a means of extracting value from a venture outside the normal venture agreement. Conversely, the international partner would also try to use his ownership advantages to influence any outcome, but as many authors have recognized, these strengths tend to diminish over time. Nevertheless, the fact that one of the most successful international JVs in Russia, TNK-BP, was a 50:50 venture would seem to contradict the theory that lower or higher stakes are to be preferred.

Joint ventures and bargaining

As has already been mentioned, much of the early foreign investment in the Russian oil and gas sector took the form of joint ventures, and indeed the majority of the greenfield or acquisitive investments that have taken place over the past decade have also contained elements of joint venturing. Shell's commitment to the greenfield development of the Sakhalin 2 project involves a partnership group, and BP's major investment in the assets of TNK and Sidanco has taken the form of a 50:50 joint entity with the Alfa-Access-Renova consortium. As such, it is valid to consider in some detail the nature of joint venture agreements and how the balance of bargaining power and management control tends to shift over time.

Bruce Kogut (1988)[134] provided an overview of the different rationales behind joint venture formation by identifying transaction costs, strategic behaviour and organizational knowledge and learning as the three main catalysts. According to the transaction cost theory of the firm as proposed by Williamson (1981),[135] firms seek to minimize the sum of production and transaction costs by either carrying out activities using the market place or by internalizing them within a firm. The theory in particular highlights that in cases of asset specificity, when protracted negotiations can take place between two agents concerning gains to be made by each from even small trades (i.e. small number bargaining), it may be cheaper for one agent to bring the whole transaction within one entity (a firm) to reduce the transaction costs. In other words a firm may choose to produce a component itself even though a supplier could do it cheaper, because this cost saving is outweighed by the transaction costs. As an alternative a joint venture can straddle the boundaries of two firms and may avoid this issue, being of benefit if it can reduce the production costs of at least one partner. An alternative view, rather than seeing minimization of costs as the main goal of a joint venture, is to view strategic behaviour as the main catalyst. This theory regards the aim of joint ventures as the maximization of profits through improving a firm's competitive position, and many views of joint ventures see them as motivated by strategic behaviour to deter entry or to erode a competitor's position (Vernon, 1983).[136] Joint ventures in the Russian oil and gas industry can to an extent be interpreted in both these ways. For the foreign investor a joint venture with a domestic partner is needed both to reduce transaction costs (the costs of doing business in the asymmetric Russian business environment) and as a strategic ploy to optimize the foreign investor's position in a country where access to huge hydrocarbon resources is possible. For the domestic investor the joint venture reduces transaction costs by introducing modern technology and management skills from the foreign partner, which can then give it a strategic advantage over its domestic peers.

A third view is that joint ventures are a means for firms to learn or seek to retain their capabilities, and is based on the resource-based view of the firm as first outlined by authors such as Penrose (1959).[137] If firms are seen as a knowledge base (or set of competencies) which cannot easily be diffused across the boundaries of the firm (McKelvey, 1983),[138] then joint ventures can be a vehicle through which this tacit, organizationally embedded, knowledge can be transferred. From this perspective a joint venture is encouraged if neither party owns each other's technology or underlying 'competencies', nor understands each other's routines. Alternatively, one firm may wish to retain an organizational capability while benefiting from another firm's current knowledge or cost advantage for potential use in a third market. In a Russian context, we will argue that foreign partners formed joint ventures in order to gain access to the competency of their domestic partner concerning how to operate in the local business environment. We will further argue that the most successful foreign partners then tried to learn this competency for themselves in order to improve their bargaining position and reduce their overall transaction costs.

Harrigan and Newman (1990)[139] provide a further comprehensive overview of the initial motivations for and the subsequent forms of joint venture creation. They argue that the most important element of the bargaining framework is the propensity of the partners to co-operate with each other, which will be based on the resources which each can bring to a new joint venture and the costs for each party to form that venture. In addition, each party's potential alternatives will be a key consideration, and will help to define the strategic importance of the venture to them. Harrigan and Newman see this strategic importance, or centrality, as being based on necessity (which can be mitigated by availability), urgency (the longer the planning horizon the more chance to look for alternatives) and interdependence (how many of a firm's activities are connected to the resource in question). Necessity has been particularly relevant in the case of oil and gas investment in Russia, although at different times for the domestic and foreign investors, but urgency also has a key role to play as perceptions about the need to invest in Russia have changed over time. Initially Russia appeared to be one of a number of options for investment for the international oil majors, but as many Middle Eastern countries then refused to grant broad IOC access to their huge resources, Russia became one of the few regions of the world that could provide large-scale opportunities for overseas investors in the oil industry. The emergence of Iraq as a new IOC opportunity and the new opportunity offered by unconventional oil in the US have started to undermine Russia's position somewhat, but it still remains the case that it offers one of the world's largest oil resource opportunities where it is possible for IOCs to invest.

The bargaining process then involves attempting to reach a consensus on an outcome that is acceptable to partners who are viewing the combined effort from a number of different perspectives (Pettigrew, 1977[140]; Fouraker and Siegal, 1963[141]). Bargaining power is gained by the ability to withhold or extend a particularly attractive input, which could ultimately be used to force a partner into an action that is unattractive to it (Bacharach and Lawler, 1980[142]; Pfeffer, 1981[143]; Hambrick, 1981[144]). In the context of a joint venture, bargaining power is based on the fit of the propensity in two specific firms (Nierenberg, 1968[145]), and power arises when one firm can withhold or dispense something that is attractive to another firm (Jemison, 1981).[146] The issue of data availability is also very important, as each partner may not have a full understanding of what the other wants or needs. In such cases perceptions of power are as important as the actual power itself, although firms, industries or national cultures may differ in the way that they use or display this power; some firms may be reluctant to use power for fear of undermining future co-operation, while others may be keen to increase the perception of how much power they wield through acting more aggressively to demonstrate the value of their input.

Relative bargaining power in joint ventures

Yan and Gray (1994)[147] pick up the theme of bargaining power in their case study of US-China joint ventures. They distinguish between context-based and resource-based bargaining power, with the former involving the stakes of the bargainers and their alternatives (Bacharach and Lawler, 1984).[148] A stake is a bargainer's level of dependence on the negotiation and its outcome, and is negatively correlated with bargaining power. Availability of alternatives, on the other hand, is positively related to bargaining power, as the negotiator with alternatives can threaten to walk away (Fisher and Ury, 1981).[149] Resource-based bargaining power, meanwhile, involves the possession or control of a critical resource that gives more power in a relationship. The relative bargaining power in a joint venture is related to who brings what and how much to the venture. As a result, a partner gains bargaining power if it brings resources that are costly or impossible for other partners to replace (Root, 1988)[150] and are critical to the venture's success. In this context the authors identified that the foreign partner generally brought technological and management know-how, while the local firm brought knowledge of how to get things done domestically, which they defined as local knowledge. In our analysis we will show that these were the resources contributed by foreign and domestic partners in the Russian oil industry, and we will also show that the more successful foreign partners attempted to change the balance of bargaining power by acquiring some of the resource of local knowledge for themselves. In this way they increased their alternative options by giving themselves the opportunity to walk away from their domestic partner. Conversely we will also show that their domestic partners were playing the same game through learning technical and management skills so that they could, if necessary, walk away from their foreign partners. As such the balance of the relationship inside a joint venture between a domestic and foreign partner can be to an extent defined by the competition for knowledge that is inherently taking place between the two parties.

Taking the analysis a step further, Yan and Gray (1994)[151] considered not only the bargaining positions of the venture partners, but also the management control that each had and the performance of the venture itself in order to reach a conclusion about the relationship between the three parties. Essentially they proposed that the bargaining power of a potential joint venture partner will be positively related to the extent of its managerial control over the joint venture's operation, while also arguing that the division of management control between joint venture parents will be related to the performance of the venture. Their research did confirm the positive relationship between bargaining power and management control, but also found that the relationship between management control and performance was not as straight forward as higher management control did not always provide better performance for both partners. (The authors acknowledge that performance is difficult to define, as it depends on what perspective one takes, but they argue one should essentially ask how much the joint venture has managed to achieve in terms of the strategic goals set by each of the partners). In addition, it would seem that shared control is not the problem that others have identified (Killing, 1983),[152] which may reflect the fact that the partners are not both from developed countries. It may be the case that resources brought by partners from developed and developing countries are more likely to be complementary, and that in such a situation the foreign partner may be allowed to dominate. However, it would then seem that a high level of mutual trust and shared objectives are vital to the success of the venture. On this issue Yan and Gray raise the very relevant point that the strategic goals of the domestic and foreign partners often differ significantly. The foreigners are generally looking for market entry and profit, while the domestic players want technology, and both partners want control in order to achieve their own goals. Initially the foreign partner will take control because of his superior management skills, but over time the domestic partner will expect this control to be passed over. As a result the foreign partner will then have to make greater resource commitments in order to maintain the balance of power.

This emphasizes the dynamic nature of international joint ventures, with changes in the experience levels of both partners (effectively learning from each other and from the process of running the JV) leading to shifts in bargaining power within the joint venture, normally in favour of the domestic partner. It is particularly interesting that the domestic partner would appear to be the main beneficiary of the learning process, as learning technological and management skills is easier for the domestic partner than gaining local knowledge is for the foreign partner. Importantly, too, the growth of the joint venture also changes the bargaining position, as the joint venture generates the critical mass to allow it to become less dependent on its parents, normally favouring the domestic partner who had less influence in the first place.

Finally, and also very importantly in a Russian context, sometimes contributions that were not recognized as important at first come to be seen as vital, which also leads to a shift in bargaining power.[153] Over time domestic players in Russia have come to appreciate both the increasing value of their resource base in an international context and the true importance of their local knowledge, and thus re-assessed their own bargaining strength relative to their international partners.

The instability of international joint ventures and the importance of learning

The issue of shifts in bargaining power leading to the instability of international joint ventures (IJVs) is explored further by Inkpen and Beamish (1997),[154] as they analyse how knowledge acquisition by joint venture partners can eliminate partner dependency and make a joint venture bargain obsolete.[155] Quoting Hamel (1991),[156] who described alliances as a "race to learn", they argue that whichever partner learns fastest will dominate. This concept of learning is a core part of the rationale for the formation of IJVs is grounded in a wide body of research (Young and Olk (1994)[157], Bacharach and Lawler (1980)[158], Hamel (1991)[159], Pfeffer (1981)[160]). Importantly the pace of learning is identified as a key element in the shift in bargaining power as it can erode the resource advantage brought by either one of the partners, and eventually can undermine the need for the JV by eliminating any dependency. In particular Inkpen and Beamish focus on what the foreign partner can do to make the bargain with the local partner obsolete. They argue that access to local knowledge is a key driver for a foreign company to form an IJV and suggest that as local knowledge increases and commitment to acquire it grows, the instability of the IJV grows too because the local partner becomes dispensable. However, from the international partner's perspective it is also recognized that the establishment of a suitable knowledge management and creation process is then the key to acquiring available local knowledge (Kogut (1988)[161], Parkhe (1991)[162], Pucik (1991)[163], Dodgson (1993)[164], Hamel (1991)[165], Inkpen (1995)[166], Inkpen and Crossan (1995)[167], Simonin and Helleloid (1993)[168]).

Conversely, while it is acknowledged that the local partner's acquisition of technological knowledge is another potential force in the joint venture, it is asserted that it is less likely to cause instability. This is justified by citing Hedlund (1994)[169] who defines three forms of knowledge – a) cognitive, b) skills and c) knowledge embodied in products and services. He argues that skills knowledge (i.e. the technical knowledge brought by the foreign partner) is the most difficult to acquire because it is ingrained within organizational routines and therefore is difficult for another firm to extract (also see Nelson and Winter, 1982).[170] According to Inkpen and Beamish[171] the most likely end-point for most international joint ventures is therefore that the foreign partner will acquire the business, implying that it has attained the local knowledge it needs. However, a contention of this book will be that in a weak state environment local knowledge is difficult to obtain, among other things because both domestic players and employees of state institutions are incentivized to maintain asymmetries in the domestic business environment. Furthermore, the allocation of responsibilities during the formation of the joint venture can also play a key role in reinforcing the difficulty for a foreign partner to gain local knowledge. If the local partner is given full responsibility for all local activity then the foreign partner will have less incentive to acquire local knowledge. As such one would expect a competitive local partner to attempt to take all responsibility for local activity on itself, and also to make a big effort to ensure that the value of local knowledge did not deteriorate over time.

In contrast, a number of the skills brought by foreign investors can either be imitated by the Russian oil companies or brought in via contractors or the direct hiring of expatriate employees. This point is highlighted by Hamel et al[172] who note that western companies generally face a disadvantage because their skills are more easily transferable, and also that western companies often need to overcome "an arrogance born of decades of leadership". Both of these issues are relevant in the Russian context, as western oil technology was assimilated by the Russian industry much more quickly than anticipated, and by their own admission western companies did arrive in Russia with a somewhat inflated view of their ability to operate in an unknown environment. However, it is interesting to note that despite the issue of skill transferability, IOCs have maintained a number of ownership advantages that have become more obvious over time. Although specific technical skills have been provided by contractors, and domestic partners have been able to learn specific management skills (e.g. finance, corporate governance, investor relations), the value of an IOC's experience in managing the overall process of oil exploration and development is still valued. As Mikhail Fridman, a core shareholder in TNK-BP, stated in 2003 on the formation of the company: "BP brings its technical and operational skill to the joint venture, but importantly will also contribute its lengthy oil industry experience and its ability to optimise the processes embedded in the oil and gas value chain."[173]

Conclusion on bargaining and joint venture theories

The first theories on bargaining in the oil and gas industry focused on the interaction between the state and an international oil company, analysing the competitive strengths of each to determine the likely outcome of any negotiation. The knowledge-based ownership advantages brought by the IOCs were contrasted with the locational advantages of the host country where the oil resources were located, and a bargain was generally struck to allow a foreign-owned subsidiary of the IOC to control the development of oilfields while benefitting both parties through the use of its firm-level skills. However, the result was generally viewed as a static agreement, negotiated once and expected to remain in-force for the duration of the life of the asset.

Authors such as Vernon (1971)[174], Moran (1974)[175] and Smith and Wells (1975)[176] recognized that any bargain was dynamic in nature and was likely to be adjusted as the bargaining positions and strengths of the parties evolved. In particular they highlighted that the bargaining position of the state was prone to improve over time, leading to a growing tax take. In addition, all the analysis was focused on the bi-partite relationship between the state and the foreign investor, with very little attention paid to a significant role for domestic investors.

Similar issues of bargaining strengths and weaknesses and the dynamic nature of any agreement feature in the analysis of joint ventures, and a significant body of research has examined the ability of the different partners to improve their bargaining positions. In a Russian context it is clear that the initial reasons for joint venture co-operation have changed over time, shifting the bargaining power of the domestic and international partners. As Harrigan and Newman (1990)[177] define it, in the early post-Soviet years the "relative bargaining power" lay with the foreign investors, as they were perceived to bring greater benefits and at the time had a greater range of alternatives. The domestic partner at least appeared to be more dependent on the outcome of any joint venture negotiations and was therefore in a weak bargaining position (Yan and Gray, 1994).[178]

Over time, though, the domestic and international partners went through a learning process (Hamel, 1991[179]; Inkpen and Beamish, 1997[180]) that helped them to understand both about the skills that constituted the bargaining strengths of their partners and about the value of their own skills and their potential impact on any bargaining process. A number of authors (Inkpen and Beamish, 1997[181]; Hedlund, 1994[182]) see this process as favouring the foreign investor, but we will demonstrate (along the lines of Hamel et al, 1989[183]) that the foreign partners are in fact at a disadvantage because some of their skills are more easily transferred or imitated. Further, we will show that domestic partners have a large incentive to protect the value of their local knowledge by keeping the investment environment as uncertain as possible. This not only strengthens their bargaining position with their foreign partners, but also enables them to build domestic business empires through the exploitation of the weak state environment they helped to create. We will also show that many foreign investors have found their bargaining strengths gradually eroded by the development of technical networks between the Russian oil companies and western contractors. Indeed the emergence of these new external economies of scale[184] has raised questions, at least among some domestic players, about the need for an IOC presence in Russia. Meanwhile the Russian oil companies have come to realize the true value of their assets to the IOCs, and the vital importance of their local knowledge to any international joint venture. As such, much of the instability in international joint ventures in Russia is derived not from the increasing dominance of the foreign partner (as seen by Inkpen and Beamish, 1997[185]) but from the growing strength in the position of the domestic partner, who had an ever decreasing need for the skills and capital offered by the IOCs. In this context, the competition for knowledge which we see as being at the heart of joint venture relations appears to be easier for the domestic partner to win because their knowledge skills are easier to protect and, as we will hope to demonstrate later, because they understand the need to defend them as part of the bargaining process.

In the context of Dunning's eclectic paradigm we will essentially argue that while foreign partners have brought their knowledge-based ownership advantages to a bargaining process with the host country, which has the locational advantage of access to oil and gas resources, the negotiations and ongoing partnership have historically been complicated by the presence of a third party, the domestic partner. In the weak state environment that existed in Russia after the end of the Soviet era, this domestic partner possessed a skillset unavailable to any foreign investor, namely local knowledge and influence essential to operate in the asymmetric business environment. In terms of the OLI framework, this local knowledge adds a new dimension to the process of a foreign investor gaining the full benefit of the potential internalization advantages. In effect the need for local knowledge hinders the ability of a foreign investor to gain the advantages of internalization, because he cannot bring the full benefits of his ownership advantages to bear without it. As a result, the domestic partner, with his local knowledge, becomes a key part of any bargaining process and a source of potential instability.

Overall conclusions – Is this all relevant to Russia today?

Figure 2.2 summarizes our conclusions on how Dunning's OLI paradigm can be used to describe the interaction between foreign partners, domestic partners and the State in a weak institutional environment. The domestic partner effectively inhibits the ability of the foreign partner to internalize his ownership advantages in negotiation with the State, which has the locational advantage. In essence, local knowledge (and therefore generally a local partner) is required to complete any bargaining process and then to keep it in balance.

However, a valid question could be raised concerning the robustness of this argument in Russia in 2013, given that a) outside observation of President Putin and his current government would suggest the growing strength of the

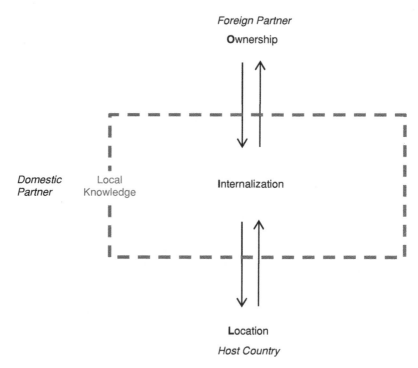

Figure 2.2 How local knowledge interrupts Dunning's eclectic paradigm

State over the past decade and b) the fact that foreign companies are once again forming ventures directly with State institutions, in particular the increasingly powerful National Oil Company, Rosneft, and therefore appear to be excluding the use of a third domestic actor. How can Figure 2.2 describe a situation in which the domestic partner no longer appears to be so relevant?

The answer, we believe, lies in the recent academic literature on Russia under Putin, which identifies both the continuing weakness of state institutions and the development of a dual state system. Pirani (2010) argues that although Putin is often identified with a strong state, in fact it would be more accurate to say that he made the state strong only in comparison with the chaos into which it descended under Yeltsin, while Mendras (2012) takes this one step further and states that although Putin promised to restore the authority of the State when he came to power, "10 years later the public institutions are all weakened and subject to the arbitrariness of the Kremlin system". What has resulted is an environment within which Putin has exercised control not through support for strong independent institutions but rather by exercising his personal authority on those around through the creation of a vertical power structure that requires all major decisions to be made, or endorsed, by him. Within this environment "secrecy, manipulation and arbitrary decision-making remain the hallmarks of the administration more than transparency, justice and consistency" (Jack, 2004).

As a result, while it is undeniable that Putin and his team use the power inherent in their political offices to exert control over social, commercial and economic life in Russia, it can also be argued that they have not done this by strengthening the institutions of power but rather by dominating those institutions and using them as a source of personal influence. As described by Sakwa (2010, p. 31) the Russian presidency remains the source of vitality within the political system, but its very pre-eminence paralyses all other institutions and creates a system where initiative from below is inhibited, with the result that all significant decisions need to be made at the top. Indeed Sakwa describes two parallel institutional networks operating within Russia's political system, with the formal order of the institutional framework being characterized as the constitutional state, but with the real power and influence being wielded by the administrative regime, characterized as "both a network of social relations, in which political and economic power are entwined in a shifting landscape of factional politics, and also an actor in the political process" (Sakwa, 2010, p. 42). As a result, although Putin's re-concentration of power in the hands of the state was designed to counter the "institutional nihilism" of the Yeltsin era, it has in fact produced a new form of nihilism, one in which "para-constitutional institutions" have continued to undermine the formal institutional system.

Kononenko and Moshes (2011) interpret this parallel institutional state in a rather more pejorative way, describing it as "a sort of symbiosis between informal groups and formal institutions of the state...in which elite groups foster their own special interests by infiltrating institutions". The elite groups then keep the institutions of state "afloat as a sort of institutional carcass that the networks need" but to which they are themselves unaccountable, effectively leaving the State "chronically weak". Tompson (2007) then suggests that this weak institutional environment prompts political leaders to choose alternative, sub-optimal, methods of exerting control, which in the case of the oil sector has been a reliance on direct control via the National Oil Company (Rosneft) rather than via contracts, regulation and taxation. However, Tompson suggests that "the creation of large state companies is likely to be associated with high levels of opacity, corruption and rent-seeking by insiders" and that they "are run for the benefit of insiders and their patrons in the state administration...and also tend to be financially opaque, which makes them attractive sources of funding for informal political or policy initiatives" (Tompson, 2007, pp. 6–9).

This parallel structure of formal, constitutional, institutions and less formal power structures behind the scenes and in state corporations has been described by Mommsen (2012) as "a system characterised by the opacity of the decision-making process and the interpenetration of the political and economic realms". The cross-over between the political and economic realms is exemplified by the fact that "no other country in the world has so many top government members who also serve on the boards of major corporations" (Inozemetsev, 2009), and Goldman (2010) has gone so far as to argue that: "Putin has instituted the practice of appointing his former colleagues not only to the most senior positions in government but also to senior and lucrative posts in the business world." As a result one can see glimpses of "the acquisition of great wealth by KGB veterans or what we have called the second generation of oligarchs" (Goldman, 2010, p. 195).

The result is that the Russian political and economic sphere arguably gives the impression of "a Putin family corporation...with a high degree of family and personal relations amongst the leaders of the top state departments and large corporations" (Mommsen, 2012, p. 78). Furthermore, "the expanding powers of the security services and the extent to which its former staff have been appointed to senior positions in a wide range of institutions...and are prominent in the world of business, in private and state-owned companies...creates a risk that they will become a state within a state" (Schneider, 2012). Again we can see the description of parallel states within Russia, incorporating both the political and commercial spheres, with Putin's authority then being built around his ability to act as an efficient referee with the "unofficial oligarchy" of vested interests beneath him, acting, as Mommsen describes him, as a "patronal president".

Given this depiction of the Russian environment as being made up of two parallel power structures that cross-over between the political and commercial worlds, one rather weak (the constitutional structure) and one rather strong, or even dominant (the administrative regime or the unofficial oligarchy), we would then argue that it is possible to re-cast our alternative version of Dunning's OLI paradigm for the Putin era. In a situation where a foreign partner forms a joint venture with a domestic partner that is not directly controlled by the state (for example Total's JV with Novatek at Yamal LNG described in Chapter 1) then the relationship as described in Figure 2.2 can still apply, with the domestic partner being a vital source of local knowledge of how to do business in the current commercial environment in Russia. However, in a scenario where a foreign partner has transacted directly with the state or with a state-owned institution, then the relationship can be re-cast to replace the domestic partner with one of the parallel institutional structures described above. In essence, the traditional relationship between the foreign partner and the constitutional state that one would expect in a strong state

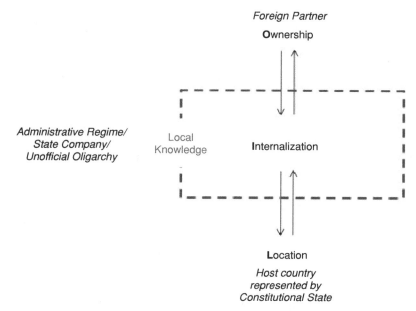

Figure 2.3 How local knowledge interrupts Dunning's OLI paradigm in a para-constitutionalism environment

environment is interrupted by the unofficial oligarchy of vested interests described by Sakwa, Mommsen and others as a parallel institutional structure in the interests of the political and commercial elite. It is the local knowledge of this new oligarchy that is now vital to a foreign partner if he wants to do business in Russia, and is best encapsulated by the decisions of Exxon, ENI and Statoil to partner with Rosneft in exploring Russia's continental shelf and its unconventional oil resources. The interests and local knowledge of this parallel institutional structure interrupt the ability of the foreign partner to internalize its ownership advantages through a traditional negotiation with the State to get access to the resources granted by the locational advantage which the latter possesses. Figure 2.3 describes this alternative description of the OLI model.

As a result, although the new political environment under President Putin appears to be remarkably different from the somewhat anarchic Yeltsin regime, we would argue that the difficulties and issues for foreign investors are very similar. A powerful group of vested interests has created a dominant position through its control of weak state institutions, and local knowledge of how to deal with this new oligarchy and the parallel institutional regime that it has created is likely to be vital to foreign investor success in Russia. Therefore, we would argue that conclusions drawn from the experiences of foreign actors throughout Russia's entire post-Soviet history remain relevant today, as the commercial environment has not changed that much. The decision-making processes remain opaque and non-transparent, the interests of vested interests remain of paramount importance, key individuals are more influential than the institutions which they represent and the blurring of political and commercial interests remains a core strategy for the Russian elite. As described by Shevstova (2001) this situation is not necessarily an indictment of Putin himself, but perhaps a reflection that on coming to power with the intention of restoring the power and strength of the Russian state he was soon forced to accept that "the only way he could secure a certain level of stability was by tolerating cosy (and corrupt) patron-client relations". Nevertheless, it would appear that local knowledge of how to deal with key "individuals within the fraternity [who] are ever changing, making it very difficult to identify the main players within this complex structure of interests" (Mommsen, 2012, p. 78) remains a vital competitive strength in Russia, and how to deal with it remains a vital issue for any foreign investor in the country.

Empirical research on the impact of local knowledge in a weak institutional environment such as Russia

In order to explore the validity of this theory about the importance of local knowledge and its relevance to foreign investors in weak state environments such as Russia we have employed a mixture of case studies and interviews with individuals who have had direct experience of the Russian business environment across the country's post-Soviet history and statistical econometric analysis based on a survey of foreign investors in the period 1990–2003. We start, in the following chapter, with a description and analysis of a number of case studies of joint ventures that stretch across the 1990s and early 2000s in order to provide what Swann (2006) describes as "a unique way of starting a research exploration into the unknown". While it is clearly important to acknowledge, as Swann does, the common criticisms of case study analysis, namely that the data collection is unsystematic and ill-defined, the possibility of investigator bias and the difficulty of generalization from a small sample, we nevertheless see value in using the studies as the foundation for initial conclusions to be drawn and then tested in more specific analysis. As Swann summarizes "the greatest strength of the case study is its ability to bring together a splendid miscellany of interesting fragments in a highly ad hoc way"[186] in order that conclusions can be drawn from as broad a spectrum of evidence as possible.

We have adopted the interview procedures advocated by Silverman (2001)[187] and Douglas (1985)[188] which see the interaction between interviewer and interviewee as an active and interactive process. Rather than have a formally structured interview with a number of standardized questions and a strict script, we adopted the approach that each interview was a social interaction where we initially attempted to encourage the interviewee to reveal their experiences within their joint entity before initiating a more interactive discussion on the conclusions that might be reached from their history. As such the interviews became a "creative search for mutual understanding",[189] with interviewee responses being challenged and conclusions established within an improvised conversation. As a result the interviews allowed us to use the case studies not just for exploratory purposes but also in an explanatory role to produce some grounded theory that could be further tested in our quantitative analysis.

As suggested by Foddy (1993)[190] we then used the initial research and preliminary conclusions established through the case studies to help define the topics for a survey analysing the drivers of foreign partner performance in joint entities in the Russian oil and gas industry that is then analysed statistically, with the results presented in Chapter 4. We designed a questionnaire that comprised a combination of 16 open and closed questions (see Appendix for full details), which was then tested on various individuals with relevant industry and country experience to ensure that the questions were comprehensible and interpreted in a similar fashion. The survey was then carried out largely through individual contacts with identified respondents, with the questionnaire being transmitted by post or electronically and being followed up by a telephone call or visit to answer any questions and if necessary to be present while the responses were filled in.

The standard criticisms of questionnaires and surveys must undoubtedly be acknowledged before analysing the results of our research. In the closed questions we asked respondents to rank various issues on a scale of 1 to 5, thus forcing them to quantify issues numerically on an artificial scale. Their responses could certainly have been coloured by their interaction with the authors or by their attitudes to our research, and given the historical nature of the events being examined their views on answering may not have fully represented their experiences when they occurred. Further, the respondents were forced to answer a number of closed questions that restricted their freedom of answer, and although we tried to address this problem by including open questions where free interpretation could be given, the analysis of the closed questions could still be regarded as an over-simplification of complex issues. All of these potential criticisms are outlined by Swann (2006),[191] but he also provides the encouraging observation that researchers using econometrics "should not overstate or understate the accuracy of measurement", because although the criticisms of this form of analysis carry some weight it is nevertheless the case that "questionnaires can discriminate between respondents and...are not just straitjackets".

Swann's main conclusion, though, and the one on which we have based the diversity of our research methodology, is that we can reasonably expect the strengths of one technique to compensate for the weaknesses of another. Of particular relevance to this thesis he states "Where econometrics is strong, case studies are weak as they can lack rigour, they are often non-quantitative, they are descriptive rather than analytic and a handful of case studies only adds up to a rather small sample. On the other hand, where econometrics is weak, case studies are strong. The Case study can reveal the workings of a specific part of the economy in some depth, is inclusive rather than selective, the structure is revealed rather than assumed and structural change can be identified – and most of all, the case study is an integrative technique, capable of adaptation to data in all shapes and sizes."[192] As such, the complementary nature of the methodologies used in the following chapters provides a robust foundation from which conclusions can then be derived.

To supplement our analysis further we then conducted a series of interviews with current participants in the Russian oil and gas sector, to test whether theories generated from historic examples would still be robust in the current business environment in Russia. The results of these interviews, which were largely conducted anonymously given the confidential nature of the views expressed, are presented in Chapter 5. Chapter 6 then presents an individual interview with one of the authors, Alastair Ferguson, who draws on his lengthy experience in Russia as both a participant in the largest foreign joint venture in the post-Soviet era (TNK-BP) as well as his more recent experience as an advisor to and participant in smaller ventures in Russia to provide an overarching conclusion on the issues facing foreign investors in Russia today.

3
Joint Ventures from the 1990s

Introduction

The history of foreign partnership in the Russian oil and gas industry during the post-Soviet era has been a chequered one, as discussed in Chapter 1. Some theoretical reasons for this outcome, including in particular the implicit bargaining between the local knowledge of domestic partners and the operational and management skills of foreigners, have been discussed in Chapter 2. However, it is now time to look at some practical examples of joint ventures in action, and to hear about the experiences of the key foreign actors who took part in them. This chapter includes three case studies of partnerships that were formed in the 1990s and operated largely in the Yeltsin era, although their activities did also spill over into the Putin era post-2000.

In a later chapter we will discuss in more detail the views of foreign players who have been active in Russia during the 2000s, but for now we plan to draw some conclusions from an era which, as argued in Chapter 2, provided a clear example of a weak state environment but also offered a business environment that is not so very different from that faced by foreigners in Russia today. All the case studies are presented on an anonymous basis for two reasons. Firstly, to protect the identity of participants and secondly because the intention is not to draw any pejorative conclusions about the Russian or international companies involved, but rather to draw relevant lessons from their respective actions and reactions during the life of the joint ventures being considered.

The first case concerns a joint venture between a small North American independent oil company and the subsidiary of a vertically integrated Russian oil company. After being formed as a 50:50 JV just after the end of the Soviet Union it operated in West Siberia, but initial operational success descended into legal dispute over non-payment of costs, legal disputes in regional courts, armed intimidation as the JVs offices were taken over by the domestic partner and finally legal proceedings in an international court. The final outcome was that the foreign partner was forced to accept a much diluted stake in the joint entity, succumbing to the pressure exerted by his domestic partner's weight of local knowledge and influence in a business environment without strict rules.

Case study two relates to a similar JV, again between a North American oil company and the subsidiary of a major Russian oil company. It was formed later in the 1990s and focused on the re-development of a mature field in West Siberia, and again was an operational success much lauded by the domestic partner as a model for field rehabilitation in Russia. However, a change in ownership at the Russian oil company left its foreign partner exposed, having previously relied entirely on its domestic partner for local knowledge and influence. When the new owners of the Russian oil company decided to use their local know-how to gain a better deal at the JV, the North American partner was faced with an unequal battle in the bankruptcy courts, and after numerous legal proceedings finally agreed to sell its interest to its Russian partner for less than half the value of its overall investment in the joint entity.

The third case study then focuses on a joint entity formed via the merger of a Russian company and US-based vehicle, in which both parties contributed all their Russian assets to the new company, and made significant efforts to ensure that the split of equity between all the parties reflected their contributions to the business. In addition, the foreign partners were very focused on "Russifying" the company as soon as possible and also on having a short-term goal of an IPO (Initial Public Offering) on the London Stock Exchange in order to provide a visible exit route and financial target for all the shareholders. The result was that all the shareholders were committed to the success of the joint entity and devoted their skill-sets to achieving it, resulting in the ultimate sale of the company to a US integrated oil company for a significant profit.

The chapter then concludes by using an interview with another anonymous foreign partner with experience of all of the features of the joint entities mentioned above to provide an overview of the conclusions that can be reached from the stories of foreign partner success or failure in Russia from the 1990s and early 2000s.

Case study one

This first case study concerns a joint venture which was formed in the early 1990s between a small North American oil company (we shall call it Texas Oil) and a Russian state-owned production association (named by us Moscow Oil). The joint venture was based on a relatively small but nevertheless significant field in the Tyumen region of West Siberia. The field had been discovered in 1969, but was left undeveloped by the Soviet authorities due to its size (particularly in comparison to its neighbours, which included the giant multi-billion-barrel Samotlor field) and the complexity of its hydrocarbon reservoir, which made oil recovery difficult and expensive. However, by 1983 production declines in West Siberia forced the local production association to turn its attention to the field, and production steadily increased over the next four years. A shortage of funds for investment and a lack of adequate technology then saw the field go into a sharp decline and by 1991 the field had become uneconomic to produce, with the result that Moscow Oil began the search for an international partner who could provide funds and expertise to turn the field's performance around.

The international company (Texas Oil) that it found was one of a number of North American oil service and exploration companies that were investigating opportunities in the former Soviet Union at that time with its primary expertise being the provision, application and management of advanced technology to enhance oil and gas well productivity, using techniques such as hydraulic fracturing and acidizing to increase hydrocarbon flows. Texas Oil could also provide financing, backed by a guarantee from its home government, and so was an ideal partner for Moscow Oil as it sought to improve the performance of one of its key assets. The joint venture (JV1) was therefore created, with the interests being split 60% to Texas Oil and 40% to Moscow Oil, and with both parties committed to providing just under $6 million of charter capital to the venture.

Initially JV1 proceeded well, with Texas Oil building a new production site at the field base 90 kilometers north of Nizhnevartovsk, flying in four plane-loads of equipment from North America in 1992 and bringing a further 174 railroad cars of facilities from Europe in 1993 in what was claimed to be the largest single shipment to Russian since the Second World War. The improvement in output from the field was almost immediate, with production increasing from just over 6,000 barrels per day (bpd) in 1992 to almost 10,000 bpd by 1996, as Texas Oil's technology increased the recovery factor for the field while its financing paid for the equipment needed to exploit this improvement. In addition Texas Oil brought in around 25 expats to supplement the 110 field workers from Moscow Oil in order to manage the correct application of the technology and to pass on their skills to their Russian colleagues.

The first changes in JV1 came as a result of the hostile takeover of Texas Oil by one of its competitors in 1995. As part of the transaction a new company was created, Houston Oil, which would take on Texas Oil's 60% interest in the JV, leaving it as Moscow Oil's partner at the joint venture, with Houston Oil's main shareholder as its CEO.

Of greater concern, however, was Moscow Oil's inability to fund its ongoing expenses at the JV. Over the period 1993 to 1995 Texas Oil had to lend Moscow Oil 300,000 tonnes of crude oil (worth approximately $50 million) in order to allow it to raise funds for continuing development work both at the joint venture and at its other fields. This oil was to be paid back over time out of the joint venture's production, but in 1995 Moscow Oil refused to make any more repayments while 170,000 tonnes was still outstanding. This led to a legal dispute which Houston Oil (the new international partner) won, but repayment of the oil remained outstanding for another three years. By 1999 Houston Oil was resolved to take more proactive steps and decided to dilute Moscow Oil's interest in the JV by the amount of its outstanding debt, which at the time totaled $7.2 million. This led to Moscow Oil's interest being reduced from 40% to 2.4% and Houston Oil's interest increasing from 60% to 97.6%.

At approximately the same time Moscow Oil, and its parent company, Moscow Neft, came under threat from another direction, in the form of a major vertically integrated Russian oil company (we shall call it Kompaniye). During 1998 Kompaniye started to use Russia's new bankruptcy law to acquire assets in the oil and gas sector, and after the financial crisis of August 1998 Moscow Neft's subsidiaries became its primary targets. In essence, the new Bankruptcy Law allowed unpaid creditors to bankrupt a debtor on the basis of very small debts and then petition the courts for the appointment of an external administrator who would either ensure the debt was repaid, or more often sell off the assets of the company.[1] In this bankruptcy sale it was very often the creditors who had initiated the bankruptcy who bought the assets at relatively low prices, having encouraged the administrator to hold the sale rather than try and recover the company under his control. This was exactly what happened at Moscow Oil, which had an outstanding debt to Kompaniye that it either could not, or perhaps was encouraged not, to repay. Kompaniye then initiated bankruptcy proceedings and as one of the largest creditors had significant influence over the creditors' committee. It managed to persuade the external administrator to hold a sale of Moscow Oil's assets where it was the only bidder and thus took over the company.

By January 2000 Kompaniye had therefore become Houston Oil's partner at JV1, albeit with only a 2.4% stake, as well as the owner of Moscow Oil, the company which still owed the JV 170,000 tonnes of oil. Houston Oil petitioned Kompaniye for the return of this oil to JV1 but was refused, and indeed in order to put pressure on Houston Oil to withdraw its claim Kompaniye is alleged to have used its influence at the Ministry of Natural Resources to initiate a full inspection of JV1's licenses and its compliance with the terms of them. At the same time Kompaniye is also alleged to have chosen to expose JV1's complete reliance on the oil transfer and treatment facilities at another of its (Kompaniye's) recently acquired companies, and by refusing to process JV1's crude effectively prevented it from accessing the Transneft pipeline system that transports all Russia's crude oil to both domestic and export markets. As a result JV1 was no longer able to sell any of its output.

Kompaniye then began the process of trying to gain control of JV1 entirely. Firstly, in 2001 it initiated court proceedings in a West Siberian regional court alleging that the reduction in Moscow Oil's stake in the JV was illegal. In a separate case it also alleged that Texas Oil's initial contribution to the charter capital of the JV was also invalid, claiming that "the know-how Houston Oil brought to the venture could have been found in any text book and was worth considerably less than the amount recorded on customs declarations". As a result of these cases the courts invalidated around 80% of Houston Oil's shareholding in JV1.

Despite the dilution of its shareholding, Houston Oil still owned the majority of officially recognized shares in JV1, and in June 2001 decided to call a shareholders' meeting to confirm its control over the joint venture. At the meeting, which was attended by Kompaniye observers but not by representatives of the actual shareholder Moscow Oil, Houston Oil proposed that the existing General Director of JV1 be re-appointed with immediate effect. The proposal was carried unanimously (as only the Houston Oil shares were available to vote) and the CEO returned to his post at the JV's headquarters. However, unbeknown to him or to Houston Oil, Kompaniye had held an alternative extraordinary shareholders' meeting at which they had used their 2.4% stake to unanimously approve the appointment of an alternative General Director.

Both sides (Kompaniye and Houston Oil) claimed that their meetings were legal and that they had been illegally kept in the dark about the alternative meeting, and both later managed to get court rulings in their favour. It is difficult to judge who was in the right, although most press reports backed Houston Oil's right to appoint the General Director as it was still the majority shareholder even after the dilution of its stake, and so it would appear that it was Kompaniye that was using dubious tactics and exploiting its influence in the West Siberian region. However, any uncertainty about the legal rights of the parties was overwhelmed the next day, when Kompaniye allegedly took control of the JV by force. In the words of the Houston Oil CEO: "Eight guys with machine guns came into the office. Four jeeps came with another fifteen with machine guns and took the perimeter." Despite attempts by JV1 employees to assert their rights at the company, Kompaniye's influence over the regional authorities appeared to carry more weight than any court ruling. JV1's General Director claimed that he got no operational support from the Khanty-Mansiisk prosecutor's office during the takeover, even though they sent her a letter affirming that Kompaniye's actions and the shareholders' meeting were "illegal". Not surprisingly Kompaniye denied all of Houston Oil's claims, stating that "contrary to media reports, Kompaniye has not used force to take over JV1, no workers are being prevented from doing their jobs and normal oil production is continuing", but comments such as those from one observer close to the issue that "it looks like something illegal has been done" suggest that, at the very least, Kompaniye was exploiting legal loopholes with aggressive commercial tactics. In addition, Houston Oil employees reported harassment at the JV's operational sites, with the workers' camp being reported to be "under siege since security guards...arrived unannounced on June 28 and took over the property at gunpoint". Indeed, one expat employee was quoted as saying, "There is no direct threat to us in our camp, but our work is hindered whenever we try to go out and do our work... Kompaniye has no oil people here, but its private security people are checking our documents. It's like a stalling tactic."

Following the physical takeover of JV1 by Kompaniye staff and the installation of their representative as General Director, the Head of the Local Administration was then allegedly "persuaded" by Kompaniye to issue a duplicate corporate seal of JV1 to him. This allowed the new General Director to access the joint venture's accounts and to take control of the company's oil sales, which he did in July 2001. According to Houston Oil $8 million was immediately transferred from the company's account at a local Russian Bank and transferred to an alternative institution, one of Kompaniye's major shareholders. As Houston Oil's CEO described the situation: "They now have all the documents. They're taking money out of our accounts. They put in a new financial director."

However, not only did Kompaniye manage to take physical control of the JV, but they also persuaded the regional courts to hand over voting control as well. The Khanty-Mansiisk Autonomous District Arbitration Court finally ruled that the initial contributions by Houston Oil and Moscow Oil entitled them to 20% and 80% shares in JV1 respectively, and with Kompaniye then winning more than 20 court cases and appeals in the local and regional courts they effectively claimed victory over Houston Oil. As one Kompaniye vice president summarized: "We have all the necessary documents to prove our work."

At the end of 2001 all the expatriates from Houston Oil decided to leave Russia and return to continue their fight against Kompaniye from North America. As one of them described the situation: "Given the level of personal intimidation I've had from the police and even judges, I don't feel safe in Russia." In February 2002 Houston Oil launched a multi-billion dollar law-suit against Kompaniye in the US courts, and the legal wrangle continued for a further four years until the issue was finally resolved because the US legislature decided that it did not have jurisdiction over the case. In essence it decided that the legal decision must be made in Russia, effectively forcing Houston Oil to temporarily give up its suit. However, in 2011 Houston Oil initiated another claim for $1 billion of damages caused by the loss of its controlling interest in JV1, but in 2012 the New York State Supreme Court dismissed the claim saying that it was "clearly untimely" and should be barred under the statute of limitations. Houston Oil has reserved the right to appeal this decision, but as of 2013 Kompaniye continues to own 80% of JV1 with Houston Oil owning the remaining 20%.

It is clear from this historical account that Houston Oil encountered a number of key issues in its partner relations over JV1, with the main one being that its original partner was taken over by Kompaniye, a Russian organization described by at least one reputable source as a company "with a reputation for aggressive innovation". Given the lack of a strong institutional environment in Russia at the time it is perhaps no surprise that Houston Oil suffered in the way it did, and as such, it is clear that one element in its downfall as a shareholder at the JV was the misfortune of an unanticipated change in its domestic partner. However, it is nevertheless instructive to consider how Houston Oil behaved with its original partner Moscow Oil, and also to consider its attempts to protect itself when it eventually came under attack from Kompaniye.

The CEO of Houston Oil has in the past discussed his business in Russia, and in many of his comments has been effusive about the initial success of the JV1, especially during the early partnership with Moscow Oil. "We started operating in 1992 [and soon]...we managed to turn this oil field around... We produced more oil per worker than any other company...in other words we were the most efficient oil company in Russia... We were indicted into Russia's business recognition programme...that was a great recognition and a great testimony to western know-how and our perseverance." In terms of partner relations, though, Houston Oil clearly relied on the Moscow Oil management for its links to the local and regional administrations, in particular because the company was initially state-owned. As a result, it appears that Houston Oil saw little need to develop its own local network of contacts, preferring to rely on its original bargaining strengths of technological and operational expertise. As the CEO was keen to emphasize "we are the most efficient oil company in Russia". In terms of influential contacts the focus of Houston Oil and its chief executive was mainly on the international business and political communities throughout its time in Russia, with the CEO continuing to emphasize the need for his domestic government "to provide protection" by empowering their embassy staff to "fight tooth and nail for every dollar and to...play the role of enforcer" in relations with the Russian authorities. The emphasis was therefore clearly on using inter-governmental politics and international relationships as a key bargaining strength, but as Houston Oil was to discover these high-level connections carry little weight in an environment described even by some Russian officials as a "shadow economy and a...shadow justice system". It is probably fair to say the Houston Oil, as a North American company, had little choice in its use of tactics, and the point here is not to criticize its management's decision but rather to highlight the problems that occurred as a result, and the way in which the local knowledge of a powerful domestic actor could undermine the theoretical rule of law in a weak state environment such as Russia.

The difficulty with using a focus on international engagement and rules of business in an environment such as Russia was first exposed when Houston Oil decided to dilute Moscow Oil's stake in JV1 when the Russian company failed to pay its oil debts. Although international auditors actually recommended the change in the charter capital and structured the process, with the result that it was all done legally, the move could of course have been interpreted as aggressive and obviously left Houston Oil as the almost 100% owner of the JV. Once Moscow Oil's stake was down to 2.4% the incentive for them to help their foreign partner in any local issues was greatly diminished, and despite Houston Oil's frustration concerning their partner's refusal to pay off the debt they could perhaps have reacted in a less commercially aggressive fashion, and possibly would have done so had they understood what the consequences might be. With hindsight their lack of local knowledge and influence was exposed, as although the use of international business rules was perfectly legitimate and logical, the debate it initiated later came back to haunt them. According to legal representations made at the time, it was suggested that Kompaniye ultimately decided that dilution of the Houston Oil stake was a good way to respond, specifically using the alleged tactics of "corrupting Russian court proceedings and government officials in an attempt to decrease Houston Oil's ownership interest in and voting rights over JV1, forging documents, and ultimately sending armed private militiamen carrying AK-47 machine guns to storm JV1's corporate offices and oil field in June 2001".

Indeed, the emergence of Kompaniye as the owner of Moscow Oil in 1998/99 completely exposed Houston Oil's lack of local, regional or national influence. As Houston Oil's CEO described in later statements, "The chairman of the board of Kompaniye at that time became a governor in a [West Siberian] region. In the Russian system all the judges in [West Siberia] regions are appointed by the governor. That means that the courts are absolutely 'independent'...their judgements do not depend on any facts...it makes no difference what you tell them." The clear implication of the CEO's statement is that the independence of the courts means an independence from the facts of the case, thus allowing influential domestic companies to gain favourable results. He later went on to describe further the use of the bankruptcy law: "the [domestic] company goes to a friendly court in their region and, in one day, the court rules that you are bankrupt and insolvent".

He has also offered a number of other statements citing examples of tactics used in this kind of legally nihilistic environment. One somewhat melodramatic, and perhaps apocryphal, quote suggested that "they [domestic company representatives] would intimidate the people by calling late at night and saying 'You have a very nice daughter. I see you taking her every evening to the ballet classes. You must be very proud of your family.' The next day they would say 'Your daughter is taking swimming lessons. Oh, that is nice... You must be proud of your family. They are very nice. I saw your wife with your daughter yesterday. They are a really nice family.' When the guy comes and wants to buy, who would not sell to such nice people who are so happy about your family?" On using their political influence, the CEO also commented on Kompaniye's links with the Ministry of Natural Resources – "During this time they tried to put all kinds of pressure on us. The vice-chairman of the company went to the paper and said 'They will not smarten up, so then we will look into the validity of their license'. Sure enough, in three days the Minister of Natural Resources sent us a commission. [We made a fuss] and told him that I am not afraid to speak up...and they backed off, but [the issue] is still kind of in suspense."

Finally, Kompaniye allegedly used their economic power to prevent JV1's crude oil being sold – "Another matter concerned our pipeline. We bought a piece of property and built the infrastructure during the old Soviet regime. We produced oil mixed with water and gas and we do the treatment to bring the oil up to around 96% of oil and 4% water. Then we pump it to a central facility, also used by other companies. It is all mixed together. Moscow Oil would do further cleaning and pump it through. That way I am involved in a pipeline and have access to the market. [But then] they told us [that] we had a bad metering system. But we had the most sophisticated metering system available. We had the first micro-motion metering system, which was brought from North America right at the start. They said 'No, we will not give you oil.' Then for six months they basically were stealing all our oil."

In the face of these attacks the CEO realized that his lack of local knowledge and influence meant that he needed to turn to international sources for help. With even local domestic actors admitting that "Russia is still not run under the rule of law and that in such a climate it is necessary to play rough from time to time since to ignore the realities of the Russian business world is to invite disaster" there was a clear need for wider support for his company. Indeed, amid claims that Kompaniye allegedly had "its own people at all levels of government" and that it "controlled Russia's supreme Arbitration court" and could "run over JV1 like a steamroller", further pressure was placed on Houston Oil's CEO to seek outside help. As a result he turned to his domestic embassy and ultimately to his country's political leader who was leading a trade mission to Moscow in 2001.

Firstly an ambassador in Moscow from Houston Oil's home country sent letters of complaint to Russian Deputy Prime Minister Viktor Khristenko, and this was followed up with a similar letter from a Minister for International Trade, who co-chaired a bilateral International Economic Commission with Mr. Khristenko. However, as neither letter elicited a positive response the CEO turned directly to his domestic politicians and focused on their forthcoming meeting with the Russian President Vladimir Putin. As the CEO described "I [wanted] my political leaders to tell Mr. Putin that we're looking for their legal system to work", and indeed he initially received a positive response. International officials publicly described the JV1 takeover by Kompaniye as "a major negative signal" to foreign investors and a political spokesman was quoted as saying: "We're obviously following this issue very closely. We're hoping for some kind of resolution and hoping to see that some basic standards of corporate governance are observed."

However, when it finally came to the meeting with Putin, it appears that Houston Oil was too small an issue to trouble the respective country's leaders and the international politicians refused to intervene on the company's behalf. Speaking to reporters after the meeting one said "What can I do? I've raised the question with the authorities. We have to be realistic. We're not going to declare a war if they don't do what this gentleman wants."

Ultimately, Houston Oil was forced to fight its own battle and returned to the local courts, but in the end was forced to accept the dilution of its stake in JV1 down to 20%, albeit that it has continued to pursue its partners through the US legal system. In conclusion, one commentator summarized Houston Oil's plight in 2001: "The CEO of Houston Oil is not the only North American businessman battling his way through Russia's capricious court system in an attempt to hang onto Russian assets. In a country where new laws regulating foreign corporations are written almost daily, and where local laws often conflict with federal legislation, a disturbing trend has emerged: after the North American firms spend millions of dollars getting the projects off the ground, their Russian partners exploit legal technicalities in court to break the contracts and take control." In other words, the domestic partner used his local knowledge to disenfranchise his foreign partner when he had the bargaining power to do so.

Case study two

The Joint Venture under consideration in our second case study (Ventura) was formed as a 50:50 joint venture between a Russian oil company (Nefteyanik) and another North American independent oil company (Independent Oil) in 1996. Ventura was founded with a small amount of charter capital, with the partners then contributing $50 million of assets and cash each to bring the total value of the JV to just over $100 million. Independent Oil's contribution was made up of exploration and field development equipment plus cash while Nefteyanik brought oil wells and production facilities as well as the licenses to one oil field and one exploration block (both located in West Siberia). Importantly, Nefteyanik and Independent Oil registered the new joint venture with the Russian Ministry of Economy, and under the agreement Nefteyanik guaranteed that it would transfer the two licenses for the blocks to the JV in conformance with Ministry of Natural Resources rules on license transfer to a new venture.[2]

The foreign partner, Independent Oil, had been formed in early 1996 by a wealthy North American businessmen and his partner, a former senior executive at an oilfield service company. This latter company had been involved in a number of service joint ventures in the CIS since the late 1980s, whereby oilfield service companies had provided new technology to improve field performance for Russian oil companies in return for a share in any production increases. Indeed Ventura was formed using many of the team from this service company because they were keen to become involved in a production, rather than just an oil service, JV. As the CFO of Ventura stated when the joint venture was formed, "Compared with service ventures, producing companies encounter fewer problems in Russia…[and] being registered as a production JV…has many more benefits." The main benefits were eligibility to hold mineral licenses and a consequent right to export crude oil, although as Independent was to discover to their cost these benefits only accrued to those foreign investors who could assert their rights.

The Russian partner, Nefteyanik, was a subsidiary of a major Russian oil company (Bolshoi Oil), having become a joint stock company during the privatization process of the early 1990s. The company's general director fully understood the need to bring in foreign partners in order to boost immediate performance and to learn how to produce oil profitably in a tough geographic and fiscal environment. "We welcome the willingness of the Americans to apply their experience and technology to the project", he stated in 1997. "[Our oil field] is our testing ground for modern operations based on project economics."[3] At the time Bolshoi Oil was still largely state-owned, as the holding company's privatization had not been completed, and so although Nefteyanik was 51% owned by Bolshoi Oil it was in effect still a state-controlled entity. As a result it was still largely being run by the oilmen who had been in charge since the Soviet era, many of whom were now beginning to realize that they would need foreign partners to provide capital and expertise if their companies were to survive in an environment of lower oil prices and high taxes. As such they were generally pleased to welcome a company like Independent who had undertaken to bring investment funds and technology and had also agreed that if the technology being used on the wells didn't work and the project was discontinued, it would assume full financial liability.

The joint venture commenced operations on January 1ˢᵗ 1997, although the licenses were not officially transferred until the end of March. The application of new technology and working practices by Independent Oil saw an immediate improvement in the venture's production efficiency and overall output, with average well productivity increasing from the West Siberian average of only 70 barrels per day to 210 barrels between January 1997 and August 1998. During the same period 18 new wells were drilled, 45 workovers were completed (on a total well count of 48) and 14 hydro-fractures were carried out to enhance well productivity. As a result total production from Ventura increased from just under 4,000 barrels per day (bpd) at the start of 1997 to 11,500 bpd by August 1998, and the JV's total revenues climbed by 23% between first half (H1) 1997 and H1 1998 despite an 18% fall in the average price of oil from $12.17 per barrel to $10.02. Indeed commentators at the time praised the JV's successful performance, noting the doubling of production at the main oil field and the beneficial impact from the introduction of international technology.

Despite this operational success, Ventura's western partners were about to find themselves exposed to the risks of the fluctuating Russian political and business environment. Firstly, a new shareholder purchased a controlling interest in Bolshoi Oil in one of the last privatization auctions. Having purchased its stake, the new shareholder began an extensive review of its operations and resolved to take full control of the best performing assets in its portfolio, of which Ventura was clearly one. It argued that the terms of the deal struck between Independent Oil and Nefteyanik were too favourable to the western investors because, amongst other things, it had not taken into account a significant amount of investment by Nefteyanik between 1995 and 1997.

Bolshoi Oil then made an offer to Independent Oil that would see it (Bolshoi Oil) increase its stake in Ventura to 51% in return for repayment of Independent Oil's past costs, thereby giving it control over the marketing of all Ventura production (for both the domestic and more lucrative export markets). In order to put pressure on Independent Oil to concede to its demands, Bolshoi Oil also initiated legal proceedings in which it argued that the transfer of the licenses from Nefteyanik to Ventura was illegal, because federal law only permitted license transfer when a company was being reorganized.[4] Although the issue of license transfer and ownership was clouded by a clear conflict between laws (the Law on Subsoil and the Ministry of Natural Resources rules on license transfer),[5] Bolshoi Oil used its greater understanding of the uncertain legal situation to gain injunctions against Ventura to prevent it producing or transporting any crude oil without its approval. Furthermore, an arbitration court in West Siberia then annulled the license transfer from Nefteyanik to Ventura, meaning that the JV lost control of the licenses, which were re-registered to Bolshoi Oil by the end of 1998. Despite this annulment, Ventura continued to operate the oil field but was forced to sell the oil directly to Bolshoi Oil under a sale and purchase agreement that effectively allowed Bolshoi Oil to pay an artificially low price at the field before selling the oil on the open market at a huge profit. As a result, despite the fact that Independent Oil won the backing of the Ministry of Energy and the Ministry of Natural Resources for its claim that the license transfer had been approved, and also asserted that Bolshoi Oil should have warned it of the risks when it made its original guarantee to contribute the license to the JV, continuing production at Ventura became unsustainable from both an economic and a political perspective. As the situation was described by an unidentified North American official at the time "it appears...the Russian partners are using the pretext of small administrative details...to carry out expropriation without compensation", although one could equally argue that Independent Oil had exposed itself to its losses through a lack of local knowledge of the legal uncertainty surrounding its license claim.

With numerous legal cases being brought in federal, regional and local courts the dispute between Independent Oil and Bolshoi Oil dragged on into 2000, when Independent Oil's original backer took over the case and decided to refer it to the court of arbitration in Stockholm. By that stage Independent Oil had invested almost $100 million into Ventura, which it sought to claim back from Bolshoi Oil. However, Bolshoi Oil had in the meantime used the increasingly common tactic of launching bankruptcy proceedings against Ventura and putting it into administration. As described earlier, Russia's bankruptcy law meant that any creditor with even a small outstanding debt could force a company into bankruptcy (and could even refuse to receive its outstanding monies owed), have a receiver appointed and then insist that the bankrupt company's assets be sold off.[6] This process was initiated by Bolshoi Oil in late 1999, and by mid-2000 Independent Oil had succumbed to the pressure and agreed to sell its stake in Ventura to Bolshoi Oil for less than $30 million, effectively around half its total original investment in the joint venture. As one commentator concluded: "The joint venture was a bad investment for Independent Oil... Operationally it was very successful, but Independent Oil did not only not earn any return on its investment but [was] expropriated from its initial investment due to political problems."

When analysing the partnership structure at Ventura and its consequences for the foreign partner, it is perhaps important to note first that the senior management of Independent Oil had already gained significant experience of operating joint ventures in Russia. The CEO and many of his team had worked on the numerous JVs set up by international oil service companies in the early 1990s and clearly felt that they had a good understanding of how to make JVs with Russian partners work. As the CEO himself stated in the late

1990s: "It's no secret that the business climate is harsh here, especially where taxes are concerned, but it is still possible to work successfully as a JV."

However, it is also clear that in applying their previous experience from the oil service JVs they failed to appreciate the fundamental difference between that experience and the situation facing Ventura, namely that Ventura would own Russian hydrocarbon resources while all the service company JVs had seen the foreign partner acting as a contractor only. This difference was very important in the Russian oil business environment of the 1990s because only license holders had the right to market their crude domestically or for exports, accessing the huge margins that could potentially be made. In contrast any international service company, acting as a contractor, had shared in the upside in production it had brought to various oilfields on a fixed margin basis, meaning that the Russian partner had control of all crude oil marketing and the upside that implied. At Ventura, the ex-oil service team was in a subtly different situation – its role was still to improve field performance, but the benefits to be won could potentially have been much greater thanks to its greater exposure to oil sales. Of course, this was why the CEO and his team decided to break away from their previous oil service employer and develop a new JV strategy in the first place, but it also meant that their previous experience was less relevant than they perhaps perceived, with the result that they underestimated how much more local knowledge they would need in a JV involved in much larger cashflow generating opportunities.

Independent Oil's strategy with regards to forming Ventura was bold for its time, as the company decided to ignore potential Production Sharing status and opt for a classic JV under the existing licensing and taxation rules. At that time many foreign companies were holding out for the introduction of a Production Sharing Agreement (PSA) law that would effectively have ring-fenced oilfields that had been granted PSA status with their own fiscal and legal rules enshrined in an individual contract. As discussed in Chapter 1, many Russian players saw the PSA law as a huge threat to their bargaining power with foreign investors and did their best to prevent its passage (ultimately successfully). At the time of the formation of Ventura, though, foreign investors still had some hope of a PSA law being passed, as the debate on it was continuing.

Following its previous success in oil service JVs, the Independent Oil management team took the view that waiting for a PSA law was a waste of time. As the CEO explained, "the development of large deposits on PSA terms is only a dream in Russia today", but he continued to believe that profitable business could still be carried out. Indeed another executive, interviewed at the same time and also preferring to remain anonymous, emphasized his view that a JV philosophy could work in Russia: "Russia is quite an acceptable place for JV's to work... The key to success, in our opinion, is to be extremely cautious in selecting projects and to keep a tight rein on the project's economics. While there are certainly risks, profitable projects are still possible on this basis."

Despite this confidence, it is clear that the JV strategy chosen by the CEO of Independent Oil and his key executives was based on the oil service JV model, with specific roles for the foreign and domestic partner. The foreign partner's role was to improve field performance and control the economics of the project, while the domestic partner was responsible for ensuring that the local business environment was managed in order to allow the foreign partner to get on with his work unhindered by bureaucracy. This view is reflected in further comments from the CEO and representatives of his original domestic partner Nefteyanik.

Firstly, the CEO's view: "As [the Russian partners] chose us, so we chose them with similar care. Without the help of our Russian partners and their knowledge of the local system we would have had to waste our time solving bureaucratic problems of secondary importance instead of doing our job." It was clear that the bureaucratic problems would be large from the attitude of some of the local officials at the time. A typical quote came from the regional Head of the Foreign Economic Relations Department who stated: "Of course, the profit for western companies is obvious. They get our oil, which we badly need ourselves, but it's still unclear whether this JV will bring any benefits to our region. Our experience with most JVs...is that they fail to yield anything tangible to us."

Consequently Independent Oil's Russian partner at Ventura did have a significant role to play. As a representative of Nefteyanik explained later, "we made an unimaginable effort to persuade local bureaucrats that the JV should be formed – the wells [were] shut in and yielding nothing, but the officials kept saying that 'the oil will escape abroad'. We had to be extremely persistent and persuasive in order to get their formal blessing to set up the JV." Thus it is clear that Independent Oil's Russian partner was solely responsible for managing the local business environment using its influence and local knowledge, while Independent Oil continued in its traditional role of oilfield operator and technical expert without making any effort to become involved in local business relations. As one Independent Oil executive summarized the situation: "Foreign investors can work virtually anywhere in Russia where you can find oil and a Russian partner on whom they can rely."

However, this reliance on Nefteyanik for all its local business knowledge left Independent Oil unfortunately disadvantaged when the partner environment changed. Unforeseen circumstance undeniably played a role in the company's downfall, as one of the bolder companies in the Russian oil industry became its partner when Bolshoi Oil took control of Nefteyanik. Nevertheless, it does seem that Independent Oil's management was not prepared for the change in partner philosophy and did not anticipate the impact of its claim on the ownership of Russian assets as opposed to the contractor-style relationships it had been involved with during the earlier oil service company operations.

From the start Bolshoi Oil made it clear that control of Ventura asset base was its primary goal in order to improve its performance and ultimately impress international investors to whom it planned to ultimately sell itself. As one unnamed Bolshoi Oil official was quoted at the time "securing control over the company's efficiently operating Ventura JV will improve Bolshoi Oil's financial position by consolidating its oil and gas resources and adding them to its own balance sheet". Initially Bolshoi Oil's tactics involved trying to persuade Independent Oil to give up majority control of the JV and also to change the marketing strategy, in effect reducing export sales from 50% to 30% of total output and sending more crude to local refineries. As these refineries were controlled by Bolshoi Oil this would effectively have given the Russian company the option to take extra margin from the refining process or else export the crude itself without giving any benefit to the JV.

Independent Oil's management clearly saw the negative impact this would have on their business, but had limited ability to respond given their previous reliance on their Russian partner for all local business negotiations. "If we accept the new terms of the Russian side, the economics of the project will prove to be simply unacceptable to Independent Oil", said the company president when interviewed at the time. "[Independent Oil] views the legal proceedings and the requests for change in control of the JV [initiated by Bolshoi Oil and Nefteyanik] as an opportunistic attack in an attempt to gain an advantage in the ongoing management of the JV." However, the company's only response, given its lack of local business or political influence, was to appeal to international style arbitration. Financial and oil industry auditors were hired to give a fairness opinion on the value of the contributions made to the JV by the respective partners, in order to demonstrate to Bolshoi Oil that they had no legal case to reduce Independent Oil's equity stake.

In the event, though, the audit demonstrated again how much greater Bolshoi Oil's local business influence was than its foreign rival. At the initiation of the audit Independent Oil claimed in a press release that "the financial audit is expected to clarify for the new management of Bolshoi Oil the terms and conditions of the participation [of the original parties in the JV]". Furthermore it believed that the audit would "provide for Bolshoi Oil and Nefteyanik to take the necessary steps to resolve any remaining uncertainties surrounding the license transfers that are currently the subject of proceedings in the Russian courts. Any necessary amendments can then be properly executed and filed to definitively confirm the validity of the Joint Venture's licenses." However, the Bolshoi Oil and Nefteyanik response was anything but conciliatory, as the companies not only refused to acknowledge any commitment to confirming license ownership, but also continued to pursue their aims in the local courts, with the goal of confirming Nefteyanik's rights to a majority stake in the licenses and to control over Ventura.

Rulings continued to be made in local courts against Independent Oil, with Bolshoi Oil's local influence again alleged to be a key factor. As summarized by one of the major shareholders in Independent Oil, "Suffice it to say that it's not clear what it takes to buy a judge in remote areas of Siberia." As a result, despite numerous attempts at appeals the foreign company found itself fighting a losing battle. Its local business influence was so limited that it had to resort to international sentiment and blaming its partner for not explaining the law properly, in effect admitting that it might have acted unlawfully. "It may be that it [the license transfer] violated federal law, but at that time they [Nefteyanik] tried to convince us of the opposite", was the statement made by one Ventura official employed by Independent Oil as the legal proceedings continued, which only encouraged the Russian side to increase its efforts to convince the courts that the initial JV formation should be unwound.

Finally Independent Oil resorted to a direct appeal to the Kremlin and to Russia's image in the world financial community. Not surprisingly the Kremlin authorities declined to act on such a small case and were not impressed by Independent Oil's claims that "this action could have a negative effect on Russia's financial interests and its international image". With these final attempts at appeal proving fruitless Independent Oil was left with little option but to settle and agree to a price of less than $30mm for its 50% stake in Ventura Petroleum, incurring a substantial loss on its original investment... Needless to say, as the announcement of the deal was made the company also confirmed that it "had ended its involvement in Russia for the time being".

The CEO's conclusion from the ongoing litigation that had engulfed Independent Oil following the takeover of Nefteyanik by Bolshoi Oil was that "Russian companies are taking advantage of the maturing legislation to find loopholes for their financial gain", and officials at Ventura itself described Bolshoi Oil's actions as tantamount to robbery. Independent Oil commentators took a similar view, with one journalist describing the situation thus: "Bolshoi Oil...simply kicked Independent Oil out of Ventura. It...bankrupted the joint venture and bought up all its assets for less than $10 million... [When] the original backer of Independent Oil tried to get compensation for its losses – which, with lost profits factored in, were valued at $100 million – at the International Arbitration Court in Stockholm...it was forced to give up and...to part with its business in Russia for [less than $30 million]."

Case study three

The joint entity in our third case study (we shall name it Bureniye)[7] had its Russian origins in a West Siberian-based geological exploration enterprise formed in the Soviet Union. Having been purely focused on exploration activity during the Soviet era, this enterprise (which we can call Geologiya) was privatized, became a joint stock company (JSC) and began to focus on generating production and cashflow from its licenses. However, in common with many of its peers, it struggled for finance in the early 1990s and began to come under pressure from the Ministry of Natural Resources to fulfill its license commitments or lose its acreage. Consequently the company ran an investment tender, which was won by a small Siberian oil producer (here called Neft)[8] run by a local entrepreneur. Neft won a 61% stake in Geologiya and proceeded to provide investment funds that led to output rising from almost zero in 1995 to 2,000 barrels per day (bpd) by 1997.

However, the Russian owners decided that further development of the company would require a foreign investor to provide access to more capital, as well as the technical expertise and international management experience that generally came with it. The company CEO summarized the situation: "We needed money for the company to flourish and it did not matter to me if the money was foreign. We wanted to become a Russian major...and now we had access to cheaper foreign capital. As a result, Bureniye can become 'a fruitful marriage' of Russian assets and industrial expertise with Western capital and management know-how."

The search for a foreign investor led Geologiya to ally with an international investment company controlled by a North American and European consortium. This firm (which we shall call Consortium) had been formed in the US in the early 1990s as a consulting company advising potential investors in the Russian oil industry. The company's CEO had been an advisor to the Russian government and in 1995 decided to re-focus Consortium on direct investment in the Russian upstream business. Having raised $300 million of investment funds, his first deal was the purchase of a 22.3% stake in an existing Russian production JV, acquired from a US Independent Oil producer. However, as Consortium's CEO described it, this investment revealed to him the limitations of the JV model because "although operations were profitable, the limitations of the joint venture – mainly its slow recuperation period on its initial investment – proved frustrating. Another problem was that the interests of the shareholders tended to differ drastically, limiting the overall growth potential of the project, particularly since the Russian partner held the majority stake and thus essentially controlled its course." He was therefore "keen to create a Russian company that would operate in accordance with Western-style management and business practices in order to turn a profit as quickly as possible".

In fact the CEOs of Neft and Consortium met by chance in Moscow in 1997, but according to both quickly struck up a good relationship based on mutual respect for each other's business cultures. As a result Geologiya and Consortium were merged to form Bureniye in October of that year, with the new company being led by a combined Russian-Western management team and backed initially by funds from the original shareholders in Consortium.

Both the Russian and western partners were keen to emphasize what they saw as the unique structure of their venture and how it aligned the interests of both parties. Geologiya's CEO described Bureniye as "a new type of company that [had] never existed in Russia before. The interests of both partners were aligned so that they were exactly the same, so we became one team." Consortium confirmed that this was also the view taken by the western investors – "we're striving for a complete alignment of interests between all of the shareholders. The bottom line is that the [project participants] understood that we could never have done this without each other. We trust each other."

Essentially Bureniye was structured so that the providers of the asset base (Geologiya and the Russian partners), the providers of management and technical expertise (Consortium) and the providers of the finance (the original Consortium shareholders) were represented in the equity base of the company according to their contribution to the venture. As a result they were all motivated to work for the development and growth of the company as a whole, without the potential conflict of personal objectives outside the corporate structure. Essentially both Geologiya and Consortium had contributed their entire Russian portfolios to Bureniye, leaving them focused 100% on the new entity, while the other shareholders were clearly motivated to see their investment returns maximized.

As all the partners confirmed, once their interests were totally aligned they could be trusted to use their business skills for the benefit of the company as a whole. As might be expected, the domestic contribution was described as follows: "an alliance with a reputable Russian partner [which] will give access not only to significant hydrocarbon resources but to solid relations with local administrations". Indeed Neft's CEO, now the vice chairman of Bureniye, had served in the USSR's foreign ministry during the Soviet era, located overseas for most of that time but spending the vital years before the break-up of the Soviet Union in Moscow, where he had made many contacts within the oil and gas bureaucracy. As a result he had acted as an advisor on a number of oil industry privatizations, in particular that of Geologiya. One other key Russian partner was the former general director of Geologiya, who had led the company until mid-1997. As a result of his extensive experience in West Siberia he wielded considerable influence with the local authorities and the regional administration, which were vital for the ongoing success of Bureniye's existing business and for the provision of new growth opportunities via license and corporate acquisitions.

Meanwhile the western partners brought finance and management expertise. The finance was largely provided by a consortium of investors organized behind the investment fund that was now backing Bureniye, whose chairman became chairman of Bureniye's board of directors. The presence of this fund, and in particular of its chairman, who had a significant reputation in the European banking community, brought the management credibility necessary not only to raise short-term finance but also to make the objective of an Initial Public Offering (IPO) on western stock markets a realistic goal over the two years following the formation of the company. As all the partners explained, it was this goal of monetizing their investment in the relatively short-term that provided the joint motivation for all of them to work for a common cause. The western investors also provided the traditional management and technical expertise, although they were keen to transfer this to their Russian colleagues as quickly as possible. As Consortium's CEO explained: "the role of the foreign management was to establish western management practices and to provide critical access to foreign capital... [As a result] the characteristics of the company in terms of transparency, operating efficiency, reserve reports and management structure is all western... [However], we think of ourselves as a Russian company and we'll become more like a Russian company in terms of senior management over time... And our objective is to replace all the foreigners with Russians as quickly as we possibly can." Neft's CEO also recognized the skills brought by his western partners as access to capital and select applications of western management and technology, with the heavy emphasis on the participation of Russian professionals being encouraged by all parties as the best way to develop the company. Essentially it appears that the western shareholders were happy to share their expertise with their Russian partners confident in the knowledge that the corporate structure they had created meant that the efforts of all the participants were targeted at a common goal. It was also clear that the input of the western management would always be essential for the ultimate value realization of the project, namely an IPO or sale to a strategic investor. As he also acknowledged, the presence of western partners was also vital to win the trust of foreign investors and to ultimately raise the substantial sums of capital needed to realize the company's value.

The skills of both sets of partners were put to good use within a very short time after the formation of Bureniye. The company immediately began negotiating to expand its portfolio of local oilfields, and thanks to the Russian partners' influence managed to acquire 100% interests in two producing entities over the next three years. On the operational front a combination of knowledge of local assets and the introduction of new oilfield technology led to a sharp jump in production from around 2,000 barrels per day (bpd) in 1997 to 14,500 bpd by mid-2002, with reserves more than doubling from 118 million barrels to 284 million barrels in the same time period. Both the production growth and the reserves growth were due in part to the acquisitions mentioned above, but improved technology, especially with regard to waterflooding techniques and improved reservoir management, also played a major role. Indeed more than 50% of the reserve growth came from reserve upgrades due to improved development techniques.

The combination of Russian access with western experience also quickly became of interest to international investors. A number of financial institutions were attracted by the upside potential of the Russian oil industry and in Bureniye found an entity where the involvement of well-known international businessmen such as the chairman provided a level of confidence in the security of their investment. International oil companies were also attracted by this lower risk entry platform to Russia, and in particular one UK exploration and production company was keen to participate in the "unique blend of Western expertise on the one hand and political ties as well as access to hydrocarbon resources on the other". This company (UK Oil) invested $25 million in the late 1990s to take a small initial stake in Bureniye, and then increased its interest to 29% in 2002 and finally to 45% by the end of the same year. As an executive from this new strategic investor said at the time of the initial investment "although we were immediately attracted by Bureniye's asset base, it would have been difficult for us to invest with the Russian partners alone given our lack of experience in the country. We might have taken the risk, but the presence of international investors with much greater experience than ours was a great help in convincing our own shareholders that we were controlling the risks in the acquisition."

At the same time Bureniye's shareholders were also considering the option of an IPO on the London stock exchange, and proceeded as far as hiring investment banks and preparing all the necessary documentation. However, two events caused the company to change strategy. Firstly, UK Oil was itself taken over by one of the oil majors, who then announced that it would take its time to decide on its plans for its 45% stake in Bureniye, and insisted that any IPO plans be delayed. Secondly, with the other partners becoming frustrated at this new investor's procrastination, a second sale option became available in the shape of a North American integrated oil company (North Oil). North Oil was attracted by the same combination of Russian and western expertise that had led to UK Oil's initial investment and as a result insisted that "Bureniye and all its subsidiaries will retain their identities" after any acquisition in order to "continue the pioneering role in developing oil and gas fields in Russia...and...providing a new core area for [North Oil] with substantial near and medium-term growth". As a result of negotiations between all the parties, North Oil ultimately paid almost $300 million to purchase 100% of the company and took full ownership in 2003. Although it bought out all the existing partners (foreign and Russian) and therefore initially changed Bureniye into a completely internationally owned company, North Oil continued to view the corporate model as a good basis for future partnership with domestic players. Indeed in its post-acquisition presentation it announced that Bureniye would be the foundation for North Oil to "continue to develop partnerships with key Russian companies" and that it would "plan to work with companies operating in the same region as Bureniye, potentially sharing equity in various entities".

Overall, then, it would seem fair to categorize the Bureniye partnership as a success for all the original partners in the venture, both international and Russian. Over a period of six years the company managed to more than double its reserve base, increase production by a factor of five times and turn approximately $80 million of investment in 1997 into a $300 million company in 2003. While the growth in the oil price from 1999 certainly played a role in this increase in value, Bureniye's shareholders firmly believed that the corporate structure they had created was the main reason for their success in an era when many other ventures failed to produce similar returns or even collapsed completely.

In analysing the choice of partnership structure made by the Bureniye partners, both the CEOs of the Russian and foreign companies involved agreed on their view that the traditional JV based on a single asset was fundamentally flawed. Consortium's CEO summarized his overall view that "many of the classic joint ventures struck in the 1990s have been operational successes, but they have invariably turned into financial disappointments". He identified two main causes of failure. "The partners often fell out because cultural differences proved too great, or else the local tax authorities viewed the JVs as cash cows and destroyed their economics."

Neft's CEO elaborated further on the problems he saw with the traditional JV model. "Many Russian companies wishing to work together suffer from the 'mermaid' syndrome: although both sides may be attracted to each other, it is difficult to consummate their relationship". He viewed JVs as having inbuilt strains "because each partner has different priorities. The foreign partner wants ownership of reserves to bolster its balance sheet; the Russian partner wants quick cash. Russian companies do not want to cede control, while their foreign partners are reluctant to carry them [financially]. Moreover, a joint venture is a static structure that does not have the flexibility to grow. There is always tension about whether each partner should inject new assets into the joint venture or keep them entirely for themselves."

The Bureniye solution to this problem was to create an entity into which both parties committed all their Russian oil assets and where the ownership structure reflected the relevant contributions. As quoted above, Consortium's CEO was determined to create complete alignment of partner interests in order to provide a platform to which all the shareholders would be fully committed, and his Russian partner Neft's CEO underlined how well he felt that this model had worked. He underlined that "the interests of both partners were completely aligned so that they are exactly the same", and believed that this was reflected in the fact that "I no longer thought of ourselves as partners but as the same team."

This bond was forged both economically and culturally. As Neft's CEO stated at the initial formation of Bureniye "the company is 50:50 owned and operated by the Russian interests at Geologiya and their western partners", which he felt reflected the balance of contribution at the time. This balance was underlined by the partners' appreciation of what the other was bringing to the venture and their mutual understanding that the influence of different business cultures was essential to the success of Bureniye. Consortium's CEO saw that Neft's CEO and his companies brought "access not only to significant hydrocarbon resources but also to solid relations with local administrations" and appreciated the fact that "our Russian partners have a long-standing history in the region which brings clear advantages in terms of their strong ties with the local authorities". Neft, meanwhile, clearly understood that Bureniye could be a new "template for how to structure joint ventures" and both partners also believed that using western management methods, including "audited accounts, a clean balance sheet, and a clear management structure" could lead to a financial exit in terms of "an initial public offering within 18 months" if they could use an international governance model to "win the trust of foreign investors".

Part of the western partners' sympathetic cultural response was also reflected in their desire to make Bureniye as Russian a company as possible. Consortium's CEO was keen to emphasize that "Geologiya, the principal operating company, was always a Russian oil company", with the role of the western partners being to establish management practices that would enable it to "compete head to head with strong Russian competitors who will inevitably be well managed and capitalized themselves". Indeed, despite the fact that Bureniye was itself registered abroad and was targeting an IPO on the London stock exchange, Consortium's CEO insisted that "irrespective of where our company was registered, we thought of ourselves as a Russian oil company" and "became more and more like a Russian oil company as we replaced western managers with Russian managers as quickly as possible".

This alignment of partner interests, combined with a commitment to implementing the best practices from the western and Russian business cultures, led to all the shareholders being motivated by the growth of the corporate entity. Neft's CEO certainly had grand ambitions for Bureniye – "we wanted to become a Russian major. We had a good reserves base and were aggressive in bidding for new tenders and looked to buy assets from other companies." This ambition was certainly reflected in the acquisitions that Bureniye made in its early years, and Consortium's CEO underlined the matching ambition of the western partners – "our objective was to build a model that worked and then to concentrate on making it as big as possible, and not vice versa as was more common in the Russian oil sector".

One final point on the Bureniye partnership was made by Neft's CEO relating to the choice of Russian partner. He identified the fact that "Russian geological companies were generally more open [than domestic producers] to co-operating with foreign investors". The reason for this, he believed, was that "these entities were especially strapped for cash because the government was no longer providing financing for exploration" and with little production experience the geological companies had no other immediate source of financial resources. As such "the equity in geological companies was much cheaper to acquire" and their owners were more amenable to partners with access to cheap capital who were prepared to recognize the benefits of having a domestic partner with a strong asset base. However, having available funds was not enough to create a strong partnership, Neft's CEO pointed out. Even cash-strapped geologists would only agree to a deal if they believed in their partners' integrity and commitment to the overall venture. As Neft's CEO concluded on the formation of the Bureniye deal "we [the Russian partners] were impressed by their [the western partners'] open-mindedness and cultural understanding. They were extremely tough negotiators, but they delivered on everything they promised, in contrast to other foreign investors who promised the world but delivered nothing."

Overall conclusions

These three case studies provide examples of two joint ventures that ended in relative failure for the foreign partner and one that had a successful conclusion for all the parties involved. In drawing some initial conclusions from these stories we believe that it is relevant to compare them with the experiences of a fourth foreign investor, a British oilman who worked in partnerships in the Russian oil industry for over twenty years. He was interviewed extensively by one of the authors in Moscow but has asked to remain anonymous due to his continuing involvement in the industry, but his experience of all the issues touched upon in the three case studies above allows us to create a solid foundation for the analysis undertaken in the subsequent chapters. We will call him Mr. A for the purposes of his commentary, and his history in Russia included being a foreign partner in a joint venture with a Russian oil major at a field in West Siberia, being a major shareholder in a company jointly owned by Russian and foreign strategic investors and acting on behalf of a domestic investor in a joint venture with an international oil major on a new field development begun in 2003.

Mr. A's first comment, which is perhaps rather obvious but is nevertheless worth reiterating, was that in a business environment such as that seen in Russia in the 1990s a domestic partner is essential for any foreigner wishing to do business in the country. As he put it, he "immediately identified the need for a domestic partner in a business environment such as Russia in the 1990s, both to facilitate access to opportunities and to provide some 'political' insurance, mainly protection against the vagaries of a system with little institutional control and huge potential for corrupt practices". However, having made this initial observation he also came to realize that any partnership agreement between a foreign and domestic player was not a static arrangement, stating that he "came to understand the bargains that were continuously being struck between JV partners and then re-modeled as each side came to understand the strength of its position and the changing value of its role in the venture". As a result of this continuing bargaining process he then asserted that "the domestic partner is the biggest business risk to any joint venture between an international and domestic player. If the joint venture is not structured correctly the domestic partner can easily develop two distinct strategies to create value for himself – develop the JV to its maximum potential using the skills of both parties to maximum advantage, or use his own skill of 'domestic knowledge and influence' to maximize his own returns by disenfranchising his international partner at the appropriate time." Mr. A's own experience of this problem had come in a joint venture on a West Siberian oilfield, where as the foreign partner he had committed his financial support to the project on the understanding that licenses would be transferred to the newly created JV by the domestic partner, and also brought significant amounts of new technology to improve field performance. However, once money had been committed and it had also become clear that the technology being used could be purchased from contractors, Mr. A's domestic partner decided to use his local knowledge not to benefit the JV as a whole but to disenfranchise Mr. A and improve its own position through a series of contentious court cases.

Mr. A's experience is clearly very similar to the Houston Oil and Ventura case studies described earlier on the chapter and leads to a number of conclusions. Firstly, although a domestic partner appears to be a necessity, overreliance on him can leave the foreign partner very exposed if circumstances change. Secondly, it would seem to be certain that circumstances will change because, as Mr. A highlights, the joint venture agreement is not static, with the balance shifting according to the bargaining options available to the different partners and their perceptions of their own best interests. In the case of the domestic partner, if he discovers that his foreign partner's skills have either become less valuable or can be replicated at lower cost, he may well decide to reduce the value of his own skill (local knowledge) to the JV and instead use it to his own advantage by disenfranchising his foreign partner and taking a larger share of the partnership for himself.

Alternatively, as happened in the Houston Oil and Ventura cases, the domestic partner may change and the new partner may perceive a different balance of bargaining power with his new foreign partner. If he perceives that the value of his local knowledge is greater than that of the previous domestic partner, and therefore that the balance of power in the JV has shifted in his favour, then once again he may be inclined to ignore the previous agreement and use his core skill to gain most advantage for himself. In this case a certain element of bad luck is involved as far as the foreign partner is concerned, as the introduction of a new domestic partner could not have been anticipated, but nevertheless it still raises the issue of the vulnerability of foreigners in a business environment such as Russia's.

The potential for misfortune to occur is also highlighted by the fact that within an asymmetric commercial environment such as Russia, where the rule of law is weak and institutions cannot be fully trusted, business tends to be based on relationships and trust. As Mr. A describes "In general senior Russian businessmen do work on the 'my word is my bond principle' and trust is very important to them. Many deals are done via non-related companies in order to avoid related company law, and as such Russians are used to the concept that many deals rely on a relationship broader than the specific deal in question. In a western business context, this often means taking a certain leap of faith in a relationship." However, the introduction of trust and friendship, and in some cases even mutual respect and genuine affection, does not mean that a balance of interests and bargaining strengths can be removed from the partnership equation. Again from Mr. A – "the most important element of any deal is to work step-by-step towards a structure where both partners have stakes in an entity where the risks and rewards are similar for both".

This statement again chimes with the example case studies discussed above. In all the JVs the skills brought by the foreign partner of management experience, technical expertise and financing were initially balanced by the domestic partner's offering of local knowledge, that included not only an understanding of how to do business in Russia but also access to assets. However, in two cases this balance did not last as it became clear that the domestic partner's local knowledge had a consistent value while the foreign partner's skills started to become less valuable once they had been used, or at least were perceived to become less valuable. Once technology had been applied to a field and output had improved, once cash had been invested, once new management techniques had been put in place the foreign partner's bargaining position weakened as his skills were either viewed as having been learnt by the domestic partner, or as being replicable (either by use of a contractor or from a new partner), or as no longer relevant (for example when the oil price rose and financing became less of an issue). Once the balance was lost, then the domestic partner became incentivized to use his enhanced bargaining power to optimize his own position and not that of the JV, and used his local knowledge against his foreign partner rather than for him.

Once the balance of bargaining power in a joint venture has shifted, the foreign partner clearly needs to consider his response and tactics for reversing the trend. The North American investors in Houston Oil and Independent Oil both decided to resort to international political pressure and appeals to Russia's standing in the international financial community. Neither of these approaches was remotely successful, and it is relatively easy to understand why. In the first case, as the domestic political leader explained in the case of Houston Oil, governments are hardly likely to create a diplomatic rift over a small commercial venture in which the owners either knew, or should have known, the risks that they were taking. In the second case, the issue of potential negative international reaction towards Russia was raised, but again this is hardly likely to overcome the chance of domestic financial gain. Furthermore, in a weak state environment the higher authorities are unlikely to be able, or even want, to overrule court decisions even if those decisions are being taken in favour of vested interests, as those vested interests may be the same ones that are helping to keep the higher authorities in power.

As a result, the necessary foreign partner response would appear to be to not an international one but one that enhances its position in the domestic market where it is operating, either by acquiring local knowledge itself or by enhancing the skill-set that it is offering. In other words, as a foreign partner you either need to acquire some of your domestic partner's skills (as he is acquiring yours) or you need to bring some better skills of your own to the table. One option, as highlighted in our conversation with Mr. A, is to develop one's own local knowledge network. This can involve finding an individual or group to provide political protection or cover, known in Russia as "kreesha",[9] or more broadly it can be achieved by putting oneself in a position to make domestic contacts that can be critical for the survival of any business in Russia. Clearly one has to make judgments about the potential value of any contacts before trusting them in order to decide whether to take advantage of the opportunity for local knowledge, and one also has to invest a significant amount of time to maintain what are likely to become personal relations within a social environment and network. It is also important to recognize that this relationship-building does not necessarily involve any exchange of money, and indeed this would often be regarded as completely inappropriate. Trust and friendship play key roles in cementing senior contacts, and if handled correctly can become enduring relationships based on mutual respect and genuine affection rather than just business-related contacts only. This form of local knowledge takes a long time to develop, but can ultimately provide the strongest security for any joint ventures in Russia.

An alternative, or even a complementary, response is for the foreign partner to maintain his bargaining strength by enhancing his existing skills, or at the very least re-emphasizing their importance on a regular basis. One specific example drawn from the author's own analysis rather than any interviews, highlights the relationship between Evikhon and Shell at the Salym project in West Siberia as a good example of how this can work to maintain balance in a JV. Development of the Salym fields was initiated in 2003, with Evikhon, a subsidiary of Sibir Energy, acting as Shell's domestic partner. Total capital expenditure of $1.5 billion saw Salym become one of Russia's most successful onshore developments of recent years and certainly the largest onshore project involving an international company.[10] The field began production in 2005, and by the end of 2007 output had reached 110,000 bpd, with a targeted peak of 160-180,000 bpd by 2009. Indeed, so successful was the development that it became a model for other companies in the region, with Evikhon's role as a key negotiator with local contractors, politicians and bureaucrats being fully acknowledged by Shell as one of the keys to success. However, Shell maintained its own bargaining position in the JV through a variety of tactics. Firstly, it created a JV with a 50:50 split between the partners, offering both an equal incentive in the event of success and preventing either from taking voting control. Secondly, its position as a major oil company with vast operational and technical experience allowed it to maintain bargaining leverage from its initial offering to the JV. If it had removed its skills from the JV the much smaller and less experienced Evikhon would not have been unable to keep the Salym field operating successfully, and the continuing success of the field further enhanced Shell's bargaining position. Furthermore, the long-term potential to develop tight and shale oil resources in the Salym licences provides Shell with an additional technological offering, given its experience with unconventional fields, allowing it to demonstrate its continuing operational relevance to the joint venture.[11] Finally, following almost 20 years of business in Russia Shell has established its own network of political connections and influence that can be used to offset any possible threat from its Russian partners. Shell's relationship with the Russian state was strengthened by the 2006 deal with Gazprom at Sakhalin 2 and by the 2010 agreement between the companies to deepen their partnership in Russia and overseas,[12] and Shell has also worked hard to ensure that political relations between Russia and the Netherlands are strong. As a result, it has developed a level of "domestic knowledge" that can be used as a deterrent against any threat to its economic interests at Salym, and has combined this with its clear operational expertise to maintain its position even after the acquisition of Sibir Energy, and therefore Evikhon, by Gazprom Neft in 2009.[13]

However, the example of Bureniye in our third case study suggests another alternative partnership model that can perhaps create more stability from its inherent structure rather than through a constant re-balancing of partner bargaining strengths. This is what we might term a corporate partnership model, in which the foreign and Russian partners become shareholders in a company that is formed to develop one or more assets together. Our conversation with Mr. A, who also experienced this type of arrangement, highlighted the potential benefits. He argued that preferably "the international partner has to be part of a Russian company, as the business model for both parties must be the same. The key is that any troubles must hit you both equally so that you both respond in a way that maximizes the value of the business entity rather than one or other of the partners." In practical terms this meant "structuring any deals in a lock-step fashion in terms of equity ownership and control, in order to work step-by-step towards a structure where both partners have stakes in an entity where the risks and rewards are similar for both. The key is therefore to tie your domestic partner into a business relationship where he is incentivized to use his influence and business skills in the interest of a jointly-owned company, and always feels that his contribution has been rewarded with a commensurate shareholding."

These views mirror the opinions of the key foreign and domestic shareholders at Bureniye, who understood that although trust between the partners is vital, in reality it is only created if they all understand that they have a common goal and that their interests are aligned to achieve that goal. Furthermore, it is enhanced if the vehicle in which they have invested has longer-term growth potential and is not focused on just one asset. They argue that the normal JV model does not provide as close alignment of partner interests as the corporate model because its focus on a single asset is more likely to mean that the partners will also have other divergent interests that could conflict either with each other or the JV itself. The interests of the partners can be more completely aligned within a corporate structure where the partners contribute all their relevant assets and are allocated equity according to their contribution. Furthermore, the JV model's single asset focus is more static and provides little scope for growth as introducing new assets or financing acquisitions is difficult for both partners as they always have the option to act alone rather than with their JV partner. The corporate model has more scope for expansion beyond the initial investment as all growth decisions are taken jointly, with the company then making investments or acquiring assets on behalf of all the equity-holding partners. This tends to reduce the risk of partners acting individually in conflict with the jointly-owned company and also encourages all partners to introduce growth opportunities to the corporate entity to ensure its continued expansion.

Overall, then, the analysis of Bureniye and our conversation with Mr. A can be summarized as follows: "The traditional JV model is fundamentally different because just sharing one asset increases the potential for conflict with your partner, particularly if the two of you do not have equal amounts to lose. Specifically this is because the longer-term nature of the relationship is not important because there is no future for the partnership beyond the life of the single asset. In contrast the corporate model provides the foundation for a longer-term relationship over the life of multiple assets where each partner can continue to add value as the entity grows. Both partners are therefore interested in the growth of the corporate vehicle to maximize joint value rather than just reaping the largest benefit for themselves out of one asset."

However, this ringing endorsement of the corporate-style partnership model cannot be taken as definitive, as the answer is clearly not so black and white. As Mr. A has also pointed out, it is possible to make money as a foreigner in a JV in Russia if you are prepared to develop your local knowledge skills. Furthermore, even the largest example of a corporate-style JV, the partnership between AAR and BP at TNK-BP, can have turbulent times if the shareholders feel that their individual objectives are not being met or if they perceive that the equity in the company has not been distributed appropriately. As a result, the next chapter provides a brief statistical analysis of the key drivers for foreign partner success in a weak institutional environment, in an attempt to provide some objective analysis to support, or disprove, the more subjective and personal conclusions reached in this chapter. We will ask how important local knowledge is to both domestic and international partners in Russia relative to the other contributions that they make, and will also seek to establish whether there are other key factors that can contribute to foreign partner success. We will also examine the possible differences between the performance of normal "single asset" joint ventures and more corporate-style partnerships, in order to establish whether the corporate model really is to be preferred.

4
The Key Drivers of Foreign Partner Success – A Quantitative Analysis

Introduction

The case studies in Chapter 3 have established a number of key themes regarding partnership relations between foreign and domestic investors in a business environment such as Russia's. The first and most significant is that in order to be successful for all the parties involved, partnerships need to remain in balance such that the bargaining power of the partners is relatively equal. If balance is lost and one partner establishes that, or even perceives that, his bargaining power is in the ascendancy then it is likely that the JV will fail and the "weaker" partner will lose out. In a Russian context it has been argued that a vital element in this balance is the issue of learning, and in particular the different learning patterns of the domestic and foreign partners about each other's skills and key contributions to a joint venture. It was pointed out that foreign partner skills are relatively easy for the domestic partner to learn, or acquire, and that the foreign partner did not object to this learning, and indeed often encouraged it. Conversely, the foreign partner appeared to find it more difficult to acquire his domestic partner's core skill, local knowledge of how to operate in an "asymmetric" business environment. However, as was also demonstrated, those who make the effort to increase their local knowledge tend to reap the benefits.

A second main conclusion, suggested in particular by the third case study, is more tentative but nevertheless potentially relevant, namely that a foreign partner's need for this local knowledge can be mitigated by the use of a different form of joint entity, namely one created using what might be described as a corporate model. In this type of entity the foreign and Russian partners become shareholders in a corporate structure, and this appears to create a greater incentive for the skills of each to be used for the benefit of the entity (and therefore all of its shareholders) rather than for one of the partners individually. In this case the skills of the foreign partner can complement the local knowledge of the Russian partner to create a greater chance of a successful outcome for both.

However, having established these two key themes via a qualitative analysis that is clearly based on the subjective reasoning of a few key individuals, we will now aim to provide a more quantitative analysis based on a survey of foreign participants in partnerships in Russia during the period 1991–2003. In carrying out the analysis we have used many of the standard survey-driven techniques advocated by numerous academic studies (for example Foddy,[1] Dijkstra,[2] and Brenner[3]) but in the description of our findings in this chapter we have attempted to reduce the statistical detail to a minimum for ease of reading. The details can be found in Appendix 1. For those readers only interested in the conclusions of the analysis, we would advise turning to page 179 for a summary that captures all the highlights of the chapter, but we hope that the main contents of the analysis will provide enough other interesting detail as we seek to back up our initial subjective conclusions with some further objective proof.

The survey of joint ventures

The quantitative analysis is based upon a survey of the foreign partners in a number of joint entities that were formed and operated in the Russian oil and gas industry in the period 1990–2003. The overall goal was to attempt to establish the drivers of foreign partner success as viewed by the foreign partners themselves. 33 responses were received from 31 of the 64 entities identified as being a true partnership between foreign and Russian investors (as opposed to being an essentially Russian company with shares held offshore). 90% of the respondents were senior managers (including a General Director), and represented a broad spread of joint entities on a number of criteria such as location, partner size and foreign partner origin. We therefore feel that, although there is inevitably some risk of bias in the analysis, the responses do represent a reasonably accurate sub-set of foreign investment in the Russian oil and gas industry at the time.[4] One caveat is the obvious fact that there are no Russian respondents, as it proved to be practically impossible largely because none of the potential Russian respondents was prepared to answer specific questions about their activities in the period under review. The most common Russian response was that the events were no longer relevant and that all parties had moved on to a different business model, and so they were no longer prepared to discuss the issues or have any responses recorded. However, as the point of the analysis is to establish drivers of foreign partner success as perceived by the foreigners themselves, this caveat is not a fundamental problem, in particular because the findings of the survey were subsequently discussed with Russian players and their observations (discussed in the next chapter) largely support our findings.

The survey contained a mixture of 16 open and closed questions, with respondents asked to rank various statements on a scale of 1 to 5, with 1 being a low rating and 5 high.[5] As one example, question 6 asked respondents to rank their contribution to the joint entity under various categories, with 1 being a minimal contribution and 5 being a high contribution.[6] Overall the questions were aimed at discovering what the key drivers of foreign partner success might be, and also to establish what foreign partners thought about the success or otherwise of their domestic partners. Following the three introductory questions the first set of exploratory questions (nos. 4 to 6) attempted to establish foreign partner perceptions of the motivations of both the foreign and Russian partners for the formation of a joint entity, and then to identify the contributions of each party to the established entity. These questions were aimed at confirming the assertions in the literature on foreign investment in the oil and gas industry by authors such as Watson (1996),[7] who identified management, capital and technology as the key contributions of foreign investors with assets and local knowledge being brought by the domestic players. Confirmation of these findings could then provide a foundation for questions on how knowledge transfer might then impact foreign partner success in a joint entity. Two open questions on foreign and domestic partner objectives were therefore followed by a closed question asking the respondents to rank their own and their partner's contributions to the joint entity in question.

The next set of questions then attempted to explore the issues of partner knowledge and learning to see how this might have impacted both initial control of the JV and any ongoing change in control over various business areas and responsibilities. The literature on joint ventures discussed in Chapter 2[8] identified the "race to learn" between partners as a key driver of success or failure, with the partner who can learn fastest being able to improve his bargaining position and take greater control of any joint entity. Therefore the respondents were first asked a direct question ranking the level of their domestic partner's learning in various areas during the life of the joint entity. Then they were asked less direct questions related to their own knowledge acquisition, based on a ranking of their own confidence on various issues as the joint entity progressed and of the control of both partners over various business areas. The respondents, being the foreign partners, were not asked a direct question about their own learning in order to "reduce question threat",[9] in other words to avoid the risk of them answering in a biased fashion because they wanted to be seen as having won the implied competition with their domestic partner. In this section an open question about partner conflict was also asked to explore if there had been any particular areas where the partners had been especially reluctant to co-operate and whether these related to any of the sensitive learning or control issues.

A further two questions were then asked concerning corruption and state influence, in order to establish if any external factors concerned with a weak state environment might have impacted the success of the joint entity from a foreign partner perspective. Respondents were asked to rank levels of state and administrative corruption they experienced during their involvement in the joint entity, and also the levels of state influence they perceived in four different areas. The final three questions then asked the respondent to rank his perception of his own and his partner's success over the life of the joint entity, while also providing the respondent with the opportunity to offer an open opinion on the key success factors for foreign partner success in a joint entity in Russia. The survey questionnaire can be seen in full in Appendix 1.

The survey results – Initial findings

The contrasting objectives of each partner

The first goal of the survey was to establish why each partner might want to form a joint entity and what each then made as its initial contribution of skills or assets. The clearest initial conclusion is that gaining access to assets in Russia was a key objective for many of the foreign partners, with two thirds of the respondents identifying it as an important goal as part of their entry strategy into Russia. This should perhaps be no surprise as Russia is a resource rich country containing 5% of the world's oil reserves and 21% of its gas reserves.[10] The opportunity to explore for and develop oil and gas fields had not been available to foreign companies during the Soviet era, but in the early 1990s foreign investors were encouraged to think that their help in rebuilding the Russian oil industry would be welcomed. With growth opportunities for exploration and production in areas outside the Middle East becoming harder to find, and with access to hydrocarbons in the Middle East being fraught with political difficulty, potential investment in the Russian oil and gas industry therefore became a key strategic theme for many international oil companies. The results of the survey confirmed this view with 22 of the 33 respondents mentioning themes such as reserve discovery, field development, hydrocarbon production and specific reserve acquisition as key objectives for their entry into Russia.

As far as domestic partner objectives are concerned, the survey supports the assertions of numerous commentators[11,12,13] that three core attributes were sought from foreign investors, namely management, technology and capital, and that of these the most important was gaining access to new technology.

As the case studies have already highlighted, foreign participation was seen as a vital way to access the international oilfield management techniques that could reverse the decline in post-Soviet oil production through the introduction of new equipment that had been widely used in the global oil industry but had not been available during the development of the Soviet oil industry. Complimenting this response, 50% of respondents also mentioned gaining management expertise as a key objective for domestic partners.[14] As with technology this was seen as one of the core skills brought by foreign companies in the post-Soviet era as domestic oil companies struggled to address both operational issues at their declining fields and more general management of an oil business that had previously been controlled by the state and its central planners. A third of respondents then also specifically mentioned a desire to access foreign capital as an objective for their domestic partner. Given the scarcity of investment capital in Russia during the immediate post-Soviet period, it is not very surprising that a number of domestic partners were seen as hungry for an injection of funds, especially as this was regarded as one of the core foreign partner contributions.

Apart from the three key goals suggested by the standard literature, other domestic partner objectives focused mainly on financial issues. These included the generic goal of "creating a profitable business" or simply "making a profit", but also highlighted the desire of some domestic investors to "cash out" their investments to a foreign buyer, either in the short or the long term. However, it is interesting that the goal of gaining the support and credibility of an international partner is also mentioned, which was especially important for domestic partners seeking either debt finance for projects or equity finance in IPOs or other share offerings. Other respondents noted protection and political support as a further perceived benefit of having a foreign partner in a business environment where high levels of political and institutional risk were being taken. Finally we would also note that two respondents cited outright theft as an objective for their domestic partner. Although this is not a broad theme in the written responses, conversations with a number of the respondents did reveal a perception that the attraction of foreign capital, in particular, was seen by a number of domestic partners as an opportunity for deception and diversion of funds.

What each partner brought to the table

Each respondent was asked to rank their own and their domestic partner's contribution in 11 different areas ranging from access to markets to provision of specific skills or assets, access to capital, and knowledge of formal and informal issues in the domestic (Russian) and international arenas. Figure 4.1 below summarizes the results and demonstrates not only that on average the

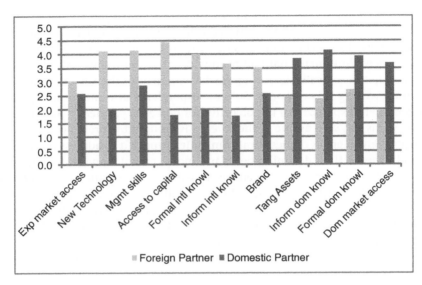

Figure 4.1   Comparison of foreign and domestic partner JV contributions

contributions blended well, with very little overlap of high contributions from both partners, but also that the contributions corresponded well with the objectives of both partners respectively.

The major foreign partner contributions clearly emerge as access to capital, management skills and new technology. To underline their importance it is interesting to note that 70% of respondents gave "access to capital" the maximum score of 5 out of 5, while 58% of respondents gave the same score to new technology and 94% of all respondents gave management skills a score of 3 or more. Conversely, and perhaps not surprisingly, the least important contributions by the foreign partner concerned the domestic market, where both ability to gain access and knowledge of local issues were scored low. Indeed the contrast between the high and low foreign partner contributions is statistically significant enough to conclude that most foreign partners had very little knowledge of local issues to contribute at the start of a joint entity in Russia.[15]

Figure 4.1 also shows that the contribution of the average domestic partner is in sharp contrast to the foreign partner offering. Experience and expertise in informal domestic issues gains the highest average score, followed by expertise in formal domestic issues, provision of tangible assets and access to domestic markets. However, domestic partners were not perceived as contributing much in the way of capital or technology, and had little to offer in international markets. Furthermore, they also scored lower for management skills, although the contrast was not quite as great as in other areas perhaps because their local skills were valued here too. An initial conclusion, though, is that there is a statistically significant difference between the domestic and foreign partner scores for every contribution (including the average overall contribution) apart from export markets, where the foreign partner scores a higher mark on average than the domestic partners, but not to a significant degree.[16] Foreign partners made significantly greater contributions of capital, management skills, technology, brand and knowledge of international markets while in contrast, domestic partners made significantly greater contributions of domestic market access, tangible assets and knowledge of local markets than their foreign partners, thus providing a complimentary skill-set in the formation of a joint entity in Russia.

Grouping the contributions using factor analysis

Before moving on to the rest of the survey, it is important to ensure that the results to date are simplified in such a way that further statistical analysis can be enhanced by grouping together responses that are very closely related. We will use this procedure with future sets of responses as well, to identify general themes and also to make sure that variables that are closely correlated do not undermine further analysis by giving excessive weight to one theme. The technique that is used is Principal Component Analysis (also known as Factor Analysis), and its purpose is to group together sets of responses that correlate closely, in effect providing sub-sets of responses that can be expected to react in similar ways when used in further statistical analysis. In this way it is possible not only to reduce the number of variables but also to discover if there are new latent variables which underlie the existing data but which are not exposed by the individual responses alone.[17] It is perhaps easiest to explain the technique using the example of partner contributions.

As mentioned above, 11 possible Partner Contributions were included in the list to be ranked by the survey respondents, and with regard to foreign partners six of these were found to correlate closely enough together to allow for possible grouping as "factors".[18] In fact two statistically significant groupings were found, creating two new factor variables that could be used in future analyses.[19] The first contains the contributions which most foreign partners appear to have regarded as their core offering in the formation of a joint entity in Russia, namely Management Expertise, Capital and Technology. For future reference we have named this factor "FPC Factor – MCT", and it is perhaps no great surprise that these three contributions, which are widely regarded as the key to the value of bringing a foreign partner into an oil and gas venture in Russia, are sufficiently closely correlated to be regarded as one variable in their own right.

The second factor groups informal and formal knowledge about international markets together, and is perhaps a more obvious single variable as it combines two attributes that one would clearly expect an international company to bring to a joint entity in Russia, which would have been useful both in facilitating export sales and in raising capital outside Russia. As a result, we can say that we have created two new more generic variables, which combine a number of closely related "sub-variables" that can be used to simplify further analysis.[20]

Domestic partner contributions were analysed in a similar fashion, with seven of the 11 variables being correlated closely enough for analysis, and three groupings were then identified as specific factors.[21] The first grouping covers the domestic contribution of access to domestic markets plus formal and informal knowledge of how to operate in them. We have called this factor "Local Knowledge and Markets". The second factor groups management and access to export markets. Although this is a slightly awkward grouping, we suggest that it could cover management of local business issues, one of which importantly included access to the export system in order to create sales to foreign markets at much higher prices than could be achieved in Russia. Gaining access to export pipes and port facilities was supposedly done on a quota basis but was more often related to management of relationships at the pipeline company Transneft and with the port authorities, and so it is possible to argue the logic of this factor grouping, which we have called "Management and Pipeline Access". The third factor groups Tangible Assets and Brand, both of which can be seen as domestic assets as they include both the physical assets needed to produce oil and gas and also the reputation and image needed to bolster an entity's ability to do business and create opportunities in a business environment relying on local influence and recognition. We have called this factor "Domestic Assets".

As a result, an initial conclusion from the survey is that overall both foreign and domestic participants in the joint entities appear to contribute what their partner is looking for. Foreign partners offer the much documented technology, management expertise and access to capital that were sought after by domestic partners looking to use these skills to catalyse the recovery of the Russian oil industry. Foreign partners also brought the knowledge of international markets that was useful not only for marketing hydrocarbons but also for bringing new capital from overseas investors. For their part the domestic partners generally brought access to the asset base in Russia, where foreign investors could find reserves and production that were becoming increasingly difficult to invest in across the globe. The domestic partner also brought the vital knowledge of how to operate in the local business environment, including informal knowledge of "how to get things done" as well as formal understanding of operational and legislative processes.

What the domestic partner learnt

Having established the key contributions made by each partner, as well as their objectives for creating a joint entity, the next aim of the survey was to establish the role of learning between the partners, in order to investigate whether the balance of bargaining power between them was based on what some academics have called a "race to learn"[22] but which we would identify as a less overt competition for knowledge. Our goal was to establish how each partner may have learned new skills from the other and how this might have been reflected in control over various aspects of the joint entity, and in light of this the respondents were directly asked how fast they felt their Russian partner acquired knowledge in three areas of capability. These areas were defined as operational (physically operating an oil and gas field or other oil asset), management (controlling the entity as a whole or the major projects within it) and technical (implementing the new technology and managing its ongoing application).

The responses suggested that the Russian partner did acquire knowledge in all three areas, but that no one area stood out significantly above the others. The difference between both the average scores for each type of learning was minimal, ranging from 3.13 to 3.25 out of 5, and furthermore the split of the scores between the different ranks suggests that where learning occurred it occurred across all three areas rather than in one area alone.[23] Indeed further tests showed that there was no significant difference between the scores for any of the areas of domestic partner learning,[24] and this result was confirmed by attempts at factor analysis which revealed that all the learning scores were so closely correlated that a simple average of the three would provide an adequate simplification for use in further analysis. The essential conclusion, therefore, is that on average domestic partners did make progress in acquiring knowledge in all three areas of operational, management and technical capabilities, but that there was no significant difference between the areas of learning.

Foreign partner learning and control

The issue of foreign partner learning or skill acquisition was addressed in a rather different manner, in that the survey did not ask a straight question about what the respondent felt he had learnt as a foreign partner but rather attempted to establish the changing levels of foreign partner control and confidence in a number of diverse areas. This rather more subtle approach was adopted in order to avoid the risk of competitive responses (i.e. a response biased by the perception of competition between domestic and foreign partner learning). Instead the idea was to demonstrate whether foreign partner skills had been developed enough over the life of a joint entity to allow greater involvement in areas where control had been low at the start. In

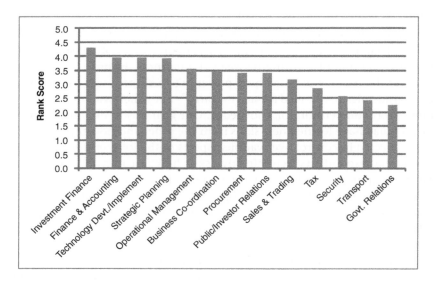

Figure 4.2   Ranked scores for initial foreign partner control

other words, did the foreign partner learn enough to gain the confidence to take on new responsibilities and did he in fact then increase his control in areas where he had initially delegated responsibility to his domestic partner?

In order to answer this question it is important to establish how much control the foreign partner had at the beginning and the end of the respective partnerships being examined, in order to measure the difference. As far as initial control is concerned, it is clear from Figure 4.2 that foreign partners are de facto most in control of "Investment Finance" (providing and/or raising capital), "Technology Development and Implementation", "Finance and Accounting" and "Strategic Planning", all of which gained average scores from the 33 respondents of close to 4 out of a possible 5.

The results point to two important conclusions. Firstly, there is a significant difference between the areas where foreign partners felt in control and those where they did not. It is interesting to note, for example, that 55% of respondents scored investment finance a 5, while 0% scored government relations a 5 and only 3% scored security a 5. Other less dramatic results saw only 15% of respondents scoring transport in the 4–5 categories, compared with 69% for finance and accounting and 78% for technology development and implementation, but overall the difference between the areas where foreign partners felt that they exerted control and where they did not is confirmed as statistically significant. Essentially foreign partners felt that they had significantly more de facto initial control over strategic planning than over government relations, over finance and accounting than over security, over technology development and implementation than transport and over investment finance than over tax.[25]

Secondly, and perhaps not surprisingly, it would seem that foreign partners felt especially in control of areas where they brought significant contributions. The lowest scores, by contrast, were in areas where knowledge of formal and informal domestic issues was most important, namely government relations, security, transport and tax, which all scored well below the median level of 3. Indeed a statistical comparison between the foreign partner's areas of greatest control and those areas where he made the greatest contribution shows that there is no significant difference.[26] A further comparison between areas where the foreign partners made low contributions (knowledge of domestic markets, experience in informal and formal domestic issues and a contribution of tangible assets) and areas of low control (government relations, transport, security and tax) shows a similar result. There is no significant difference between low foreign partner contributions and low foreign partner control, and it is interesting to note that both the contributions and the control in this case are focused on issues of a domestic nature where local knowledge is required. As a result, one can conclude that overall foreign partners felt most in control at the initial stage of their joint entities in areas where they had made the greatest initial contribution, namely management (control of finance and accounting and strategic planning in particular), capital (control of investment finance) and technology (control of technology development and implementation). In contrast, foreign partners felt least in control where they made little contribution and where knowledge of informal and formal domestic issues was required – in particular in government relations, security, transport and tax.

The impression of foreign partner control over management and technology issues is reinforced by a factor analysis of the survey responses on this issue. Eight of the 13 variables correlated adequately but not excessively, allowing the three factor groups to be created within acceptable statistical boundaries.[27] The first of these concerns "Business Management" as it includes control over the running and co-ordination of business activities, including specifically sales and trading and procurement, as well as the more generic operational management and business co-ordination. Essentially foreign partners, having brought management as one of their core skills, were generally entrusted with running the operations of the joint entity into which they had invested. The second can be labelled "Local Business Issues", with tax and security regarded as elements of operational management that needed to be dealt with using elements of local knowledge as well as general business acumen. The third has been labelled "Long-term Development", including strategic planning and technology as two areas where the foreign partner would bring longer-term benefits to a partnership through a more thorough planning of investment and the introduction of technology to improve operational performance over time. Interestingly the first and third groups concern areas where the foreign partner has a high level of control, while the second (Local Business Issues) is an area of low control. Factor analysis is not designed to create groups of variables with high scores, but rather groups where the scores are closely related whether high or low. As a consequence these results show us that there were two areas in which the foreign partner generally felt in control (management and long-term planning) and one where he generally felt he had little control (local business issues).

Having established the areas of high and low initial foreign partner control, the survey then addressed the issue of how this control changed over time in an attempt to see whether foreign partners were able to take practical steps to play a greater role in areas where they had previously lacked knowledge and skills. The ranking system for this question was somewhat different in that a score of 3 meant no change in control, with 1 meaning a large decrease in control and 5 a large increase, and as can be seen from Figure 4.3 below, the first main conclusion is that although all but one of the scores are at or above 3, the range is narrow and no score is above 3.45. Therefore on average foreign partners saw little overall change in control over the life of their joint entities in Russia.

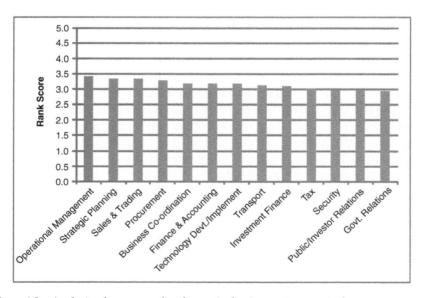

Figure 4.3 Analysis of responses for change in foreign partner control

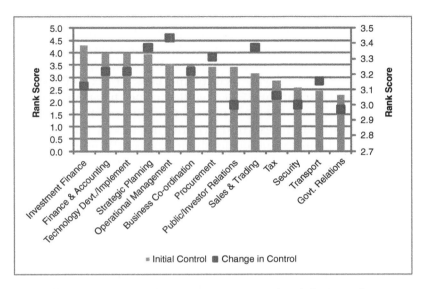

Figure 4.4   Comparison of initial foreign partner control and change in foreign partner control

A second conclusion is suggested by Figure 4.4, which compares initial partner control scores with the change in control scores. The four highest scores for increased foreign partner control are for operational management, sales and trading, procurement and strategic planning, and these results closely correspond with the previous results for initial control. Indeed strategic planning had been one of the areas where foreign partners felt they had very high initial control, while operational management and procurement had also scored above the mean for initial control, and as a result one conclusion is that three of the areas where foreign partners most increased control were also areas where they felt that they already had more than the average level of control.

In contrast, three of the functions where foreign partners achieved least change in control were the areas where they were weakest to start with, namely government relations, security and tax. In addition, the other area where the foreign partners originally had a low level of control (transport) also ranked below the mean of the scores on change in control. A clear conclusion from this is that the foreign partners, on average, made least, and effectively zero, progress in the functions where their domestic partners had most initial control and where any progress they might have made could have helped them to undermine their domestic partners' bargaining strength. Furthermore the lack of progress made by foreign partners in the functions that concerned informal and formal knowledge of domestic issues is high-lighted by the range of responses in each of the key functions related to these areas. For example, 75% of respondents said that the foreign partner had no increase in control or lost control in the area of government relations, with 78% concluding the same with security and 69% for tax. Interestingly, a similar number of respondents (75%) highlighted no change in control over investment finance, with the result that the functions in which foreign part-ners had the most and the least initial control had exactly the same level of change in control. One would obviously not expect the foreign partner to increase his control of a function such as investment finance, which they clearly dominated from the start, but it is interesting that no progress was made in three areas where the foreign partner had obvious weaknesses.

Factor analysis then confirmed the areas where the changes in foreign partner control appeared to be linked. The analysis allowed three factors to be extracted at acceptable levels of significance and accuracy.[28] The first can be identified as "Business Planning and Management" as it includes a number of elements involved in the management of a joint entity, including the financial management of Sales and Trading, Tax and Procurement as well as the implementation of new technology and the long-term issue of Strategic Planning. The second factor can be labelled "Financing issues", as it covers the raising of investment finance and the ongoing interactions with investors, both of which are linked to the foreign partner's core skill of providing capital to the joint entity. A third factor groups government relations and security and can therefore be described as "Issues involving Local Knowledge", and it encapsulates the core strength and contribution of the domestic partner, and therefore any increase in the foreign partners' control of this factor would indicate a change in the bargaining strength between the partners.

Combining the answers for initial foreign partner control and change in foreign partner control can then create a final control measure for each area. We have done this by adjusting the initial control scores (in Question 8) according to the response to the change in control question (Question 9) in the following way. If a respondent replied that the change in control had been a large decrease (a score of 1 in my initial methodology) I have adjusted it to –2. Correspondingly a score of 2 (small decrease in control) has been adjusted to –1, 3 (no change) to 0, 4 (small increase in control) to +1 and 5 (large increase in control) to +2. I have then added these scores to the original initial control scores to give a final control score. For example, if a respondent answered that their initial control of tax had been 3, but that its control had decreased slightly (a score of 2 in my 1–5 range) then the final control would have been calculated as 2 (3 + –1). This methodology has led to the range of scores for final control being broader than the range for initial control, as the minimum score for final control is now –1 (initial control scored at 1 followed by a large decrease in control scoring a further –2) and the maximum is 7 (an initial score of 5 combined with a large increase in control scoring a further +2). However, this does not cause a problem for our analysis as the statistical tests we ran allowed for this difference.[29] The results for final control compared to initial control are shown in Figure 4.5 below, which confirms that there appears to have been little change in control across the business areas. Indeed a statistical analysis underlined the lack of change in most areas, as there are only two in which a significant difference between the initial and final scores has been registered – strategic planning and operational management. In both cases, however, although the foreign partner's final control is higher than his initial control the result shows only a medium significance score,[30] while in all other areas there is no significant difference between the initial and final scores.

This is an interesting result, because there is clearly less room for increase in control in areas where initial control is already high. Strategic planning and operational management ranked 4th and 5th out of 13 areas for initial control, with scores well above the average level, and so one might have expected these areas to show low and insignificant levels of change in control. That this did not occur points to a potential conclusion that where the foreign partner contributed management expertise and had a high level of initial management control he managed to increase it over time. In contrast in other areas, including all the areas where the domestic partners had made high contributions and had a higher level of initial control, the foreign partner made no

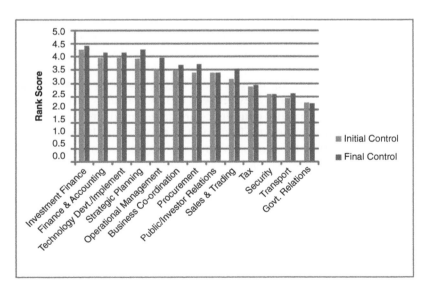

Figure 4.5   Final foreign partner control compared to initial control

significant progress in gaining extra control. In particular, foreign partners gained no effective extra control in three key areas where formal and informal knowledge of domestic issues are important, namely government relations, security and tax.

An analysis of foreign partner confidence

However, while it would appear that foreign partners achieved no practical change in their ability to influence issues and business areas that were initially controlled by their domestic partner, they may nevertheless have felt that their experience and learning in a joint entity improved their future ability to operate in the Russian business environment. In order to test this possibility survey respondents were asked about their level of confidence now (or at the conclusion of their joint entity) with regard to operating in various functions without a domestic partner. A high level of confidence would indicate either that a foreign partner had maintained or enhanced its ability to function in an area or that the business environment in which it was operating had become less difficult. A low level of confidence would imply either that the business environment in certain areas had deteriorated or that the ability of the foreign partner to function in that area had declined. The discussion of corruption and state influence in Box 4.1 suggests, however, that foreign partners' perceptions of the external environment remained very similar across the life of the joint entities under discussion, implying that any change in confidence would largely have been the result of their internal experiences within their joint entity. As a result, the conclusions drawn from the analysis of confidence scores can be interpreted as referring to changes (or lack of them) in foreign partner ability rather than being the result of significant external forces.

It is therefore interesting to note from Figure 4.8 below that the split of foreign partner confidence scores between business areas is very marked. The areas of least foreign partner confidence are government relations, transport and security, with sales and trading and tax also scoring below the median rating of 3. Conversely the areas of highest confidence are investment finance, finance and accounting, technology and strategic planning. In terms of the spread of results, no respondents scored their confidence in government relations, procurement or transport with the highest rating of 5, while only 3% rated their confidence to run security in the highest bracket. Conversely 55% rated their confidence in running investment finance a 5, while at least 65% of respondents placed finance and accounting, technology and strategic planning in the 4–5 range.

A subsequent factor analysis highlights the split of the confidence scores into various themes, as it allowed two factors to be extracted at acceptable

Box 4.1   The External Environment – Corruption and State Influence

In order to test the possible impact of the external environment respondents were asked for their opinion on the levels of state and administrative corruption* at the beginning and end of their involvement in their joint entity. As can be seen from Figure 4.6 below, the levels of corruption in both areas were regarded as relatively high (approximately 3.8 out of 5 for state corruption and 3.9 for administrative corruption), but hardly changed over the period in question.

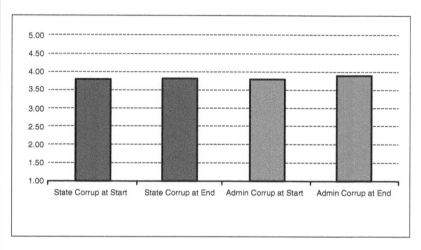

Figure 4.6   Results for perceptions of state and administrative corruption

Respondents were also asked for their opinions of state influence on their joint entity in the areas of governance, administrative issues, commercial issues and technical/operational issues. While the levels of influence in the four areas were very different, the key finding was that again they did not change significantly over the life of the respective joint entities. Figure 4.7 below shows that, while state influence on governance issues such as equity ownership and management control was much lower than influence on administrative issues such as taxation and pipeline access, both stayed relatively constant in the perceptions of the foreign partners.

Indeed statistical analysis of the difference between the corruption scores and the state influence scores at the beginning and end of the joint entities confirms that in both cases the change was not significant. As in other tests described earlier, a Wilcoxson Signed Rank test was run and all the r scores were below 0.3 (indicating a small effect using Cohen's criteria), with the significance levels being >0.1.

Box 4.1   The External Environment – Corruption and State Influence
– continued

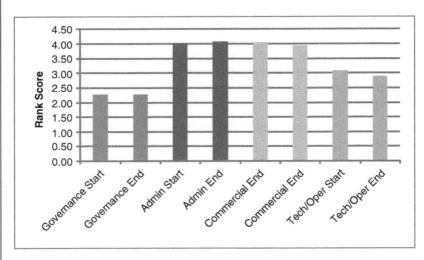

Figure 4.7   Results for perceptions of state influence

Conclusions on External Environment
The results of the survey indicate that the foreign respondents' perceptions of corruption and state influence did not change over the period of their involvement in various joint entities in Russia. Given the relatively high levels of corruption identified in the responses, this could be interpreted as a somewhat depressing commentary on Russia's progress during the initial transition period from 1991–2003. However, in terms of its relevance to this analysis it demonstrates that changes in the external environment are unlikely to have played a significant role in affecting partner relations in the joint entities being studied. The external environment may have been poor but it did not change, and so any differences in a foreign partner's position in a joint entity or confidence in certain business areas must have been caused by changes to the internal environment of the joint entity.

State corruption is defined as the provision of unofficial payments, gifts or private benefits to public officials to gain advantages in the drafting of laws, decrees or regulations and other binding government decisions that have a direct impact on the provider's business (The World Bank gives the example of a powerful oil company bribing legislators to vote for or against PSA legislation). Administrative corruption is defined as the provision of benefits to influence the implementation of the established rules (The World Bank gives the example of a shopkeeper bribing an official to overlook minor infractions of existing regulations or to avoid extra unauthorized checks on his business)

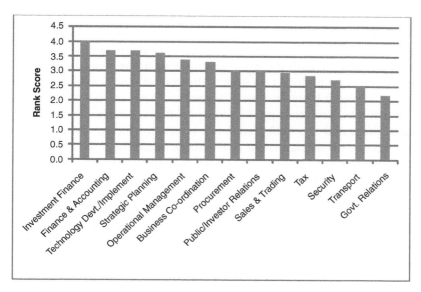

Figure 4.8   Results for question on foreign partner confidence

levels of significance and accuracy.[31] The first grouped the traditional foreign partner strengths in areas such as management, finance and technology, where the foreigners had made the highest initial contributions to the JV and clearly still felt confident about their ability in these areas at the conclusion of their partnership. The second, by contrast, grouped themes where local knowledge would have been needed to facilitate operational processes such as procurement, transport and sales and trading as well more general issues such as government relations, and could therefore be defined as an assessment of confidence in "local knowledge issues" where the domestic partner made the greatest initial contribution. As a result, although the factors do not demonstrate in themselves high or low levels of foreign partner confidence, they would appear to capture different ends of the scale of foreign partner capabilities at the start of his involvement in a joint entity in Russia. Factor 1 would appear to cover confidence in issues where the foreign partner felt he was making a contribution at the start, while factor 2 would appear to cover many of the more domestic issues where the domestic partner was generally seen to make a greater contribution at the start.

As a result, it is relevant to investigate the relationship between foreign partner confidence and the initial contributions of both partners to the joint entity, and the statistics interestingly reveal the lack of variation between the confidence results and the initial foreign partner control results, but a significant variation between the confidence and domestic partner contribution results. Figure 4.9 below shows a pictorial comparison of the initial foreign partner control scores and the foreign partner confidence scores. As can be clearly seen, both the scores and ordering are very similar. The top four and bottom three positions are exactly the same and no area is more than one position different between initial control and final confidence. A statistical comparison between the specific results for initial foreign partner control in various areas and the final confidence results for foreign partners in those same areas shows no significant difference between the results, leading to the conclusion that foreign partner confidence neither increased in areas where it had low initial control nor decreased where it had high initial control. While the latter result might be expected, it is interesting that foreign partner confidence was low in areas where domestic partners had more initial influence (in particular government relations, security and other local issues). One clear interpretation of this would be to imply that there was little transfer of knowledge in these areas to allow foreign partner confidence to increase.

This conclusion is supported by Figure 4.10, which shows the significant variation in the results for domestic partner contribution and final foreign partner confidence in areas related to local knowledge. I have compared the domestic partner contributions of informal domestic knowledge, formal domestic knowledge and domestic market access with final foreign partner confidence in the related areas of government relations, security, tax, trans-

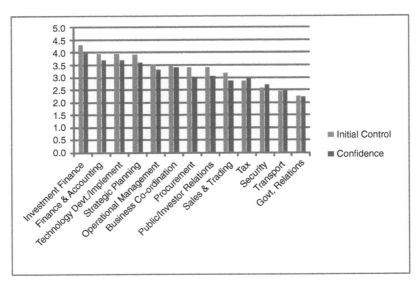

Figure 4.9   Initial foreign partner control compared to final foreign partner confidence

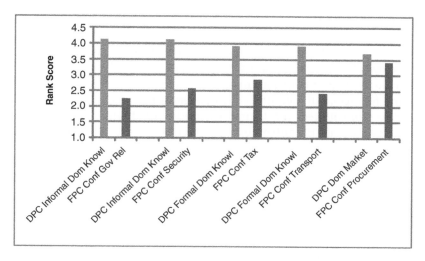

Figure 4.10 Comparison of high domestic partner contributions and foreign partner confidence

port and procurement. In all cases the scores for final foreign partner confidence are significantly lower than the scores for domestic partner contribution,[32] implying that the foreign partners remained reliant on their domestic partners at the end of their partnerships and that little significant knowledge had been transferred.

In conclusion, foreign partners seem to be most confident in running investment finance, finance and accounting, strategic planning and technology, but have least confidence in the areas of government relations, security, transport and tax. Furthermore, there appears to be no significant difference between the scores for initial foreign partner control and final foreign partner confidence, and as a result foreign partners do not appear to have become significantly more confident in areas where they had low initial control. In addition, there is a significant variation in the scores for domestic partner contribution of local knowledge and final partner confidence in areas where local knowledge is required, with the confidence scores all being low, implying that little transfer of knowledge from domestic to foreign partners took place in these areas.

Overall conclusions on learning and change in control

From the analysis outlined above it would therefore seem reasonable to draw a number of key conclusions. Firstly, domestic partners do appear to have been able to learn from their foreign partners to a reasonably high level across a broad range of topics from management expertise to technical skills. In contrast, a more practical analysis of levels of control over and confidence in certain business areas suggests that foreign partners made less progress in acquiring new skills. An analysis of the levels of initial control of the joint entities reveals that foreign partners tended to have high control where they had made the largest contribution (mainly in areas of management, technology and finance), but had little control over areas where their domestic partners had contributed most (mainly areas involving the use of local knowledge). While this outcome might have been expected, it is particularly noteworthy that the analysis of change in control over the life of the joint entities reveals very little movement. Essentially there was no significant change in foreign partner control in any business area, and while this might have been expected in areas where the foreign partners were already strong, it is surprising that none occurred where control had previously been low. As a result, the scores for final control show no significant change from those for initial control, showing that foreign partners made no practical gains with regard to using newly acquired skills.

Furthermore, the results for foreign partner confidence following their involvement in the joint entities also suggest that little knowledge acquisition took place. Foreign partner confidence remains high in areas where initial contributions were made and initial control was taken, but is low in areas where the domestic partners made the highest contributions. As the external domestic environment in terms of corruption and state influence was shown to have been stable and therefore not a great influence, it can perhaps therefore be concluded that the lack of any increased control or confidence in areas requiring local knowledge was the result of internal factors at the joint entities and a lack of skill acquisition by the foreign partners.

One final conclusion on learning as a key element in establishing bargaining power within partnerships might also be gleaned from a subjective analysis of another question from the survey that we have not yet discussed, which concerned partner disputes. Respondents were asked to identify any areas or issues that had brought them into conflict with their domestic partner, and the most frequent response was that disputes had occurred over management issues such as allocation of roles, use of management techniques and control over various functions. Given that management was one of the areas in which domestic partner learning did occur, and also given that control over sensitive business functions, government relations and security allowed domestic partners to maintain their local knowledge and prevent foreign partner learning, it is perhaps possible to interpret the conflict over management control as evidence that the partners were indeed in some form of competitive race to learn. Further, the initial conclusions from the survey would suggest that it was a race that the domestic partners were rather adept at working to their own advantage.

Foreign partner success and its key catalysts

Ranking foreign and domestic partner success

The overall goal of the survey was to establish if foreign partner success in a weak state environment such as Russia could be influenced by partner learning in a joint entity between foreign and domestic partners. As such a key question for the respondents was to rank the level of success that they felt they had achieved as a result of their involvement in their joint entity. They were asked to rank their level of success on a scale of 1–5 in four areas – financial, asset acquisition, production and overall – with 1 being low success and 5 high success. The results are shown in Figure 4.11 below, which shows that on average foreign partners achieved a fair degree of success across all areas.

While it is possible to debate the difference between the scores for the various measures, and to perhaps ask why overall success is ranked below the other three more specific measures, in fact the variances are not statistically significant.[33] As a result, we have created a simple average of the four scores for use in our analysis, as this ranking would seem to represent a reasonable measure of foreign partners' perceptions of their overall success.

Figure 4.11 also shows the score for domestic partner success, as perceived by the foreign partner in the joint entity. The foreign partners in each case were asked to assess how well their domestic partners had done in achieving their objectives for the joint entity, again on a scale of 1–5 with 1 being very few achieved and 5 implying all achieved. The result, at just over 3, again

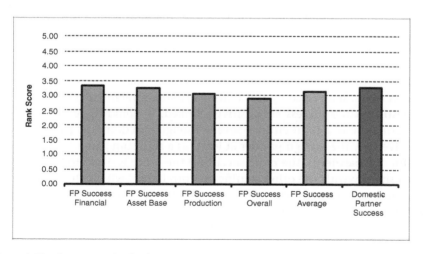

Figure 4.11   Survey results for foreign partner success

indicates a moderate level of success and one that is not significantly distinguishable from average foreign partner success.[34]

The catalysts of foreign partner success

The scores for foreign partner success can then be compared with the other variables established from the results of the survey in order to identify potential catalysts of foreign partner success. Box 4.2 summarizes the new variables that were identified as factors in the Principal Components Analysis carried out earlier in this chapter, and these new variables were included in the following correlation analysis with all the other individual variables that could not be summarized into smaller sub-sets.

In the analysis we have attempted to correlate[35] all the factors generated above with each other and with the various measures of foreign partner success (including the average), domestic partner success, foreign partner perceptions of corruption and foreign partner perceptions of state influence. Given that the aim of the research is to establish how a foreign partner can be successful in a joint entity in Russia, we have largely focused on the significant correlations with the success variables.

The first conclusion from the correlation analysis is that there is one outstanding result with regards to foreign partner success. This is that average foreign partner success is significantly and positively correlated to the factor of "Change in Foreign Partner Control over Issues Involving Local Knowledge".[36] Although it is not possible to conclude a directional causal link between the two variables, it is nevertheless possible to say that there is a clear link between a foreign partner's ability to increase his influence over issues involving local knowledge and his success. Further, given that local knowledge has been established as a key domestic partner contribution and a foreign partner weakness at the start of any joint entity, it is also possible to say that foreign partner success in the joint entity is linked to a change in the balance of influence over issues involving local knowledge.

There are only two other significant correlations with foreign partner success that are revealed by the analysis. Firstly, foreign partner success and domestic partner success are positively linked. It would therefore seem that the formation of a joint entity between foreign and domestic partners is not perceived (by the foreign partner at least) as a zero-sum game. The more successful one partner is, the more successful the other is likely to be. This contrasts sharply with the other significant correlation, which shows that State Influence over Governance Issues is significantly and negatively correlated with foreign partner success. There is therefore a clear negative link between state interference in the establishment of management structures, procedures and incentives at a joint entity and the success of the foreign partner. Table A2.1 in Appendix 2 shows all the significant correlations with average foreign partner success in detail.

Box 4.2   Summary of Factors extracted during Principal Components Analysis

The table below summarizes the factors extracted via principal components analysis on the responses to all of the closed questions analysed in this chapter. As can be seen from the table, the responses to a number of the questions (on foreign and domestic partner success, corruption and state influence) were too closely correlated to allow adequate factor extraction, and in these cases appropriate simple averages have been used to summarize the data where relevant. Variables that were excluded from the factor extraction analysis, where it took place, have been included separately in the correlation analysis alongside the factors themselves.

Theme	Factors
FP Contribution	1. Management, Capital and Technology 2. Knowledge of International Markets
DP Contribution	1. Local Knowledge and Markets 2. Management and Pipeline Access 3. Domestic Assets
FP Initial Control	1. Business Management 2. Local Business Issues 3. Long-term Development
Change in FP Control	1. Business Planning and Management 2. Financing Issues 3. Issues involving Local Knowledge
FP Confidence	1. Foreign Partner Strengths 2. Local Operational Issues
FP Success	Results too highly correlated to justify factor analysis. Further tests suggest averaging of scores for Production, Financial and Asset Success is justified.
DP Learning	Results too highly correlated for factor analysis. Averaging of all scores justified by further tests.
Corruption	Results too highly correlated for factor analysis. Averaging of all scores justified by further tests.
State Influence	Factor analysis not justified, but further tests suggest four separate averages for influence over governance, administrative issues, commercial issues and technology issues.

One further correlation between change in foreign partner control of issues involving local knowledge is also of potential interest, as it is significantly and positively correlated with foreign partner confidence,[37] suggesting that increased influence and participation in local issues has a significant link to how positive a foreign partner feels about his investment in Russia and his ability to deal with issues on his own. Interestingly the confidence question relates to how confident a foreign partner feels dealing with various issues at the end of his involvement in the joint entity in question, while the change in control over local issues occurs during the course of the life of the entity, so although it is not justified to draw a direct causal link from the correlation analysis itself, it seems fairly clear that a change in foreign partner control over local issues is associated with higher foreign partner confidence, as well as a higher foreign partner perception of his own success.

Towards a regression analysis – Identifying other possible influences on success

Having established that there is a link between three key variables and foreign partner success, the next logical step is to try and establish a causal relationship between the dependent and independent variables using regression analysis. However, before attempting this analysis it is also important to establish if there are any other identifiable elements that may also have an impact on foreign partner success and which should be used as control variables in the regression analysis. For example, the academic literature discussed in Chapter 2 has raised the possibility that a domestic partner with links to a Business Group may be detrimental to foreign partner success because of the heavy reliance of many entrepreneurs forming business groups on local knowledge and their use of this skill as a competitive weapon. This would suggest "domestic partner link with a business group" (or not) as one potential dummy variable in a regression analysis, and other possible variables include the size of the foreign or domestic partner (large or small), the type of domestic investor (oil-based or not), and whether the joint entity ultimately succeeded in producing oil or not. One final variable suggested both by the literature review and by the case studies is the type of investment model used in forming the joint entity, with the contrast between a classic JV model (for example in the first and second case studies) and a corporate model, such as that identified in the third case study. Use of a corporate model (or not) would then appear to be a final important variable to be analysed. A summary of the number of survey respondents that belong to each of the groups defined above can be seen in Figure 4.12.

In order to establish a preliminary assessment of the potential impact of these categories we ran a series of statistical tests[38] looking for differences between two independent samples (e.g. small or large foreign partners).[39] However, the overall conclusion from the tests was that the only significant difference between the joint entities in relation to foreign partner success was caused by the investment model used. As shown in Figure 4.12, 24 of the joint entities that were represented in the survey were identified as classic JVs, with

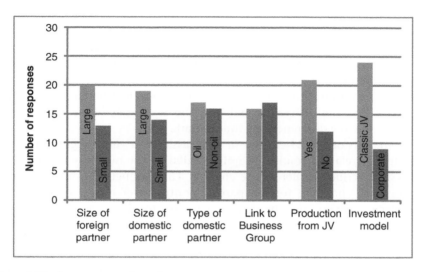

Figure 4.12 Survey respondents by category

nine as corporate vehicles, and when the statistical tests were run the results suggested the corporate vehicles generated significantly more success for foreign partners than the classic JV model.[40]

Indeed this conclusion would seem to fit well with the case studies in Chapter 3, where a number of the survey participants identified problems with the classic Joint Venture model, in as much as it is focused on one asset and provides little incentive for sharing of skill-sets, in particular from the domestic investor's point of view, as it generally makes up only a small part of his overall portfolio. An alternative corporate model was suggested, especially by the foreign partners in the third case study, whereby the foreign and domestic partners become shareholders in an entity that itself can then own a broader portfolio of assets and where the incentives of both partners are more equally aligned. This is seen as a model that creates less competition between the partners and encourages both to act in the best interests of the joint entity. As a result, although it is not possible to draw specific conclusions on any causal links between FP success and investment model at this stage, the test nevertheless suggests that impact of the Investment Model could be a significant factor and should be considered further in our analysis.

How does the concept of local knowledge fit with our conclusions on business models?

We described earlier how the overall correlation analysis demonstrates that foreign partner success is linked positively to change in foreign partner control over local issues and domestic partner success and negatively to state influence over governance issues, but it now also appears that success is also significantly differentiated by the type of corporate structure involved in the joint entities under analysis. As demonstrated above, joint entities using a corporate structure were significantly more successful than joint entities using a classic joint venture structure. As such, an obvious next step in the analysis is to investigate the differences between the two types of structure, and as shown below the differences are indeed stark.

An analysis of the 24 entities in the classic joint venture group indicates that the correlation results are quite similar to the outcome of the overall analysis described earlier in the chapter. The link between foreign partner success and changing foreign partner control over issues involving local knowledge remains positive and is actually stronger than in the original analysis.[41] Foreign and domestic partner success also show an even stronger and more positive link,[42] while foreign partner confidence also remains significantly correlated with control over issues relating to local knowledge, with the strength of the positive link again increasing. The only major change is that the impact of state influence over governance declines and is no longer a significant negative factor on foreign partner success.

In complete contrast, the results for the corporate structure group show a starkly different result, with no correlation at all between foreign partner success and local knowledge issues, domestic partner success, state interference or foreign partner confidence. Indeed there are no significant links between foreign partner success and any of the other variables generated from the survey and used in the overall analysis. As a result it would appear that the only significant driver of foreign partner success when a corporate model is used is the structure itself.

Initial conclusions on the catalysts of foreign partner success

Interpretation of these key differences requires reference to the case studies discussed in the previous chapter. If we can understand the relationship in a classic JV as a competitive situation in which each partner is incentivized to learn the skills of the other as fast as possible in order to improve his own bargaining position, then it is clear that for the foreign partner to be successful he must improve his position with regard to local knowledge, which is his domestic partner's core strength. The statistics suggest that a change in the foreign partner's control over issues involving local knowledge is the one strong and positive link with his own success, and as local knowledge is the domestic partner's core strength then it would seem that there is a link between an improved foreign partner bargaining position and foreign partner success. In addition, it also seems that the foreign partner is more confident of his ability to operate in the domestic environment the more he is involved in local knowledge issues, and although this is not correlated with success it may help to explain a foreign partner's more positive attitude towards the outcome of his involvement in a joint entity.

Conversely, it appears that when a corporate structure is used, that fact alone is enough to increase the foreign partner's success, as there is no other correlation between success and any of the other variables in this case. This would appear to coincide with the views expressed in the case studies, which explained the benefits of the corporate model as reducing competition between the partners and encouraging each to contribute their core skills in a win-win situation.

Therefore, although the correlation analysis does not allow us to make definitive causal conclusions about what leads to foreign partner success, there would appear to be two tentative links that can be established. In the case of a classic JV structure, foreign partner success is linked to greater foreign partner influence on issues involving local knowledge over time, implying a weakening of the domestic partner's core bargaining strength. Alternatively, when a corporate structure is formed no such link exists, and yet these corporate entities appear to be significantly more successful than the classic joint ventures. From the case studies we can conclude that this is because the corporate structure incentivizes both partners to use their skills for the benefit of all shareholders in the joint entity rather than competing to get the best individual result out of the joint venture.

Finding a causal link using regression analysis

In order to attempt to establish some causal explanation of foreign partner success in joint entities in Russia it is necessary to run multiple regression analysis using the variables identified in the correlation analysis above. As with the correlations, our initial analysis examined the overall results for all of the joint entities included in the survey, with a subsequent analysis examining the results split by the type of entity structure used – classic joint venture or corporate model. Even before we begin, though, we must first acknowledge that the data we have gathered is not ideal for a standard regression analysis, and as a result we have used three forms of regression analysis in an attempt to provide a secure foundation for our conclusions.[43] Nevertheless, we must stress that although we believe that our analysis is robust, the context for this latter part of our statistical analysis is that it should provide more evidence to support the ideas generated from the literature review and the case studies rather than being seen as definitive proof in itself.

Having made this caveat, we have structured our regression analysis to test which variables can be identified as significant contributors to foreign partner success in partnerships in Russia. Therefore we have chosen Average Foreign Partner Success as the dependent variable in our model and have used the three variables revealed by our correlation analysis – the Factor "Change in Foreign Partner Control – Local Knowledge", Domestic Partner Success and State Influence over Governance Issues – as our potential predictors. We have also included two dummy variables, namely domestic partner link to a Business Group, as this was suggested as having a potential impact by the literature review, and Investment Model, as the Foreign Partner Success outcome was shown to be significantly different for the classic JV and corporate models. The step-wise method of regression was used to ensure that predictor variables were only added if they would make a significant contribution to the analysis.[44] On this basis the dummy variable of domestic partner link to a Business Group was excluded from further analysis because it showed insufficient correlation to foreign partner success, thus confirming the findings of the Mann Whitney analysis above.

The full results of the model are shown in the Statistical Appendix (in Table A2.2), but the overall conclusion is that when all 33 survey responses are analysed the three key variables make significant contributions to the regression, with Change in Foreign Partner Control of Local Knowledge Issues and Domestic Partner Success having a positive impact on Foreign Partner Success and State Influence on Governance having a negative impact. However, when the dummy variable JV Investment Model is added to the fourth regression model it does not make a significant contribution, suggesting that it should be ignored when trying to explain foreign partner success in an overall analysis of all 33 joint entities in the survey. Nevertheless, the model does confirm that the Investment Model can make a significant contribution on its own (just not in combination with the other variables) and we shall therefore return to this theme later in the analysis.[45]

In terms of explaining foreign partner success the overall model shows that the most important predictor is "Change in Foreign Partner Control – Local Knowledge" which accounts for 34% of the variance in foreign partner success (see results for Model 1 in Table A2.3 in Appendix 2), while the addition of domestic partner success as a predictor then increases the predictive capability to 47.3%. Finally the inclusion of State Influence over Governance Issues increased the overall explanatory power of the analysis to 60.7% of the variance in foreign partner success.[46] However when the dummy variable of Investment Model is included the predictive power reduces to 59.3% and the change in the model is not significant,[47] reinforcing the conclusion that the variable Investment Model does not add to the predictive power of the other three variables in an analysis of all the joint entities.

If we focus on the regression model that includes only the three relevant predictors we can actually produce a mathematical formula to explain at least some part of the catalysts for foreign partner success. Having established the reliability of the model with a number of tests,[48] we can use the results of the regression analysis (to be found in Model 3 in Table A2.2 of Appendix 2) to show that Foreign Partner Success = 2.926 (a constant) + (0.460 x "Change in Foreign Partner Control – Local Knowledge") + (0.319 x "Domestic Partner Success") – (0.314 x "State Influence over Governance Issues"). Furthermore, we can also conclude[49] that for every 1 standard deviation increase in the Local Knowledge score, Foreign Partner Success increases by 0.5 standard deviations. Given that the standard deviations for Local Knowledge and Foreign Partner Success are 1.02 and 0.94 respectively, we can conclude that each 1.02 increase in the score for Local Knowledge leads to a 0.47 increase in Foreign Partner Success, on a scale of 1 to 5. In other words, for every 25% increase in foreign partner control over local knowledge issues gained during the life of a joint entity, there is a 12% increase in the success of the foreign partner.

Domestic partner success has a slightly lower impact, with a 1 standard deviation change leading to a 0.41 standard deviation change in foreign partner success, while a similar increase in State Influence on Governance causes foreign partner success to decline by 0.39 standard deviations. Given the standard deviation of domestic partner success of 1.21 and for State Influence on Governance Issues of 1.16, on a scale of 1–5 we can further conclude that each 1.21 increase in Domestic Partner Success leads to a 0.38 increase in foreign partner success, and each 1.16 increase in State Influence on Governance Issues leads to a 0.37 decrease in the score for foreign partner success.

Conclusions from initial multiple regression analysis

However, while it is interesting to be able to generate specific numerical formulae to explain foreign partner success, the core finding is to establish that three key variables can be used to create a significant explanatory model. The variables "Change in Foreign Partner Control of Local Knowledge Issues", "Domestic Partner Success" and "State Influence on Governance Issues" all contribute to a significant regression model, through which it is possible to explain 61% of the variance in foreign partner success as a combination of the three. The highest contribution comes from the first predictor (Change in Foreign Partner Control of Local Knowledge Issues), indicating that as a foreign partner improves his position in the area of greatest domestic partner strength he improves his chances of success. However, he clearly cannot ignore the success of his domestic partner, possibly because a more successful domestic partner will be less likely to try and undermine any joint entity. Finally the foreign partner must also try to avoid interference from the state in the structuring and management organization of any joint entity, as this would seem to undermine the chance of success.

The other key findings from the regression model were to confirm that exposure to a domestic partner who is part of a Business Group is not a significant cause of success or failure for a foreign partner, and also that the use of different investment models is not significant when combined with the other predictors. Nevertheless, the use of a corporate model would seem to be a significant predictor in its own right, and therefore once again we can usefully attempt an analysis of the different types of partnership structure to see whether more detailed results can be derived.

Regression analysis to explain success under different business models

Firstly we simply conducted a multiple regression analysis using all 33 responses, using foreign partner success as the independent variable and JV Investment Model as the dependent variable (the predictor), and this demonstrated that even in an overall analysis the use of corporate structure alone does make a significant contribution to foreign partner success (see Table A2.4 in Appendix 2). A number of other "dummy" variables were also included, to ensure that the analysis was not biased, but none of them had any significant effect.[50] In numerical terms the regression analysis showed that use of the corporate model accounted for 10.5% of foreign partner success, and when this result is combined with the split file correlation analysis completed earlier, which showed that joint entities using a corporate model had no other links to foreign partner success, it can be concluded that the use of this model has some significant and unique explanatory power.[51]

We then split the responses from the joint entities into those using the corporate model and those using the classic JV model, and ran a multiple regression analysis on each. Once again, average foreign partner success was the independent variable, while the dependent variables (predictors) were the three variables that contributed to the overall regression analysis above plus the dummy variables of foreign and domestic partner size, link to a Business Group, type of domestic investor and production. As expected, the joint entities using the corporate model produced no significant regression model related to foreign partner success because there were no other variables that were correlated with success under this model. This confirmed the conclusion that use of the corporate model alone is one unique explanation of foreign partner success.

In contrast, when the joint entities using the classic JV were analysed it became clear that their success is significantly linked to Change in Foreign Partner Control over Local Knowledge and with Domestic Partner Success, but is no longer significantly linked with State Influence over Governance Issues and was also not related to any of the dummy variables.

In a similar conclusion to the correlation analysis that we carried out earlier, it appears that the results for the classic JV emphasize to an even greater degree the importance of local knowledge to foreign partner success. This can be seen in the results of a new statistical model that can be derived from the regression analysis. In our earlier model, change in local knowledge accounted for 34% of the variance in Foreign Partner Success, but in this new more focused analysis it accounts for 46%, while the inclusion of Domestic Partner Success as a variable increases the predictive ability of the model to 58%, compared to 47% before (see Table A2.5 in Appendix 2). Using the statistical results we can confirm not only that the results are significant and relevant,[52] but also explain the contribution of each predictor to the final regression model. In the final analysis, which includes both predictors, "Change in Foreign Partner Control – Local Knowledge" makes the largest contribution, but overall the model can be summarized as follows: Foreign Partner Success = 2.104 (a constant) + (0.627 x "Change in Foreign Partner Control over Local Knowledge Issues") + (0.312 x "Domestic Partner Success").[53] In a more general interpretation a 1 standard deviation in CPFC Local Knowledge leads to a 0.697 change in Foreign Partner success, or a 0.65 increase on the 1 to 5 scale for FP success, while a 1 standard deviation change in Domestic Partner Success leads to a 0.363 change in Foreign Partner Success, implying a 0.34 increase on a 1–5 scale. We can therefore conclude that a 25% change in FP control over local knowledge issues leads to a 16% increase in FP success while a 25% change in Domestic Partner Success leads to a 9% increase in Foreign Partner Success in joint entities using the classic JV model.

Conclusions from multiple regression analysis

Initial multiple regression analysis covering all 33 responses from joint entities revealed that three variables made a significant contribution to Foreign Partner Success, namely Change in Foreign Partner Control of Local Knowledge Issues, Domestic Partner Success and State Influence over Governance Issues, which together were shown to account for 61% of the variance in Foreign Partner Success. However, a further conclusion was that although the dummy variable concerning choice of Investment Model did not make a significant contribution to the regression model, its correlation with Foreign Partner Success merited further investigation.

A second regression analysis using this Investment Model variable revealed that it could, on its own, account for 10.5% of the variance in Foreign Partner Success across all 33 joint entities, but given the lack of correlation to other variables the next obvious step was to split the joint entities by Investment Model and re-run the regression analysis. The inability to create a regression model for those joint entities using the corporate model under this split file scenario confirmed again the unique contribution of this Investment Model to Foreign Partner Success.

For the joint entities using the classic JV Model, further analysis was carried out using the three variables that were correlated with foreign partner success in the overall analysis as well as a number of dummy variables. However, although the results showed that only two make a significant contribution to a regression model using foreign partner success as the independent variable, it is nevertheless clear that "Change in Foreign Partner Control – Local Knowledge" and "Domestic Partner Success" can explain 58% of the variance in foreign partner success. The highest contribution comes from the first predictor, further confirming that when a classic JV is used and a foreign partner improves his position in the area of greatest domestic partner strength he improves his chances of success. However, the model again confirms that he cannot ignore the success of his domestic partner, as to do so would likely create competition between the partners which has been shown by a number of the case studies discussed in Chapter 3 to be the main cause of disruption in joint entities in Russia.

Alternative regression analysis to confirm the results

As we mentioned when starting the regression analysis, one criticism of the type of model we used[54] is that our data is not necessarily well suited to it.[55] As a result, although the results of the analysis we have shown so far are interesting they really need to be confirmed using alternative regression models. Therefore we have also run our analysis through two other forms of model, a logistic regression model and a truncated regression model, in order to provide a firmer foundation for our conclusions. If the details of this secondary analysis are of no interest then we would advise the reader to skip this section and move on to the conclusions of this chapter, where we confirm that the two new models do confirm our initial thoughts.

In brief, then, logistic regression is useful because it allows us to answer one criticism of our original regression model, namely that it defines success using an arbitrary scale when in fact a better definition would be dichotomous, in other words the outcome is either success or failure. However, if success is a dichotomous outcome then the direct application of a standard linear regression model is not appropriate[56] as the relationship between the outcome and predictor variables is not linear. As a result logistic regression can be used as an alternative as it expresses the regression equation in terms of logistic function or probability. In this way it can overcome the problem of the variables violating the assumption of linearity in a traditional OLS regression model.

In simple terms, we have essentially defined each of the joint entities in our survey as being either a success or a failure, rather than grading them on a scale of 1 to 5, with reference both to foreign partner success and domestic partner success. We have then compared this success or failure with the three variables used in the previous analysis to understand how the probability of foreign partner success increases with the inclusion of the other variables.[57] The model showed that without the predictor variables the probability of success was 74% but that this increased to 91% when the predictor variables were included, and various subsequent statistical tests showed that this was a significant change in the results and that all the predictor variables made a significant contribution to the new model.[58] As a result, the logistic regression model would appear to confirm the importance of the predictor variables identified in our initial standard regression. We can therefore conclude that Change of Foreign Partner Control over Local Knowledge Issues and Domestic Partner Success are significant predictors of Foreign Partner Success, confirming the conclusions reached in the earlier regression analysis.

A truncated regression model was then also used to help confirm our results, as it further addresses the somewhat arbitrary nature of the 1–5 scoring method we used in our survey by acknowledging the artificial cut-offs that we imposed on the respondents.[59] We therefore created a truncated regression model[60] to check the significance of the relationship between foreign partner success and the variables Domestic Partner Success and Change in Foreign Control over Local Knowledge. The lower limit of the model was placed at 1, in line with the lowest score on the Survey, with the upper limit at 5, and 23 of the 24 classic joint ventures were included in the analysis. The results once again confirmed a statistically significant relationship between the variables,[61] with a 1% change in domestic partner success and "change in foreign partner control over local knowledge issues" leading 0.43% and 0.33% changes in the predicted foreign partner success, respectively. Therefore we can again conclude that the two predictor variables do have a significant effect on foreign partner success, confirming the results generated from the initial standard and logistic regression models.

Overall conclusions on the joint venture survey results

The case studies described in Chapter 3 suggested that a foreign partner's success in any joint entity in the Russian oil industry was closely tied to his ability to increase his local knowledge or create a governance structure for the joint entity that minimized the potential to use local knowledge against him. The survey of joint entity participants analysed in this chapter supports these findings, identifying "Change in Foreign Partner Control over Local Knowledge Issues" as a key driver of foreign partner success in a classic JV structure and also showing that use of a corporate model that incentivizes all shareholders to act for mutual interest can also lead to success for the foreign partner.

The survey established that the foreign and domestic partners tended to be well matched in their goals for the joint entity and the contributions they brought. Foreign partners mainly contributed the management skills, technology and capital sought by their domestic partners, while the domestic partners brought access to assets in Russia as well as vital knowledge of how to operate in the local business environment, including informal knowledge of "how to get things done" as well as formal understanding of operational and legislative processes.

The literature on partner learning in joint ventures suggested that there would be a "race to learn", or as we have now termed it a competition for knowledge, between the partners in order to increase bargaining strength by acquiring the other partner's skills, and the survey confirmed that domestic partners were able to learn from their foreign partners to a reasonably high level across a broad range of topics from management expertise to technical skills. Furthermore, in some areas this does seem to have caused partner conflict (particularly over management issues), suggesting that the process of learning was competitive in nature. However, for foreign partners, a more practical analysis of levels of control over and confidence in certain business areas suggests that they made less progress in acquiring new skills. Indeed the overall conclusion was that they retained control and remained confident to operate only in areas where they made high initial contributions and brought their original skills, and made little or no progress in areas that required the acquisition of domestic partner skills such as local knowledge.

The acquisition of local knowledge was then shown to be linked to foreign partner success, with the two being significantly and positively correlated, while foreign partner confidence was also shown to be significantly correlated to all the variables involving local knowledge. It therefore appears that a foreign partner feels more confident in his ability to execute his core abilities if he is more involved in domestic issues involving local knowledge, and that his involvement in these issues is linked to increased success. However, a series of tests on a number of dichotomous variables suggested that a further variation of the analysis would be to differentiate between joint entities using a classic JV model and a corporate model, as this variable appeared to be linked with foreign partner success on its own.

An analysis split by investment model (classic JV or corporate model) then confirmed that the success and confidence of foreign partners in a classic JV structure are significantly and positively linked to a foreign partner's involvement in local issues. It appears that in a classic JV a change in the foreign partner's control over issues involving local knowledge is the one strong and positive link with his own success, and as local knowledge is the domestic partner's core strength it would seem that there is a link between an improved foreign partner bargaining position and foreign partner success. In addition, it also seems that the foreign partner is more confident of his ability to operate in the domestic environment the more he is involved in local knowledge issues, again suggesting that local knowledge acquisition gives him the ability to operate in an area of domestic partner strength.

In stark contrast the success of foreign partners in joint entities with a corporate structure does not appear to be linked to anything other than the fact that the entity does have a corporate structure. Furthermore the confidence of the foreign partner is linked to his own control over all business issues rather than his initial and increasing influence over local issues. This would appear to coincide with the views expressed in a number of the case studies in Chapter 3, which explained the benefits of the corporate model as reducing competition between the partners and encouraging each to contribute their core skills in a win-win situation.

Multiple regression analysis then established a causal link between the variables using the different investment models. When a classic JV model is used, only two variables make a significant contribution, with "Change in Foreign Partner Control – Local Knowledge" and "Domestic Partner Success" explaining 58% of the variance in foreign partner success. The highest contribution came from the first predictor, further confirming that when a classic JV is formed a foreign partner improves his chances of success as he improves his position in the area of greatest domestic partner strength.

Meanwhile any attempt at multiple regression for those entities using a corporate model failed due to the lack of variables correlated with success. However, it was shown that use of the corporate model on its own could account for 10.5% of the variance in Foreign Partner Success across all 33 joint entities, while the impossibility of finding further correlations to success under this model suggested that it provides a unique link.

In essence, then, it would seem that foreign partners looking to succeed in an asymmetric business environment such as that seen in Russia in the 1990s and early 2000s did need to consider the importance of local knowledge when forming partnerships with domestic players. Their own skills of management, technology and financing can be relatively easily learned or acquired, and it appears that domestic partners do actively seek to gain these skills. Meanwhile the domestic partners' core skill of how to operate in the local environment (local knowledge) would appear to be more esoteric in nature and therefore more difficult to learn. Nevertheless, the survey has shown that, no matter how difficult the learning process is and despite the concern that no foreigner could ever really compete on local knowledge issues with an influential domestic player, the more that local knowledge is acquired the more successful a foreign partner is likely to be. The outcomes are all relative, of course – local knowledge does not guarantee success. Nevertheless, it would seem that the greater the effort made to acquire it, the more likely it is that a positive outcome will occur. An alternative, or perhaps complimentary, conclusion, is that the creation of a partnership structure that encourages the domestic and foreign partners to share their skills over the long term can also provide a more successful outcome, and over the next two chapters we will expand this theory in discussing the more recent thoughts of foreign players during the 2003–2012 time period, when one of the most obvious examples of this structure, TNK-BP, was in existence.

5
Experiences in the Putin Era

Introduction

In the previous two chapters we examined case studies of joint ventures during the 1990s and then carried out a statistical analysis of the results of a survey of foreign participants in partnerships in Russia in the period 1990–2003. Both elements of the research have revealed that acquisition of knowledge is a competitive process within the relationship between the foreign and domestic partner, and that from a foreign partner perspective the acquisition of local knowledge concerning how to conduct business in Russia is a key driver of his potential success. Both the case studies and the statistics also suggested that the form of the partnership could be a further crucial element, with a corporate structure offering the potential to more closely align the interests of the partners and thus remove some of the competitive pressure between them, leading to greater success.

However, these findings are all based on partnerships formed during the 1990s, when Boris Yeltsin was president and the somewhat anarchic era of the business oligarchs was the dominant feature of the Russian business environment. We have argued in Chapter 2 that, although the outward façade of the Putin era post-2000 is very different, in reality many of the same issues for business in Russia, and especially for foreigners trying to run a business in Russia, remain the same. The political and business environments appear more stable, but the institutions that underpin these environments are in fact very weak and are dominated by key individuals who exert their power by using the front of state institutions to exert their own will. The institutions themselves have little inherent power, and as a result the oligarchic elite evident in the Yeltsin era has been replaced by a new politically connected elite with similar levels of power and influence.

In order to test this theory in practice, and to see if there has been any change in the way that foreign companies perceive the business environment in Russia, we conducted a series of further interviews with senior representatives of foreign oil companies who are currently operating in the country. The spread of interviewees is broad, and although we promised all of them anonymity in order to encourage honest and forthright opinions we can say that they include the regional head of a major international oil company, a vice president from a European national oil company and the country head of a European energy business as well as a number of other senior actors in the international oil and gas community in Moscow. Furthermore, we have extended our research to include actors from the domestic oil industry, again on an anonymous basis, in an attempt to understand the tactics that they might be employing in relation to their foreign partners and also to compare their understanding of the business environment in their own country with the view of foreigners trying to do business there. We conducted all the interviews in a relatively unstructured fashion, introducing the subject as "the reasons behind the success or failure of foreign partnerships in Russia" and then allowing the respondents to give their thoughts with only a small amount of prompting from the questioner. In this way we attempted to avoid any bias in the interview process, although we did try to ensure that opinions on certain topics were given in each interview, in particular on perceptions of the business environment, drivers of foreign partner success and thoughts on domestic partner reactions within the partnership.

In total 12 interviews were conducted, seven with foreign actors and five with Russians, over the course of a month in the autumn of 2012. The responses relate to partnerships that operated during President Putin's first and second terms (2000–2008), during the presidency of Dmitry Medvedev (2008–2012) and now during Putin's third term from 2013. Some of the partnerships also existed during the Yeltsin era prior to 2000, but the questioning has mainly been about operations during the past 12 to 13 years, and any comparisons with the Yeltsin era were only drawn where appropriate. We have decided to group the findings from the interviews by theme rather than to present each interview on a stand-alone basis and then draw conclusions. This was done not only to provide a more coherent structure for the reader but also in an attempt to further ensure the anonymity of the respondents.

The business environment

A number of interconnected themes were identified by the foreign interviewees when asked about the business environment in Russia, with their answers linking both commercial and cultural issues. In general poor protection of property rights and the weak implementation of legal rights were seen as key risks in all the responses, leading to high levels of uncertainty in making business decisions. One particular direct result of this higher risk environment that was noted by many of the interviewees was a perception that domestic partners have adopted a very short-term outlook to investment decision-making, specifically because they understand that if profits are not generated now then the opportunity to do so may be removed tomorrow. It was commented that this outlook contrasted rather sharply with the view of most foreign partners in the Russian oil and gas industry, who tend to take a much longer-term view of an industry with multi-decade investment cycles.

Aggressive opportunism in a high risk environment

More specifically, one of the foreign partners made a comment that the high levels of uncertainty not only created a propensity to focus on near-term cashflow but also created a more opportunistic business environment which tended to make relationships between partners more competitive. In particular he highlighted what he saw as an "Us and Them" mentality, with protection of your own group or company as the first priority in an uncertain environment where most negotiations are seen as a "zero sum game". In this situation the focus is on ensuring that "I win, even if you lose", and when opportunities arise the general attitude is therefore to exploit them as beneficially as possible, irrespective of the potential consequences for others. This attitude was not seen as necessarily specific to relations with foreign partners, but the conclusion was reached that if a foreign partner's position in a joint venture is seen as having weakened then in general the domestic partner would have little hesitation in exploiting that situation. Furthermore, the short-term nature of domestic business focus was seen as leading to a more aggressive approach to exploiting business opportunities, in as much as deals need to be conducted quickly and without compromise, and nothing should stand in the way of a conclusion. This was generally viewed as creating a negotiating environment in which most international businessmen would feel uncomfortable due to lack of familiarity with such assertive and, as one respondent put it, "macho" tactics, giving the domestic partner an immediate bargaining advantage.

When this cultural theme of short-term focus and aggressive negotiating tactics was addressed with the Russian interviewees they generally agreed that this was an accurate interpretation and offered one explanation as domestic partner fear of being viewed as the subservient player in a partnership. Power and control are seen as vital elements in a partnership in Russia, and the domestic partner is concerned to ensure that he retains as much of it as possible. However, in general he fears that the clear advantages brought by foreign partners in the form of technical skills, management experience and often financial firepower might outweigh what he himself has to offer, and therefore he reinforces his own skill-set and bargaining power by aggressively demonstrating the value of his own core skill, local knowledge. Within a weak legal and institutional system, where all the domestic interviewees highlighted that there continues to be "little downside from misbehaving" if you have the right contacts and influence, the local partner has the perfect opportunity to show his worth. Indeed, a more aggressive stance from the domestic partner can underline two points at the same time. Firstly it confirms that the foreign partner needs his domestic partner in order to avoid attacks from third parties that are unlikely to be prevented using traditional legal tactics. And secondly, it makes the more subtle point that the foreign partner also has little chance of legal redress if his domestic partner turns against him, with the implied suggestion that he should therefore not bring about any conflict within the partnership.

Indeed, the potential for a "double-edged sword" in relations with a domestic partner in a weak institutional environment was emphasized by both the foreign and domestic interviewees. On the one hand, as one of the foreign respondents put it, "there are all sorts of risks in Russia, at all levels – federal, regional and local. You need a strong domestic partner to provide protection whether it be from the regional governor, the political centre or the local courts". The domestic partner's skill is to provide this protection by having the contacts and influence to prevent attacks occurring or to fend them off if they do occur. However, on the other hand one of the key skills in carrying out this task is to understand how to "exploit the lacunas in the legislation", as one Russian phrased it, and of course any loopholes can as easily be used against the foreign partner should the right opportunity arise. As a result, the foreign partner "is treading a fine line between wanting as strong a partner as possible to provide maximum access to opportunities and protection from attacks, but then needing to be aware that all this could be turned against him in the event of a partnership dispute".

Complexity and corruption

Having agreed that domestic partners do have a clear skill in their local knowledge and understanding of an "asymmetric" business environment, a number of interviewees then discussed one of the reasons behind this skill-set, namely the complexity of the commercial and legal systems in Russia. It was stated that, while gaining access to the appropriate information is difficult enough, the additional need to then work your way through the numerous interlinked, and sometimes conflicting, regulations allows the domestic partner to emphasize his importance to a joint venture by underlining how difficult and risky it would be for a foreigner to operate alone within such a complex commercial setting. As one domestic partner pointed out, the usefulness of this situation as a source of bargaining power is well understood by officials and domestic businessmen. As he stated "if the complexity of the issues in the legal system, and even the tax system, were really seen as unhelpful to domestic players then they would have been removed a long time ago".

This complexity, when combined with the vast layers of bureaucracy within Russian state organizations and institutions, also highlights another key element of the Russian business environment identified by all the respondents – corruption. Indeed it is on this issue that the continuity between the Yeltsin and Putin eras can be most clearly seen, as all the domestic interviewees as well as those foreigners who had lived in Russia for more than 15 years agreed that little has changed over the entire post-Soviet era. Phrases such as "the situation has not changed much from the 1990s" and "the corruption culture has remained prevalent throughout [my time in Russia]" were commonplace, with one Russian respondent even arguing that "we are returning to the 1990s" when referring to corruption in the legal system, stating bluntly that "the legal system does not work – you can corrupt the judge. As a result many agreements are effectively unenforceable." Given this situation, a number of conclusions were drawn about foreign–domestic partner relations. The first and perhaps most obvious was that a strong domestic partner is needed to try and avoid becoming involved in corruption issues or being overwhelmed by them. A second, and perhaps more subtle, point identified mainly by the Russian respondents was that foreign partners recognized that corruption was inevitable and therefore some wanted a domestic partner in order to "do what was necessary" while pretending that nothing was really going on. As we will discuss later, a number of foreign partners argue that corruption can be avoided using less underhand tactics, but nevertheless it is clear that the pervasion of corruption in Russia has further strengthened the hand of domestic partners. Finally, the multi-layered and multi-faceted elements of influencing decisions in a weak institutional environment also provide domestic partners with huge bargaining strength. While the prevalence of outright corrupt practices such as preferential allocation of contracts, illegal use of corporate wealth and even outright theft of products or cashflows have been acknowledged as general problems at the highest levels in Russia, it is really in the grey areas of influence and persuasion that domestic partners find their greatest bargaining strength. As one Russian respondent explained "we object to corruption as much as any foreigner – it costs us significant amounts of money. We see our skill as providing a 'soft licence to operate' in Russia. Our relationships allow us to both gain access to, and then protect, assets that others might not be offered. If you like, we are lobbying and using our influence on the fringes of legality in an environment in which there really are no rules."

The importance of key individuals

In relation to the concept of influence and lobbying another key element of the Russian business environment that all the interviewees recognized was the importance of key individuals within the vertical power structure created by President Putin. Examples of this power structure were offered across the political spectrum both in Moscow and the regions, with the importance of access to the most powerful people at the top of the vertical structure, whether they be the local mayor, the regional governor or the President of Russia himself, identified as a vital catalyst for business success. The identity of the key individuals for each partnership clearly differs depending upon their regional location and size, but for the larger companies interviewed strong relations with key top-level figures were regarded as essential, with a particular emphasis on Igor Sechin, as many of the foreign companies now operating in Russia have partnerships with Rosneft.

However, ignoring the specific names for a moment, the general sentiment was that certain individuals, rather than institutions, are likely to be vital to the success of any foreign joint venture and that fostering good relations with these people is the most important task for the joint venture partners. As one foreign respondent stated "It's personal", while another emphasized that "it's still all about individuals and the influence that they can exert because the institutions themselves remain inert and drowned in bureaucracy". Furthermore "there is a need to tie yourself to the theoretically strongest person or most influential party and hope that their power base can protect you", because an important individual with significant influence can "be like the remedy against any serious disease – he may not be needed but it's good to have the insurance cover". The Russian interviewees reinforced this view with comments such as "the state has influence over key issues, but in reality it is individuals who are the most important because in most instances the institutions can be manipulated", and of course it is in developing relations with these vital individuals that the domestic partner could demonstrate his value to a partnership and create further bargaining strength. As one foreign partner described, his domestic partner was "constantly developing personal contacts and friendships, and was a vital source of introductions for us", and it is clear that the domestic partners understood how much leverage this provided, with one explaining "we brought the ability to break through bureaucratic barriers and get to the people who mattered".

Change to the status quo unlikely in the short term

One final point of note about the business environment and the relevance of key individuals is that none of the interviewees foresaw any imminent change to the current status quo because it is too advantageous to the current elite. The current complexities in the system "provide the opportunity to facilitate bribes and to help intermediaries to survive" while the prevalence of corruption not only provides "rent" to multiple parties but also provides those in power with a valuable weapon with which to threaten those who might want to challenge them – as one domestic interviewee put it "they have an available accusation against everyone". Meanwhile the key individuals at all layers of the command pyramid are hardly likely to encourage any change in a system that currently provides them with so much power and influence, meaning that "the system is unlikely to change in the foreseeable future. The power of the elite is protected by the status quo."

The competition for knowledge

Chapters 3 and 4 have concluded that many partnerships can be viewed as a competition to learn. In the Russian oil industry over the past 20 years, this competition has involved domestic partners learning the new skills brought by their foreign partners in the form of technology, management and finance, and it has been argued that conversely the foreign partners have been rather less successful in acquiring their domestic partner's core skill, local knowledge. In this next section we therefore review the responses from our interviews that address this topic, to assess whether the trends that we identified in the 1990s and early 2000s are still observable in Russia today. From the previous section it would appear that little has really changed in the business and institutional environment, and so we were keen to understand whether partner relations could also be characterized in a similar fashion.

Differing attitudes to knowledge transfer

In addressing the issues surrounding knowledge transfer in joint ventures in Russia, there was a stark contrast between the apparent attitudes of the foreign and domestic partners, and interestingly the difference was acknowledged by both parties. The foreign partners generally felt that they had shared a significant amount of technical expertise and management experience with their Russian partners, and encouraged an increasing role for domestic employees in areas of the business where these skills could be learnt. As one foreigner pointed out "we had been brought in to share our experience and to help our domestic partners learn new skills. This was our value added to the joint venture, and we wanted to encourage the Russification of the business rather than have it staffed with expensive expats for a long period of time." As such the transfer of knowledge from foreign partner to domestic partner was not only easy for the domestic partner to achieve but was encouraged by the foreigners.

Conversely, there appears to have been much less transfer of knowledge in the other direction, although it is not clear whether this was entirely due to obstruction from the domestic partner or whether the unwillingness of the foreign partners to get involved in what some regarded as "shady issues" also played a part. Interestingly the Russian interviewees were fairly clear that domestic partners did not want their foreign partners to get involved in their areas of expertise, especially when it came to gaining local knowledge and experience. As described above, domestic partners seem to have been concerned about becoming more subservient to their apparently more knowledgeable foreign counterparts. They therefore encouraged a business environment in which their local abilities would be required, and it appears from responses to our questions that they defended this position quite aggressively. One Russian respondent, for example, described how he had acted as an advisor to the foreign head of his joint venture and had advised him not only to get more involved in government relations at a senior level but also, on a more mundane point, to start a meetings log in order to keep track of the main issues being discussed and the key individuals involved. However, as he described, "both initiatives were resisted by the senior Russian management. They made the role of government relations sound very complex and difficult and emphasized how it could only be carried out by a senior Russian. And as far as the meetings log went, they definitely resisted any attempts at transparency – they certainly did not want their foreign partner knowing what they had discussed."

Another Russian interviewee emphasized that "no foreign partner was welcomed into the government relations, security or finance departments" as this would have undermined the power base of the domestic partner and potentially loosened his control over the joint venture. However, it was also pointed out by both domestic and foreign respondents that in a number of cases foreign partners did not really want to be too heavily involved in these areas, as they understood that it might necessitate their involvement in, as it was euphemistically described, "other negotiations" which they would prefer to ignore. Indeed, this echoes a number of the case studies described in Chapter 3, where the foreign partner was happy to rely on his domestic partner in all dealings involving the local business environment. As a result, it would appear that the acquisition of local knowledge by foreign partners was inhibited by two key factors. Firstly, and most importantly, by the unwillingness of domestic partners to share their core skills and to offer foreign partners the opportunity to take on roles in relevant departments such as Government Relations where these skills would be relevant. And secondly, in some instances by foreign partner reluctance to get involved in issues involving local knowledge that could have created some potentially uncomfortable complications.

As a result, the balance of learning certainly seems to have favoured the domestic partner, enhancing his bargaining power as his own knowledge and skill-set grew while those of his foreign partner remained largely static. Furthermore, an additional catalyst for a change in bargaining power appears to have been seen in attempts to undermine the value of the skills brought by the foreign partner by domestic actors who felt threatened by the introduction of new ideas. This was emphasized by the assertions of another foreign player who witnessed the attempts of a US company to offer its support to a Russian major in which it had purchased shares. He described a situation in which the link between the foreign and domestic partner had been consummated by the strong personal relationship enjoyed by the CEOs of the two companies, but where lower down the organization there was much less cooperation. "One example was a colleague who had been sent to work in the Business Development department, but who never sat in the same office as his Russian counterparts. He would send presentations to the Head of the Department but no feedback was ever received or even a comment given. He effectively acted as a consultant whose advice could be taken or ignored at will, and if it was taken no credit was given to him."

"Another more technical example concerned the pressure of the liquids column in producing wells that was restricting the oil flow. A technical expert from the foreign partner suggested a very simple solution that could have caused a significant and immediate increase in production, but it was rejected on the excuse that it did not fit the Energy Ministry plan. However, we suspect that the real reason was that it would have exposed flaws in the previous system and undermined the power and influence of a local employee."

This attitude towards foreign partner contributions was confirmed by a Russian interviewee who commented that "the foreign partner often comes with well thought out business processes and corporate governance rules that do not always suit the domestic partner", in particular because they might expose failings in previous methodologies used on the Russian side. As our interviewee explained "the general attitude here [in Russia] is rule by fear, and the main fear is a fear of failure. As a result, anything that might expose past or present failures is not welcome." A further conclusion about the skills and knowledge brought by the foreign partner, then is that it can be deliberately undermined by the domestic partner for "internal or external political factors, which act as the real incentives for action or lack of action on any particular issue, with the overall prosperity of the company or joint venture as a very low priority".

In this case the knowledge brought by the foreign partner could be seen as unwelcome, with its relevance being called into question by domestic partners in order to avoid comparisons with past performance, again undermining the foreign partner's bargaining position. Furthermore, even in a more positive scenario where the advice was accepted, the benefits to the foreign partner's position in the joint venture were not always very long-lasting. As one foreign player described it "we brought technical skills to improve well performance and production, but as soon as they had been used a few times the continuing benefits of our contribution were soon forgotten. It was as if we had nothing more to offer, and the fact that we made an on-going contribution in the form of optimising the utilisation of the new techniques seemed to be irrelevant." This view was underlined by a Russian interviewee who stated that "we expected the foreign partner to bring new technology, but once it had been introduced and our employees had learnt how to use it the participation of the foreigners became rather redundant. In fact, we had cheaper people to do the same jobs, and in some instances we felt that they did a better job than the foreigners."

As a result, the balance of bargaining power in the transfer of knowledge appears to have been weighed heavily in favour of the domestic partner. Foreign partner skills appear to have been readily transferable, with the encouragement of the foreign partner, but once they had been learned by the Russian partner the continuing contribution of the foreign partner was no longer recognized. Furthermore, in some instances the new knowledge was also resented, and even ignored, if it exposed previous flaws in domestic techniques that could have embarrassed the employees of the domestic partner. In contrast, domestic partner skills and local knowledge were much more difficult for the foreign partner to acquire, due both to domestic partner obstruction and in some instances to foreign partner reluctance to become involved.

Quality of foreign employees

One final point concerning knowledge and skills that was also pointed out by both foreign and Russian interviewees concerned the quality of the employees sent to Russia by the foreign partner. While a number of the foreigners we interviewed made comments such as "the foreign partner needs to be visible and to make smart contributions" and "success has a lot to do with the quality of the people that the foreign partner sends out", a number also conceded that "the best people aren't always available for postings like Russia, especially if they perceive that it's not a major priority for the company and that their careers might be better enhanced elsewhere. You need to be very careful that you don't just get average people looking for the financial benefits of a hardship posting." This topic was picked up very specifically by a number of the Russian interviewees, who made comments such as "the foreign partner did not always send their best people – a common theme that was quickly spotted by the Russians who exploited it", and "second rate people were sent out at very high cost and not contributing any value". This appears to have been a particular source of frustration to some Russian partners who were expecting the cream of the international oil industry to arrive in Russia, but who found what they perceived to be "relatively poor quality expats who were not really accountable or responsible for anything and therefore could not be correctly incentivised".

Clearly these statements come from a small sub-set of domestic partners in Russia, but they do at least exemplify another way in which the value of foreign partner knowledge and its consequent bargaining strength could be undermined. Whether in reality or just in perception, it certainly appears that some domestic partners felt that they were not getting value for money from the foreign partner, and as a result did not rate their contribution to any joint venture as highly as might have been expected. In contrast, it appears to have been much more difficult for the foreign partner to measure the value of his domestic counterpart's contribution. Not only were the results from issues involving local knowledge much less transparent and measurable than the impact of the foreigner's skills, which could be seen in the form of changes in production or enhanced cost efficiency, but the foreign partners also appear to have had much less ability to even tell what their domestic partner was doing at all. As one outside observer of a number of partnerships put it "in order to protect himself the foreign partner needs to know more about his domestic partner, to understand how the system works and what the domestic partner's position within that system is". As we have seen, the domestic partners appear, at least in some instances, to have been keen to prevent this from happening. However, we will discuss in the next section how some foreign players claim to have kept themselves relevant in Russia over a long period of time and to have gained the levels of knowledge required at least to understand what contribution their domestic partner is making, even if they can never hope to match it themselves.

Foreign partner strategies in a weak institutional environment

"When you are working in Russia it is important to become actively involved rather than to just manage the issues that you already know about. In particular, this means building relationships with the key individuals who have influence over your business." On the surface this might appear to be a standard piece of business school advice for use in any country or operating situation, but it takes on more resonance in an environment where the power structure is vertical and where very few people hold significant power and dominate the state institutions. The quote above is actually from a Russian employee of an international joint venture, who claimed during our interview that he had tried without success to persuade his foreign colleagues to take a more active role in meeting with state officials "if only to make sure that nothing bad was being said about them behind their back". Although in this case the foreign partner appears to have ignored the advice, others with whom we spoke had taken a much more proactive role and claimed to have reaped the rewards from it.

Relationships with key individuals

Given the perception described earlier that only very few people make the most important decisions in the Russian oil and gas sector, with Igor Sechin and Vladimir Putin being the most obvious, one general theme in our discussions with foreign partners was the need to "anchor relationships as high up the vertical power structure as possible". One country head of a major international oil company which has developed a close relationship with one of the Russian state energy companies over the past few years described in detail how his company made this happen. "I have a very close relationship with their CEO and I manage it very carefully. No-one else from our company is allowed to meet with him unless I am in attendance, apart from our Chief Executive and the Head of our Upstream Business. We monitor who in government and business he likes and dislikes, and we make a point of not being seen to associate too closely with people he doesn't like. In the past we have had comments from him such as 'why did you meet with X or Y – he is our enemy' and we don't want issues like that to cloud our own relationship. I also have to ensure that the rest of the organisation keeps in step with this strategy. In the past I have had to veto deals with other Russian companies that could have potentially upset our core relationship. It is vital to retain your focus on the key people and to ensure that you do not inadvertently upset them. They tend to have other options available to them (i.e. other potential foreign partners), so you need to make sure that you don't give them an excuse to exercise those options."

Clearly this type of very high-level relationship is critical in order to ensure continued alignment with the leaders of the domestic companies with which foreign entities are partnering. However, such relationships are often hard to achieve, especially if the foreign partner is relatively small or if the joint venture he is involved in is not particularly significant. In this case a broader approach to gaining local knowledge and building relationships was suggested by our Russian interviewees. In particular, one Russian respondent who worked for a Japanese conglomerate with partnerships in the Russian oil sector emphasized that any foreign partner "can rely to an extent on their domestic partner, but should gain enough of a network of his own in order to double check what is going on and to be able to assess what value his domestic partner is really adding". This advice is similar to the conclusions from the case studies discussed in Chapter 3, where it was asserted that although a foreign partner could never compete with his partner's local knowledge and influence he could manage to build sufficient relationships of his own to provide some intelligence on his evolving situation and also some level of protection against commercial assault. As another Russian interviewee put it, a key tactic is to "trust but check" – in other words to know enough to ensure that your partner's local knowledge is being used for you rather than against you.

This more broad-based and lower-level relationship building was also highlighted as important even for those larger companies who have access to high-level individuals, as any reliance on a few key relationships carries the inherent risk of leaving the foreign partner very exposed if his main contacts leave or are replaced. In order to counter this risk, two of our interviewees talked of building "relationship models" through which a broad range of interactions between the foreign and domestic partner, and between the foreign partner and other important external actors, can be both monitored and planned. One senior foreign executive spoke of having a "Russia Plan" which aimed to create a matrix of interactions that could filter relationships vertically and horizontally across organizations and institutions that were important to his company, with staff being allocated to specific relationships with domestic players. The key goals of this strategy were explained to us as being "the need to make sure that there are no issues with different messages being given across the organisation and also to ensure that the messages which are given and received are clearly understood by the intended audience". Furthermore, as the matrix spreads, the reliance on a single relationship with a key individual at the top of the organization is somewhat mitigated. We will explore this theme further in Chapter 7 as we develop the concept of an engagement model aimed not only at protecting a foreign investor from the risks of a business environment in which local knowledge is so vital but also at allowing him to proactively build competitive advantage with his domestic partner.

Mutual learning as a tool for relationship building

However, talking about the theory of relationship building in order to gain local knowledge and experience is one thing, but finding a way of putting it into practice in a business environment where the domestic partner is often incentivized to create barriers is quite another. Therefore it was interesting to hear three of our foreign partner interviewees address this issue by combining it with their search for a solution to the problem of knowledge transfer that we have discussed above, as they advocated a strategy of joint learning on specific, mainly technical, issues. For example, one European respondent described how his firm's entire Russian business plan was based upon the development of a wet gas strategy in tandem with his Russian partner, starting from a base where neither had any particularly significant experience in that area. He reiterated the point that a common problem for foreign partners, whose perceived added value is the provision of new technology, is that when new equipment has been provided and used a few times then the domestic partner often views the job as done and the foreign partner as redundant. The further skill involved in the continuous optimization of the use of the equipment is often ignored, leaving the foreign partner as a frustrated observer of a sub-optimal process and searching for a new skill to offer.

The process of mutual learning about a new process of field development technique can help to mitigate this problem. Our European interviewee explained that "my company believed that scientific technological cooperation would be vital to make its wet gas project a success and so we put an education system in place that allowed an intensive dialogue on both technical and operational issues. As a result the partnering companies got to know each other on many different levels, with personal contact a vital part of this as it encouraged mutual friendship and respect. Furthermore, our value to the partnership did not diminish while we continued to foster this learning environment. Indeed, if key issues emerged on specific projects it was actually very useful because they could be taken away as topics for more detailed discussion either at our home HQ in Europe or at our research centre in Russia, and we could enjoy a learning experience with no vested interests involved. Finding a solution was to our mutual benefit, and joint cultural development was also achieved as many relationships grew up across the organisations."

A similar strategy is being adopted by the companies that have recently formed partnerships with Rosneft to develop licences in the Russian Arctic. Scientific Centres of Excellence are being established in Russia to address the new technical and environmental issues that will be faced in the harsh geographical environment of the Russian Far North, and as one of the foreign partners involved pointed out "this not only provides for a mutually beneficial learning environment but also helps to avoid the issue of western intellectual arrogance. I always emphasize to new expat employees who arrive in Russia that they need to clear their minds of any intellectual prejudices they may have before they interact with Russian specialists. When they meet in our technical centres to look for solutions to new challenges together it rapidly becomes clear that the Russian scientists have a lot to offer – at least as much if not more than our own people. As a result, it is much easier to create respectful relationships across the organisations in which both sides value the other's contributions over the long-term."

As a result, it would appear that joint learning can help both to reduce the risk of foreign partner redundancy and also to assist with the building of broad relationships that can allow the foreign partner to gain more local knowledge and experience. However, a key question remains – how can the foreign partner get into a position where this mutual learning can occur, if one of his key offerings, technical expertise, is part of this learning experience rather than some extra value that he brings to the partnership. What else does the foreign partner have to offer that can catalyse the start of a long-term relationship?

Reciprocity in the relationship

"Foreign partners have a hard sell at present because they have less to offer than in the past – only technology for specific types of assets, funding for very expensive projects and the offer of international assets in which a domestic partner might be interested." This quote, from a Russian employee of a domestic state company that has partnered with a number of foreign entities, emphasizes that in addition to technological expertise, which as described above is best seen as a mutual learning process rather than an outright transfer from one party to another, a foreign partner can only offer hard cash or an exchange of assets in return for gaining access to the potentially huge hydrocarbon resources available across Russia. Financial support is clearly one important element of this equation, and has played a vital part in the recent partnerships formed with Rosneft. ExxonMobil, Statoil and ENI will all be paying 100% of the initial exploration costs in their Arctic joint ventures with Russia's state oil company, despite the fact that they only have a 33% interest in the joint ventures, with this "carry" clearly being seen as a form of payment for entry into the licences. However, this cash element is a rather unsatisfactory contribution, as once it has been spent it is gone – little, if any, credit is given for past expenditure once it has become a sunk cost.

In contrast reciprocity can provide a longer-term platform for a continuing relationship and also offers an element of balance in the partnership – assets overseas offered for assets in Russia. As another of our Russian interviewees put it "reciprocity is important in establishing a good relationship for the foreign partner – he can show that he is not just a taker but also a giver". A banker who has been involved in a number of cross-border transactions in Russia explained the situation rather more exotically – "if you go to someone's house and you expect to enjoy their hospitality, surely it is only polite to take something along that you think they might want or enjoy. Foreign oil companies cannot expect to come to Russia and gain an interest in the country's crown jewels, its hydrocarbon assets, without offering something in return, and international assets are the obvious exchange to be made."

Indeed, although in the early years of international investment in Russia the trade was very much in a one-way direction, it has become increasingly obvious to all foreign participants hoping to operate in Russia that reciprocal assets swaps are an important part of any deal. Statoil's recent joint venture with Rosneft provides access to the Norwegian continental shelf, while ExxonMobil's deal with the same company provides access to offshore blocks in the Gulf of Mexico and onshore licences in the US and Canada for the development of shale and tight oil reserves. ENI, Rosneft's third Arctic partner, is also in discussion with the Russian National Oil Company about offering shares in international assets, and BP, who have recently increased their equity stake in Rosneft to 20% following the sale of their interest in TNK-BP, have mentioned their intention to look for joint investment opportunities "both in Russia and elsewhere".

Interestingly, though, one foreign partner noted that "reciprocity is important, even if the international assets are not of equivalent value", and it would certainly seem that reciprocal assets are only one part of an overall package offered by a foreign partner in Russia. It is very unlikely, for example, that the resource potential of the international asset package offered by ExxonMobil to Rosneft will match the multi-billion barrel potential of its Russian Arctic licences, but this is perhaps to be expected given that ExxonMobil is also contributing financing and its offshore oil experience to the joint venture. As a result, reciprocity should perhaps be seen as an acknowledgement that Russian companies want, and deserve, to be welcomed into the international energy arena, and also can provide exposure for them to international assets where experience relevant to Russia can be gained. As an example, the ExxonMobil international package will give Rosneft exposure to offshore exploration and unconventional oil technology which will both be useful in the development of new assets in Russia. Furthermore, the psychological impact of making a reciprocal asset offer would seem to be quite profound – as one Russian interviewee stated "Reciprocity is a key issue – in offering it you can become more readily accepted into the club."

A final concrete example of the use of reciprocal investment was provided by our interview with a European energy company that developed strong links with Gazprom, Russia's major state-controlled gas producer and exporter. As our respondent outlined "We initially brought money to help gain Gazprom some breathing space in the 1990s at a time when it was struggling to arrange financing with banks. Then, as a customer of Gazprom's, we started with the market place and worked backwards towards our goal of an upstream partnership. We wanted to establish some value for our domestic partner before we asked for anything in return, and we managed to do this by helping them to market their gas in Europe. Then we moved to infrastructure projects to help transport the gas from Russia and finally we were offered an interest in upstream gas assets in West Siberia. We had achieved an integrated chain, starting with the asset of most interest to our partner (a market for its gas) and ending with our goal of upstream production in Russia."

A further conclusion would therefore seem to be that reciprocity can be used as a powerful lever into partnerships in Russia, if one can identify key international assets that are of value or interest to a Russian partner. The value of the reciprocal assets would not necessarily need to be equal in financial terms, as long as the international assets are perceived to have sufficient overall value to the Russian partner. This is not to say, of course, that a foreign company can simply offer the poorest assets in its portfolio and hope to make a successful deal, but it does imply that the provision of a reasonable reciprocal offer does have some intrinsic value in its own right, and can help to cement a more powerful bond between foreign and domestic partners in their domestic Russian joint venture.

Partner alignment

A constant refrain from the foreign partners we interviewed concerned strategic alignment between the partners as a necessary condition for success. A typical response from one US company was that "strategic alignment with your domestic partner is vital in order to avoid conflict. It needs to be continuously reviewed in order to ensure that some balance and joint alignment is maintained." Reciprocity can of course play a part in achieving this alignment, both as a positive force indicating a willingness to share assets across borders and also as a potential insurance policy should anything start to go wrong (i.e. if you harm my assets in Russia then I can harm yours outside Russia). This latter option is clearly a rather negative one, with little actual resonance as in most instances the assets outside Russia are much less valuable than those inside, but in any case both the positive and negative effects of reciprocity can provide some alignment between the partners.

However, much more important is the continuing alignment of mutual interests inside Russia, where the domestic partner is strongest and is most likely to have the upper hand in any partner conflict. A number of respondents underlined the need for the foreign partner to ensure that he understood if, when and how his domestic partner's goals might be changing and how he, as a foreigner, could maintain his relevance and bargaining power within the joint venture in the light of these shifts. Legal agreements were acknowledged as one important lever to keep partners working together through any turbulence, but as one Russian partner asserted "the legal system does not support partnership because shareholder agreements are effectively unenforceable". And as a long-time international oil company employee summarized the situation "legal documents are clearly vital, but if you have to turn to them you are already in trouble".

Ensuring alignment therefore becomes a continuous process of monitoring the relationship between the domestic and foreign partner, assessment of who is bringing what to the venture and whether the contributions remain balanced, understanding if goals have changed or if external forces are creating new effects and evaluation of how your partner might be assessing the relative positions within the joint venture. As another foreign executive summed up the situation "you have to be aware that your partner has options, and that if you are not matching his expectations then he may be tempted to exercise them, no matter what your agreement says". Indeed, this sentiment was backed up by a Russian respondent who believed that "in an opportunistic environment such as Russia, you will exploit any partner weakness as and when it appears, for example if you perceive that your foreign partner is relying on you too much. The domestic partner will wait for a trigger event and then attack, especially if he feels he is contributing more to the venture than his foreign partner at that stage." In effect, the foreign partner needs to continuously monitor his relevance to a joint venture, in order to ensure that balance is maintained between what he is contributing and receiving, thus reducing the likelihood of his domestic partner becoming antagonistic and using his core local skills against the interests of the partnership.

The risk of misalignment for the foreign partner would therefore seem to be large, and although a constant monitoring process can clearly provide some advance warning it cannot provide insurance against exogenous shocks that can significantly impact one partner or another. In such a circumstance a more structural form of partner alignment might be needed to keep a joint entity together, and a number of our interviewees did advocate a form of corporate structure to achieve this goal. As one foreign partner noted "since the major privatisation sales the value of owning equity in companies has become increasingly apparent", and as a result joint companies with shares owned by the different partners can offer an interesting form of partnership structure. As another Russian noted "joint ventures are hard to maintain under the current legal system, and so a corporate structure is preferable. It is more flexible and also provides a simpler exit strategy." More than that, though, a company structure can also imply a longer-term relationship than a joint venture, which possibly only contains a single asset. As another interviewee suggested "the comparison is between a letter of intent (a JV) and a firm contract (company). There is more commitment in a corporate structure." We will discuss TNK-BP in more depth in the next chapter, but it can perhaps offer an example of a corporate structure, with a 50:50 shareholding for the domestic and foreign partners, that survived and prospered for a decade despite the significant turbulence between the partners. Even with BP at its weakest, following the Macondo tragedy in the Gulf of Mexico in 2010, the partnership stayed together, with the company structure and the corporate governance rules implied by it arguably providing the foundation for both parties to exit on equal terms in 2013.

Full engagement and delivery on promises

Finally, almost all of the interviewees discussed, in a number of different ways, the need for the foreign company to be fully engaged as a partner in its Russian joint venture. A clear implication is that this must start at the top of the organization, with the foreigners we talked to noting the importance of senior board members at the parent company being involved, or at least fully supportive of, the Russian joint venture and also having a deep understanding of the reality of the business environment in the country. On a positive note, one mentioned the active participation of his CEO, who had previously been directly involved in Russian operations, while another discussed the active work of his Board of Directors concerning the detailed operations of their jointly-owned Russian company. This was noted as vital to the success of a foreign joint venture in Russia, because "when we need to find a way around problems this is often done by escalating them to the top. If our senior management are not engaged then this is very difficult to achieve." Others, however, were less complimentary, noting that expatriate employees in joint ventures often felt isolated from their parent company and undermined by a lack of support from senior executives who appeared to have little grasp of the real issues involved in doing business in Russia.

Indeed, one of the Russian respondents specifically commented on this issue, saying that "support from the foreign partner HQ is a decisive factor. It is clear when this is not forthcoming, and then the expats often feel isolated and this can be exploited by the domestic partner. Eventually the expats get tired of fighting in a constant battle, while the people in HQ are just waiting to step in at the last moment once the situation has escalated. In this situation poor decisions can slip through, normally to the advantage of the Russian partner."

This ability to make key decisions, especially when they involve turning down deals that the domestic partner was keen on, was another theme highlighted by our foreign respondents. Although many discussed the need to be flexible, and to take into account the relationship and alignment issues noted above, a number were also very keen to emphasize the importance of being tough at the appropriate time. As one European described, "the first asset we were offered was originally on the PSA list, but the lack of any final agreement led us to withdraw. We were always firm in refusing assets that we did not regard as suitable, and we believe that this gained us the respect of our Russian partners." An equally determined US company asserted that "we always made it clear that we would probably be seen as difficult to deal with, that we are stubborn and that sometimes we would say no. But when we say yes we will mean it and we will deliver."

One final point, allied to the ability to make decisions and to understand the Russian way of doing business, is that longevity of senior staff retention in Russia was also viewed as an important issue. The country head of one European company we spoke to with partnerships in Russia had been based in Moscow for 15 years, while the foreign general director of a US company had been working in Russia for 20 years, and although this is clearly not the only criterion for understanding and working in Russia it was highlighted by a number of Russian interviewees as an important issue. "When we are doing business with a foreign company it can of course be frustrating if the key people change every three years. We have just built a relationship and then we have to start all over again. Of course it is the same company, but the personal relationship is gone. Also, it leads us to ask ourselves how seriously these people are taking our partnership. For them it sometimes seems just like a short posting and a step on their career ladder while for us it is our core business. Perhaps the answer would be to put a Russian in charge of their Russian operations."

Conclusions

Our interviews with a broad range of foreign and Russian participants in international joint ventures during the past decade have revealed important themes concerning the business environment in the country, the attitudes of both partners towards the sharing of knowledge and tactics that both partners have used to optimize their positions. We believe that the main conclusion from all our conversations is that the evidence drawn from our analysis of joint ventures in the 1990s and early 2000s has been further corroborated, and that the business environment for partnerships in Russia has not altered dramatically over the past decade. Of course there have been changes, and Russia is certainly a much healthier and stable economy in 2013 than it was in the 1990s, but the evidence suggests that many of the underlying business trends are the same. Indeed a number of our respondents, both foreign and domestic, used phrases such as "we are going back to the 1990s" or "nothing much has changed in the past 10 years". This does of course beg the question as to why, if the environment is still so difficult, an increasing number of foreign partnerships have been formed since 2012, in particular with Rosneft. We shall return to this question at the end of this chapter.

With regard to the business environment, it certainly appears that property rights remain weak, the legal system is not trusted to enforce laws fairly and corruption remains rife. In that sense it would seem hard to argue that much has changed since the 1990s. The Kremlin and the Russian Government might argue that stability has been restored, and it is certainly true that the risk of systemic economic and political collapse has been reduced (although this perhaps has as much to do with rising oil prices as political and economic management). However, our interviews would suggest that the institutional environment has not altered very much – the institutions themselves remain weak and are dominated by key individuals who make all the important decisions. In the case of the oil sector two men are seen as the main decision-makers – Igor Sechin and Vladimir Putin.

Within this environment of reliance on individual decision-makers and arbitrary application of laws, uncertainty is high and the domestic business outlook is focused on the short term, as few are prepared to take long-term investment risks. To further compound the ambiguous nature of the business environment, the complexity of tax rules, commercial laws and information sources is a further complication for any foreign investor who lacks experience in Russia, making the need for a domestic partner essential. Furthermore, it would seem that most domestic partners clearly understand that this is their main competitive advantage and are not unhappy that the commercial asymmetries should continue. Indeed, their aggressive tactics in conducting business are not only used to emphasize their importance as a partner but also as a form of threat to their foreign partner not to cross them, as there is no doubt who would be the winner of a dispute in Russia. Finally, none of our interviews suggested that there was much hope of change in the short term. The status quo benefits the political elite and their associated vested interests too much to believe that anyone with any power or influence is likely to suggest serious reform.

Within this environment, local knowledge and influence are clearly vital commodities, as was suggested by the case studies in Chapter 3 and the statistical analysis in Chapter 4. This local knowledge is a skill brought to any joint venture by the domestic partner, while the foreign partner brings his technical, management and financial advantages. Our hypothesis to date has been that the competition to learn these skills is very important to the success or failure of a partnership from both partners' perspectives, and we have suggested that the domestic partner has generally been in a more favourable position. The interviews conducted for this chapter have suggested a reason for this, namely that foreign partners appear to have seen part of their role in any partnership as the sharing of their skills, while the domestic partners have been more inclined to preserve their competitive advantage.

In particular, it would seem that foreign partners have been keen to "russify" their partnerships by encouraging their domestic partners to increase their involvement in all the technical and management areas where they (the domestic partners) had originally been less experienced, thus allowing them to actively absorb new skills. In contrast, it appears that the Russian partners have been much less keen to share their skills, and have not welcomed foreign involvement into areas such as government relations, security, legal and finance. Indeed, some of our Russian respondents confirmed the view that even encouraging transparency in these areas through the use of tools such as a meetings log was not welcome, as this could undermine their ability to take advantage of their local knowledge. However, it is also fair to add that on occasion foreign partners were willing participants in this allocation of responsibilities, not wanting to become involved in the uncomfortable world of Russian politics, but in either case it seems clear that the acquisition of local knowledge by a foreign partner has been much harder than the acquisition of international skills by the Russians.

Two final conclusions on knowledge and skills were also seen as potentially undermining the foreign partner position. Firstly, the knowledge brought by the foreign partner was not always welcome, especially if it exposed past or present flaws in business practices. In this case it would often be deliberately undermined or ignored, with the consequence that the perceived value of the foreign partner contribution was reduced. Secondly, the perceived low quality of some expat employees sent to work in JVs in Russia also reduced the credibility of the foreign partners, as the domestic partner would often claim that he was paying a high price for a less than first-class service. Again, this could undermine the bargaining power of the foreign partner.

Given this situation, the interview discussion turned to foreign partner strategies for successful involvement in partnerships in Russia. The first, and perhaps the most obvious conclusion is the need to build core relationships with the key individuals at the top of the "power vertical", with those key individuals varying from the CEO of Rosneft to regional governors or local mayors depending upon the size and location of the respective joint venture. Beyond this initial conclusion, though, was a broader view that a deep horizontal and vertical relationship building exercise is needed within relevant companies and institutions, with a specific plan to link foreign actors with appropriate Russian contacts and encourage a continuous process of engagement and interaction. In Chapter 7 we will outline a detailed methodology for creating such an "Engagement Plan", with the overall goal not necessarily being to compete with your domestic partner's local knowledge and influence but at least to know enough to assess his real contribution to the partnership. As one Russian put it, a foreign partner needs to "trust but check".

One means of facilitating this relationship building as well as addressing the issue of knowledge transfer was then suggested in the form of mutual learning. Essentially it would seem that if an area of collaboration can be established where both parties have the opportunity to develop new skills to the mutual benefit of the partnership, then this can provide the basis for strengthening the business and cultural relations between the foreign and domestic actors. Examples of the development of a wet gas strategy and innovation in the Arctic were cited, and importantly while neither completely excluded the possibility of technical expertise being contributed by the foreign partner, the key element of both was the sharing of a learning experience rather than the transfer of knowledge from one partner to another.

However, if a foreign company is to gain access to potentially valuable hydrocarbon assets in Russia then he must make some valuable, sustainable offer of his own. If technical skills become a smaller part of the offer in a mutual learning process, then two obvious alternative contributions are financing and reciprocal international assets. The former is clearly being used in a number of current joint ventures, but is ultimately quite unsatisfactory as a partnership building tool – once the cash is spent the foreign partner credit is gone. Reciprocity, on the other hand, is seen not only as having an overt value in terms of the assets contributed, but also an intrinsic value in the acknowledgement of the Russian partner's right to operate overseas and in the proof that the foreign partner is not just here to acquire Russian assets but also to give opportunities to his new partners. This process can provide powerful leverage into Russian assets as well as providing some token insurance against foul play, but its main value is to provide a firmer foundation for the partnership in Russia through its creation of a mutually beneficial asset swap – both parties are giving and receiving domestic and foreign assets, and are welcoming each other into a new club.

This reciprocal arrangement can also play a vital role in another important issue brought up in the interviews, namely partner alignment. However, the most important place to ensure that this occurs is in Russia itself, with the maintenance of a balance of interests being seen as the key to foreign partner success. Legal constraints were acknowledged as one means of keeping a partnership together, but in reality once you have gone to court your partnership is already in big trouble. Therefore the foreign partners we interviewed emphasized the need to constantly monitor the continuing contributions being made to the partnership, the potential changes in their domestic partner's goals and the possible reactions to exogenous shocks that might disturb the equilibrium – essentially to monitor the foreign partner's continuing relevance to the partnership. Of course this is difficult to assess accurately all the time, and so a further conclusion was suggested in the form of an alternative corporate structure, where each partner would have an equity share in a joint company rather than a joint venture. This was seen as potentially creating a greater commitment between the partners and an increased chance of a long-term alignment of interests.

A final conclusion on commitment was then also raised by both the Russian and foreign interviewees, concerning the full engagement of senior management both in the home country of the foreign partner and in Russia. The importance of active management participation, or at least full support, from the foreign partner HQ was highlighted as a key issue, with any wavering of enthusiasm or activity likely to be seized on by a domestic partner looking to exploit a competitive advantage. Furthermore, long-term commitment of senior management in Russia was also noted as important, with the constant rotation of leading staff bringing into question their real commitment to the country.

These conclusions include some new thoughts on potential routes to foreign partner success in a business environment such as Russia's, but also have enough similarity with our earlier views to suggest that our initial theories on the importance of local knowledge and the competition over learning have some validity. However, they do also highlight that Russia is a difficult place for foreign companies to gain a long-term competitive advantage, which returns us to our earlier question as to why a number of new partnerships have been formed over the past two years. The answer, we believe, is that, as discussed in Chapter 1, Russia is entering a new phase in its oil industry development as the older "Soviet era" fields in West Siberia move into their decline phase and new regions need to be explored and developed in order to ensure that overall Russian oil production does not go into serious decline. These new regions, such as East Siberia, the Arctic and in offshore waters around Russia's entire coast are more technically challenging and expensive to develop than the country's traditional hydrocarbon regions, which has led to a search for companies with relevant expertise to provide both financial and technical assistance. As a result, foreign companies with broad global oil industry experience have found that their expertise and financial strength provide them with a competitive advantage in Russia once more, especially if it is combined with the offer of reciprocal international assets. ExxonMobil, Statoil, ENI and BP have all formed partnerships with Rosneft in the past two years, while Novatek and Gazprom have also brought in new foreign partners to help solve some of their more challenging issues. However, it appears to the authors that one key question remains – how long will this competitive advantage last and what will happen when it starts to become less relevant? We have seen a similar trend in the 1990s, when foreign technical, financing and management expertise was highly valued for a while but was then gradually undermined by exogenous factors such as a higher oil price and endogenous factors such as the ability of the Russian partners to acquire their foreign partners' skills. It appears to us that the pattern could certainly repeat itself again, unless the foreign companies adopt a different strategy this time around, involving the acquisition of local knowledge, a continued process of mutual learning and a constant process of ensuring that they maintain their relevance through partner alignment over the long term.

As we have discussed, one of the methods suggested as a foundation for partner alignment is the use of a corporate structure rather than a traditional joint venture. Our hypothesis is that this form of partnership may help to encourage commitment and longevity and has led us in this chapter to a brief mention of TNK-BP, the largest foreign partnership in the history of post-Soviet Russia. Therefore it seems logical that our next discussion should be based around this entity, which was described both as a joint venture and as a joint stock company, and did indeed include a major subsidiary company that was quoted on the Russian stock exchange. The next chapter is therefore devoted to a conversation with a foreign employee who spent eight years as a senior manager at TNK-BP and who since his departure has also spent a significant amount of time working with and analysing other partnerships in Russia.

6
Reflections on Partnership at TNK-BP

Introduction

After the turbulent experiences for overseas companies in Russia during the 1990s and the hiatus in foreign investment activity in the aftermath of the 1998 financial crisis, BP's decision in early 2003 to take a 50% interest in TNK-BP not only marked a dramatic turning point but also created a company that would become a bell-weather for foreign investors in Russia for the next decade. Officially created in the presence of Russian President Vladimir Putin and UK Prime Minister Tony Blair at a signing ceremony in February 2003, the company instantly became by far the largest example of FDI in Russia, bringing together one of the world's largest oil companies and a group of Russia's most influential and assertive entrepreneurs (AAR). Although the new entity they created was often called a joint venture, the main holding vehicle was actually a company based in the British Virgin Islands in which both groups had a 50% shareholding (interestingly against the advice of President Putin, who thought that one side should have control),[1] and so provides an interesting, and very large, example of the corporate structure that we discussed earlier. However, as we shall also discover, although this did help to keep the partners together over a decade of turbulent interaction, local knowledge also played a key role in determining the outcome of a number of disputes.

Following a long career at BP during which he experienced working life in many of the world's major hydrocarbon provinces, Alastair Ferguson, one of the co-authors of this book, worked at TNK-BP from its inception until 2011, with his main role being the Head of the company's gas business, reporting directly to one of the Russian shareholders, Viktor Vekselberg. Since leaving TNK-BP he has remained in Russia as an independent consultant, where he has offered advice to many foreign companies on the best tactics for doing business in the country. As a result of both these roles he is very well placed to provide a detailed assessment of the pitfalls that can befall foreign investors entering partnerships in Russia and can also offer some practical thoughts on how to improve the chances of, if not guarantee, a more successful outcome. This chapter is based on a series of discussions between the authors as they began their collaboration on this book, and is presented as a conversation in the hope that it can provide a more intimate view of Alastair's relatively unique insights into the day-to-day experiences of an international partnership in Russia during the 2000s. It should be made clear at the outset, however, that we draw no pejorative conclusions about the behaviour or actions of any Russian or foreign participant in the ventures we discuss. The purpose is not to provide a sensational account of partner disputes or nefarious activities but rather an attempt to assess the tactics used by both parties to adjust their bargaining positions, adapt to changing external factors and ultimately to maximize their returns from what has arguably been Russia's most successful oil company in the post-Soviet era.

A brief history of TNK-BP

BP's initial exposure to Russia began in 1995 and took the form of petrol retail sites built in Moscow,[2] but its decision to invest heavily in the country was actually sparked by its interest in the Chinese gas market, which emerged during a visit by then CEO John Browne to Beijing in 1997.[3] Noticing the growing demand for gas in China, and seeing the potential to link it to the huge Kovykta field in eastern Russia that BP had identified some years before,[4] he decided to investigate the possibility of gaining an interest in this significant gas asset. Having established that Kovykta's owner was the Russian oil company Sidanco, whose main shareholder was the Russian entrepreneur Vladimir Potanin via his industrial holding company Interros, BP entered negotiations to make an investment and in September 1997 announced the purchase of a 10% stake in Sidanco itself for $571 million.[5] Importantly, though the deal also included a promise to purchase 45% of Sidanco's 60% interest in Rusia Petroleum, the subsidiary that operated the Kovykta field, providing BP with what it really wanted, namely access to the gas field that it believed could be a source of gas exports to the growing Chinese market.

However, Kovykta was to remain in the background for some time, as BP's main focus soon became protecting its investment in Sidanco. The financial crisis of 1998, which involved the default of Russian government debt and a huge devaluation of the rouble, placed significant financial strain both on Sidanco and its main shareholder Interros, putting it at risk of bankruptcy. This was seized on as an opportunity by Sidanco's other key shareholder, the Alfa Group led by another influential Russian businessman Mikhail Fridman. Fridman was unhappy with the situation at Sidanco as he believed that he had been cheated by Potanin during the sale of 10% to BP, and he planned to get his revenge using his own oil company TNK as the vehicle for his attack.[6] Using Russia's bankruptcy law, which, as described in Chapter 1, allowed anyone owning even a small amount of debt in a Russian company to place it in receivership, TNK began the process of bankrupting Sidanco's main subsidiary, Chernogorneft, while other Sidanco subsidiaries also came under attack from various domestic competitors. Potanin, weakened by the financial crisis and focussing more on his other main industrial assets, including the mining company Norilsk Nickel, left BP and Sidanco to fend for themselves, and as John Browne himself described (Browne, 2010) the situation soon degenerated so much that "Sidanco was little more than a skeleton with hardly any assets. We were a naïve foreign investor caught out by a rigged legal system...BP had been made to look ridiculous."[7]

BP had a choice to make: accept defeat in Russia's anarchic commercial environment as TNK gradually won case after case in the Russian courts, or fight back using alternative tactics. It chose the latter option, and attacked TNK by having one of its international loans cancelled, thus demonstrating its ability to hurt TNK outside Russia if TNK continued to create difficulties inside Russia.[8] This strategy of "negative reciprocity" worked well enough to get both parties to the negotiating table by the end of 1999, and although it took a further two years to hammer out the details of a resolution, by 2001 the Chernogorneft assets had been returned to Sidanco[9] and in 2002 BP paid $375 million to increase its stake in the company from 10% to 25%.[10]

Having re-committed itself to Russia, BP realized that it needed a strong partner if it was to both survive in the asymmetric business environment and also take advantage of the continuing opportunities for the re-development of Soviet era oil assets that it hardly had a chance to exploit at Sidanco. On the other side, TNK and AAR had begun to understand the potential benefits of partnership with an international oil company in bringing new technology, operational skills and management techniques to enhance the performance of TNK's oilfield portfolio. As a result, negotiations between the two parties continued through 2002, and by February 2003 they had reached an agreement on the formation of TNK-BP, with BP paying $8 billion in cash, assets and its share of Sidanco for a 50% stake in the new entity, that would also include all of TNK. At a presentation to investors in London, John Browne underlined the importance of the deal for BP in establishing its presence in "one of the great natural resource centres of the world".[11] TNK-BP would now account for 11% of the BP Group's total proved reserve base and 15% of its production, and as a company generating a positive net cashflow at oil prices as low as $13 per barrel would also provide significant dividend income for the company.

During the presentation the potential for reserve and production growth over the subsequent few years was also underlined by TNK-BP's new CEO, Bob Dudley.[12] He detailed the opportunity for BP technology to enhance field performance across the new company's asset portfolio to improve recoverability and to increase output per well to an extent that overall production was estimated to rise from 1.2mmbpd to around 1.4mmbpd in just three years, while increased efficiency was also expected to see lifting costs per barrel on a declining trajectory. It was precisely these performance enhancements, as well as the international and domestic credibility brought by partnership with an IOC, that attracted AAR to BP, and Mikhail Fridman and his fellow investors at AAR made it clear from the outset that they were looking forward to improved performance from the joint company.

And indeed, the initial results were impressive, with oil output growing by 14% in 2003, 13% in 2004 and 6% in 2005, while the company replaced more than 100% of its production in each of these years by focussing on the redevelopment of the enormous brownfield resource at its disposal.[13] However, inevitably these rates of growth were unsustainable over the longer term as the impact of new techniques such as horizontal drilling and hydraulic fracturing became less dramatic once the initial gains had been made, and by 2007 TNK-BP's production growth had effectively slowed to around 1% per annum.[14] When this slowdown in output growth from the company's brownfields was combined with the fact that significant investment was also needed in new "greenfield" developments to sustain the long-term production outlook, it meant that returns to investors were bound to decline. The Russian shareholders were not pleased with this outcome, especially as they saw what they regarded as very highly paid BP expats being employed by their company and not generating the expected return. This situation began to catalyse heated debates within the TNK-BP management team, and the potential for a partner dispute was further fuelled by three other key issues.

The first was related to the expat issue, in that AAR believed that BP were treating TNK-BP as a subsidiary of the BP Group and not as an independent entity, and thus felt that they (AAR) might risk losing control of the company. Indeed, German Khan, a senior figure in the AAR consortium and a director at TNK-BP, made very clear in public interviews that two key issues for him in 2007 and 2008 were management costs and the development of TNK-BP as an independent entity, not a subsidiary of BP.[15] However, a second issue presented perhaps even more of a challenge to AAR in the form of the emergence of Gazprom as a potential alternative partner for BP. In 2006 Gazprom had been given the responsibility for the export of gas from East Siberia into Asia, and as a result had taken an interest in gaining a share in the Kovykta field, now owned by TNK-BP and of course a key part of BP's longstanding plans in Russia. In 2007, BP, TNK-BP and Gazprom signed a strategic agreement on the involvement of Gazprom in the field, but negotiations on the cost of entry and the final terms were never concluded.[16] As a result, Gazprom started to use external pressure to threaten TNK-BP's ownership of the license, in an attempt to force a deal, but rumours also abounded in Moscow that BP and Gazprom might be trying to tie up a bigger deal that could have included Gazprom's participation in TNK-BP.[17] The original 2007 MoU had mentioned international co-operation, which of course only BP could offer, and the thought that BP might attempt to usurp AAR in a new relationship with Russia's state-controlled gas company was a clear threat to the Russian entrepreneurs.

In addition, the fact that TNK-BP had no international exposure while BP was potentially going to offer overseas assets to another Russian company was a further bone of contention, and highlighted a key difference in strategic alignment between the partners. BP clearly saw TNK-BP as a vehicle for Russian and CIS business only, and increasingly appeared to have eyes on other possible partners in Russia. For AAR, TNK-BP was a vehicle to generate cashflow in Russia but also to provide opportunities outside the country, and they resented being denied these by BP. As a result, what appeared to be a concerted attack on TNK-BP, and in particular BP employees within the company, began. It included the arrest of a TNK-BP employee, an inspection by the environmental agency, a claim for back taxes, a failure to renew the visas of 148 expatriate employees and their forced exit from Russia and most seriously an open attack on the position of Bob Dudley as CEO of the company. Indeed by July 2008 he had felt the need to leave Russia, and ultimately to resign from his post, due to the threat of personal prosecution in Russia.[18]

Adding to the complications caused by this dispute, BP was also going through some turbulence of its own in 2007 and 2008, with the resignation of CEO John Browne in 2007 marking the end of a period in which BP's reputation had also suffered from the explosion at its Texas City refinery.[19] Furthermore, the global financial crisis was also building out of the US housing crash in 2008, leading to dramatic share price falls around the world and bringing the valuations of both BP and TNK-BP sharply lower. AAR may have tried to combine all these factors in their negotiations with BP's new CEO, Tony Hayward, and the pressure they brought to bear certainly yielded a positive result in the resolution that was reached in October 2008. A new management structure was put in place that contained far fewer expats and the Board of Directors was also re-modelled to include four directors each from AAR and BP plus three independent directors, providing a balanced situation on the surface but one that was in reality now dominated by the Russian side.[20]

Having weathered this first major shareholder dispute, and also the low oil prices seen in 2009 as a result of the global financial crisis, TNK-BP continued to report impressive financial results, reporting record profits and paying out significant dividends to its shareholders. In addition, it also began to invest overseas, taking advantage of BP's sale of non-core assets following the Macondo disaster in the Gulf of Mexico to buy assets in Vietnam, Venezuela and Brazil. However, the impact of the dispute had not entirely dissipated, and BP's view that it now wanted to expand its partnership options with a state-controlled company had not diminished. The rise of Rosneft in the Russian oil industry since 2004 had resulted in a decline in the opportunities available for private companies such as TNK-BP, and BP clearly decided that it wanted to further its relations with this emerging state champion, initially entering negotiations during 2010 on partnership in the German refining sector.[21] However, the ultimate goal of these discussions became apparent in January 2011, when a deal for BP to take an interest in three large Arctic off-shore licences controlled by Rosneft in the South Kara Sea was announced in London, combined with an agreed share swap between the two companies. The strategic nature of the deal[22] posed a clear threat to AAR's position as the dominant local partner for BP in Russia, but also offered them a route to respond. The founding shareholder agreement for TNK-BP, signed in 2003, had included a clause that limited the activities of both BP and AAR in Russia, ensuring that either would have to offer any significant opportunities in the country to the other, with specific permission being needed before proceeding alone. AAR argued that the BP-Rosneft deal broke both the spirit and the letter of this agreement, and took their case to the courts. The High Court of Justice in London issued a temporary injunction blocking the deal,[23] which was subsequently confirmed by an arbitration panel in Stockholm.[24] No final ruling was ever reached on the rights and wrongs of the situation, but the debate continued long enough to prove terminal for the deal. By the middle of May it had officially collapsed,[25] and then in August 2011 Rosneft announced that it had effectively replaced BP in its South Kara deal with ExxonMobil (minus the share swap).[26]

Having effectively conceded defeat, BP was left to patch up relations with its partners at TNK-BP once again, but this time it appeared that any fix would only ever be temporary. After a year of continuous negotiations about the future of the company, BP announced in June 2012 that it was putting its 50% share in TNK-BP up for sale.[27] By October a deal with Rosneft had been agreed, with both BP and AAR selling their stakes to the Russian national oil company for a combined total of $55 billion, with the deal being finally completed in March 2013.[28] And so a unique partnership in the Russian oil industry ended, following a decade of volatile partner relations during which corporate performance had surpassed expectations in spite of the difficulties experienced by the shareholders. Production had increased from 1.2 million boepd in 2003 to over 2 million boepd by 2012, while the company's reserve base had expanded to almost 14 billion barrels of oil equivalent,[29] with reserve replacement having accounted for more than 100% of production in every year since inception apart from 2008. From a financial perspective the company had also been a triumph, with profits jumping from $2.4 billion in 2003 to $7.6 billion in 2012,[30] while total dividends paid out to both shareholders amounted to $19 billion each over the life of the company.[31]

As a result, from an initial investment of $8 billion, BP has received $19 billion of dividends plus a final settlement in the sale to Rosneft of $27.5 billion, comprising approximately $12.5 billion in cash and an 18.5% equity stake in Rosneft (purchased from Rosneft itself and from another state-owned holding company Rosneftegaz).[32] The company has therefore made a total return on its investment of almost 500%, and retains an ongoing interest in Russia via a 19.5% stake in Rosneft,[33] through which it also hopes to generate additional asset-based opportunities for investment. By any stretch of the imagination this should be deemed a commercial success, and yet during the life of TNK-BP many of the headlines concerned BP's troubles in Russia – "BP's Russia dream turns into nightmare",[34] "BP: Roughed up in Russia"[35] and "Why its Russia mess should not surprise BP"[36] being three prime examples. In part these headlines certainly seemed to reflect reality, as BP's business in Russia did face significant turbulence throughout the 2000s. However, another explanation for these headlines is that the noise surrounding the inter-partner relations was part of the exploitation of local knowledge being used by the domestic partners as part of their bargaining game with BP. They understood that BP and its investors, and therefore the company's share price, would be far more sensitive to domestic problems in Russia than AAR themselves would be, therefore providing another upside from any potentially chaotic situation. And it is at this point, as we try to understand the rationale behind the actions of both partners in the joint company, that we can benefit from the views of an insider who witnessed the interactions between the partners personally and was intimately involved in the successes of TNK-BP for more than eight years.

A conversation with Alastair Ferguson, former Head of Gas at TNK-BP

James Henderson (JH): Having just talked about the history of TNK-BP, perhaps you could start from the beginning and give your perspective on the initial goals of the two partners and what the company was like back in 2003?

Alastair Ferguson (AF): In general I would say that there was good alignment over what the partners wanted at the start of the JV. AAR had seen the success at Sibneft and Yukos in terms of exploiting the upside from brownfield recovery and owned a share in two oil companies (TNK and Sidanco) that had the same turnaround potential. BP was already a shareholder in one (Sidanco) and had started to demonstrate how it could help and so it made sense to get it involved in a broader context. In addition, TNK was a somewhat chaotic company back in 2002/03 – a number of disparate assets that had been brought together in a relatively random fashion that was run as a series of fiefdoms with no overall corporate culture. So AAR looked to BP to bring not only the technical expertise to turn the fields around but also the management and organizational experience to create a true corporate vehicle with international governance rules and processes. More subjectively, AAR also may have hoped that an alliance with a major IOC would provide some political cover too. From a BP perspective, the formation of TNK-BP provided a unique opportunity to access huge reserves and resources with significant upside in production potential in tandem with a partner that had already proved itself to be a true survivor in Russia's chaotic business environment. BP knew that it had the skills to make a huge difference to TNK and Sidanco's asset bases, but it needed the opportunity to access them and the protection to make the most of its investment in the long term. As a result, TNK-BP brought together the best skills of both companies in order to maximize the operational and financial returns for all the shareholders, initially providing ideal stakeholder alignment over the company's ultimate objectives.

JH: The cultures of the two partners were very different though. What impact did this have?

AF: The cultures were indeed very different, but in a way they complimented each other, with certain caveats. BP brought an entrepreneurial but strategic culture, with a view towards the long-term development of TNK-BP's business, as one might expect from an international oil company used to developing assets with a 20 to 30 year investment horizon and production cycle. Of course this is what AAR were looking for in order to transform their business and bring it some longer-term commercial focus. However, although they wanted to change TNK from being a collection of assets into an organized vertically integrated oil company with a multi-year business plan, at heart I believe that they continued to reflect the much shorter-term nature of most Russian entrepreneurs. TNK was a very transaction-based company and AAR were opportunistic and much more focused on the next deal rather than the day-to-day running of the company. They also had a much more ruthless business style, and were very tough in their business dealings. In general I would say that Russian domestic players can be very aggressive and confrontational in defending their bargaining position and their competitive advantages, and this would not just be with regard to foreigners. I would often watch interactions between domestic actors both inside and outside of TNK-BP and the analogy of watching dogs fight under the carpet would come to mind. You often cannot understand exactly what is going on but you can see that an almighty fight is taking place.

Another cultural point to make here is that the relationship between senior management and employees is very feudal in nature, where the system works on the basis of fear. If a senior person orders you to drop everything and come to his office, then you do it without hesitation. If you are a more junior employee you do not criticize your boss or even contradict him, especially in a meeting or any open forum. As a result, initiative is not really encouraged at all. Many Russian staff that I have encountered won't do something unless they are specifically asked to do so, and are very keen to ensure that they cannot be blamed if anything goes wrong. The sense is that if you are found to have made a mistake then you are in big trouble, even if decisions were made for all the right reasons. This is very different from the culture that most expatriates have experienced, where the generation of new ideas is encouraged and open discussion in meetings is also welcomed, even if it does contradict the consensus view.

However, it would be wrong to characterize the foreign, more strategic, open and long term, model as the right one and the more aggressive and short-term Russian model as wrong, especially in a domestic Russian context. The domestic actors that I have met and interacted with have often pursued their goals in a much more antagonistic way than I had been used to in other international markets, and this can obviously cause a very uncomfortable environment for expatriate employees of international joint ventures, but on the flip side of the coin it does bring an urgency and focus to discussions that can be beneficial. The domestic partners had a "cut to the chase" mentality which forced discussions to be more efficient and to focus on the end result. Again, though, there is a balance to be struck. Often the desire to get to the conclusion would be to the detriment of the analysis that went into the discussion, and this is where the more methodical IOC approach to decision-making would act as a counterweight, by forcing the discussants to take a step back and consider the more analytical detail. Overall, though, I would say that elements of both cultures are needed in a commercial environment like the one seen in Russia over the past 20 years. One clearly needs to think before acting, but the rapid changes and levels of uncertainty and unpredictability involved in operating there do also require a more clinical and rapid decision-making culture.

The commercial environment and local knowledge

JH: So perhaps you could talk some more about the commercial environment and what the main challenges and implications were?

AF: I would characterize the commercial environment as a triangle of business, political and vested interests, with an underlying context of very influential individuals and rather weak institutions. In practical terms this means that getting anything done requires you to have relationships with the right people and to sustain those relationships in a variety of ways. Which leads us to the elephant in the room, of course – corruption. The statistics will tell you that corruption is rife in Russia, and both President Putin and Prime Minister Medvedev have acknowledged it as a huge problem that needs to be addressed, but it is interesting to consider exactly what forms it takes. Personally I neither witnessed nor was directly aware of any specific corrupt practices such as blatant transfer of funds or theft of assets. However, I was constantly aware of an underlying sense of inter-related activities outside of the operations of the joint company. In other words deals might have been going on, perhaps not even in the oil and gas sector, that were in some way related to deals that TNK-BP was carrying out. As a result, some form of value was possibly being created for individuals who worked for TNK-BP, but behind the scenes.

Defining exactly what this value was and how it was ultimately realized is impossible to determine. However, I would relate it to the fact that individuals are so important within the political and economic environments in Russia. Individual influence and authority is a hugely valuable commodity within such an environment, and therefore I would say that power in itself is more important to many Russian businessmen than revenues, particularly short-term revenues, because of its huge longer-term relevance. If the completion of a transaction can help to sponsor a vaguely related external deal and thereby create some form of obligation from the individual who has benefited from that second deal, then your own power base and influence has been enhanced even if you have made no immediate personal cash return. This, it seems to me, is a very important driver for many domestic actors, and can help to explain a number of the "apparently sub-optimal" commercial decisions that I saw being made.

Creating this obligation and power base is important in a number of contexts. Firstly, the feudal system that I described above works from the highest level in Russia. The most senior people pass down edicts from on high, and it is important to know when this is likely to happen so that you can be prepared to respond or react. You need influence and relationships to be able to meet these powerful decision-makers, and hopefully to influence their decisions, but you also need to know when their gaze is likely to be focussed on you so that you are ready. One of the obvious failings of a quasi-imperial system like Russia's is that the key individuals have far too many issues to address and cannot focus on them all at once. They will only have a fleeting moment to focus on you, so you either need enough influence to catalyse when that moment will be and what the specific issue will focus on, or you just need to know when to be ready. Within this context, having a powerful domestic ally is vital, and of course this gives your partner a huge competitive advantage.

Furthermore, the weakness of the institutions compared to the key individuals also provides powerful domestic businessmen and companies with an opportunity. It would appear that many people within even important institutions such as the Ministry of Energy are simply waiting to be told what to do, and as a result there is often a knowledge vacuum. This provides the opportunity for businesses to fill that vacuum by providing assistance and attempting to manage the agenda to ensure that the issues most important to them are at the top. Of course, this is a rather random process as the key players may ultimately decide on something completely different, but nevertheless there is a sense of working both to use influence at the bottom of the power base in order to try and understand what is going on and to shape the discussion, and also at the top, so that you can understand when and how the decision-makers may react. Within this context, any deal or transaction, large or small, that can give you leverage over relevant individuals is useful, and this is where I got the greatest sense of corruption – a deal being completed where I suspect that the value being created was not only in a monetary form to TNK-BP but also in the form of personal power or leverage to key individuals.

This form of leverage also appeared to be very applicable to the law courts, where on a number of occasions decisions were made which seemed to have no basis in legal fact. Of course there are numerous examples in a broader Russian context where accusations of legal impropriety have been alleged, but I have no direct examples to offer of this in practice from my own experience. All I can say is that I got the general sense that if we needed a decision to go in our favour in a Russian court, then it could be arranged, and also that if a law-suit was brought between an influential Russian and a foreigner then there would only be one winner, at least initially. To be fair, if pushed through an appeal process many initial decisions could be reversed, but I think that many Russians felt that if a foreigner saw initial judgements going against them and started to feel an inevitability about the ultimate outcome then they would return to the negotiating table in a weaker position or just give up. Ironically, those who didn't do this and decided to fight actually gained respect from the Russian side for having the determination to do so and the courage to operate in a more Russian-business style.

JH: So any foreign partner needs a domestic partner to help him manage a business through this maze of asymmetric business practices. In your experience, does the domestic partner fully understand that this is his most significant competitive advantage and therefore exploits and even protects it?

AF: I think that it is possible for a foreign company to operate alone, but having a domestic partner presents you with much greater access and opportunity. A foreign company operating alone would have to work extraordinarily hard to develop its network of relationships and contacts to allow it to even understand how the system works, and I don't think that on any reasonable timescale it could hope to compete with a powerful domestic player when it comes to gaining access to opportunities and then successfully exploiting them. In the oil industry, of course, there are also legal restrictions on the size of deposits that can be accessed by foreigners without a Russian partner, but irrespective of this in any industry it would be very difficult to extract the full potential of a business in Russia without a domestic partner. BP certainly understood this when they initially took a stake in Sidanco, with Potanin and Interros as the partner, and then continued the theme in the formation of TNK-BP. Many analysts looked at the latter deal and wondered why BP chose to partner with AAR after so many years of dispute, but in my opinion it was certainly a case of "better the devil you know, than the devil you don't". BP had seen the worst of what the Russian business environment could throw at it and was very realistic about what protection it would need going forward. AAR had proved that it had the skills to get things done on the ground where any foreign partner would have encountered major difficulty.

Inevitably, it is of course natural that the domestic players not only understand this but also protect their competitive position. The perpetuation of the chaotic business environment was clearly to their advantage, and I would say they were happy to make it difficult for any foreigner, including their partner, to operate in that environment. I think that there is another cultural point to be made here, that there is a tradition of deception in Russia that is not well understood by foreigners. Russians, and in particular the security services, have long prided themselves on their ability to dissemble and disorientate, and they put a huge amount of work into creating an appearance of what is going on whereas in fact the real game is happening somewhere else. This is very confusing for foreigners and often makes them believe that they cannot operate alone. I certainly feel that the Russians exploit this fact, perpetuating the view that it is all very difficult, that there is a "special Russian way" and that no foreigner can hope to understand how the system as a whole operates. While I think that this is partially true, I also believe that it is not as complicated as domestic actors might have us believe. My own experience, in a TNK-BP context, was that the senior Russians did constantly try to keep the foreigners confused and off guard, using deception and misinformation as key tools. They also understood that in any difficult situation, the more chaotic things became the more likely they were to win, and so this was also used as a key tactic to disorientate anyone from outside the system.

The importance of learning

JH: Earlier in the book we addressed the issue of the roles that domestic and foreign partners might take in joint ventures based on their initial skill-sets, and we also suggested that knowledge transfer might be reflected in a gradual change in these roles. Given what you have said so far about AAR and BP's offerings to TNK-BP, was this reflected in the responsibilities that both partners took within the organization and was there any change over time?

AF: The organization was really set up around the technical skills that were BP's main contribution to the new company. A technology group was set up that provided functional technical support throughout the organization, and was headed by a BP person. This group drove technical change throughout the organization, from the upstream to downstream and marketing, and was a key vehicle for the transfer of technical knowledge. BP also brought management and governance skills and so departments that were involved with this expertise were also generally led by BP people. The Head of Strategy and M&A was a BP person, as was the Head of PPM (Planning and Performance Management), which was the department that implemented the key governance change by introducing the concept of the Investment Committee, where the commercial case for any new project had to be presented and approved. As a result all the areas where the traditional foreign partner skills were most relevant were run by BP people. However, we should point out that when we say BP people, what we mean is staff sourced from BP, because the majority of the senior staff who came to work for TNK-BP actually resigned from BP and signed new contracts with the joint company. TNK-BP was an independent company in its own right and that was a key point made by the Russian partners. Loyalty should be to the new entity, not to BP.

The roles taken up by the Russian employees also reflected their initial strengths. The Head of Upstream, for example, was a domestic employee because it was perceived that a tough manager was needed in a fairly tough environment, and without doubt the Russians did bring some strong on-the-ground operational management skills in both the upstream and downstream businesses. However, the real areas of domestic partner responsibility were government relations, security, legal and tax, where they really dominated the business. The first two departments reported directly to German Khan, the Executive Director of TNK-BP and one of the main shareholders, and you could say that he effectively ran the company through his control over these issues. Bob Dudley, a former BP employee, was the CEO and did wield considerable power through this office, but in practical terms German Khan would oversee the entire business and controlled all the external relations with the key people in the government and the ministries.

JH: In practical terms what does government relations and security actually mean? What did these departments actually do?

AF: TNK-BP, but in reality AAR, had a huge network of contacts and relationships with influential people within ministries, companies and government offices that would provide them with data, access to relevant people and the opportunity to not only know what was going on regarding most issues but also the ability to influence outcomes. In practical terms, at a senior level they would constantly be meeting with high-ranking government officials and business leaders in order to position the company and themselves to take advantage of relevant opportunities. On a more mundane level, TNK would have representation in almost every Ministry, with at least one employee whose job it was to work the corridors, know all the relevant people, organize meetings, manage communications, deliver messages and ensure that they were read by the correct people. This was a very intensive and high pressure job, as there was a lot of interaction and both the issues and the personalities involved were in a constant state of flux.

The overall goal was to be able to interpret messages coming out of the various institutions and to place them in a context of what the key power brokers might also be thinking, to find routes for lobbying for TNK-BP's interests, to get improved access to things such as new licences and export approvals, and to manage other administrative or legislative issues. This really was a unique domestic partner offering and one which would have taken any foreign partner a huge amount of time and effort to match. In fact it would probably have been impossible to achieve because of the enormous relationship history that was the foundation of AAR's and other domestic actors' competitive advantage in this field.

JH: So did BP try to get involved in this area and what was the reaction of their partners if they did?

AF: I would say that both BP and senior foreign staff within TNK-BP did try to get involved in building relations and gaining local knowledge but that they met some significant resistance as they tried to do so. For example, at the highest level BP set up a shareholder team in 2005, when it became clear that it would need to actively manage its interest in TNK-BP and in Russia generally. The objective of the team was to build up the company's forensic capability with regards to the situation in Russia on a macro political and commercial basis as well as on an industrial and corporate basis. There was a clear attempt to understand the overall context behind decisions that were being taken or proposed at TNK-BP in order to inform the Board members representing BP so that they could react appropriately. Part of this process was an attempt to establish BP's own links with Russian government officials and corporate executives at all levels of the power structure.

However, there was tremendous reluctance from the Russian partners to allow BP to build independent relations within Russia. Even if meetings were organized between BP officials and the Russian authorities, a representative of AAR, or even one of the partners themselves, would often be found outside the room in advance in a clear attempt to prevent new individual relationships being built. Furthermore, AAR offered no encouragement to introduce BP to Russian officials even if it could have benefited TNK-BP. For example John Browne was widely respected in Russia, and although many senior people in the country would have welcomed meeting him, AAR were reluctant to allow him free access to meetings. They always tried to be in attendance in order to prevent him increasing BP's local knowledge and thus reducing their own competitive advantage.

On a more personal level, I also experienced the same effect many times in my attempts to build a relationship with Gazprom. The domestic TNK-BP representatives always guarded their relationships with Gazprom staff at all levels very jealously, and even if a joint meeting had been planned I would arrive to find that they had been there first to have a preliminary meeting. Sometimes I would be told what had been discussed and sometimes not, but often I would go into my own meeting and find that certain decisions had already been taken. I then had to endorse them or face the embarrassing situation of having to argue against an agreement that had already been made with a senior TNK-BP executive, which was of course normally impossible to do. Even more frustratingly, and annoyingly, meetings would sometimes be interrupted so that the leading Russian participants on both sides could have a side discussion, reach a decision and then return to the meeting to confirm the details. When challenged after the meeting my TNK-BP colleagues would often argue that this was done because "we have the relationship" and that it was in the best interests of the company for deals to be done like this. The real frustration, though, was that in the case of Gazprom I didn't feel that the relationships were actually that strong, and that I and my expat colleagues could have added some significant value if we had been given the opportunity. Instead we always felt that our Russian partners were constantly trying to defend their own core relationships and guarding their competitive advantage, with the added suspicion, of course, that side deals might have been negotiated without our knowledge.

Interestingly, it also seemed as though Gazprom were party to this game. Despite the fact that their relationship with AAR and TNK-BP did not seem that strong, there were still occasions when the presence of foreigners in the room would limit the freedom of the conversation. It seemed as if the whole process of negotiation was meant to be opaque, and transparency was not encouraged from either side if it meant sharing information with expats. As a result, even though Gazprom might have benefited from a more open discussion, there appeared to be an implicit understanding that certain issues were better discussed outside the room in order to continue the theme of keeping some knowledge between locals only.

This concern over foreigners starting to understand the situation in Russia was also demonstrated in many other ways when we started to build a picture of the financial and operational situation at Gazprom and across the domestic gas sector as a whole. It showed, I believe, a systemic concern about local knowledge being acquired by foreigners or those working for them, and aroused general suspicion about how we had acquired any information, even when it was publicly available.

JH: What happened in terms of roles and responsibilities inside the company then? Was there much evidence of knowledge transfer in the movement of partners between departments?

AF: I'm not aware of an expatriate getting fully involved in government relations or security, and the only external communications that foreigners were responsible for was in public relations, where the head of international PR was a foreigner. However, that clearly wasn't a role which had any domestic influence and wouldn't have disturbed any of the Russian partner relationships. Domestic PR was obviously run by a Russian.

Conversely, the sharing of technical and management knowledge was a key plank of the BP offering and was encouraged from day one. From a technical standpoint there was a specific goal to ensure that Russian staff were trained in using all the new techniques that were brought into the company, and this included both education and working together in Russia as well as reverse secondments to allow Russians to work in relevant BP subsidiaries overseas. As far as I am aware there was no obvious obfuscation from BP, and my reading of the situation was that it was quite the reverse, as BP were keen to encourage increased Russian participation across TNK-BP. This also stretched into the various management and governance departments, in particular PPM, through which BP's organizational and performance management experience was also brought into the company. I have mentioned portfolio and investment management before, and you could say that investment governance was a piece of kit that was brought in, and was used initially by expat employees but was soon shared with domestic employees. Indeed Russian employees were introduced to this department on a regular basis, and as a secondment it became a part of the overall training process for the highest quality staff. Russian staff began to take control of the department over time and also to become much more actively involved in the Strategy and M&A departments as they gained more expertise in these areas. So it was certainly my impression that BP made a big effort to share its skill base and to not only train domestic employees but also to get them heavily involved in the actual management of relevant business areas.

JH: So it would appear that there was a mismatch of learning within the joint company. Would you say that there was a competition to learn, and if so did BP or

AAR make any overt efforts to change the way that learning was taking place? And did the varying levels of learning create any conflict within the joint company?

AF: On the AAR side there was not much to complain about, at least initially. BP was introducing its new techniques which were demonstrably having an effect not only on the company's production but also on the way that TNK-BP was being managed. Furthermore, Russian employees were being introduced to these new techniques and learning how to run the business according to a more "international" standard, if I can call it that. In effect BP was keeping its promises. The problems came when the impact of these changes started to become less dramatic. Over time the results from the rehabilitation of the company's brownfields naturally started to become less impressive – the first horizontal wells and frac jobs had a much bigger impact than those being carried out three years later, as you always start with your best prospects and then move down the list. As a result, AAR became rather frustrated that the cost of the secondees from BP and the expats that TNK-BP was directly employing was no longer reaping the rewards they had seen in the first few years. A similar pattern happened on the management side. Once new accounting and performance management techniques had been put in place and Russian staff had been trained how to use them, BP's value added was perceived to fall and questions were soon asked about why so many expat employees were involved. So I'd say that the perception of BP's contributions declined over time, and the Russian side certainly felt that they were learning less as the joint company matured, and they were not happy about this. This is partly a function of not understanding how long it takes to learn and imbed these skills in the organization.

From a BP perspective, I would say that there was much less complaint about a lack of learning. Individual frustration was expressed about not being introduced to key individuals or getting access to certain meetings, but I would not say that it was brought up as a general issue. There was an overall acceptance that this was the domestic partner's role and I think that there was little expectation that foreigners would be involved. However, I think that this situation raises a number of key issues. Firstly, and perhaps most obviously, it left BP at a significant disadvantage when it came to the shareholder disputes, and also when it came to fully understanding what value AAR were really adding. I think this is important because of a second issue, which is that there is a certain hypocrisy from many foreign partners about the role of their domestic partner. On entering Russia, or any country with a similar commercial environment, there is an acknowledgement that a domestic partner is needed to deal with the "difficult issues" that are thrown up in a weak institutional environment, including corruption. The foreign partner feels that it does not have the expertise to play the necessary games initially, but then over time often continues to leave the dirty work to its domestic partner, happy to reap the rewards without fully acknowledging the value being added. As a result it implicitly weakens its own bargaining position by limiting its involvement in, and acquisition of, local knowledge that could either help it to operate alone or allow it to more accurately value its domestic partner's contribution. As a result, when conflict arises it is not in a very good position to respond either by fighting back or by accepting that the contributions of the two partners have got out of balance and, having acknowledged this, then addressing the issue.

JH: So how did BP cope with its lack of local knowledge?

AF: Externally I have mentioned that a shareholder team was formed to help with decision-making and data provision at Board level. This team worked in conjunction with senior TNK-BP and BP executives to try to establish a network of contacts within the Russian establishment and also used consultants and other external sources to try to build up a picture of the overall commercial environment and also about specific issues affecting TNK-BP and the deals that it was trying to do. However, I have also mentioned that this process was somewhat undermined by the domestic partners' constant efforts to ensure that BP did not get any unique access to key government or corporate decision-makers. They always seemed to be present when important meetings were due to take place, and their network of contacts meant that they often knew about things before the senior expat staff. On more than one occasion I was summoned to meet one of the AAR partners to be asked why a senior BP executive was meeting someone in Russia and I had to admit that I did not even know that the meeting was taking place.

Internally within TNK-BP, we needed to develop a capability to deal with the lack of information we were receiving on certain issues and on some occasions the misinformation that we were receiving. Essentially we had to establish a model of utilizing BP-related people in key senior positions, what you might term 'organizational nodes', in order to both monitor and triangulate what was happening and develop options to deal with specific initiatives and poor quality investment decisions that were being put forward. The CEO was clearly the most senior of these positions, but BP-related people also occupied the posts of COO, Head of Downstream, Head of Strategy, Head of PPM and Head of Gas and could act as listening posts within the organization to provide feedback and oversight on major investment decisions. For example as the Head of Gas, I was involved in other business streams, including Upstream, and if I saw investment proposals being made that I thought were wrong I could make an intervention by asking appropriate questions about these projects to reveal any problem areas.

And it was this questioning of investment proposals which was the real weapon in our armoury. As part of the management processes that AAR wanted BP to bring to TNK-BP the governance of investment decision-making was a key tool that I have already alluded too. However, once the process of developing an investment case for each major proposal had been introduced, it not only brought more rational behaviour to the allocation of the capital expenditure budget but it also allowed the Board and senior executives to keep an eye on deals that appeared to have "additional features", if I can use that euphemism. I have talked about the fact that the Russian partners often seemed to be holding side meetings with key contacts and reaching decisions without the participation of the foreign partner, and of course this often led to suspicion that side deals might have been cut which brought no value to TNK-BP. This was of course frustrating, but the interrogation of investment cases at least gave us the opportunity to spot anomalies and interrogate the rationale for any deals that appeared to lack commercial logic. I remember various occasions when the numbers on a specific deal just did not seem to add up, and the only explanation was that some other agreement might also have been reached. A question and answer session would then take place and would sometimes get quite heated, especially if the initiator of the deal could not offer logical answers to our questions or adequately defend the investment proposal. On more than one occasion the debate would end in a major confrontation, and we then had a difficult choice to make in deciding which battles to fight to their conclusion and which to concede. We couldn't hope to win all the time, and didn't want to cause a complete breakdown in partner relations, and we knew that on occasion an apparently illogical decision might produce a result that could actually benefit TNK-BP as a whole. However, our lack of local knowledge made it very difficult to decide which decisions to concede and which to fight.

JH: So what happened if there was a stalemate? How was a final decision made?

AF: The vertical power structure prevalent within any Russian company meant that all the major battles had to be fought at a senior level, either at a meeting of top management or at the Board. The CEO was expert at bringing together parties who were in dispute, as he had extraordinary diplomatic skills and a huge amount of patience, even under the most extreme duress. His consensual view of management was the reason that more conflict did not occur within the company, but occasionally even his skills were not enough and the issue had to be pushed higher to the Board of Directors level. Essentially most of the disputes centred around power and influence. Most of the deals that were challenged had been proposed because they would allow one of the Russian partners to gain some form of external advantage that would enhance his power base. Furthermore, the fact that these deals had then been questioned by a TNK-BP employee, normally an expat, created a threat to his internal power which he would normally not be prepared to tolerate. As expats we were used to giving our view and challenging perceived wisdom or decisions that we believed were made based on flawed logic. However, this is often not welcomed in a domestic context, and I remember being accused by senior Russian executives of "blocking my agenda" and threatened with "you know what happens to people who block my agenda". This would happen in front of a meeting of senior TNK-BP executives in order to cause maximum psychological effect, and you had to be particularly thick-skinned not to crack.

It is perhaps worth discussing at this stage how difficult things could get if as an expat you tried to oppose certain decisions or if you were felt to know too much about how the system was really operating. We would regularly see expats being targeted by the Russian partners if they were felt to be getting in the way. If, for example, they were blocking a deal, the first tactic would be to swamp them with information and advice in favour of the proposal. Numerous Russian employees from different departments would appear with supposedly rational arguments about why the deal should go ahead. The expat's time would be taken up either responding to all this "advice" or analysing the new data that he had been given. This would undermine his ability to do his normal job and leave him open to criticism, thus weakening his opposition to the main issue under debate.

If this didn't work then attempts would be made to neuter his authority and destroy any respect for his position. This tactic essentially involved breaking down the model of organizational nodes that we set up by creating a parallel organization that could by-pass the "problem individual". One of the Russian partners would propose a Russian employee to sit next to the expat inside the Business Unit, ostensibly as a learning experience in the development of an up-and-coming employee. However, almost immediately he would begin to exert his authority by going around the existing management structure and starting to brief the Russian staff separately that he was going to be running the Business Unit, and would begin to set up a second organizational structure to undermine the expat's position. Then in meetings the expat would be aggressively challenged by various Russian staff who had been specifically told to oppose his views, openly showing disrespect in front of colleagues who were too afraid to support him. He would be constantly criticized and attempts were made to highlight even the smallest mistakes in order to destroy his credibility. They didn't actually try to get rid of the person; that is never the intention as they want to avoid appearing too aggressive. The idea is to establish the foreigner as a highly paid consultant whose advice they can take or ignore as it suits their purpose. They would go to extraordinary lengths to try and achieve this goal and get BP staff into trouble. It sounds almost too apocryphal to be true, but I saw it happening in front of my own eyes.

However, we have got a bit side-tracked from the original question, which is how are decisions ultimately made when conflict cannot be resolved at management level. The answer is that they would ultimately be escalated to Board level, where the shareholders could reach a final resolution. This at times was very "political" and would rely on the BP board members being tough enough to support the internal expat view and having the information available to argue their case. However, this raises the overall issue of the quality of staff allocated to TNK-BP by BP and the willingness of HQ in London to support the people that they sent over to Russia.

JH: As we get into the issue of shareholders and the Board, perhaps now is the time to discuss the impact of the overall corporate structure of TNK-BP. It was a BVI-based company owned 50:50 between AAR and BP, with corporate governance structures and even a subsidiary that was quoted on the Moscow stock exchange. Did the fact that it was a corporate entity rather than a JV have a material impact on the longevity of the partnership and its ultimate success?

AF: Personally I think that the corporate structure was vital to the survival of the partnership and the 50:50 share split was also key. Right at the start John Browne would have preferred to take a 51% stake for BP but was told that there was no chance of achieving that, and he fully understood that taking a 49% stake would leave BP open to minority shareholder risks. Therefore, although Putin warned him that 50:50 would lead to lots of disputes I think that he was absolutely right to go for 50%. It gave us the opportunity to have a proper discussion about the important issues rather than being told "we're in control, so this is what we are doing".

As far as the corporate form of the partnership is concerned, it provided both the basis for the shareholding structure and also created a vehicle which provided long-term opportunity, growth potential and obvious financial returns in terms of dividend payments and a final exit strategy. I think that this was very important when it came to resolving conflicts – at the end of the day the structure incentivized both shareholders to come to the table to negotiate and ultimately to keep a unique investment vehicle together for their mutual benefit. Importantly it also created an environment where international corporate governance rules could form the basis for these negotiations, which helped in part to counter the "local knowledge" advantage of the domestic partners.

However, it wasn't perfect for one fundamental reason. Both shareholders were not equally represented inside the company. Specifically, AAR had direct shareholder representatives in management positions in TNK-BP, with German Khan as Executive Director, Viktor Vekselberg as the Director in charge of the Gas Business and ultimately Mikhail Fridman taking over from Bob Dudley as CEO after he left the country in 2008. Meanwhile BP did not have such direct representation, as all the expat employees were either directly employed by TNK-BP (for example Bob Dudley, myself and circa 15 others) or were secondees with no real seniority or responsibility. All the senior BP executives were on the Board of TNK-BP and not inside the company.

I think that there were two main consequences of this situation. Firstly, when big decisions were being made inside the company the AAR managers could, with some justification, say "I own half this company and this is what I want to do". Of course in extremis the response could be "but BP own the other half so we have to ask them too", but in reality you are not going to escalate every decision to Board level and so the owner-managers always had extra power inside the organization. Of course this was a clear conflict of interest, and I believe that John Browne anticipated the problem right at the initial formation of TNK-BP, but ultimately he conceded that AAR shareholders could have management positions. As a result, they could create an almost unstoppable momentum towards certain decisions being made through the force of their personalities and the fact that they were owners of the company.

A second consequence was that at Board level AAR generally had more direct information with which to make their arguments than the BP representatives. Of course the BP Board members had the support of the Shareholder Team, who did a good job of providing as much insight as possible, but there was always an advantage for the Russian Board members who had direct involvement in the business. This is not to say that they always got their way, as on many occasions normal governance rules and procedures allowed BP directors, and ultimately the independent directors who were appointed after the 2008 dispute, to veto decisions. However, the reality of the situation was that AAR were often better informed not only with their local knowledge of the situation in Russia but also thanks to their management roles inside TNK-BP, which meant that they were involved in company issues all the time, and this gave them a stronger bargaining position. When this was combined with their very aggressive attitude towards negotiation, their ability to force through decisions was rather powerful. In contrast BP Board members not only spent much less time at TNK-BP but also sometimes preferred to take a less confrontational approach to meetings, but this did not always create the right impression with the Russians, who tend to respect businessmen who are prepared to fight their corner. BP did do this occasionally, but not often enough in my opinion.

The shareholder disputes

JH: So the corporate structure helped to keep the partnership together, and ultimately it was very successful financially for both parties, but there were significant conflicts along the way. The first major shareholder dispute was in 2008. Can you talk about the causes of that and how you interpreted the ultimate outcome?

AF: The first thing to say was that the major shareholder dispute that you are referring to in 2008 did not just appear out the blue but was the culmination of a number of internal and external catalysts coming together at that time.

I would say that the partnership was never completely smooth, even at the beginning. There was no honeymoon period, although the partners were most aligned in the period 2003–2005 when the operational metrics were improving rapidly and the financial returns were impressive. However, as we have discussed above, around 2005 a slowing of production growth and the completion of the initial introduction phase of the new governance procedures started to create the impression that BP's influence and added value were declining. At around the same time, BP's frustration at not getting sufficient access to AAR's local knowledge was also starting to create some strains, as the perception that side deals were being done in meetings where we were not in attendance led to increasing mistrust and a gradual decline in confidence that AAR were the ideal domestic partner.

With this background, the major source of internal dispute was over investment decisions in capital projects. Proposals would come forward to the Investment Committee, which had been put in place as part of the BP-inspired governance initiative and was much more rigorous than the system in TNK, and more often than not would be turned down, mainly because there was a feeling that in a number of cases the full picture was not being revealed and as a result the economics just did not stack up for TNK-BP. A lack of trust on the foreign side always inclined us towards a negative interpretation of any discrepancies in the investment case, while on the Russian side the new governance rules were seen as an increasing hindrance to their objectives. Again, the supposedly value-adding process introduced by BP did not seem to be adding much value. Furthermore, whenever we tried to get access to more data that could have allowed us to make a more informed decision and perhaps be more positive, we were often blocked. This could happen either at a Head Office level or in one of the subsidiaries, where the issues were exactly the same.

There was also a lot of friction about the implementation of projects as well as their approval, with questions about what individuals were actually doing, where expats could add value, how much independent verification of information there was and also very specific debates about whether Russian or international techniques should be used in field development. People in the subsidiaries clearly did not always see it as a good thing that expats were arriving to tell them how to improve their operational procedures, as they saw this as an explicit criticism of past working practices and an implicit threat to their current position. There were clear examples of projects that could have been implemented more efficiently if new individuals had been given responsibility or if new techniques had been used, but these were blocked by the incumbent management and staff.

It is with this background that one needs to interpret the 2008 shareholder dispute at TNK-BP. To start with, investment in international assets became another source of friction at the Investment Committee level, with AAR very keen to see the company expand its sphere of operations as it was becoming clear that the best domestic opportunities were being reserved for the state companies. However, many of the international proposals were opportunistic and did not make economic sense, and from a BP perspective were not part of their plan for TNK-BP, which they saw as a Russian investment vehicle. As a result BP was seen as blocking TNK-BP's international plans for selfish reasons and not allowing the partnership to fulfil its full potential. Furthermore, AAR then skilfully managed the PR of the situation to portray BP as a foreigner that was preventing Russia's expansion onto the international stage, against the express wishes of President Putin himself.

As this issue over international assets was developing, a second debate emerged in the form of BP and TNK-BP's relationship with Gazprom. In 2006 Gazprom had been granted the monopoly for gas exports from Eastern Russia and as a result had decided to open discussions over the Kovykta field. TNK-BP controlled the field via its subsidiary Rusia Petroleum, and was keen to involve Gazprom in the field development as it understood that this would be the best way to facilitate gas exports to China. However, given the growing dominance of state companies in Russia's energy economy, the suspicion also emerged that BP might be planning a broader alliance with Gazprom, and had offered not only international assets but also potentially its share of TNK-BP as part of a partnership deal. This clearly worried AAR as it could see itself being usurped as BP's domestic partner of choice and would also have been concerned that, if left in a partnership at TNK-BP with Gazprom, its local knowledge would no longer be as valuable compared to that of a company with close links to the Kremlin.

All these issues came together at one time and led to the major shareholder dispute that emerged in 2008. Three major accusations were laid at BP's door. Firstly, it was blocking TNK-BP and Russia's legitimate desire to invest internationally. Secondly, it appeared to be betraying its Russian partner, AAR, by trying to form an alternative partnership with state-controlled Gazprom. And thirdly, it was openly accused of turning TNK-BP into a BP subsidiary, bringing in expensive expat staff who were adding less value than before and undermining the concept of TNK-BP as an independent entity. All three accusations appear to have had a certain validity, but as someone working inside the company I can only really comment on the third, with the observation that we had warned senior BP management both about the need to be seen to be keeping TNK-BP independent and about maintaining BP's relevance in terms of the technology and capabilities that they provided to the company. To be honest, it was not so much about the quality of the staff that were arriving, as they were all very good at their jobs and had a lot of international experience. The real issues were more that there were an increasing number of

Russian employees who could do the job equally well and at lower cost, and that a number of the foreigners who were arriving did not really understand the Russian context, how to build relationships in Russia, and therefore undermined the overall perception of expat staff in the company. I would say that some of the new arrivals just did not "get it", by which I mean that they could be rather patronizing and would criticize the existing working practices without fully understanding the context and the history of TNK-BP itself and of the Russian oil industry as a whole.

Furthermore, a number of the foreign staff that I interacted with also failed to get to grips with the working environment. There is a need to be prepared to do business in a tougher manner than you might be used to outside Russia, but also to build relationships across an organization in order to understand which battles to fight and which to let go. This relationship building, in essence creating your own internal local knowledge, also allows you to gain the respect of the domestic staff by showing that you understand what is going on, and that you recognize the games that are being played around the side of negotiations or deals. Then, without necessarily exposing them, you can demonstrate your knowledge in a manner that can achieve your goals without destroying the respect of your Russian colleagues. I would term this "constructive engagement". However, if you respond to the more aggressive Russian way of doing business in an antagonistic fashion, without at least acknowledging some respect for the domestic rules of the game, then a dispute can easily escalate. I think that this is what happened in 2008, as BP's tactics on a number of issues combined to put AAR on the offensive in an attempt to defend their position both inside TNK-BP and in the Russian business and political environment as a whole.

This broader context is important because often people analysing the situation cannot understand why a Russian partner might act in a manner that would appear to harm his own, as well as his foreign partner's, interests in a joint venture. The answer, I believe, is that most conflicts in Russia are actually about power rather than creating value and profits, as the former certainly mattered more than the latter. Both were clearly important, but I think that over the long term it was felt that if one's power was maintained then revenue opportunities would always emerge in a country with a political structure like Russia's. Therefore a Russian partner would be prepared to risk the entire partnership if necessary, with the understanding that he could most probably rebuild his business in Russia using his power and influence while his foreign partner would have much more difficulty. As a result the foreign partner is more likely to yield in any negotiation, knowing that the domestic partner is less likely to blink if the joint venture between them is put at risk.

In 2008 this negotiating tactic was enhanced by one other factor external to TNK-BP but very relevant to BP, namely the resignation of John Browne from the company in early 2007, which brought about a major change in the relationship with AAR. Tony Hayward took over as CEO, and while I certainly have no criticism of the job he did at the head of the company through some incredibly difficult years, there is no doubt in my mind that the Russian partners did not respect, even fear, him in the way that they did John Browne. As a result, the 2008 shareholder dispute provided AAR with an opportunity to test the mettle of BP's new CEO, and to potentially extract some concessions from him. And I believe that they feel they achieved this. TNK-BP's governance structure was overhauled and the membership of the Board of Directors was made more balanced. Furthermore, AAR also managed to secure the resignation of TNK-BP's CEO Bob Dudley, who was ultimately viewed by them as the symbol of BP's influence within the organization. Finally they also managed to demonstrate the extent of their local knowledge and influence through the various practical issues that inconvenienced both the company and its expat employees.[37] TNK-BP also started to plan for an international strategy that culminated in it buying overseas assets from BP and others over the next three years. And finally, the potential for a wide-ranging alliance between BP and Gazprom was effectively halted, with Gazprom pulling out of an agreement over the Kovykta field by the end of 2008 and having no further negotiations with BP concerning a broader partnership.

JH: The second shareholder dispute seemed to have many of the same issues, albeit with some different characters involved. Do you interpret the causes and effects of that 2011 dispute in the same way?

AF: To a certain extent yes, in as much as a number of the same characteristics were involved, but the issues were not all the same. I think that the 2008 dispute, and especially the way it ended with Bob Dudley's departure from Russia and the embarrassment caused over AAR's overall tactics, convinced BP that they needed a new partner in Russia. The need to calm the situation at TNK-BP, combined with the additional necessity to survive the 2009 economic crisis and the slump in the oil price, meant that nothing happened for a while, but by 2010 it is well known that BP was in discussions with Rosneft. Again, the motivation was to have a stronger state-sponsored partner who could provide access to the new opportunities that were increasingly being offered only to state-controlled companies. In this instance the Arctic licences in the South Kara Sea were the main goal, with a share swap between Rosneft and BP planned as a further confirmation of their plans for a long-term alliance.

AAR's reaction was not a great surprise to those of us watching the deal unfold from our position inside TNK-BP. I was not party to the BP discussions at all and so I have no idea what was discussed or not discussed with AAR before the deal announcement, but I think that the threat to AAR's position was pretty clear from the "strategic" nature of the deal between BP and Rosneft that was announced in their joint press release. Although BP attempted to reiterate that it remained committed to TNK-BP, AAR could no doubt envisage a scenario in which, once again, its position as BP's preferred partner was under threat and one in which its local knowledge advantage would be significantly undermined. Even if TNK-BP had progressed alongside a new BP-Rosneft alliance, BP's relationship with a state oil company with close links to the Kremlin would have transformed its position relative to AAR. And it was very clear from the negotiations after the deal was announced that Rosneft did not want anything to do with AAR, underlining again the likelihood of its increasing isolation if the deal did go ahead.

Therefore, the aggressive reaction from AAR was to be expected, and of course it was to their tremendous advantage that BP had left a legal route open for them in the international courts. As a result, they were able to argue strongly that they should be allowed to pursue their commercial rights through the legal processes in the UK and Stockholm, while they also had the further option, during the delay that this caused, to use their local influence in Russia to undermine BP's cause. I think that most people, myself included, expected that AAR would be allowed to pursue their case to a certain extent, extract some value from BP and then back down, allowing the deal to go ahead. However, it would seem that the issue of their position being undermined was so vital to their future interests that they were prepared to pursue the destruction of the deal to the bitter end, with a number of other local factors coming into play that undermined BP's plans.

The first was the political dispute that appeared to be taking place ahead of the Duma and Presidential elections at the end of 2011 and the beginning of 2012. In early 2011 the political elite seemed to be manoeuvring ahead of a decision about whether Putin would stand for President again or whether the incumbent Dmitry Medvedev would be re-nominated. Within this debate it seems that Medvedev was keen to reduce Igor Sechin's power base, and he forced him to leave his position as chairman of Rosneft.[38] Although it is not clear how the BP-Rosneft deal figured in the political sphere, it is not beyond the bounds of credibility to suggest that certain political figures may have been happy to see the deal fail, while others may have decided not to expend too much political capital defending it.

The second factor was that, faced with the need to fight to save the deal and also to negotiate with AAR, Sechin ultimately had another easier option, namely a deal with another IOC. Ultimately, of course, he exercised this option when after a four and a half month struggle with AAR, Sechin and BP ultimately announced the collapse of their deal and Rosneft went on to sign an Arctic agreement over the same licences with ExxonMobil in August 2011, and then to sign further offshore deals with Statoil and ENI in the subsequent

12 months. The most extraordinary thing, though, in many people's eyes was that AAR was prepared to take its fight to the limit and ultimately to break a deal that had initially been supported by both Igor Sechin and Vladimir Putin. I think that this demonstrates two things. Firstly, just how strong their local knowledge and influence was. This was clear to me from inside TNK-BP just from the number of times that I was aware that various of the AAR partners were meeting with Sechin and other government officials even as they were putting the biggest deal in Russian oil history under threat. The interaction appeared to be happening on an almost daily basis, and certainly trumped anything that BP could have hoped to achieve. And secondly, as we discussed earlier, it showed that at the end of the day they were prepared to cause chaos and put the entire partnership at risk rather than lose out in a battle of local power and influence. They must have been very confident about their ability to recover from the chaos that they were causing to have gone so far, and I think that this illustrates once again how many of the big disputes are really about power rather than revenues.

Finally, one other factor that undermined BP's position was the impact of the Deepwater Horizon tragedy. I am not talking here about BP's reputation as an operator in the aftermath of the disaster, as both AAR and the Russian authorities were actually rather supportive of their largest international investor – the fact that they were prepared to sign an Arctic deal shows you that. However, the weakness of BP's share price, the possible threat of a bid by one of its major competitors and the clear indications from shareholders that another big corporate problem would not be tolerated for long clearly undermined BP's bargaining position. As a result, although it is not obvious whether it was a deliberate tactic or not, it must have been clear to AAR that any lengthy delay to the deal completion, especially if it was accompanied by the threat of legal action, could ultimately weaken BP's resolve, and eventually that is what happened. Rosneft and Sechin had expended enough political capital defending the deal and took an alternative route while BP could not sustain a protracted legal dispute any longer. And so AAR won.

JH: But the miraculous thing, it seems to me, is that although AAR got their way in 2011, by the end of 2012 both BP and AAR were bought out on equal terms and BP managed to retain a significant position in Russia. From a position of fairly devastating defeat BP seems to have found a route to a very profitable exit – how did that happen?

AF: I think that BP had one significant advantage and made one very smart move. The advantage was in the corporate structure of TNK-BP and the fact that it had 50% ownership of the company. This meant that it could ultimately constrain AAR's actions via the corporate governance of the company and also benefit in the same way as AAR from any outcome. Of course this was not a perfect situation and I wouldn't want to suggest that there were no major rows and disputes between the shareholders as each tried to get the better of various situations. But at the end of the day they were tied together by their ownership of a company with multiple assets, long-term growth prospects and importantly, a transparent financial structure and a market valuation. As a result it was something that clearly had an open market value, offering an exit strategy for either partner in extremis. And this led to BP's move, which was to announce the sale of its 50% share in TNK-BP. This essentially forced AAR's hand, leaving them with a stark choice. Exercise their right to match any offer made to BP and own 100% of TNK-BP, or accept that BP would probably have to sell to Rosneft or Gazprom, thus leaving AAR in the position it had rejected in 2008, or sell their own 50% stake alongside BP.

The risk for BP, of course, was that there was a limited range of buyers, but once Rosneft's interest had emerged and AAR had decided to sell it was in a strong position. As they were selling the same asset BP could benefit from AAR's obvious desire to maximize its valuation, if necessary by using its local knowledge in any negotiations. The corporate nature of the deal, and the transparent financial history of the company, also meant that a reasonable value range could be established with relative ease, reducing BP's risk of receiving an unfair price. Finally, BP's desire to reinvest a large part of its proceeds in Rosneft shares also helped to facilitate the deal, as it reduced the amount of cash that Rosneft needed to raise.

Overall, then, I think that BP got as good a deal as was possible in the situation, largely as a result of its ability to take AAR's local knowledge out of the equation by turning the transaction into a large, but relatively straightforward, corporate M&A deal. In the end it would have been very difficult for it to receive anything other than a fair price, and I think that it certainly achieved that as well as maintaining a rather unique position in Russia as a major shareholder in Russia's National Oil Company. We will have to wait and see if this ultimately provides the financial and industrial dividends that BP is no doubt hoping for, and also whether it might set a new paradigm for IOC/NOC relations across the global energy sector. However, it certainly provided BP with a significant return on its initial investment and made its Russian strategy to date an undoubted success.

Conclusions

JH: And so to conclude, what are the main things that you have learnt both from your experience at TNK-BP and also from your involvement with other partnerships in Russia since you left?

AF: Firstly, the commercial environment in Russia is a complex triangle of business, political and vested interests, dominated by a relatively small number of key individuals but ostensibly run by government institutions whose inherent weakness can be exploited by those with power and influence. Within this environment, local knowledge of how to operate, who to have close relationships with, how to gain access to opportunities and how to protect any assets that you have managed to acquire is vital. Entrepreneurs in Russia exploit this local knowledge, as they have used it to build their domestic businesses in the first place, and they know that it is a core competitive advantage when it comes to dealing with foreign partners. They see that foreign partners can bring new skills and also a form of protection from the risk of asset appropriation via the link they bring to the international market place, and the domestic partners not only value these attributes but are also slightly threatened by them. They feel that they need something to counterbalance the perceived strength of their foreign partner, and this balance is provided by their local knowledge. Domestic partners understand this and protect their advantage by emphasizing how difficult it is to do business in Russia and by encouraging an asymmetric environment. It is to their advantage that the system is a maze of different interests and power bases, where their relationships are vital to provide access and protection. As a result it is important to see local knowledge as the key bargaining strength of the domestic partner in countries with business environments like that in Russia, and also to understand that it is balanced by the technical and management skills brought by a foreign partner. This balance is generally clear at the start of a partnership, but the key is to maintain it over an extended period.

Secondly, this rather chaotic and confusing situation has helped to create a business and relationship culture that is very different to that which most foreigners have experienced before. Due to the riskier environment in Russia, domestic businessmen can tend to be more short term in their outlook and "deal driven" rather than strategic. This can be reflected in a more opportunistic approach to business and a less rigorous analytical focus on the specifics of individual transactions. It is possible for this attitude to be complimented by a foreign partner who takes a more long-term view, especially in the oil business, with a greater inclination to base business decisions on detailed economic and commercial analysis. In an ideal world the best of both approaches can lead to a vibrant atmosphere in which there is a full understanding of the key issues and the long-term goal but also a desire to be proactive and get things done in a commercial environment where change is frequent and rapid and where too much delay and over-analysis can lead to opportunities being missed.

However, the clash of cultures can also cause significant friction, especially because the Russian management system is somewhat feudal in nature. The boss rules and his subordinates do what they are told, and wait to be told what to do. There is not much initiative used and avoidance of blame is a key objective for many more junior and mid-level staff. In contrast many expat staff are used to expressing their views openly and even contradicting their senior management if appropriate, and this can lead to clashes. The situation can get particularly difficult when there is a sense, as I often experienced, that a deal is not just being driven by a profit motive. Apparently sub-optimal deals for the partnership can often have side benefits for the domestic partner, often based on creating obligation to enhance power and influence rather than for the creation of extra revenues. In these cases, where debates over the commercial rationale for a deal are muddied by other issues that cannot be mentioned, the atmosphere can get very aggressive, and Russian businessmen are not afraid to test the mettle of their foreign partners in a heated argument. This can make things very uncomfortable for some expats, and it is important for any foreign company to find the right kind of people who can deal "constructively" with these types of situation.

A third conclusion is that knowledge transfer really can be seen as a competition between the partners, with the domestic side in particular keen to absorb knowledge but not keen to share it. This was clearly exemplified in the changing responsibilities of the Russian and foreign employees over the life of TNK-BP. Russian staff were encouraged to learn about technology, management, strategy and governance, and over time were given roles that reflected their newly-acquired skills. In contrast, I don't know of any BP employees who took on significant roles in the main "local knowledge" departments such as government relations and security. Indeed, I would say that attempts to become more informed in these areas were actively blocked, with even the CEO of BP sometimes struggling to have an independent meeting with senior government officials. At a lower level within TNK-BP, expat employees who were seen to be "blocking agendas" or learning too much about how the system really worked were actively targeted and undermined in order to remove them as a threat.

BP certainly took steps to improve its local knowledge, primarily through the formation of its shareholder team, but I would say that it never really had a chance of success because it did not employ full-time senior Russian staff as BP, rather than TNK-BP, employees. As a result, it was normally at least one or two steps behind the domestic partner on every issue. Internally at TNK-BP we tried to control the situation by having expat employees in important organizational nodes, so that we could stay informed and block poor quality investment proposals. We also used the new governance rules, in particular the interrogation of investment cases, to expose flaws in deals and to highlight areas where "side deals" seemed to be prevalent, but even if we managed to do this we still had to make a difficult choice as to whether to block every apparently sub-optimal deal or to let some through. At the end of the day, because of the vertical power structure in the company, many of these decisions became subjective calls for the Board to make, and then the outcome depended upon how much reliable information the BP representatives had and how tough they were prepared to be at that time. In this regard there were often trade-offs at the Board level.

A fourth conclusion is that, although it was not a panacea, the corporate structure of the TNK-BP partnership provided the basis for its longevity and the ultimate exit on profitable terms for all the partners. When the Board had to make tough decisions, the governance rules of a company, rather than a simple JV, created a solid foundation. When disputes between the shareholders had been taken almost to breaking point, the long-term nature of the business and its clear value as a corporate entity brought them back to the negotiating table. And finally, when it came to the ultimate sale, the transparency of the governance structure and the financial position of the company ensured that both partners optimized the exit price for each other, ensuring that both got a good deal, in my opinion.

Within this positive view, one negative stood out, which was that the involvement of AAR shareholders in executive management positions within TNK-BP significantly increased their bargaining position. Using their constant involvement in the company and the power of their official positions they could create initial momentum towards an objective within the company which would then be difficult to stop at Board level. Equally, in any arguments at Board level they would have additional information and experience from their internal roles at TNK-BP to add to their existing "local knowledge" advantage. John Browne certainly saw the problem at the formation of TNK-BP, and tried to change the situation on more than one occasion, but it remained an issue throughout.

Another specific issue which caused a major problem, especially during BP's attempts to do the deal with Rosneft, was the AMI (Area of Mutual Interest) clause in the original shareholder agreement. Initially it had been inserted by BP to prevent AAR from working with other IOCs in Russia, as it asserted that all opportunities in Russia must be offered to the TNK-BP partnership. However, it came back to haunt BP when the opportunity to partner with Rosneft was offered, but AAR were not included. It highlights the risk of unintended consequences as you put the initial agreements together, and although it is of course easy to be wise with hindsight, it is a point worth considering for future entrants into similar partnerships.

The change in the dynamic of the AMI also highlights perhaps the most interesting, and final, conclusion to be drawn from the TNK-BP partnership, which is that as a foreign partner there is a need to constantly monitor the balance of the relationship between you and your domestic partner. In the case of TNK-BP, the partnership started in reasonable balance, but as the domestic partners acquired the skills brought by their foreign partner the balance shifted in their favour, especially as BP failed to acquire similar amounts of local knowledge. I have outlined how BP and the expats within TNK-BP tried to address this issue, and how the domestic partners tried to block them, but essentially I think that one of the main causes for the disputes in 2008 and 2011 was the fight over the shifting bargaining power. One interpretation might suggest that BP did not realize until it was too late how the balance of bargaining power had moved against them, and then were forced into the somewhat drastic action of trying to find alternative partners (Gazprom in 2007/08 and Rosneft in 2011) to address the situation. AAR's reaction to this threat was very aggressive, and twice exposed BP's lack of local knowledge as they essentially failed to achieve their objectives in both cases. However, the corporate structure of TNK-BP, combined with BP's strategy in exploiting the governance and valuation implications of it, ultimately saved the day and ensured a profitable exit.

In the next chapter, though, we will outline some more generic conclusions that we believe might help to secure a more stable ongoing relationship between foreign and domestic partners in Russia. We will suggest that a consistent process of monitoring balance within a joint entity and acquiring sufficient local knowledge to do this can help to avoid the worst forms of partnership turbulence. While acknowledging that this acquisition of local knowledge is not easy, to say the least, we will offer suggestions about how it can be achieved so that there is enough information to both assess your domestic partner's value and also to acknowledge a key feature of learning in environments like Russia – knowing where the gaps in your knowledge are and having a plan to address them.

We will also suggest that the foreign partner needs to consistently assess its own contribution to the partnership, its relevance to the various stakeholders and at times to adjust it to take into account the changing internal and external circumstances surrounding the partnership. We will also argue that it needs to carry out the same assessment for its domestic partner, which again will require an increased level of local knowledge and insight that must be acquired on a continuous basis. And finally, we will argue that, while BP managed to exit its partnership with a significant return on its initial investment thanks to the corporate nature of its venture, the structure of the latest international partnerships in Russia is returning to the joint venture model seen in the 1990s, increasing the risks for the latest wave of international investors in Russia.

7
Conclusions on a Strategy for Foreign Partners

Introduction

Over the course of the past six chapters we have laid out a number of themes and ideas about the relationship between the partners in international joint ventures in Russia. We began with a brief history of the Russian oil industry and the role of foreign actors within it, highlighting the varied fortunes of large companies such as Shell and BP down to the smaller players such as the Canadian independents who formed JVs in the early post-Soviet period. We discussed the fact that, after an initial surge in activity in the 1990s, there was a hiatus in significant foreign company activity after 1998 (with the notable exception of TNK-BP), but over the past two to three years IOCs have once again begun to focus on Russia as a core part of their global growth strategy, making an analysis of the key drivers of successful partnership a very relevant and current topic.

We then presented a theoretical debate about the formation of joint ventures in the oil and gas industry, and discussed the factors which influence the bargaining power between the partners. We did this in the particular context of a weak institutional environment, which we argued has been prevalent in Russia throughout the post-Soviet era, although in different forms under the three presidents who have been elected in that period. We argued that local knowledge of the business environment, and in particular the use of contacts, influence and relationships, is a key skill used by domestic entrepreneurs to build their businesses, and is also used as their core offering to any joint venture formed with a foreign company. Meanwhile the foreign company brings their more international skill-set of technical expertise, management experience and, where needed, financing. Our analytical interpretation of the relevant academic literature then suggested that the balance of bargaining power within joint ventures was established in an implicit "race to learn" in what is effectively a "competition for knowledge", with the winner likely to be the partner who could most quickly acquire his counterpart's skills. We further suggested that, given the complex and enigmatic nature of local knowledge, this competition was more likely to be won by the domestic partner, giving him an inherent competitive advantage in any joint venture.

We then used a number of case studies and interviews with foreign and domestic actors in the Russian oil and gas industry to support the concept of the importance of local knowledge as part of the relationship between the two partners. All the foreign partners, whether successful or not, acknowledged that an understanding and ability to deal with local political, operational, financial and other business issues was vital to the ongoing development of their business in Russia. Furthermore, some foreign partners also recognized that they had relied too heavily and for too long on their domestic partner, and had ultimately been undermined by their inability to demonstrate an increase in their own local knowledge. Others decided either to make a big effort to develop a personal local network, and thus balance their domestic partner's biggest strength, or to try and provide an ongoing incentive to their partner to use his abilities for the general benefit of all the shareholders in a corporate structure.

Statistical analysis of a survey of foreign joint venture partners who operated in Russia between 1991 and 2003 also helped to provide some numerical evidence to support our theories. Local knowledge was identified as the most important contribution made by domestic partners, and the importance of this local knowledge was emphasized by the manner in which more successful foreign partners harnessed it. Across all the joint entities that we analysed, the most important catalyst of greater foreign partner success was an increase in foreign partner control over local knowledge issues, and this was especially true in traditional single asset joint ventures. Meanwhile, a potential alternative route to success was seen as the use of a corporate model in order to create a structure within which all the partners were encouraged to direct the use of their skills towards the overall success of the entity rather than compete with their partner for greater individual success.

In this concluding chapter we will therefore attempt to re-define the bargaining model for international companies in the Russian oil and gas industry, to identify the key drivers for success and to outline the strategic thought process that we believe can lead not just to greater achievement of an IOC's objectives but also to a mutually beneficial outcome for both parties that can enhance the long-term relationship between foreign and domestic actors. In addition, we will also outline some tactical steps that we believe can help to form an analytical foundation for foreign companies seeking to build a profitable and sustainable business in settings such as Russia, where local knowledge is clearly a key element of the commercial and political environment.

An analytical framework for thinking about the Russian business environment

Before we embark on our conclusions about partnerships between foreign and domestic investors in Russia, it is important first to summarize our thoughts on the business environment in which this co-operation is taking place. Throughout the preceding chapters we have outlined various theoretical descriptions of the political and commercial situation in the country over the post-Soviet era and have also heard first-hand from businessmen who have experienced the problems of running a company or a joint venture during this period. In brief, the theoretical analysis suggests that during the 1990s a small number of very influential business entrepreneurs exploited the weakness of state institutions as they were first formed and emerged in the immediate aftermath of the collapse of the Soviet Union, through a process that is often referred to as state capture. In essence these entrepreneurs had sufficient influence to ensure both that new laws were created that could benefit their businesses and also that existing laws were interpreted in a favourable way, using various incentives to tempt public officials who were poorly paid and unclear as to their exact role in the developing Russian political and economic environment. Essentially, a business elite dominated the state, with the clearest example of this being their support for the re-election of Boris Yeltsin as president in 1996, when their money and media connections effectively won the day.

During the Putin/Medvedev era post-2000 the situation has changed somewhat, in that the state has re-emerged as a powerful force in Russia, with the example of a resurgent Rosneft in the oil (and now gas) sector as the clearest example of this trend. However, we have argued, using a number of academic references, that in fact the situation has not altered as much as one might think, once one delves underneath the surface. The institutions of state remain relatively weak, as it is the individuals who control them who are the dominant force in Russian society, creating a new political elite. As one commentator described the situation – "the state is thus chronically weak and subordinate to the networks [of key individuals], yet it is kept afloat as a sort of institutional carcass that the networks need".[1] Furthermore "the system is characterised by the opacity of the decision-making processes and the interdependency of the political and economic realms"[2] with the result that, although in 2000 Putin promised to restore the authority of the State "10 years later the public institutions are all weakened and subject to the arbitrariness of the Kremlin system", which is a system of managed tension between competing groups.[3] Within this environment "corruption has flourished because...money and gift exchange are the currency of business and power"[4] and "the enforcement of property rights is also a major barrier for business development...with violations common and the business community often opting for informal resolution of conflicts rather than using formal institutions".[5]

We have also discussed numerous practical examples of foreign companies attempting to operate within this environment, both in the case studies from the 1990s and in the discussions with foreign actors in the 2000s. The case studies offered us examples of the Russian bankruptcy law being used to disenfranchise both the owners of assets and their shareholders, while other tactics involved overt threats and opportunistic use of the opaque and complex commercial situation. Interviews with later participants in the sector suggested that little had changed, with quotes such as "we are returning to the 1990s" and "the legal system does not support partnership because shareholder agreements are effectively unenforceable". In particular the importance of key individuals was emphasized time and again, as was the link between business and politics, with interviewees claiming that "it is still all about individuals and the influence they can exert because the institutions themselves remain inert and drowned in bureaucracy". The complexity of the linkages between individuals and institutions was also highlighted as was the overall confusion surrounding the vast quantities of data that could be used to obscure key decisions. The higher risks that this implied meant that many Russian businessmen focused on the short term and on taking opportunities as they arrive, in particular by exploiting the "lacunas in the legislation". For any company hoping to prosper in this environment the key strategy was therefore summarized as "a need to tie yourself to the theoretically strongest person or most influential party and hope that their power base can protect you".

Pulling all of these strands of theoretical and practical evidence together, we believe that it is useful to create a simple image of the main forces at work in the Russian business environment, indeed in the business environment of any country with a weak institutional framework, which we can then use as the foundation for our further conclusions on partnership and foreign company strategies. We show this image in Figure 7.1, and we believe that, although it clearly needs deepening in any specific situation, it can help as a reminder of the three key issues that are held in a "managed tension" in commercial environments like Russia.

Of the three elements in the Triangle of Tension, the business section is perhaps the easiest to understand. In any venture there will be a commercial negotiation around the value of contributions, assets, and work carried out, and all the parties will have a view about the returns they expect to make given the financial commitment they are making and their perceptions of the risks involved. This negotiation will not always be easy, of course, and in a Russian environment may be hindered by a lack of available data, the

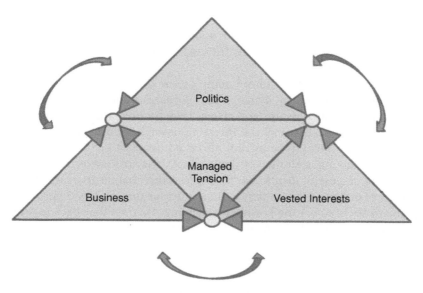

Figure 7.1 "The Triangle of Tension": Explaining the interconnection between politics, business and vested interests in a weak institutional environment

exploitation of information asymmetries or even outright deception. Conversely, it may also be complicated by a scarcely comprehensible overflow of information that has to be filtered and analysed, often under extreme time pressure that adds further stress. Nevertheless, a final decision to proceed with the venture or not is likely to be reached on recognizable commercial parameters.

These negotiations may bring an initial level of complexity and difficulty, but further complications can then be added by the introduction of the political element to any discussion. In any country, of course, there may be a political dynamic to a large business deal, with the dispute over CNPC's $18 billion bid for US oil company Unocal in 2005 being one example where, even in the world's leading free market economy, political opposition interfered with commercial strategy due to fears over national security.[6] In a country like Russia, where the state has re-asserted its control over strategic industries such as oil and gas and where power has been increasingly concentrated in the hands of a few people who are involved in all key political and economic decisions, the situation is magnified many times. This is especially true where the National Oil Company (Rosneft) and the National Gas Company (Gazprom) are more than 51% owned by the State, giving any move they make an inherently political overtone, with implications both domestically and overseas. Deals with overseas companies have clear foreign policy and geo-political implications, but they also play to a domestic audience in terms of boosting the standing of politicians who are seen to be re-establishing Russia on the global stage. They can also have an obvious impact on the economies of various regions in Russia, depending upon where investments are to be made and how tax revenues are to be distributed, which again can have important political consequences.

It is no surprise, then, to hear many of our interviewees referring to the importance of the political dynamic in their business dealings in Russia, both when initiating partnerships and also as they progress through their various milestones. Indeed, many of the interactions we have discussed highlighted not only the political dynamic but also the impact of just a few very senior politicians who made all the key decisions. As one senior executive described the closing of a major deal to us: "We agreed the final terms of the deal with the CEO of our partner company at 4am one morning, and by 5am he was on a plane to Sochi to get the President's blessing. He then flew back to Moscow the next day to consult the Board of his company before announcing the deal the following day. However, it was clear that only one person had the ultimate say on the deal – the country's most senior politician." Given that this one person, Vladimir Putin, is seen as being so influential, it is also interesting to note that one of the key foundations of his power is often seen as being the ability to balance the rival political clans that surround him.[7] In this sense the entire political system can be seen as a form of managed tension, to which foreign companies and individuals find themselves exposed as soon as they start to negotiate for business opportunities in Russia.

If one can then conclude that the politics are relatively easy to understand, given the small number of individuals involved, although very difficult to influence, one cannot say the same about the third element of the "Triangle of Tension", namely Vested Interests, which are both challenging to untangle and equally troublesome to affect. As has been identified by a number of authors cited in earlier chapters, the nature of Russian politics tends to create an atmosphere in which the satisfaction of the needs of influential, wealthy and potent individuals is vital in order to sustain a political power base. It also inspires the potential for high levels of corruption inherent in an institutional environment which is heavy on bureaucracy and light on legal enforcement. Although the corruption is not necessarily of the most obvious type, many of our interviews touched on the side deals, special treatment and related transactions that sit at the heart of a society such as that in Russia. Indeed, one of the most insightful books on Russian society, Ledeneva's "Russia's Economy of Favours",[8] captures the essence of the situation in its title.

However, much of the foundation and structure of the networks of vested interests in Russia are desperately difficult for a foreigner to understand. Many connections have been formed out of Soviet-era contacts, university friendships, family ties or early working associations, and it requires a huge amount of research in order to unearth not just the top layer of connections but also the multiple tiers of inter-related ties that form the overall web of influence, reliance, responsibility and loyalty. Nevertheless, if any business is to be successful in Russia, and if any major deal is to be completed, then it is necessary to at the very least understand as much of this complex issue as possible, as it is relevant for each transaction or ongoing commercial enterprise. This is vital because, if any one part of the Triangle is not held in balance, then any deal can collapse for what may seem an inexplicable reason. For example, when BP finalized its Arctic deal with Rosneft in January 2011 it clearly believed that it had the three parts of the triangle in the correct balanced tension. The commercial deal had been struck, political support from Igor Sechin and Vladimir Putin had been won and it appeared that the key vested interest, AAR, had been mollified or at least by-passed. It also appears to have been assumed that any problems in this direction would be resolved by the political elite in Russia, who would also play a role in keeping any other vested interests satisfied. However, the triangle clearly became unbalanced rather rapidly as AAR responded in an unexpectedly aggressive style, Vladimir Putin was not prepared to expend excessive political capital to defend the deal and Igor Sechin ultimately had other options to pursue. The major failing, though, was a lack of understanding as to how far AAR would be allowed to push their objections, and it seems clear with hindsight that they had a much more powerful network of vested interests supporting them than had been anticipated.

Some other conclusions on the Russian business setting are also worth noting, as they relate to the difficulty of keeping the "Triangle of Tension" intact. These relate to the more detailed elements of the working environment that led Alastair to describe it as "probably the most complex business and political situation I have ever worked in". This complexity is founded on a number of cultural factors that make it difficult for foreigners to adapt to the Russian commercial world. The first is that this world is very factional and fragmented, almost tribal, in how it works, meaning that it is sometimes difficult to understand individual views and motivations. This is true both at a high level and also within companies, where there often appear to be cases of continuous managed tension between factions which are controlled through various trade-offs between connected interests whenever a major decision is made. This tension is exacerbated by the generally confrontational and aggressive attitude that can be taken by many domestic players in negotiations in order to gain dominance and exploit weakness. Furthermore the level of tenacity and persistence in pursuing goals, if necessary by obfuscating and blocking decisions on unrelated issues to gain leverage, is also exceptional.

In addition, the experience of a number of our interviewees has been that conflict and mistrust are often the norm, and that the preferred outcome appears to be "win-lose" rather than "win-win". Trust is elusive, and often deception is used to confuse and outmanoeuvre opponents, with parallel control systems also being set up to by-pass problems and reduce the influence of those who appear to be getting in the way of decisions being made. As a result much of our analysis would suggest that what you see and hear on the surface is rarely a true reflection of what is really happening in a particular situation, implying a continuous need to check facts, build up sources of information and develop networks of influence in order to understand and triangulate as much of what is actually happening behind the scenes as possible. As we will discuss next, this is what domestic actors in weak institutional environments such as Russia are expert at doing, indeed it is the very foundation of their competitive advantage, and it is why foreign players believe, correctly in our view, that they are needed as partners in new foreign ventures in Russia.

A new model to describe relationships in a weak institutional environment

In Chapter 2 we identified Dunning's eclectic (OLI) paradigm as a good structure on which to base a discussion of foreign investors' participation in the Russian oil and gas industry. On the one hand foreign investors bring their ownership (O) skills of management, technology and in some instances capital, as outlined in the literature on foreign investment in the resources industry.[9] On the other hand the State which controls the natural resources has a significant locational (L) advantage, thanks to its geological and geographical good fortune. In a traditional negotiation the foreign investor then attempts to gain access to these resources by acquiring a licence to explore and develop them, thereby internalizing (I) his ownership advantages for his own benefit and also, via the payment of taxes, for the benefit of the State.

However, although this model provides a good description of the process in a strong legal and institutional environment, it ignores the participation of a third domestic actor in a weak state environment. Building on the work of various academics,[10] we have argued that domestic entrepreneurs in a weak state environment, with a poor legal and judicial system and weak governance rules, use state capture as a core strategy, with local knowledge as a core competence. Ledeneva (2006)[11] has defined this competence as an understanding of the informal processes that allow an economy and a political system to operate in a weak institutional situation, and it is clear from the literature on Business Groups in particular that it was used by entrepreneurs to acquire assets and build businesses in Russia in the 1990s. We have explored this notion both empirically and analytically, and evidence from the case studies in the 1990s, the interviews with foreign actors in the 2000s and the survey of foreign partners confirms the importance of three actors in joint entities in Russia and highlights the use of local knowledge as a core competence and a bargaining tool by the domestic investors.

However, not only was this "local knowledge" a core competence of the domestic actors in Russia, it was also used as an aggressive bargaining strength, as suggested by the many interviews we conducted when every foreign partner acknowledged the importance of his domestic partner's local skills. One quote from a senior international executive captured the overall theme of the responses – "We obviously joined with a Russian partner in order to access Russian assets and to join forces with a company who knew how to operate in the local business environment. When we first started it was obvious that local knowledge would be essential to operate in what was a very fluid and uncertain business environment. Contacts and local influence were hugely valuable, and we had none of these." Many of our other conversations with foreign partners essentially outlined the same views in their own words.

That these skills were actually used as a bargaining tool can be seen by further reference to the case studies and the interviews, where it is clear that the domestic partner could and did use his skills to generate extra personal value from a joint entity. More than one foreign actor pointed out that the domestic partner always had a clear choice between working for the joint entity of which he was a partner or "using his domestic knowledge and influence to maximise his own returns by disenfranchising his international partner at the appropriate time". Furthermore, many interviewees discussed the sense that relationships were built and sustained on "inter-related" deals, with influence and power being generated for the domestic partner through his use of transactions connected with joint venture activities. Furthermore, the fact that foreign partners appear to have been excluded not only from these side deals (not surprisingly) but also from much of the relationship-building that is a core part of establishing influence in Russia demonstrates that the domestic partner was keen to keep his competitive advantage to himself.

One clear example of where local knowledge was used against foreign partners can be seen on the debate over the PSA law in the 1990s. The passing of a PSA law would have allowed oil and gas field developments to be carried out under specific rules that would have guaranteed both their fiscal terms and the contractual rights of their partners, and would have established a framework that is commonly accepted throughout the global energy industry.[12] This would certainly have encouraged greater foreign investment in the Russian oil and gas industry, as it would have dramatically reduced the risks perceived by potential foreign investors.

However, as one of the foreign partners in Chapter 3 noted when he was considering his investment in a joint venture in the 1990s, "the development of large deposits on PSA terms is only a dream in Russia today".[13] This was because of active lobbying by the Russian oil majors, and in particular Yukos, against the passing of a law that would have made life easier for foreign investors.[14] As recognized by a number of commentators, the main objection raised against the PSA law (namely that it reduced the potential tax take for the Russian government) actually masked the real reasons. As concluded by Andrei Koplianik (2003)[15] "the real reason why PSAs have been torpedoed is that they would introduce a competitive threat to Russian firms and could erode their value". Essentially the passing of the PSA law would have encouraged foreign investors to enter the Russian oil and gas industry, not only increasing competition for access to licenses and fields as well as to the domestic transport system (essential to be able to sell oil production both in Russia and overseas) but also reducing the value of partnership with a domestic player. This would have clearly undermined the bargaining position of any potential domestic partner, so they lobbied against it in order to maintain an institutional environment within which their local knowledge remained an essential asset.

As a result we believe that this and other examples show that in a weak state environment, with Russia being one example, the classic bargaining process between foreign investor and State is interrupted by domestic entrepreneurs. We would therefore re-draw the model of Dunning's OLI paradigm to describe FDI in a weak state environment as shown in Figure 7.2 below, where the core

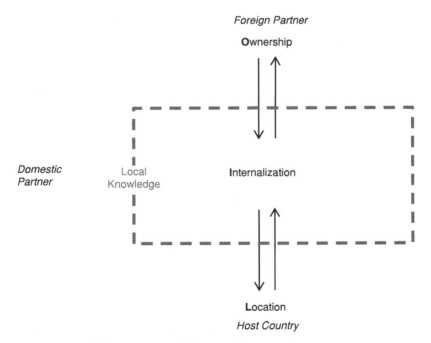

Figure 7.2   The OLI bargaining model in a weak state environment

competence of the domestic partner (his local knowledge) is shown as preventing the internalization of the foreign partner's ownership advantages. Essentially, in a weak state environment the foreign partner cannot bring his skills to bear on the country's natural resources (the source of the State's locational advantage) without a domestic partner's local knowledge. We believe that it is fundamental for any foreign partner to acknowledge that this is the situation in an asymmetric business environment such as Russia's before he can hope to develop strategies to counter the innate competition with any domestic partner that this model inherently creates.

The importance of learning – A domestic partner objective

We have identified how the domestic partner comes to play a vital role in FDI decisions in a weak state environment, and now we can assess his additional role in catalysing a potential shift in bargaining power in a joint entity via the learning process. It is clear that domestic partners in Russia viewed the assimilation and use of their foreign partner's skills as a key part of any joint venture, with the importance of the foreign partner contributions of technology, management skills and capital being confirmed not only by the literature on the Russian oil industry[16] but also by direct quotes from domestic partners. Some of the earliest work on FDI in the oil and gas industry[17] identified that the foreign partner's position is based upon technological complexity, the degree of concentration of the global industry and each investor's own financial and managerial strengths. This was particularly true in Russia, where many commentators have noted that the state of the oil and gas industry at the end of the Soviet era necessitated the introduction of new technology and management techniques and the capital to fund them.[18]

Our own analysis has confirmed this view, with both foreign and domestic interviewees acknowledging the contributions of the IOCs. The Russian evidence is perhaps the most compelling, with the domestic partner in the third case study in Chapter 3 asserting that his foreign partner was essential in bringing "access to capital and select applications of western management and technology"[19] and even German Khan at TNK agreed that bringing BP in as a partner was important as "the best means of getting access to world-class international energy experience".[20] Meanwhile our survey of foreign investors, while clearly reflecting the views of the foreign partners themselves, nevertheless also underlined the view that their key contributions were management skills, technology and capital.

However, in terms of our thoughts on what we have defined as "the competition for knowledge", the key question is whether the domestic partner actively tries to acquire, or learn, his partner's skills as part of a process of improving his bargaining position. Academic literature would certainly suggest that the answer is yes, as for example Radosevic and Henderson (2004)[21] provide two case studies of Russian oil companies where the use of alliances and partnerships was a core strategy to improve their bargaining position and "to get access to resources they lack, especially to technology." The Yukos oil company in particular was seen as using technology alliances while looking to create "in-house expertise", with the ultimate goal of "alleviating some problems inherent with technology alliances, in particular the risk of growing dependency".

Our statistical analysis of foreign partners in joint entities in Russia also supports the suggestion that domestic partners did successfully learn about the skills brought by international investors. When asked whether their partners had learned about operational, management and technical skills during the life of the joint entities, the average score (on a scale of 1–5) was 3.2, suggesting learning had taken place. Further, there was no significant difference between any of the types of skills learned, implying a general acquisition of knowledge by the domestic partner. Our conversations with foreign and Russian players who have participated in joint ventures during the past 20 years also pointed to domestic partner learning of foreign partner skills not only being a key domestic goal but also one that was encouraged by the foreign partner. The discussion about TNK-BP in Chapter 6 particularly highlighted that the transfer of skills was a main focus at the company, with Russian staff encouraged to participate in areas of the business where they could both acquire, and ultimately use and manage application of, new technologies and management skills.

An additional feature concerning foreign partner skills was also highlighted by the case studies and subsequent interviews, namely that the potential disenfranchisement of a foreign partner, where it occurred, could happen not only as a result of learning but also as a result of the gradual obsolescence of its offering after its skills had been successfully implemented and utilized. In the case of a number of the early JVs, for example, the marginalization of the foreign partner occurred when a domestic partner saw the success of the JV but was no longer prepared to recognize the contribution of the foreign partner towards it, and saw no further added value in the foreign partner's presence. At this point it used its local knowledge and influence to force the foreign partner out. A later example was seen at TNK-BP, where in Chapter 6 Alastair Ferguson discussed the changing perception of BP's contribution to the joint company, with the perceived value falling sharply once new technologies and management concepts had been incorporated into the working practices of the Russian employees.

As such it would seem that the balance of bargaining power is not just driven by an increase in domestic partner understanding and knowledge of foreign partner skills, but is also impacted by the change in the perceived value of these skills as the joint entity progresses. Once production has been improved and management performance has been upgraded, then the key problems for the domestic partner have been solved. Unless the foreign partner can demonstrate his ongoing value and relevance (either because the problems will re-occur without him or because he has some extra skills that can improve performance further) then his value to the JV will start to obsolesce. Domestic partner learning therefore concerns both actual assimilation of knowledge of a foreign partner's skills, and also an understanding of when the benefits of those skills have largely been reaped. The case studies and the subsequent interviews suggest that, in a weak institutional environment, once the foreign partner has applied his skills, increased the experience of his domestic partner and brought operational and technical benefits to the JV, his bargaining position has been weakened if his domestic partner's local knowledge remains a vital necessity for the joint entity.

The importance of foreign partner acquisition of local knowledge

It is clear then that domestic partners actively seek to learn the technical and management skills brought by their foreign partners, and in doing so they increase their bargaining leverage of the joint ventures that they have formed. Academic theory has suggested the clear logic for this strategy, with Hamel (1991)[22] introducing the idea that whichever partner in a joint entity could acquire the other partner's skills the fastest would be in the best position to "succeed" because he could essentially remove the need for partnership and take over control of any joint entity using his enhanced bargaining power. Yan and Gray (1994) then linked this potential for increased bargaining power and success not just to knowledge but also to management control, and Ledeneva (2006) confirmed the importance of active participation, rather than just learning, in her definition of local knowledge. The clear message, then, is that if the domestic partner is actively acquiring his foreign partner's skills, then one obvious response is for the foreign partner to level the bargaining playing field by acquiring his domestic partner's core skill.

A definition of local knowledge

However, before we discuss how this might be achieved we should perhaps reiterate a more detailed definition of this core domestic skill of "local knowledge". In her book "How Russia Really Works"[23] Ledeneva identifies local knowledge as the use of informal practices involving a "know-how of post-Soviet Russia...that is implicitly endorsed by the state and is divisive in its implications, serving and sustaining insiders at the expense of outsiders".[24] Using this know-how, competent players can manage and manipulate the system to their own advantage as they use personal networks to exploit the inadequacies of the market mechanisms and political institutions prevalent in post-Soviet Russia. We have argued in Chapter 2 that this definition is not only relevant to the Yeltsin era of the 1990s but also to the Putin/Medvedev era of the 2000s, as although the nature of business-state relations have clearly changed between the two eras, the strength of key individuals compared to the inherent weakness of state institutions remains. As a result, local knowledge and influence are as important today as they were a decade or more ago.

Local knowledge is not just an understanding of the situation, though, but an active skill to be employed in the building and exploitation of core relationships and influence over domestic situations. This is confirmed by our interactions with foreign and Russian interviewees in this book, who all identified the contacts and influence of their domestic partner as a vital factor in their joint entities. As one foreigner put it, his domestic partner brought "the most precious asset of excellent personal relationships with officials and local oil industry barons", essentially identifying the key knowledge as being the ability to use these contacts to further the business interests of the jointly-owned entity. Another described his domestic partner as bringing "political insurance...in West Siberia and Moscow", in order to protect the company from the vagaries of the business environment. More specifically another described the local knowledge of his domestic partner as dealing with "local politics, tax, transport and sales and marketing issues", and that the use of contacts and influence was directed at resolving issues in these areas.[25] Other quotes defined the local knowledge of a domestic partner in the broader context of "solving bureaucratic problems in the regional and federal administrations", while a more generic feature of local knowledge was seen as the ability to operate in an environment based on mutual trust rather than legal certainty. The widespread prevalence of the "my word is my bond" principle in business dealings, often driven by a desire to avoid official documentation that might attract the attention of the authorities, means that it is vital to understand which relationships can be relied upon and which cannot. This implies, therefore, that local knowledge also extends to a broad understanding of how networks of influence operate within a weak institutional environment.

The survey of joint entities has also helped to provide a definition of local knowledge based on the domestic partner contributions to the joint entities and on the areas which foreign partners initially left under the control of their domestic partner. The key domestic partner contributions were identified as knowledge of formal and informal domestic issues and access to domestic markets and these skills were vital to any joint entity operating within the domestic Russian market as it enabled it to navigate between the formal and informal rules prevalent in the local business environment. However, the survey also highlighted the important point that foreign partners had least control (and so de facto domestic partners had most control) over areas where these local knowledge skills were most relevant, including government relations, tax, legal, transport and security.

The importance of using, as well as acquiring, local knowledge

We argued earlier that domestic partners not only acquire foreign partner skills but also put them into practice as part of their increasing bargaining leverage. As a result, it would seem logical to argue that in an equal and opposite strategy foreign partners need to ensure that balance in their joint entities is maintained by both acquiring and being in a position to use the local knowledge that is the main bargaining strength of their domestic partners. They need to do this both to balance the domestic partner's learning of their own skills of management, technology and capital raising and also to counterbalance the potential obsolescence of their own skills once they have been applied to a venture and achieved success.

Again, the evidence to support this hypothesis is provided by both our empirical and statistical analysis. In particular the case studies in Chapter 3 underline the view that a foreign partner can increase his chance of success by acquiring local knowledge. As one foreign partner explained "we decided that we had to make some effort to build a local network and establish contacts in the region and at the Energy Ministry" in order to provide routes to senior influencers within the Russian administration that could provide some balance with the contacts and influence being used by his domestic partner. In the end he was convinced that the local network he had established was the key reason why he was able to exit his joint entity with a profit. Despite feeling at risk of financial and physical harm, he was finally able to sell his entire holding to a foreign buyer, but stated that "I was told by various third parties after the event that even this would not have been possible without my contacts, who were working on my behalf behind the scenes."

Perhaps more important than the testimony of the interviews, though, the link between foreign partner success and his ability to become involved in issues involving local knowledge is confirmed by the analysis of the survey of foreign investors. Firstly principal components analysis, which is used to group variables with close connections, revealed that local knowledge included formal and informal understanding of issues such as government relations and security, confirming our earlier definition. Furthermore, the overall factor of "change in foreign partner control over local knowledge issues" was shown to have the strongest correlation with foreign partner success, implying that increased local knowledge and the willingness of a foreign partner to use it is correlated with greater success in a joint venture. All the other statistical models also confirmed that this factor is the strongest predictor of foreign partner success, and indeed accounted for almost half the variance in foreign partner success, with domestic partner success being the only other significant predictor.

As such, it would seem to be clear that if a foreign partner can establish a greater individual capability to operate in a local business environment, and understands how this needs to change and develop over time, then he has a greater chance of success. This may just be because his domestic partner is less inclined to use local knowledge against him, or because he may actually have to actively use local contacts and influence to defend his position. In either case, though, the fact that the foreign partner has attempted to re-dress the balance of bargaining power in the relationship with his domestic partner has increased his chances of a successful outcome. In effect, the foreign partner's contributions to the joint venture (and therefore his bargaining strength) can become obsolescent over time, and one way of balancing this process is to ensure that the domestic partner's contribution of local knowledge also becomes less vital to the joint entity over time. In other words one core strategy for the foreign partner is to acquire the local knowledge that is his domestic partner's core competence, in order to maximize his own potential for success.

A model to describe foreign partner engagement strategies

Having laid out our theories concerning the importance of learning in joint ventures and in particular the vital role of local knowledge in a weak institutional environment such as Russia, we are aware that the practical steps needed for a foreign actor to acquire this skill-set are not easy to achieve and need to be examined in more detail. We have also seen, from the case studies and interviews in previous chapters, that the acquisition of local knowledge is not the only way that a foreign partner can hope to keep a joint venture in Russia in balance. Indeed, if it was the only strategy then all foreign actors in joint ventures would struggle, as the very nature of local knowledge in a weak institutional environment suggests that, almost by definition, a foreigner will never be able to fully compete with his domestic partner. Indeed, our conclusion thus far has been that foreign partners need to make their best effort to acquire local knowledge and take an active role in areas where it is used in order to provide an element of balance in their joint venture, even if this balance is in reality just the ability to assess how valuable their domestic partner's contribution is.

As a result, foreign partners would appear to need a multi-layered strategy in order to maintain the stability of their joint ventures in commercial environments such as Russia. Acquisition and use of local knowledge is an important strand in this strategy, providing an increased level of protection against possible disenfranchisement. However, our interviews and case studies have

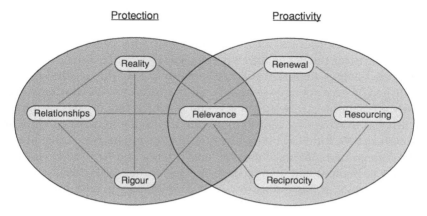

Figure 7.3 The "7R" Engagement Model

suggested that there is a more proactive strategy that foreign partners can and do use in tandem with their increased local knowledge, namely to maintain their relevance by bringing further new skills and opportunities to the joint venture. We believe that this overlap of protective and proactive strategies can be best summarized in an outline which we have entitled the "7R Engagement Model", because it includes the seven key features which can underpin a successful foreign partner strategy in Russia or countries with similar business environments (Figure 7.3).

The focus of the model is on maintaining the relevance of the foreign partner in his engagement both with his domestic partner and with the broader political and economic community in the country where he is operating. We see this first "R" – *Relevance* – as being the most important goal for any foreign actor looking to create a successful partnership in an asymmetric business environment, although it is also perhaps the most difficult to define. In the broadest sense it is about "what you bring to the table" in the joint venture and how you prove your worth both to your domestic partner and to the relevant state entities with some influence over your business. It is important to emphasize that this is not just about what assets you contribute, although that may play some part, but is also about bringing good ideas and thoughts on key issues as well as building your credibility and the confidence that domestic actors have in you. As we will go on to describe, a foreign partner's relevance is about the protective measures he takes in boosting his local knowledge and also about the proactive measures he uses to enhance his contribution to a joint venture, both of which increase confidence and credibility in different ways. If you can demonstrate, through your increased local knowledge, that you understand the business environment and can deal with it, then your credibility as a business partner is increased. Equally, if you demonstrate that you are continually looking for ways to bring new opportunities to the venture, and most importantly to enhance the revenue generating capacity for the benefit of all parties, your relevance is maintained and enhanced. Having said this, it is also important to note that credibility is also established by being clear on what you do not bring, as well as what you do. Clearly a balanced partnership is not one in which one of the players consistently has to bring new contributions out of fear that his partner will otherwise turn against him. Firm boundaries need to be established, and a number of the foreign participants whom we have interviewed have been very clear that they have often had to say a firm "no" when their boundaries have been crossed, but that, if handled correctly, this can enhance, rather than undermine, a partnership relationship.

As a result, we believe that relevance sits at the heart of the engagement model because it characterizes the essential balance between the protective and proactive dimensions of foreign partner strategy in a weak institutional environment. On the one hand increased local knowledge is vital in order to understand the commercial and political situation in which a venture is operating both because it can protect a foreign partner in an asymmetric environment and because it can help him to understand what proactive contributions he needs to make to keep his partnership in balance. On the other hand, the proactive contribution of new ideas, assets, people and opportunities can provide further evidence of commitment to a partnership, can enhance credibility and can help to create an atmosphere of increased mutual confidence that in itself can allow the foreign partner access to greater local knowledge. All of these elements, if kept in balance, can maintain and enhance the relevance of a foreign partner and keep his position in a partnership secure.

However, any attempts to keep the engagement model in balance are hindered by the very dynamic internal and external forces that create a constant state of flux in business environments that are dominated by key individuals who are prone to change their minds or who have to deal with their own ever-changing circumstances. As a result, it is necessary to discuss the detailed work that is needed to provide the foundation for a successful engagement strategy. This involves a process of constant monitoring and assessment to ensure that you consistently remain relevant to your domestic partner and the appropriate government authorities and are also clearly differentiated from your competition (other foreign companies) who could ultimately replace you as a preferred partner.

As a result the first element of the protective dimension, where the aim is to undertake the detailed acquisition of local knowledge, is **Reality**, by which we mean establishing as clear and accurate a picture as possible of what is really occurring both within the venture and in the external environment where it is operating. A number of our interviews have revealed that deception and deceit can be important elements in commercial environments such as Russia, and also that preventing foreigners from getting access to local knowledge is another key strategy. As a result, establishing the reality of any situation is not a trivial undertaking, and is made even more complicated by the fast changing nature of relationships between key players and factions in a dynamic business environment. Information that may have been given with full integrity and honesty one day may become irrelevant within weeks, or even days, as new domestic priorities emerge or alternative options become available.

We would assert that the important foundations for establishing a clear picture of reality are firstly to acknowledge that there is likely to be a lot more going on beneath the surface than you might expect; secondly to accept that finding out the truth may not be a pleasant experience and may reveal inadequacies in your own position as well as difficulties with your partner; and thirdly to create an information gathering and analysis strategy that involves triangulation of data from multiple internal and external sources, including third party advisors. Given the dynamic nature of the environment it will of course be necessary to constantly update and review information sources, opinions and conclusions, and inevitably it will take considerable time and management resource to do this well. Historically, many companies, in particular those in relatively small ventures, have appeared reluctant to make this commitment, and of course it makes sense for the effort to be commensurate with the importance of the JV. Nevertheless, it seems to us that if a company is going to make the strategic decision to enter a country such as Russia then it should also be prepared to make the commitment to understand the reality of the environment it is getting into. The model of establishing a strong shareholder team, outlined by Alastair Ferguson in Chapter 6, is a useful benchmark, with a central unit co-ordinating the search for information as well as the analysis and interpretation of it, using multiple internal and external resources. In this way it is possible to start building an integrated picture of what is really going on inside your partnership and also a broader view of the political and commercial drivers of the business. It may never be possible to get a complete understanding of all the issues, given the often murky landscape, but the experiences of many of our interviewees would suggest that achieving 80% visibility is a realistic goal and one that can provide a satisfactory platform for sensible decision-making.

Given the importance of key individuals within the Russian political and commercial worlds, however, this level of clarity would be almost impossible to achieve without establishing an intricate network of **Relationships** – our third "R". Having the right contacts and personal relations with relevant and influential individuals is a cornerstone of the local knowledge that we have established to be the main competitive advantage of domestic actors in Russia, and in order to create balance foreign actors need to build their own networks. These need to be both formal and informal connections at both corporate and individual levels, and can be professional and personal in nature. In an ideal situation this would create a web of relationships which could be used to cross-check information, to provide multiple sources of data and to increase confidence in the picture of reality being built up. Many of our interviewees have particularly mentioned the importance of the personal element in relationships in Russia, and it would appear to be the case that developing a closer bond away from a work context has allowed foreign partners to gain a greater understanding of Russian business culture and methods as well as a more general appreciation of domestic thought processes.

The archetypal "out-of-work" activity is of course well known, and tends to involve the consumption of large quantities of food and alcohol, in particular vodka. However, although this still seems to be a preferred method of building friendships, it is by no means a pre-requisite to creating a good impression. In fact a number of our interviewees stated bluntly that they were not prepared to "drink to oblivion" and often expressed a preference for wine or cigars over vodka, as they felt that the key to creating a close bond was to be seen to be natural and at one with the domestic environment – to appreciate the Russian way of doing things but not to be afraid to state your own boundaries and preferences. In this way a true friendship based on mutual respect can be built, and it is from this base that a strong link can be forged. The real test of whether this has been achieved is whether you can get down to discussing the serious issues in a cordial fashion, whether you can give and receive bad, as well as good, news without fear of spoiling the relationship and overall whether you can send and receive messages accurately and know that they have been understood by the right people.

Relationships, then, are a vital tool for gaining knowledge, for creating confidence and credibility with partners and external actors, for establishing bonds that could lead to guidance and influence at important moments and for building the bridges that can be used to send and receive important messages. However, the ability to do all these things, and in particular to ensure that the correct messages have been heard by the correct people, can only be achieved through the use of a detailed and comprehensive process of relationship planning and monitoring, using our fourth "R" – *Rigour*. The processes of building a clear picture of reality and of establishing meaningful relationships are hard enough work in themselves, but would effectively be meaningless if they are not co-ordinated in a meticulous fashion to guarantee that the process is handled efficiently and to ensure that mistakes of collation or interpretation are not made. Again, this requires commitment to a systematic process that is difficult to implement and requires consistent updating, essentially involving a plan of action to identify key individuals, to allocate relationship responsibilities, to record messages and information received, to understand where there are holes in the data and to create a plan for addressing them. Rigour is also about developing 'forensic capability' to understand what is going on and to build up a real time understanding of respective stakeholder positions. In the next few paragraphs we outline one model for dealing with this process. While we fully recognize that it is not the only solution, we offer it as an example of the type of thorough process that we believe needs to be adopted if local knowledge is to be acquired and used successfully.

A relationship map to underpin the engagement model

In our research into the proactive development of relationships for business purposes we initially focussed on examples of partnerships built in the oil and gas industry.[26] A wide range of literature exists, but having examined a broad spectrum of theories we would acknowledge one book as the foundation of the process outlined in the next few pages – The New Strategic Selling (1998) – as it illustrates the thorough nature of a rigorous relationship mapping strategy.[27]

The primary goal of any relationship model, it seems to us, is to provide a stable platform to monitor connections between one company and the important players that interact with it in a world of external and internal factors that is in a constant state of flux. As such the formation of a modelling process on its own can establish a rigorous and stable method for monitoring relationships while also creating a common language with which to discuss the various individuals and interactions that are the core elements of it. Furthermore it can also establish a framework for ongoing re-assessment of assumptions, strategies and tactics through regular debate between the owners of the model, and by the very nature of this debate can enable a swift response in the light of shifts in the perceptions of key players, the actions of competitors or changes in the external environment. It is well suited to the dynamic political and business environment in Russia and the fast changing nature of relationships between key stakeholders.

Both the map and the process can be applied to an overall corporate country strategy or to a specific transaction within a relevant part of the region, but it is perhaps easier to explain how a relationship mapping exercise might work if we focus on one specific deal. The first, and perhaps most crucial, part of the process is to identify those individuals who will have significant influence over the success or failure of the deal and to categorize them so that there is a common understanding of their likely role in the completion of the transaction. In sales terminology these individuals are known generally as "buyers", but for the purposes of this book we have changed the titles slightly to acknowledge the fact that not every relationship in an international joint venture will concern a "buy-sell" motive. As a result, Figure 7.4 shows a simple categorization of the four main types of actors that can be identified – the "Decision-Maker", the "Gatekeeper", the "Associates" and the "Advisors".

The "Decision-Maker", not surprisingly, is the person who will be the key to the success of any proposal or deal, and therefore needs to be identified very accurately and very early in the relationship-building process. They are generally in a senior role and have the responsibility of plotting the strategic course for their company or organization, and have the authority to give the final approval on a proposal, but could also be a group of people (a committee or board for example) who have control over key resources. He (or they) will obviously have the power of veto over any decision, but on a more positive note will also be looking at the overall success that could be generated for their own organization from any proposal made.

The "Associates" will be those people who will have to work with the practical consequences of any deal and whose key priority is likely to be the potential impact that the transaction will have on their working life. They will be involved in (or associated with) the practical implementation of any proposal, and will want to see that it is likely to bring them personal success

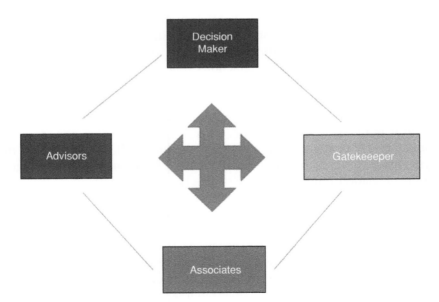

Figure 7.4 The key actors in a relationship model

before they give it any support. Although they will not have the ultimate say over whether any proposal is actually accepted or not, if they are against you then they can certainly do their best to sabotage any plans that you may have.

The "Gatekeeper" is again not the person who will make the final decision but is likely to be a senior person or persons who will have veto power. The Head of Business Development or the CFO could be an example of an individual who is responsible for analysing and screening ideas in order to establish which do not meet the necessary criteria, and so they can be seen as rather negative in their outlook. They will be judging one idea, deal or partner against competing options, likely using quantifiable standards, and their veto rights will be based on their ability to provide specific measured reasons why one concept is better or worse than another. Their relatively powerful position can sometimes make them seem like the Decision-Maker, but their approval rarely leads to a final decision being taken – it rather stops it being blocked.

The fourth key actor is the "Advisor", and this person (or persons) can be cultivated as well as identified within an organization. Essentially they can act as guides who can provide and interpret information about whether your goals are valid, what each of the other key actors is trying to achieve both for themselves and their organization, the key internal and external influences which will affect decisions being made and the progress of your strategy towards its ultimate success. To be useful Advisors must be credible with all the parties involved and must, for whatever reason, want you to be successful for some personal reason of their own. Ideally one would find more than one Advisor so that you can triangulate and cross-check what you are being told via a network of advice, with some of the Advisors being from inside your counterpart's organization and some being external.

The identification of the key actors can be a long process, especially as a debate is likely to ensue about their specific roles. In particular it is important to identify the one Decision-Maker and to acknowledge that there can only be one for any specific proposal or transaction. It may be that an overall database of key individuals within the commercial and political spheres inside a specific country or region needs to be put together, with relevant individuals then being identified from this overall database and allocated to various roles according to different proposals that are being considered. Indeed it may be important to recognize that one individual has multiple roles relevant to your organization depending on specific issues that you are addressing at any one time, meaning that it is even more important to have a stable and regularly updated modelling process in place in order to ensure that mixed messages are not being sent and that there is no confusion over messages that are being received. However, once the debate over roles has been resolved, then a process such as the one outlined in Figure 7.5 can begin.

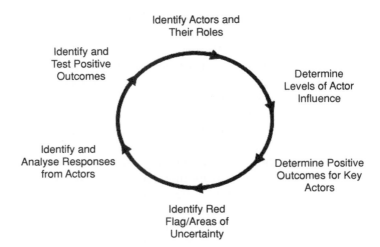

Identify Actors and
Their Roles

Identify and
Test Positive
Outcomes

Determine
Levels of Actor
Influence

Identify and
Analyse Responses
from Actors

Determine Positive
Outcomes for Key
Actors

Identify Red
Flag/Areas of
Uncertainty

Figure 7.5   Outline of the relationship mapping process

Once the key actors have been identified, the next task is to identify their level of influence on any decision being taken and to establish the factors on which this influence is based. This may be rather obvious in the case of the Decision-Maker, as his authority is likely to be based on his position and his high level of influence is taken as read. However, for the other actors the identification of influence and the reasons for it is important so that any interactions can be prioritized and the correct individuals within one's own organization can be allocated to a specific relationship. If, for example, a highly qualified accountant in the counterpart's finance department is identified as a key Gatekeeper, then you would naturally want to allocate someone of equal ability to manage that relationship and to make the building of a relationship a high priority exercise.

The third step in the process is then to identify what the objectives of the key actors are likely to be and how they might be satisfied by your current proposal, or alternatively what else you might need to do to satisfy them. These objectives will almost certainly have two dimensions, namely positive results for the counterparty organization and personal "wins" for the individuals involved as key actors. Many texts are keen to point out that "results are for corporations, but decisions are made by individuals", and as a result it is vital to consider both elements in the development of a relationship model. It may be that a successful result for the organization itself can increase the personal standing of an individual associated with it, and this may be enough for

Name	Actor/ Influencer	Role	Influence	Results/Wins	Support Level	Red Flags/ Uncertainties	Comments
Person A	Decision Maker	CEO	High	Higher share price	Supportive	Political influences	Govt relations to investigate
Person B	Gatekeeper	Head of Strategy	Medium	Active role in deal decisions	Negative	Comparison of Upstream and Downstream opportunities	Demonstrate comparative value of upstream and downstream options
Person C	Associate	Head of Upstream	Medium	Larger Upstream Business Unit	Interested	Alternative options	Analyse potential competition from other IOCs to act as partners
Person D	Coach	Non-Executive Director	High	Political influence	Enthusiastic	Vested interest in outcome?	Investigate political connections/ ambitions

Figure 7.6   A simple relationship map

some actors to support your proposal. However, others may need to see other benefits from a deal (for example greater control over others, being perceived as a leader) before they support it, and so it is important to consider the two questions "why is this good for the counterpart organization?" and "why is this good for key individuals within that counterpart organization?" together as a relationship map is built around specific proposals that are being made.

At this stage it is realistic to start to put a relationship map down on paper, or in a spreadsheet, and we offer a very simple model as an example in Figure 7.6. The individuals, the identification of their "actor type", their organizational role, level of influence and objectives are noted, as well as an initial estimate of their support for the proposal or deal. This estimate would come from an initial interaction with the individual concerned, and although we have not included it in the database this interaction would be carried out by the person within our own organization who had been allocated to this relationship. As noted above, it is very important that this relationship allocation is carried out correctly, having identified the key skills that the main actors have and also taking into account their personalities and cultural backgrounds. The psychology of relationship management is the topic for another book altogether, and so although it is important to acknowledge its importance in the allocation of individuals to specific relationships, the key point we are aiming to make here is that the Relationship Map now becomes a tool for an iterative conversation between all the individuals within the host organization that are attempting to get their proposal accepted.

Combining the messages from Figures 7.5 and 7.6, the next important step is to identify any major issues or uncertainties that could undermine the acceptance of a proposal, which some authors like to call "red flags". These could include missing or uncertain information about individuals or key issues, changes in internal or external factors, inability to make contact with important individuals or the introduction or removal of one or more of the actors from their posts, but in any case they should catalyse a debate about the steps that should be taken to remedy the situation. Continuing the iterative discussion, an ongoing process of assessment and interpretation of responses from interactions with the actors would then potentially prompt changes in any of the boxes shown in Figure 7.6 above, with the further actions then identified to progress the proposal to its next stage via the appropriate relationship managers. The ultimate goal would, of course, be to ensure that all the key actors were fully supportive of the proposal and could each see positive organizational and personal outcomes that would result from it, with no red flags or dissenting voices.

This rather brief and cursory discussion of an outline of a relationship management process is perhaps rather unsatisfactory as it would clearly need to be adapted to individual circumstances and to specific corporate objectives, but the main point of showing it is to underline that it is a difficult and complex process that needs to be undertaken with significant rigour (to return to the 7Rs) if it is to be successful. However, it is just this sort of process, we believe, that foreign partners need to undertake if they are to have any chance of acquiring, retaining and using local knowledge in an asymmetric business environment, and thus somewhat re-dress the balance with their local partners in a joint venture. While local entrepreneurs and businessmen appear to do this intuitively and without the need for a detailed work plan, this is thanks to their natural affinity with the business and cultural environment and their long history of operating within it. For a foreign company to compete with this innate knowledge base a systematic approach is required, and it will undoubtedly take a lot of time and effort over a considerable period of time to achieve it with any degree of success.

Two more proactive "Rs" from the Engagement Model

While we certainly believe that the acquisition and use of local knowledge by foreign partners in a weak institutional environment is essential to their success, we are also forced to acknowledge that it is not only a difficult and lengthy process but also that it is very unlikely that it will, on its own, achieve balance within an international joint venture. A foreigner can never realistically hope to match his domestic partner's local knowledge, not least because the country in which they are both operating is likely to be of much higher priority to the latter than the former and therefore the levels of effort put into relationship building are inevitably different. Nevertheless we still believe that any effort made by a foreign partner to begin re-dressing the balance is valid, although to be effective it must also be supplemented by other "Proactive" elements in our Engagement Model. This brings us to two more "Rs", as described in Figure 7.3 above.

The first of these is *Renewal*, which we would define as a constant review of your position within a joint venture and an assessment of what may need to be done to refresh it. We have discussed in previous chapters how foreign partner skills are learned by domestic partners, and as such their value as a bargaining chip within a venture becomes less relevant, with domestic players often encouraged to acquire technical and management skills and to put them into practice by taking on active roles that require their use. We have also mentioned that, in some instances, once foreign skills have been brought to a venture they can often be taken for granted, with the perception being that the value is in the introduction of the skill and not its ongoing application. As a result, the perceived bargaining power of the foreign partner is reduced and the balance in a joint venture is lost.

The concept of renewal therefore attempts to address this issue. It suggests that a foreign partner needs to regularly and honestly assess its continuing contribution to a joint venture, reviewing its initial offerings and evaluating whether their worth remains the same now as in the past. If the answer to this question is no, then new ideas for re-dressing the balance need to be generated and introduced to the joint venture. If the main issue is identified as one of perception, then the answer may be to underline the continuing importance of certain processes or skills that have been contributed and the ongoing relevance of foreign involvement in them. However, it may also be the case that new ideas are needed, whether they be technical, financial, corporate or human resource. It is also important that the analysis of the situation be seen in the context of the continuing domestic partner contributions, of course, which is one of the important reasons why the complimentary acquisition of some local knowledge is needed to help in this calculation. We would not want to suggest that the foreign partner should be in a constant state of providing new ideas and contributions unless a genuine imbalance in the partnership is emerging. Nevertheless, we do believe that, in an environment of constant change and fast-moving competition, foreign partners do need to think about Renewal as a core strategy to maintain and enhance their position in their existing joint ventures and also as a chance to create further opportunities to grow.

One additional method for creating balance in a joint venture, which overlaps with the concept of renewal but can also be seen as a proactive alternative to it, is *Reciprocity*, which in its most obvious form can mean offering to co-operate outside as well as inside the host country of your domestic partner. Put simply, this can be interpreted as acknowledging that "if you have welcomed me into your home, then I am prepared to welcome you into mine", but in addition it can offer some implied protection to the foreign partner as it also carries the implicit threat "if you mess with my assets in your country, then you can expect an equal and opposite reaction from me". In the case of Russia, we do not believe that the threatening part of the reciprocity equation actually carries much weight, as the assets offered to foreigners in Russia are usually of much greater value than those offered outside, but we do nevertheless very much believe in the concept of reciprocity as a part of a partnership-building strategy.

Examples of the positive impact of reciprocal asset ownership across partner geographies can most recently be seen in the deal struck between Exxon and Rosneft in 2011. Exxon has gained access to licences offshore in the Russian Arctic and onshore in West Siberia (where it will explore for oil in unconventional reservoirs) while Rosneft acquired interests in offshore licences in the Gulf of Mexico and onshore in the US and Canada (where it too will be looking for unconventional oil and gas resources). This example demonstrates two types of reciprocity, namely the swap of assets and also the provision of international experience to the domestic partner in areas where the skills gained can be used on assets back in their home market. This double reciprocal benefit can provide an even closer bond as it is likely to have a longer-lasting effect – Rosneft will want to maintain good relations not only because it has new assets outside Russia but also because it is gaining valuable experience through its continuing participation. Statoil has effectively offered the same model in its deal with Rosneft, offering access to the Norwegian Continental Shelf as it enters offshore regions of Russia, with the reciprocity enhanced in this case by the political dynamic of the deal, following the ending of the border dispute between the two host countries.

This type of double reciprocal effect also highlights the fact that the specific value of the assets in a reciprocal exchange does not necessarily have to be of equivalent net present value, as perceptions of worth can be as important as actual monetary calculations. By its very nature it is impossible to say how much subjective value is placed by domestic partners on being granted access to international assets – some may see it purely in NPV terms, but to others the implied value of becoming an international company from a political perspective, as part of a diversification strategy or to enhance the global prestige of the company may also have significant value. A number of deals involving Russian and international partners appear to have involved relatively small overseas components (for example Wintershall offered Gazprom some small upstream assets in North Africa as part of its initial deal to enter the Russian upstream while ENI offered an interest in the Elephant field in Libya as part of its deal to enter the SeverEnergia asset), but their value has clearly been enough to play a role in securing a deal. This is not to say that IOCs should just search their portfolios for unwanted assets to offer as a token international gesture – many a deal has fallen down on the insult that this can imply. It is merely to point out that one should not ignore the subjective and unquantifiable value that exists in offering a relevant international asset as part of a joint venture deal, which can bring potential benefits beyond its pure financial value.

Meanwhile the negative impact of failing to either offer or to ultimately achieve reciprocity can be seen in a number of partnership disappointments and disputes. We have already discussed, in Chapter 6, that one of the catalysts for the initial partner dispute at TNK-BP was the differing attitudes of AAR and BP towards a potential international strategy for the company, with BP ultimately conceding to AAR's desires having been cast as a block to Russia's overseas ambitions. However, other examples of failed international ambition include LUKOIL and ConocoPhillips' unsuccessful attempts to find overseas investments to cement their partnership (in particular in Iraq) and ARCO and LUKOIL's failure to agree on international expansion options for their LUKARCO joint venture. In both cases the initial promise of reciprocity turned into a failure to agree on financial terms or on asset quality, with the ultimate result that hopes were disappointed and the partnerships ultimately came to an end.

Reciprocity, however, does not just have to be of the international-domestic asset variety. It can also just mean finding areas where co-operation in new ideas and ventures can provide mutual benefit, irrespective of geography. The fact that Russian oil and gas companies have sought to expand overseas in the past decade has meant that international reciprocity has been an obvious area where this can happen, but an alternative example might be seen in Gazprom and Wintershall's co-operation in deep gas condensate development at the Urengoy field. International co-operation did certainly play a role in the formation of the Achimgaz JV, but equally important was the joint learning process that both companies went through to generate mutual advantage in the development of a new geological formation of which neither had much previous experience. In this case relations improved because neither side was teaching the other, and therefore reducing their own bargaining strength, but instead both were learning together and thus developed technical, cultural and personal overlaps that allowed the ties between them to be strengthened. As a result reciprocity can be seen not just as an equal and opposite sharing of assets but also a development of reciprocal interests that can provide both mutual benefit and a catalyst for closer connection between corporate cultures.

Resourcing – The final proactive "R"

We have included one final R – *Resourcing* – in our proactive dimension of the Engagement Model because we believe that it can be a very positive, rather than just protective or defensive, element in foreign partner strategies in countries such as Russia, although to date it has often been a foreign company failing. Our interviews with participants in international joint ventures have revealed that in a number of cases foreign partner staff have been resented because they were either not suited to working in the Russian environment or did not appear to be providing value for money, and in some cases domestic actors deliberately exploited what they saw as a lack of quality to gain competitive advantage over their foreign partner. Furthermore, a number of expatriate interviewees have emphasized how important it is to bring in the right kind of personnel, people who are recognized experts in their own field but are also sympathetic to the cultural differences that they will face. At the same time they need to be strong enough, with sufficient personal and corporate integrity, to stand their ground in a heated debate over key decisions. As a result, it appears to us that a proactive resourcing policy which identifies the right kind of expatriate employees to be brought into a new business environment and keeps them in place for an extended period in order to allow core relationships to be built and maintained can be an important source of competitive advantage. Equally importantly we also believe that companies will benefit from seeking out senior level national staff to work at a high level not just for the joint venture but also for the foreign company itself, thereby accelerating the process of local knowledge acquisition. Indeed, a number of international companies are now adopting the strategy of identifying high potential national staff, providing them with international training in the corporate headquarters and then returning them to their native environment as an ideal blend of the domestic and international business cultures. These "repats" can be trusted by the foreign companies because they have been immersed in their corporate values and principles and yet also retain the close links to their domestic society that are vital for acquiring and retaining local knowledge.

Furthermore, in a country where relationships are valued so highly and where the importance of key individuals is so apparent it should not be much of a surprise that the presence of foreign partner staff who have demonstrated their commitment to the country through their longevity in it and who speak the language fluently can also be a huge benefit. However, it is nevertheless the case that not all companies adopt this strategy, and those that do appear to generate competitive advantage from it. Wintershall, arguably Gazprom's closest international partner, had as head of its Moscow office a man who had been in Russia for 17 years when we met him in 2012, while ExxonMobil, which is arguably now Rosneft's closest international ally, is led in Moscow by a man who was worked and lived in Russia for 20 years and who has developed close personal ties with many of the country's leading figures. Meanwhile BP, a company whose financial success we have noted but whose turbulent relationship history is also very apparent, has consistently changed its Head of Russia and has had very few fluent Russian-speaking executives at the higher levels of management in its Russian operations over the course of its history in the country.

It would therefore appear to us that a proactive resourcing strategy can be a way to provide further balance in a partnership relationship in a weak institutional environment. High quality people who are ready to understand the different culture within which they are operating but who can also see when firm boundaries need to be established; who can demonstrate their relevance both by their own expertise and also by showing that they understand the rules of the game in a new environment; and who are prepared to demonstrate their commitment to a country and thereby generate loyalty and commitment in return from their domestic partners, seem to us to be a hugely valuable asset for any foreign partner in a country like Russia. Furthermore, we would also strongly advise that a number of these high quality people placed in senior positions should be Russian nationals themselves. At present this is not always the case in a number of foreign companies, with cost being one potential issue, as there is no doubt that top Russian executives now have many lucrative options that they can pursue in the country's developing economy. Trust may be another issue, as it is undoubtedly difficult to establish who can and cannot be relied upon in an asymmetric environment such as Russia's. As a result, it may be some time before senior domestic employees are seen among the higher echelons of IOC management in Russia. Nevertheless, this does not undermine our view that the search for them should continue, and that in the meantime the ideal expatriate leader should be Russian-speaking, committed to a long-term role in the country and a leading expert in his or her field in order to command the respect required to maintain their relevance in any partnership arrangement.

Two final points on resourcing also need to be made. The first is that even the highest quality employees of a foreign company in Russia will only be successful if they are fully supported by the senior management in the headquarters of their domestic organization. Our interviews have revealed many examples of foreign employees who have felt frustrated by the decisions of senior executives who appear to lack the knowledge or will to provide support at critical times, or who appear to be pursuing different agendas. Of course, in any international organization the operations in different countries will be allocated different priority at various times, but it is also clear that any perceived or actual lack of commitment from the headquarters is likely to be exploited by a domestic partner looking for competitive advantage in a specific joint venture. One possible answer to this problem is suggested by our final point on resourcing, namely the appropriate use of independent advisors. In a dynamic and unpredictable business environment such as Russia, advisors can be used to triangulate data and opinion, to provide additional contacts and to offer alternative and contradictory views that can be helpful in establishing rigorous and robust conclusions on contentious issues. They can also provide senior executives with a more impartial opinion on the state of the joint venture and the actions that may be needed to secure its success, thus helping to ensure that there is a fuller understanding in headquarters of the issues that expatriate employees are facing. In this way information flows can be improved both within the joint venture and between the joint venture and the senior executives in headquarters who will be making decisions that affect it, and who will also be interacting at Board level with the domestic joint venture partners. Ideally this would lead to appropriate support being given to expatriate employees and more informed and vigorous conversations being had with domestic partners.

Conclusions on the 7R Engagement Model

To return briefly to the original concept of the 7R Engagement Model, the underlying goal is to maintain the Relevance of the foreign partner in a joint venture by retaining the balance of the partnership. We believe that this involves developing a comprehensive engagement strategy with two dimensions – protective and proactive. The protective dimension is focused on the main theme of this book, namely that any joint venture involves at its core a "competition for knowledge", and that one of the most important objectives for a foreign partner in a joint venture in a weak institutional environment should be to acquire local knowledge and establish the ability to use it. It appears to us that the foundations upon which this learning should take place are a sound grasp of the Reality of the situation in which the foreign partner finds himself, a strategy to build Relationships with important individuals and a commitment to undertake this task of understanding the various stakeholder positions with the absolute Rigour implied by our example of a relationship mapping process.

The proactive dimension is viewed as complimentary to the protective, and acknowledges that a foreign partner is never likely to achieve the level of local knowledge that can provide complete balance with his domestic counterpart. This is recognized during the formation of most joint ventures, when the foreign skills of technology, management and financing are offered to compliment the local knowledge brought by the domestic partner. We suggest that as the joint venture develops, Renewal of these foreign partner skills is a vital strategy if balance is to be maintained, involving a constant process of assessment to understand whether the initial offerings are still relevant and their value fully understood. It is important that the foreign partner does not assume that he can stand still in the joint venture, but needs to continue bringing new ideas for revenue creation in order to provide evidence of his ongoing worth and relevance. One part of this renewal process can be Reciprocity, which in its simplest form can be the introduction of the domestic partner into foreign assets to bring a geographical balance to a relationship. In a more subtle form, it can bring complimentary skills that can be learned overseas and applied domestically, or can involve the development of mutually beneficial new ventures where neither party brings expertise but both can gain from an exercise in joint learning that can enhance corporate and cultural links between the partners.

Finally, we have also emphasized the importance of <u>Resourcing</u> as part of the proactive dimension in the Engagement Model, because we believe that it can be a source of competitive advantage for foreign partners who implement it seriously. A focus on high quality staff, committed to the country or region, speaking the language and demonstrating the value that they bring to a partnership through their individual technical expertise can dramatically enhance the relevance of a foreign partner in a country where relationships with key individuals are so important and where loyalty is valued highly. We have also highlighted that in our opinion senior national staff should play a major role in the process of sustaining foreign partner relevance, and although this has clearly been a difficult issue for many companies to solve, the increasing use of a "repat" strategy, where domestic staff are trained overseas and then brought back as international company managers, may gradually resolve it. Furthermore, we also believe that senior executive support from the domestic headquarters is vital to the success of international joint ventures, and any perceived lack of it is likely to be seized upon by domestic partners as a potential source of bargaining strength. Finally, we also see a useful contribution that can be made by independent advisors in increasing the robustness of any analysis and in providing impartial advice to senior executives.

The possible relevance of a corporate model in partnership strategies

We believe that the Engagement Model that we have outlined above is relevant for any foreign investor in a weak state environment, irrespective of the type of venture that he is undertaking. It is always important to acquire local knowledge and the ability to use it, and it is equally important to remain proactive in assessing your continuing relevance to any partnership and considering whether you need to contribute more. However, the case studies, the interviews and the statistical analysis that we have described in earlier chapters have also revealed another strategy that can be used to maintain balance between domestic and international partners, namely the use of a corporate structure. The concept is a slightly nebulous one, as it does not just mean the formation of a legal corporate entity to act as a joint venture vehicle. Rather it attempts to capture the difference between a single asset joint venture in which the partnership has a limited scope and a more wide-ranging multi-asset company in which the shareholders are incentivized to encourage long-term growth and are controlled by internationally accepted corporate governance rules.

This definition is perhaps best explained using two examples, one small and one large. In case study three in Chapter 3, both the main shareholders in the company pointed out that the issue of competition between partners can be addressed by providing sufficient incentive for both to act in the interest of all the stakeholders in a joint entity. This incentive can be created through structuring a partnership correctly, with the specific goal of encouraging a team atmosphere and providing the opportunity for growth beyond the initial investment. As the domestic partner noted "a [classic] joint venture is a static structure that does not have the flexibility to grow. There is always tension about whether each partner should inject new assets into the joint venture or keep them entirely for themselves."[28] Further the foreign partner observed that "many of the classic 50:50 joint ventures struck in the 1990s have been operational successes, but they have invariably turned into financial disappointments", and both agreed that a corporate structure created an atmosphere where the partners "no longer thought of ourselves as partners but as the same team" and therefore encouraged a "fruitful marriage of Russian assets and industrial expertise with western capital and management know-how".[29] Interestingly this marriage allowed the foreign partner to encourage the growth of a Russian culture in the joint entity, with a focus on hiring Russian staff, while maintaining western standards of corporate governance and management with the incentive of a future IPO on an international stock exchange. The potential financial rewards of the exit strategy kept the Russian partners incentivized to grow the joint entity, while the increasing Russification of the company allowed it to present itself as a domestic player and benefit from the perception this created with the domestic authorities.

A much larger example of this corporate incentivization was discussed in Chapter 6, where the fact that TNK-BP was formed as a BVI-based company with international corporate governance rules, and with its major subsidiary quoted on the stock exchange in Moscow, was seen as a major reason why the joint entity stayed together despite the turbulent relations between the partners. The corporate form of the partnership created a vehicle which provided long-term opportunity, growth potential and obvious financial returns in terms of dividend payments and a final exit strategy. It also incentivized both shareholders to come to the table to negotiate and ultimately to keep a unique investment vehicle together for their mutual benefit. In addition it also created an environment where international corporate governance rules could form the basis for these negotiations, which helped in part to counter the "local knowledge" advantage of the domestic partners. The 50:50 nature of the venture also provided a significant foundation for longevity, as it forced the partners to resolve issues through negotiation rather than have one party impose its will upon the other. Although this was seen as a source of friction by some (including President Putin himself), in reality it was probably the key feature that made TNK-BP so successful for both partners. However, this potential for friction does necessitate the appointment of appropriate foreign Board members (in particular in a Non-Executive capacity) who are prepared, both through force of character and through the weight of their international experience, to uphold governance rules and resist the often forceful arguments of domestic partners. Of course, under Russia's current Strategic Resource legislation such a shareholding structure could not be repeated today, but it nevertheless provides a useful general example for foreign investors in weak institutional environments across the world.

Other interviewees also endorsed the concept of the corporate model, in particular one who had also experienced the alternative JV structure. His anonymous conclusion was that the domestic partner is the biggest business risk in a joint entity, and therefore "if the joint venture is not structured correctly the domestic partner can easily develop two distinct strategies to create value for himself – develop the JV to its maximum potential using the skills of both parties to maximum advantage, or use his own skill of "domestic knowledge and influence". He urged that "the international partner has to be part of a Russian company" and emphasized that this was because "any troubles must hit you both equally so that you both respond in a way that maximizes the value of the business entity rather than one or other of the partners". Further, the benefit of the corporate model was also supported by the survey of foreign partners, where it was shown to have a significantly greater correlation with foreign partner success than the classic JV model. We might therefore conclude that a structure that draws all the stakeholders into a team atmosphere where they are all incentivized to work for the growth of the joint entity, and where their interests are aligned as closely as possible, can help to reduce the impact of many of the issues seen with the classic JV, in particular the potential use of local knowledge by the domestic partner against his foreign partner.

Final conclusions on partnership in a weak institutional environment

Having reached this positive conclusion about the corporate model, however, it would be wrong to herald it as the answer to all partnership problems. As highlighted earlier, it is a relatively imprecise concept and is also one that is not always available to foreign investors. Indeed in Russia today it would be impossible for any of the foreign partners who have recently linked up with Rosneft to hope to create such a structure. As a result, perhaps the most important conclusions to be drawn from the corporate model are the fundamental principles that underlie it rather than the structure itself. These are that partnerships work when all the parties are incentivized to work for the mutual benefit of the joint venture, whatever form it may take, over the long term. The incentive is created by the ongoing creation of opportunities for asset, revenue, profit and dividend growth and the greatest mutual benefit is generated when both partners continue to provide relevant skills to the venture.

In a weak institutional environment we have argued that the greatest skill provided by the domestic partner is local knowledge, and that this is much more difficult for the foreign partner to acquire in the "competition for knowledge" than it is for the domestic partner to acquire the international skills of technology, management and financing. The concept of the corporate model attempts to by-pass the competition by using governance rules to create a rigid structure where partner balance is almost enforced, but we have also argued that the foreign partner can and should aim to achieve this balance in any joint venture using the "7R Engagement Model". In particular he needs to remain relevant to the partnership he has created, firstly by ensuring that he makes great efforts to balance his domestic partner's key competitive advantage with his own networks of contacts and sources of local knowledge. Equally importantly, though, he also needs to proactively find ways to renew and refresh his own contribution to the partnership, producing new revenue-generating ideas, offering reciprocity in its many forms and providing high quality human resources. In this way a foreign partner can create the platform for long-term growth and mutual benefit that is at the heart of the corporate model concept, even if he cannot use the corporate model.

We believe that the recent Exxon joint venture with Rosneft may provide a good example of this in action. The Russian assets included in the joint venture consist of unconventional oil that could be developed before 2020, exploration assets in the South Kara Sea that will be explored in the current decade but will only produce hydrocarbons in the next, and following the supplementary deal announced in February 2013, have added exploration assets that will see activity continue in the Arctic towards 2050. Internationally, complimentary assets have been included in the Gulf of Mexico and onshore the USA and Canada which will allow Rosneft not only to increase its overseas exposure but also to gain relevant experience that can be used on its assets in Russia. Meanwhile the creation of an Arctic Research Centre[30] as the basis for the development of new technology for Russia's offshore industry will provide a platform for mutual learning that can also help to cement the relations between the two companies. In essence then, Exxon has attempted to put in place many of the elements of the corporate model without actually forming a company, as it is restricted to a 33% or 49% interest in various operating entities that are effectively acting as contractors to the ultimate licence holder, Rosneft.

However, despite our belief that Exxon has put in place many of the elements that can underpin a successful partnership, this does not mean to say that success is guaranteed. As we have constantly reiterated, the situation in any weak institutional environment is fluid and complex, and reliance on relationships with a few key individuals always carries the inherent risk that they will not be around forever. Indeed, the necessity of comprehensive relationship mapping and rigorous updating of the engagement model is even more vital in an environment where the removal of one key contact could have a dramatic effect on a foreign partner's business. There is never any room for complacency, and we have emphasized not only the detailed work that is needed to remain relevant but also the iterative nature of the engagement process. The very nature of a partnership in a weak institutional environment means that maintaining relevance is a game of perpetual motion, as there are always information gaps to be filled, external and internal changes to be analysed, partner contributions to be assessed and most importantly people with whom to build or enhance relations. As our statistical analysis concluded in Chapter 4, it is vital for a foreign company operating in an environment like Russia to get involved in this process. The more a foreign partner gets involved in local knowledge issues, the more likely he is to succeed, and he can increase his relative chances even more by proactively engaging with the partnership process and thus remaining as relevant as possible to both his commercial counterparts and the political elite who carry vital influence over his business.

Last thought – Russia is not alone in having a weak state environment

One final point is worth making as we end. Although we have focused on Russia, and in particular its oil and gas industry, as the focus for our study, we believe that the conclusions we have reached are relevant to many countries around the world with similar business environments and to many industries within them. In the World Bank database of Worldwide Governance Indicators Russia ranked in the 25th percentile for Rule of Law, in the 13th percentile for Control of Corruption, in the 39th percentile for Regulatory Quality and in the 42nd percentile for Government Effectiveness (with 0 being the worst and 100 the best),[31] while in the same institution's Ease of Doing Business Survey for 2013 Russia ranked in 112nd place out of 185 countries.[32] While these scores emphasize the points made throughout this book about the difficulty of doing business in the country, especially as a foreigner, they also underline that Russia is far from being the worst performer and that similar issues are faced by businessmen across the world. In carrying out our research we have been told multiple stories about activities in Central Asia, the FSU, Latin America and Asia that mirror the examples we have used in this book. We would therefore conclude by once again emphasizing that we are not attempting in any way to single out Russia for any specific criticism, because we genuinely believe that partnership is possible as long as foreign partners understand how business is conducted there. It is certainly different from the environment in which most international businessmen from OECD countries have worked, but in reality it is not much different from large parts of the global economy. Our goal has been to try to help explain any differences and the logical reasons for them, and therefore to encourage, not discourage, partnership with a country which we believe can offer huge opportunities for those companies prepared to embrace engagement.

Appendix 1   Survey Questionnaire for Joint Venture Statistical Analysis

1. Name of Joint Venture: ....
2. Your role in the Joint Venture: ....
3. Time spent in this role: ....
4. What were the objectives of your company in forming the joint venture?
   ....
   ....
5. What did you perceive your partner's objectives to be?
   ....
   ....
6. At the time the joint venture was formed, how do you rate the importance of the contributions made by your company and by your domestic partner(s) in the following areas (scale of 1–5, where 1 is minimal contribution and 5 is high contribution. Please tick two boxes for each contribution, one for your company and one for the domestic partner):

Contribution to:	By your company					By domestic partner(s)				
	1	2	3	4	5	1	2	3	4	5
Access to export markets										
Access to domestic markets										
Access to improved (new) technology										
Access to tangible assets (reserves and infrastructure at oil and gas fields, refineries, retail stations etc.)										
Access to capital resources										
Managing informal domestic political and social issues										
Managing informal issues in international markets										
Managing formal domestic business issues										
Managing formal international business issues										
Brand name/goodwill of firm										
Provision of management skills										

7. How would you evaluate the progress of your domestic partner in acquiring greater production capability during the course of the joint venture, from operational, management and technological perspectives (on a scale of 1–5, 1 implying minimal learning and 5 very significant learning)?

Learning by Domestic Partner in Area of:	1	2	3	4	5
Operational capability					
Management capability					
Technological capability to develop business					

8. At the time the joint venture was developed, how much control, **de facto**, did you as the foreign investor have over the following business functions (scale of 1–5, where 1 is a very low level of control and 5 is a very high level of control):

Business function controlled by:	1	2	3	4	5
Strategic management or planning					
Operational management					
Business co-ordination and integration					
Sales and Trading					
Transport					
Finance and Accounting of Operations					
Tax					
Investment Finance					
Government Relations					
Technology Development/ Implementation					
IT					
Security					
Procurement					
Public/investor relations					

9. For each business function, how did your involvement, influence and control change, **de facto**, over the life of the JV (please tick one box for each function)

Change in foreign partner role:	Large decrease	Small decrease	Remained the same	Small increase	Large increase
Strategic management or planning					
Operational management					
Business co-ordination and integration					
Sales and Trading					
Transport					
Finance and Accounting of Operations					
Tax					
Investment Finance					
Government Relations					
Technology Development/ Implementation					
Security					
Procurement					
Public/investor relations					

10. Were there any business functions/activities/events where there was significant partner friction over the allocation of roles? If so, what were those functions/activities/events?

....

11. As a result of this JV how confident would you be to operate in Russia without a domestic partner in the following areas (on a scale of 1–5, 1 implying low confidence, 5 high confidence)?

Confidence to operate without a domestic partner	1	2	3	4	5
Strategic management or planning					
Operational management					
Business co-ordination and integration					
Sales and Trading					
Transport					
Finance and Accounting of					
Operations					
Tax					
Investment Finance					
Government Relations					
Technology Development/ Implementation					
Security					
Procurement					
Public/investor relations					

12. How would you respond to the following statements: 1. "State corruption[1] was widespread in the Russian oil and gas industry during the period of our investment in this JV"; 2. "Administrative corruption[2] was widespread in the Russian oil and gas industry during the period of our investment in this JV" (on a scale of 1–5, with 1 as strongly disagree and 5 as strongly agree)?[3]

	At initiation of JV					Now, or when you left JV				
	1	2	3	4	5	1	2	3	4	5
State corruption										
Administrative corruption										

13. How would you assess the influence of the state and administration (federal or regional) on the business of the JV concerning the following issues during the life of the joint venture (on a scale of 1–5 where 1 is low and 5 is high)?

Influence of state re:	At initiation of JV					Now, or when you left JV				
	1	2	3	4	5	1	2	3	4	5
Governance issues (equity, BoD membership, management roles)										
Administrative issues (licensing, development approvals, employment and social issues)										
Commercial issues (taxation, pricing, export allocations, pipeline access, procurement)										
Technical/operational issues (devt. plans, production targets, choice of equipment and technology)										

14. From your perspective how would you assess the success of the JV, in terms of meeting your objectives in a number of areas (on a scale of 1–5, 1 implying minimal and 5 complete success):

Success of objectives in various areas	1	2	3	4	5
Financial performance					
Reserve/asset base					
Production volumes					
Overall strategic aims					

15. How would you assess the JV from your domestic partner's perspective? On a scale of 1–5 how many of their strategic objectives do you think they achieved (1 implies very few, 5 implies all).

	1	2	3	4	5
Perception of domestic partner's view of success of JV					

16. What were the critical success factors in the operation and development of the joint venture?
    ....
    ....

Appendix 2   Statistical Tables to Support Analysis in Chapter 4

Table A2.1   Significant correlations with foreign partner success

		Change if FP Control CFPC_FAC_LOC	Domestic Partner Success	State Influence on Governance Issues
Average Foreign Partner Success	Correlation Coefficient	0.33	0.39	−0.40
	Sig. (2-tailed)	0.01	0.01	0.01
	N	32	33	31

Table A2.2   Results of first regression analysis

Coefficients[a]

Model		Unstandardized Coefficients		Standardized Coefficients	t	Sig.	Collinearity Statistics	
		B	Std. Error	Beta			Tolerance	VIF
1	(Constant)	3.247	.137		23.788	.000		
	CFPC local knowledge	.557	.137	.604	4.078	.000	1.000	1.000
2	(Constant)	2.292	.356		6.434	.000		
	CFPC local knowledge	.559	.122	.606	4.573	.000	1.000	1.000
	Domestic Partner Success	.293	.103	.379	2.855	.008	1.000	1.000
3	(Constant)	2.926	.365		8.027	.000		
	CFPC local knowledge	.460	.110	.499	4.186	.000	.923	1.083
	Domestic Partner Success	.319	.089	.412	3.581	.001	.992	1.008
	Average State Influence on Governance	−.314	.097	−.388	−3.245	.003	.916	1.092
4	(Constant)	2.869	.421		6.821	.000		
	CFPC local knowledge	.463	.112	.502	4.123	.000	.914	1.094
	Domestic Partner Success	.315	.091	.407	3.449	.002	.974	1.026
	Average State Influence on Governance	−.293	.121	−.363	−2.432	.022	.609	1.643
	JV Model (Corp or not)	.088	.303	.042	.291	.774	.658	1.521

[a] Dependent Variable: FP Success Average

Table A2.3 Multiple regression model summary

Model Summary[e]

Model	R	R Square	Adjusted R Square	Std. Error of the Estimate	Change Statistics					Durbin-Watson
					R Square Change	F Change	df1	df2	Sig. F. Change	
1	.604[a]	.364	.343	.76003	.364	16.628	1	29	.000	
2	.713[b]	.508	.473	.68071	.143	8.152	1	28	.008	
3	.804[c]	.646	.607	.58797	.138	10.529	1	27	.003	
4	.804[d]	.647	.593	.59820	.001	.085	1	26	.774	2.602

[a] Predictors: (Constant), CFPC local knowledge
[b] Predictors: (Constant), CFPC local knowledge, Domestic Partner Success
[c] Predictors: (Constant), CFPC local knowledge, Domestic Partner Success, Average State Influence on Governance
[d] Predictors: (Constant), CFPC local knowledge, Domestic Partner Success, Average State Influence on Governance, JV Model (Corp or not)
[e] Dependent Variable: FP Success Average

Table A2.4 Results of regression analysis using JV investment model to explain foreign partner success

	Beta	Standard Error	Standardized Co-efficient Beta	Significance
Constant	2.988	0.195		
JV Investment Model	0.813	0.372	0.365	0.037

Table A2.5 Model summary for regression analysis of joint entities using the classic JV model

Model Summary

JV Model (Corp or not)	Model	R	R Square	Adjusted R Square	Std. Error of the Estimate
Other	1	.697[a]	.486	.461	.735
	2	.786[b]	.618	.580	.649

[a] Predictors: (Constant), CFPC local knowledge
[b] Predictors: (Constant), CFPC local knowledge, Domestic Partner Success

Table A2.6   Results of regression analysis for joint entities using JV model

JV Model (Corp or not)	Model		Coefficients[a] Unstandardized Coefficients		Standardized Coefficients	t	Sig.
			B	Std. Error	Beta		
Other	1	(Constant)	3.108	.153		20.261	.000
		CFPC local knowledge	.627	.141	.697	4.454	.000
	2	(Constant)	2.104	.405		5.193	.000
		CFPC local knowledge	.627	.124	.697	5.042	.000
		Domestic Partner Success	.312	.119	.363	2.629	.016

[a] Dependent Variable: FP Success Average

Table A2.7 Logistic regression results for classic JV when score of 3 equates to success

Variables in the Equation JV Model			B	S.E.	Wald	df	Sig.	Exp(B)
Other	Step 1(a)	DP_Success_Log	8.51	4.67	3.32	1	0.07	4950.7
		CFPC_FAC_LOC	3.66	1.98	3.41	1	0.07	38.7
		Constant	−2.25	1.66	1.85	1	0.17	0.1

[a] Variable(s) entered on step 1: DP_Success_Log, CFPC_FAC_LOC

Table A2.8 Results of truncated regression analysis

Model	
DP Success	0.43*
(robust std. err.)	*(0.13)*
CFPC Local Knowledge	0.33**
(robust std. err.)	*(0.19)*
Constant	1.84
(robust std. err.)	*(0.44)*
Standard error of estimate	0.63
Log likelihood	−18.92
chi-squared	11.88
Prob>chi2	0.003

* *significant at 0.05 level*
** *significant at 0.1 level*

Notes

Chapter 1   The Turbulent History of Foreign Involvement in the Russian Oil and Gas Industry

1   United States Geological Survey.
2   Author's estimate based on corporate presentations from Rosneft and LUKOIL.
3   Goldman, Marshall I., 1980, "The Enigma of Soviet Petroleum" (London: Allen & Unwin), pp. 13–15.
4   Alekperov, V., 2011, "Oil of Russia: Past, Present and Future" (East View Press), pp. 84–88.
5   Yergin, pp. 58–61.
6   Goldman, p. 16.
7   Yergin, pp. 60–61; Goldman, pp. 16–17.
8   Hassman, Heinrich, 1953, "Oil in the Soviet Union: History, Geography, Problems, translated from the German by Alfred M. Leeston (Princeton: Princeton University Press), p. 112 and Figure 19.
9   Goldman, p. 17.
10 Baibakov, Nikolai, 1984, "The Cause of My Life" (Moscow: Progress Publishers), p. 13.
11 Goldman, p. 21.
12 Baibakov, p. 14.
13 Goldman, p. 20.
14 Baibakov, p. 15.
15 Goldman, p. 22.
16 Sutton, Anthony C., 1968, "Western Technology and Soviet Economic Development, Vol. I, 1917 to 1930" (Stanford: Hoover Institution Press), p. 41.
17 Goldman, p. 25.
18 Sutton, Anthony C., 1971, "Western Technology and Soviet Economic Development, Vol. II, 1930–1945" (Stanford: Hoover Institution Press), p. 17.
19 Alekperov, V., 2011, p. 260.
20 Gustafson, T., 1989, "Crisis Amid Plenty" (Princeton: Princeton University Press), p. 73.
21 Goldman, M. I., 1980, "The Enigma of Soviet Petroleum" (London: Allen & Unwin), p. 34.
22 Gustafson, p. 79.
23 Goldman, p. 35.
24 Gustafson, p. 86.
25 Gustafson, p. 80.
26 Goldman, p. 41.
27 Gustafson, p. 116.
28 The USSR produced a total of 625 million tonnes, of which Russia contributed 570 million tonnes, equivalent to 11.4 million bpd.
29 Gustafson, T., 2012, "Wheel of Fortune: The Struggle for Oil and Power in Russia" (Cambridge, Mass.), p. 40.
30 Almanac of Russian Petroleum, 2000, Moscow, Energy Intelligence Group, p. 89.
31 Pravda, 26th June 1987, in Gustafson, p. 6.
32 Gustafson, 2012, p. 35.

33   Ibid., pp. 35–36.
34   BP Statistical Review of World Energy 2012.
35   Gustafson, 2012, p. 36.
36   Ibid., p. 45.
37   Oil and Gas Journal, 12 August 1991, "Profits, Progress on Soviet Ventures Outlined".
38   Gustafson, 2012, p. 46.
39   Ibid., p. 47.
40   Lane, David & Seifulmulukov, Iskander, 1999, "Structure and Ownership" in "The Political Economy of Russian Oil", ed. David Lane (Oxford: Rowman and Littlefield).
41   Lane & Seifulmulukov, in Lane, p. 16.
42   Moser, Nat & Oppenheimer, Peter, 2001, "The Oil Industry: Structural Transformation and Corporate Governance" in "Russia's Post-Communist Economy", ed. B. Granville & P. Oppenheimer (Oxford University Press).
43   Moser and Oppenheimer, p. 304.
44   Moser, N., 1999, "The Privatisation of the Russian Oil Industry, 1992–1995. Façade or Reality?", M.Phil dissertation, St. Antony's College, University of Oxford, p. 24.
45   Russian government ordinance no. 452, May 1994.
46   Presidential decree no. 327, April 1995.
47   Moser & Oppenheimer, p. 306.
48   Lane & Seifulmulukov, in Lane, pp. 19–23.
49   Allan, Duncan, 2002, "Banks and the Loans-for-Shares Auctions" in "Russian Banking", ed. Lane, D. (Cheltenham: Elgar), pp. 137–160.
50   Ibid.
51   Kommersant Daily, 5 April 1995, "Usloviya kredita banka predlagayut v pyatnitsu".
52   Allan, Duncan, 2002, "Banks and the Loans-for-Shares Auctions" in "Russian Banking", ed. Lane, D. (Cheltenham: Elgar), pp. 137–160.
53   Ibid.
54   Economist, 18 November 1995.
55   Gustafson, 2012, p. 102.
56   Ibid., pp. 324–325.
57   Nefte Compass, 25 October 2001, "Infidels: Oil Majores Revert to Corporate Shenanigans", Moscow.
58   "The Energy Dimension in Russian Global Strategy – From Rags to Riches: Oilmen vs. Financiers in the Russian Oil Sector", Dr. Nina Poussenkova, James Baker III Institute for Public Policy of Rice University, October 2004, p. 3.
59   Moscow Times, 16 January 1999, "Tensions Flare Up Between Yukos, Shareholders", Moscow.
60   Moscow Times, 21 December 1999, "Yukos, Dart End Long-Running Feud", Moscow.
61   BP Statistical Review of World Energy 2012.
62   Price for Urals Blend, the Russian export crude blend, sourced from Energy Intelligence Group database.
63   The rouble:dollar exchange rate moved from 6:1 in early 1998 to 28:1 in 2000.
64   Gustafson, 2012, pp. 185–230.
65   Schleifer, A. & Treisman, D., 2000, "Without a Map: Political Tactics and Economic Reform in Russia" (Cambridge, Mass.: MIT Press).
66   Oil & Gas Journal, 7 February 2000, "Schlumberger Helps Yukos Boost Oil Output", Moscow.
67   Data from InfoTEK and Russian Ministry of Energy.

68   Gustafson, T., 2012, pp. 221–225.
69   Ibid., pp. 225–228.
70   Goldman, M. I., 2008, "Oilopoly: Putin, Power and the Rise of the New Russia" (Oxford: One World), pp. 97–99.
71   Gustafson, T., 2012, pp. 246–249.
72   Goldman, M. I., 2008, pp. 99–102.
73   Tompson, W., 2005, "Putin and the Oligarchs: A Two-Sided Commitment Problem" (Oxford: Oxford University Press).
74   Gustafson, T., 2012, p. 292.
75   Petroleum Economist, 5 October 2005, "Russia: Gazprom Swallows Sibneft", London.
76   Ownership of 75% of a company in Russia is vital because it effectively gives the owner complete control over all strategic decisions at the company. A shareholder with a 25% plus one share stake can veto these decisions, hence the need to acquire more than 75% to assume complete control of a Russian company.
77   Financial Times, 20 April 2009, "The State's Unsated Appetite", London.
78   Press release by Sibneft and Tyumen Oil, 18 December 2002, http://pda.gazprom-neft.com/press-center/news/3439/, accessed 8th March 2013.
79   Gustafson, T., 2012, pp. 275–277.
80   Goldman, M. I., 2008, pp. 194–198.
81   Tompson, W., 2005, p. 9.
82   Pirani, S., 2010, "Change in Putin's Russia: Power, Money and People" (London: Pluto Press).
83   Gustafson, T., 2012, p. 275.
84   For example in The Economist, 10 August 2006, "Oil's Dark Secret: National Oil Companies", London.
85   For example: Henderson, J., 2011, "From Brownfield to Greenfield", FIRST Magazine, St. Petersburg; TNK-BP presentation, 2010, "Brownfield Evolution/Greenfield Revolution", http://www.tnk-bp.ru/upload/iblock/f7a/eng.pdf, accessed 11th March 2013.
86   Quotes from Vladimir Bogdanov sourced from http://www.news.kremlin.ru/transcripts/7198, accessed 11th March 2013.
87   Energy Strategy of Russian for the period up to 2030, approved by Decree No. 1715 on 13th November 2009.
88   Henderson, J., 2011, "From Brownfield to Greenfield", FIRST Magazine, St. Petersburg.
89   United States Geological Survey, 2009, "Circum-Arctic Resource Appraisal; Estimates of Undiscovered Oil and Gas North of the Arctic Circle", California.
90   Data estimated from various company reports and analyst estimates.
91   Interfax, 9 November 2012, "Gazprom Neft Expects Decision on Commercial Shale Oil Development in Russia by 2017–18".
92   Rosneft presentation, 1 February 2013, "Q4 and 12M 2012 IFRS Results", slide 9.
93   Bloomberg, 25 May 2012, "Gazprom May Invite Shell to Shtokman Group, Focus on LNG", Moscow.
94   Calculation based on data from the IFRS financial statements of the major Russian oil companies.
95   Kostanian, K., 2012, "Russia's Unconventional Future" (Moscow: Merrill Lynch), p. 4.
96   Interfax, 27 October 2009, "TNK-BP to Save $2–2.5bn from Export Tax, NRET Reductions", Moscow.
97   Interfax, 16 April 2012, "Putin Order Tax Breaks for Offshore Oil, Gas Projects – Deputy PM", Moscow.
98   Henderson, J., 2001, "Russian Oil: The Non-OPEC Alternative" (Moscow: Renaissance Capital).

99   Gustafson, T., 2012, pp. 154–155.
100   World Bank Staff Appraisal Report, No. 11556-RU, "Russian Federation: Oil Rehabilitation Project", 26 May 1993, p. v.
101   Sagers, Matthew J., 1993, "The Energy Industries in the Former USSR: A Mid-Year Survey", *Post-Soviet Geography*, 34(6), 341–418.
102   Russia Petroleum Investor Inc., 2003, "M&A Opportunities in the Oil & Gas Sector of Russia", Moscow.
103   EIA data from http://www.eia.doe.gov/emeu/jv/jvtxt.html.
104   Gustafson, T., 2012, p. 155.
105   Russia Petroleum Investor Inc., 2003, "M&A Opportunities in the Oil & Gas Sector of Russia", Moscow, p. 33.
106   IEA, 2002, "Russia Energy Survey", Paris, pp. 83–87.
107   Interview with German Khan in "Insight TNK-BP, December 2003", p. 4.
108   Gustafson, T., 2012, p. 165.
109   HSE stands for Health, Safety and the Environment.
110   Interview with German Khan in "Insight TNK-BP, December 2003", p. 5.
111   IEA Russia Energy Survey 2002, p. 87.
112   Gustafson, Thane, 1999, "Capitalism Russian-Style" (Cambridge University Press), pp. 192–194.
113   International Energy Agency, pp. 79–82.
114   Russia Petroleum Investor, May 1995.
115   Watson, 1996, p. 434.
116   Gustafson, T., 2012, p. 403.
117   Braginsky, A., 2010, "Stand and Deliver: Oil and Gas Yearbook 2010" (Moscow: Renaissance Capital).
118   Landes, A., July 2002, "Russia Oil & Gas Yearbook 2002" (Moscow: Renaissance Capital), p. 97.
119   Gaddy, C. G. & Ickes, B. W., 2002, "Russia's Virtual Economy" (Washington: Brookings Institution Press).
120   International Energy Agency, p. 95.
121   World Bank BEEPS Survey 2002.
122   McPherson, C. P., 1996, "Political Reforms in the Russian Oil Sector", World Bank Finance and Development Report, 33(2), June.
123   Pleines, p. 101.
124   Hellman, Joel S., Jones, Geraint & Kaufmann, Daniel, September 2000, "Seize the State, Seize the Day; State Capture, Corruption and Influence in Transition", World Bank Policy Research Working Paper No. 2444.
125   Gustafson, T., 2012, p. 166.
126   Landes, Adam, 2003, "Russia Oil & Gas Yearbook" (Moscow: Renaissance Capital), pp. 129–130.
127   Gustafson, T., 2012, p. 179.
128   Landes, p. 129.
129   International Energy Agency, 2002, "Russia Energy Survey, 2002", p. 85.
130   Landes, A., 2003, "Russia Oil and Gas Yearbook: Piping Growth" (Moscow: Renaissance Capital).
131   IEA, 2002, p. 35.
132   Atlantic Richfield Corporation.
133   Gorst, I., 2007, "LUKOIL: Russia's Largest Oil Company" (Houston: James Baker III Institute).
134   The History of ARCO at www.bp.com accessed 20th March 2013.
135   Daily Telegraph, 31 January 2001, "BP Sells LUKOIL Stake to Focus on Siberia Gas", London.
136   Economist, 2 December 1999, "Russia: Rules of War", Moscow.

137 IEA, 2002, "Russia Energy Survey", Paris, p. 39.

138 Nash, 2002, p. 6.

139 Ibid.

140 "TNK Strikes Deal for Sidanco", 3 August 2001, Alfa Group Press Release, www.alfagroup.org.

141 Moser and Oppenheimer, p. 320.

142 Terry Macalister, 13 February 2003, "Prime Minister Argues Case for Blair Petroleum", Guardian, London.

143 Russia Journal, 6 September 1999, "Sidanco Fight to be Test for Foreign Investment", Moscow.

144 Economist, 2 December 1999, "Russia: Rules of War", Moscow.

145 Jack, A., 2004, "Inside Putin's Russia" (London: Granta), p. 190.

146 Petroleum Economist, 1 January 1999, "Small Might Be Beautiful", London.

147 "Elf Decides Not to Pursue Its Alliance with Sibneft", Elf press release, August 25th 1998, www.total.com

148 Stern, J., 2005, "The Future of Russian Gas and Gazprom" (Oxford: Oxford University Press), pp. 73–74.

149 Moscow Times, 23 June 2003, "Yukos Market Capitalisation Hits $30bn", Moscow.

150 The Economic Times, 16 September 2003, "Chevron, Exxon Vie for 25% Stake in Yukos".

151 Gustafson, T., 2012, pp. 297–300.

152 Daily Telegraph, 8 October 2003, "Putin Confirms Exxon Talks with Yukos", London.

153 Moscow Times, 27 October 2003, "9 Years Ago a Man was Arrested: Khodorkovsky Arrested on 7 Charges", Moscow.

154 Pravda, 3 March 2004, "Exxon Mobil Likely to Buy Yukos", http://english. pravda.ru/news/world/11-03-2004/55910-0/, accessed 20 March 2013.

155 Moscow Times, 15 March 2004, "Chevron, Shell and Total All Chasing a Stake in Sibneft", Moscow.

156 Goldman, M., 2008, "Oilopoly: Putin, Power and the Rise of the New Russia" (Oxford: One World), p. 123.

157 Washington Post, 30 September 2004, "ConocoPhillips Acquires Russian Government's Stake in LUKOIL", Washington.

158 The CEOs of LUKOIL and ConocoPhillips respectively.

159 Russia Beyond the Headlines, 2 August 2012, "ConocoPhillips to Sell Its Last Remaining Assets in Russia", http://rbth.ru/articles/2012/08/02/conocophillips_ to_sell_its_last_remaining_assets_in_russia_16949.html, accessed on 20 March 2013.

160 Financial Times, 14 November 2012, "Gazprom Boost Presence in European Gas", London.

161 Petroleum Economist, 2 August 2011, "E.On and Gazprom in Gas Price Deadlock", London.

162 Platts, 3 July 2012, "E.On and Gazprom Agree on Long-Term Gas Contract Compromise", London.

163 Gustafson, T., 2012, pp. 176–177.

164 Arkhady Ostrovsky, 2006, "Sakhalin 2 Fell Foul of Zealous Official", Financial Times, 29th September.

165 "Shell Cedes Control of Sakhalin 2 to Gazprom", 2006, International Herald Tribune, 21st December.

166 Gazprom Press Release, 21 June 2012, "Gazprom and Shell Develop Co-operation in Russian and International Oil and Gas Markets".

167 Financial Times, 4 April 2007, "ENI/Enel Win Yukos Assets Auction", Moscow.

168   Reuters, 25 March 2009, "Gazprom to Exercise ENI Buyback Option in Early April", Moscow.
169   Interfax, 30 November 2010, "Novatek, GazpromNeft JV Acquires 51% of Severenergia for $1.8 billion", Moscow.
170   Reuters, 7 August 2012, "Statoil Writes Off $336 Shtokman Gas Investment", Moscow.
171   Guardian, 29 August 2012, "Plug Pulled on Russia's Flagship Shtokman Energy Project", London.
172   Reuters, 24 March 2011, "Total to Buy Novatek Stake, Join Yamal LNG Project", Moscow.
173   Gustafson, T., 2012, p. 87.
174   Reuters, 12 February 2013, "Gazprom Monopoly Under Pressure as Putin Mulls LNG Options", Moscow.
175   Rosneft Press Release, 30 August 2011, "Rosneft and ExxonMobil Join Forces in the Arctic and Black Sea Offshore", Moscow.
176   Rosneft Press Release, 13 February 2013, "Rosneft and ExxonMobil Expand Strategic Cooperation", Moscow.
177   Rosneft Presentation, January 2011, "Strategic Alliance with BP", slide 6.
178   Rosneft Presentation, 5 October 2012, "Non-Deal Roadshow", slide 9.
179   Rosneft Presentation, 1 February 2013, "12M 2012 IFRS Results", slide 9.
180   Rosneft Press Release, 25 April 2012, "Rosneft and ENI Join Forces to Explore Fields in Barents and Black Seas", Moscow.
181   Rosneft Press Release, 5 May 2012, "Rosneft and Statoil Agree on Joint Offshore Operations in Branets Sea and Sea of Okhotsk", Moscow.
182   Rosneft Press Release, 25 April 2012, "Rosneft and ENI Join Forces to Explore Fields in Barents and Black Seas", Moscow.
183   AAR – Alfa Access Renova, the consortium of companies owned by Mikhail Fridman, Viktor Vekselberg, Leonid Blavatnik and German Khan.
184   Although foreign companies did own 100% of some smaller companies such as Marathon at KMOC and ONGC at Imperial Oil.
185   Goldman, M., 2008, p. 126.
186   Browne, J., 2010, "Beyond Business", p. 146.
187   Tim Summers presentation at CERA Week, February 2007, "TNK-BP: Three Years in Russia", slide 5.
188   TNK-BP Investor Presentation, July 2010, slides 11 and 32.
189   Gustafson, T., 2012, pp. 424–426.
190   For example The Daily Telegraph, 5 September 2008, "BP's Russian Alliance with Gazprom Put on Ice", London.
191   BP Press Release, 22 June 2007, "BP and TNK-BP Plan Strategic Alliance with Gazprom", London.
192   Gustafson, T., 2012, p. 426.
193   Daily Telegraph, 24 July 2008, "Russians Issue Legal Threat to TNK-BP's Robert Dudley", London.
194   Ibid., p. 427.
195   BP Press Release, 14 January 2011, "Rosneft and BP Form Global and Arctic Strategic Alliance", London.
196   Guardian, 17 May 2011, "BP-Rosneft Deal Collapses", London.
197   Wall Street Journal, 1 June 2012, "BP Draws Russian Suitors for TNK-BP Stake", Moscow.
198   Note that BP already owned 1.25% of Rosneft before the TNK-BP sale, meaning that its total stake after the deal reached 19.75%.
199   "US-Russia Business Committee Urges Changes Aimed at Russia's Energy Sector", International Trade Reporter, 29 June 1994, p. 1033.

200 "Russia Aims for Favourable Climate for Joint Ventures", Oil & Gas Journal, 10 August 1992, pp. 19–21.
201 International Energy Agency, 2002, "Russia Energy Survey, 2002", p. 87. The three key projects were the original PSAs for the Sakhalin 1, Sakhalin 2 and Kharyaga developments.
202 Data from State Statistics Committee of the Russian Federation.
203 Nash, Roland, 2002, "Foreign Direct Investment: Ready for Take-Off?", Renaissance Capital, Moscow.

Chapter 2   A Review of Academic Theory on Joint Ventures, Partnership and the Importance of Local Knowledge

1   Dunning, J. H., 2000, "The Eclectic Paradigm as an Envelope for Economic and Business Theories of MNE Activity", International Business Review, 9, pp. 163–190.
2   Hymer, S. H., 1960, "The International Operations of National Firms: A Study of Direct Foreign Investment" (Cambridge, MA: MIT Press) (published 1976).
3   Kindelberger, C. P., 1969, "American Business Abroad" (New Haven, CT: Yale University Press).
4   Navaretti, G. B. & Venables, A. J., 2004, "Multinational Firms in the World Economy" (Princeton University Press), Chapter 2, pp. 22–48.
5   Markusen, J., 2002, "Multinational Firms and the Theory of International Trade" (MIT Press).
6   Hummels, D., 2000, "Time as a Trade Barrier", Mimeo, Purdue University.
7   Harrigan, J. & Venables, A. J., 2004, "Timeliness, Trade and Agglomeration", Discussion Paper, Centre for Economic Performance, LSE.
8   Anderson, J. & Van Wincoop, E., 2004, "Trade Costs", Journal of Economic Literature, 118, pp. 1375–1418.
9   Navaretti, G. B. & Venables, A. J., 2004, "Multinational Firms in the World Economy", Princeton University Press, Chapter 2, p. 29.
10   Knickerbocker, F. T., 1973, "Oligopolistic Reaction and Multinational Enterprise", Cambridge, MA, Division of Research, Graduate School of Business Administration, Harvard University.
11   Devereux, M. P., Griffith, R. & Klemm, A., 2002, "Corporate Income Tax Reforms and International Tax Competition", Economic Policy, 17, pp. 451–495.
12   Hines, J. R., 1999, "Lessons from Behavioural Responses to International Taxation", National Tax Journal, 52, pp. 305–322.
13   MNE – Multinational Enterprise.
14   Any field containing more than 70 million tonnes of oil or 50 billion cubic metres (bcm) of gas is classified as strategic and foreign investment is limited to below 50% – see "Law on Strategic Foreign Investments", www.russianlaws.com, March 2009.
15   Luxemburg, R., 1913, "The Accumulation of Capital" (London: Routledge and Kegan Paul) (1971 edition).
16   Frobel, F., Heinricks, J. & Kreye, O., 1980, "The New International Division of Labour" (Cambridge and Paris: Cambridge University Press and Editions de la Maison des Sciences de l'Homme).
17   Sunkel, O., 1972, "Big Business and 'Dependencia': A Latin American View", Foreign Affairs, 50 (April 1972), pp. 517–531.
18   See later discussion on JVs as a learning competition between partners in section.
19   Grossman, S. & Hart, O., 1986, "The Costs and Benefits of Ownership: A Theory of Vertical and Lateral Integration", Journal of Political Economy, 94, pp. 691–719.

20　Hart, O. & Moore, J., 1990, "Property Rights and the Nature of the Firm", Journal of Political Economy, 98, pp. 1119–1158.

21　Hart, O., 1995, "Firms, Contracts and Financial Structure" (Oxford: Oxford University Press).

22　Caves, R. E., 1971, "International Corporations: The Industrial Economics of Foreign Investment", Economica, 38, pp. 1–27.

23　Buckley, P. J. & Casson, M. C., 1976, "A Long Run Theory of the Multinational Enterprise", in Buckley, P. J. & Casson, M. C. (eds) "The Future of the Multinational Enterprise" (London: Macmillan).

24　Buckley & Casson, 1976, p. 45.

25　Navaretti, G. B. & Venables, A. J., 2004, "Multinational Firms in the World Economy" (Princeton University Press), Chapter 2, p. 38.

26　Markusen, J. R., 2002, "Multinational Firms and the Theory of International Trade" (MIT Press).

27　McKern, B., 1993, "Introduction: Transnational Corporations and the Exploitation of Natural Resources", from McKern, B. (ed.), "Transnational Corporations and the Exploitation of Natural Resources", UN Library on Transnational Corporations (London and New York: Routledge).

28　Hughes, H., 1975, "Economic Rents, the Distribution of Gains from Mineral Exploitation, and Mineral Development Policy", World Development, 3, pp. 811–825.

29　Penrose, E. T., 1968, "The Large International Firm in Developing Countries" (London: Allen & Unwin).

30　Vernon, R., 1971, "Sovereignty at Bay" (New York: Basic Books).

31　Ibid., pp. 26–59.

32　Ibid., p. 45.

33　Ibid.

34　Ibid.

35　Djankov, S., Glaeser, E., La Porta, R., Lopez-de-Silanes, F. & Schleifer, A., 2003, "The New Comparative Economics", Journal of Comparative Economics, 31(4), pp. 595–619.

36　Djankov et al, 2003, p. 17.

37　Hellman, J. S., Jones, G. & Kaufmann, D., 2000, "Seize the State, Seize the Day – State Capture, Corruption and Influence in Transition", World Bank Working Paper No. 2444.

38　Ibid.

39　1999 BEEPS survey at www.worldbank/countries/Europe&Central Asia/Anti-corruption/BEEPs firm level data

40　Sonin, K., 2002, "Why the Rich May Favour Poor Protection of Property Rights", Washington: World Bank Working Paper No. 544, December 2002.

41　Hellman, J., 1998, "Winners Take All: The Politics of Partial Reform in Postcommunist Transitions", World Politics, 50, pp. 203–234.

42　Slinko, I., Yakovlev, E. & Zhuravskaya, E., 2003, "Institutional Subversion: Evidence from Russian Regions", William Davidson Institute Working Paper No. 604, July.

43　Smarzynska, B. K. & Wei, S-J., 2000, "Corruption and Composition of Foreign Direct Investment: Firm Level Evidence", World Bank Working Paper No. 2360.

44　Nielsen, K., Jessop, B. & Hausner, J., 1995, "Institutional Change in Post-Socialism", from Strategic Choice and Path Dependency in Post Socialism, eds. Hausner, J., Jessop, R. & Nielsen, K. (Aldershot, UK: Edward Elgar), pp. 3–41.

45　Henisz, W. J. & Zelner, B. A., 2003. "Legitimacy, Interest Group Pressures and Change in Emergent Institutions: The Case of Foreign Investors and Host

Country Governments", William Davidson Institute Working Paper No. 589, May.

46   Henisz, W. J. & Zelner, B. A., 2003, p. 34.

47   For example Guardian, 1 December 2011, "Putin Prepares the Russian Empire to Strike Back".

48   Jack, A., 2004, "Inside Putin's Russia" (London: Granta Books), p. 331.

49   Daily Mail, 5 August 2009, "On holiday with Vladimir: Putin takes a dip, climbs a tree and loses his shirt – again – in back-to-basics Siberia vacation".

50   Mendras, M., 2012, "Russia Politics: The Paradox of a Weak State" (New York: Columbia University Press), p. 11.

51   Aslund, A., 2007, "Russia's Capitalist Revolution" (Washington, USA: Peterson Institute for International Economics).

52   Ibid.

53   Ledeneva, A., 2006, "How Russia Really Works" (New York: Cornell University Press).

54   Ibid., p. 194.

55   Ledeneva, A., 2009, "From Russia with Blat: Can Informal Networks Help Modernise Russia?", Social Research, 76 (1), Spring 2009, pp. 257–288.

56   Shevtsova, L., 2003, "Putin's Russia" (Washington D.C.: Carnegie Endowment for World Peace).

57   Mendras, 2012, p. 243.

58   Jack, 2004, pp. 306–309.

59   Ibid., p. 337.

60   Hanson & Teague, 2013, p. 3.

61   Ibid., p. 4.

62   Interview with Anna Nikolaeva in Moskovskie Novosti, 1 March 2012.

63   "Transcript: Dmitry Medvedev's Interview with CNN", 29 January 2013 sourced at http://russialist.org/transcript-dmitry-medvedevs-interview-with-cnn/ on 25 June 2013.

64   Vladimir Putin, 30 January 2012, "Our Task", quoted in Kinossian, N., 14 March 2012, "Strong Presidency, Weak Institutions: The Problems of Modernisation in the Russian Federation", Presentation at the Aleksanteri Institute, Helsinki.

65   Hanson & Teague, 2013, p. 6.

66   Tompson, 2007, p. 9.

67   Sutela, 2012, p. 1.

68   Mendras, M., 2012, p. 149.

69   Coase, R., 1937, "The Nature of the Firm", Economica, 4(16), pp. 386–405.

70   Williamson, O., 1985, "The Economic Institutions of Capitalism: Firms, Markets, Relational Contracting" (New York and London: Free Press).

71   Perman, R. & Scouller, J., 1999, "Business Economics" (Oxford University Press), Chapter 4.

72   Prahalad, C. K. & Hamel, G., 1990, "The Core Competence of the Corporation", Harvard Business Review, pp. 79–91.

73   Stalk, G., Evans, P. & Shulman, L., 1992, "Competing on Capabilities: The New Rules of Corporate Strategy", Harvard Business Review, March 1992, 70(2), pp. 57–69.

74   Kay, J., 1995, "Foundations of Corporate Success" (Oxford University Press).

75   Ibid.

76   Peteraf, M., 1993, "The Cornerstones of Competitive Advantage: A Resource-Based View", Strategic Management Journal, Volume 14.

77   Perman, R. & Scouller, J., 1999, "Business Economics" (Oxford University Press), pp. 199–202.

78   Kock, C. J. & Guillen, M. F., 2001, "Strategy and Structure in Developing Countries: Business Groups as an Evolutionary Response to Opportunities for Unrelated Diversification", Industrial and Corporate Change, 10(1), pp. 77–113.
79   Ibid.
80   Ibid., pp. 92–95.
81   Ledeneva, A., 2006, "How Russia Really Works (Cornell University Press).
82   Ibid., p. 2.
83   Ibid., p. 113.
84   Ibid., p. 114.
85   Ibid., p. 132.
86   Ibid.
87   Makino, S. and Delios, A., 1996, "Local Knowledge Transfer and Performance: Implications for Alliance Formation in Asia", Journal of International Business Studies, 27(5), pp. 905–927.
88   Ledeneva, 2006, p. 159.
89   Nielsen, K., Jessop, B. & Hausner, J., 1995, "Institutional Change in Post-Socialism", from Strategic Choice and Path Dependency in Post Socialism, eds. Hausner, J., Jessop, R. & Nielsen, K. (Aldershot, UK: Edward Elgar), pp. 3–41.
90   Ibid.
91   Ledeneva, 2006, p. 181.
92   Black, B., Kraakman, R. & Tarassova, A., 2002, "Russian Privatisation and Corporate Governance: What Went Wrong?" Stanford Law Review, 52, pp. 1731–1801.
93   Sergey Braguinsky, 2007, "The Rise and Fall of Post-Communist Oligarchs: Legitimate and Illegitimate Children of Praetorian Communism" (Washington: World Bank).
94   Mendras, M., 2012, p. 230.
95   Ibid., p. 236.
96   Kononenko and Moshes, 2011, p. 1.
97   Tompson, 2007, p. 6.
98   Goldman, 2010, p. 135.
99   Ibid., p. 203.
100   Mendras, 2012, p. 227.
101   Granovetter, M., 1995, "Coase Revisited: Business Groups in the Modern Economy", *Industrial and Corporate Change*, 4(1), pp. 93–130.
102   Guillen, M. F., 2000, "Business Groups in Emerging Economies: A Resource-Based View", *Academy of Management Journal*, 43(3), pp. 362–380.
103   Ghemawat, P. & Khanna, T., 1998, "The Nature of Diversified Business Groups: A Research Design and Two Case Studies", The Journal of Industrial Economics, Vol. XLVI, March 1998, pp. 35–61.
104   Khanna, T. & Palepu, K., 1997, "Why Focused Strategies May Be Wrong For Emerging Markets", Harvard Business Review, 75, pp. 41–50.
105   Prokop, J. E., 1995, "Industrial Conglomerates, Risk Spreading and the Transition in Russia", Communist Economies and Economic Transformation, 7(1).
106   Starodubrovskaya, I., 1995, "Financial Industrial Groups: Illusions and Reality", Communist Economies and Economic Transformation, 7(1).
107   Guillen, M. F., 2000, "Business Groups in Emerging Economies: A Resource-Based View", Academy of Management Journal, 43(3), p. 368.
108   Lane, D., 1999, "The Political Economy of Russian Oil" (Maryland, USA: Rowman & Littlefield), Chapter 1, pp. 15–47.
109   Boone, P. & Rodionov, D., 2001 (updated 2003), "Rent Seeking in Russia and the CIS", Paper presented to EBRD 10th Anniversary Conference in London, December 2001.

110 Freinkman, L., 1995, "Financial Industrial Groups in Russia: Emergence of Large Diversified Private Companies", Communist Economies and Economic Transformation, 7(1), pp. 51–66.

111 Black, B., Kraakman, R. & Tarassova, A., 2002, "Russian Privatisation and Corporate Governance: What Went Wrong?", William Davidson Institute Working Paper No. 269, Univ. of Michigan Business School.

112 Boone, P. & Rodionov, D., 2001, p. 8.

113 Ibid., p. 10.

114 Boone, P. & Rodionov, D., 2002, "Sustaining Growth: Three Investment Strategies – Turnarounds, ROIC Growth and Yields", Brunswick UBS Warburg research report, Moscow.

115 2005 World Bank Report "From Transition to Development: A Country Economic Memorandum for the Russian Federation", Poverty Reduction and Economic Management Unit, Europe and Central Asia Region, Chapter 4 (Washington: World Bank), pp. 97–108.

116 Freinkman, L., 1995, p. 61.

117 Kock, C. J. & Guillen, M. F., 2001, "Strategy and Structure in Developing Countries: Business Groups as an Evolutionary Response to Opportunities for Unrelated Diversification", Industrial and Corporate Change, 10(1), pp. 77–113.

118 Ledeneva, A., 2006, "How Russia Really Works" (Cornell University Press).

119 Makino, S. & Delios, A., 1996, "Local Knowledge Transfer and Performance: Implications for Alliance Formation in Asia", Journal of International Business Studies, 27(5), pp. 905–927.

120 Ibid.

121 Moran, T. H., 1974, "A Model of the Relations between the Host Country and Foreign Investors: Balance of Power, National Interest and Economic Nationalism", from "Multinational Corporations and the Politics of Dependence" (Princeton: Princeton University Press), p. 155.

122 Smith, D. & Wells, L. T., 1975, "Changing Relationships in the Concessions Process", from "Negotiating Third World Mineral Agreements: Promises as Prologue" (Cambridge, MA: Ballinger), pp. 1–25.

123 Ibid.

124 McKern, B., 1977, "Foreign Investment and Technology Transfer in the Australian Mining Industry", from Germidis, D. (ed.) "Transfer of Technology by Multinational Corporations" (Paris: OECD).

125 Hennart, J.-F. M. A., 1986, "Internalization in Practice: Foreign Direct Investment in Malaysian Tin Mining", Journal of International Business Studies, 17(2), pp. 131–143.

126 Walde, T. W., 1991, "Investment Policies and Investment Promotion in the Mineral Industries", Foreign Investment Law Journal, 6, pp. 94–113.

127 Lecraw, D. J., 1984, "Bargaining Power, Ownership and Profitability of Transnational Corporations in Developing Countries", Journal of International Business Studies, Spring/Summer 1984.

128 Fagre, N. & Wells, L. T., 1982, "Bargaining Power of Multinationals and Host Governments", Journal of International Business Studies, 13(2), pp. 9–23.

129 Killing, P., 1980, "Technology Acquisition: License Agreements or Joint Ventures", Columbia Journal of World Business, pp. 38–46.

130 Schaan, J. L., 1982, "Joint Ventures in Mexico", PhD proposal, Business School, The University of Western Ontario, London, Canada.

131 Beamish, P. & Lane H., 1982, "Joint Venture Performance in Developing Countries", University of Western Ontario, London, Canada.

132 Lecraw, D. J., 1984, p. 40.

133 Cowling, K. & Sugden, R., 1987, "Transnational Monopoly Capitalism" (Brighton: Wheatsheaf).

134 Kogut, B., 1988, "Joint Ventures: Theoretical and Empirical Perspectives", *Strategic Management Journal*, 9, pp. 319–332.

135 Williamson, O. E., 1981, "The Economics of Organisation: The Transaction Cost Approach", *American Journal of Sociology*, 87, pp. 548–577.

136 Vernon, R., 1983, "Organisational and Institutional Responses to International Risk", in Herring, R. (ed.) "Managing International Risk" (New York: Cambridge University Press).

137 Penrose, E., 1959, "The Theory of the Growth of the Firm" (New York: John Wiley and Sons).

138 McKelvey, B., 1983, "Organisational Systematics: Taxonomy, Evolution, Classification" (Berkeley: University of California).

139 Harrigan, K. R. & Newman, W. H., 1990, "Bases of Interorganisation Co-operation: Propensity, Power, Persistence", *Journal of Management Studies*, 27(4), pp. 417–434.

140 Pettigrew, A. M., 1977, "Strategy Formulation as a Political Process", *International Studies of Management and Organization*, 7, pp. 78–87.

141 Fouraker, L. E. & Siegal, S., 1963, "Bargaining Behaviour" (New York: McGraw-Hill).

142 Bacharach, S. & Lawler, E., 1980, "Power and Politics in Organisations" (San Francisco: Jossey-Bass).

143 Pfeffer, J., 1981, "Power in Organisations" (Boston, Mass.: Pitman).

144 Hambrick, D. C., 1981, "Environment, Strategy and Power Within Top Management Teams", *Administrative Science Quarterly*, 26, pp. 253–275.

145 Nierenberg, G., 1968, "The Art of Negotiating; Psychological Strategies for Gaining Advantageous Bargains" (New York: Hawthorn Books).

146 Jemison, D. B., 1981, "Organisational versus Environmental Sources of Influence in Strategic Decision Making", Strategic Management Journal, 2, pp. 77–89.

147 Yan, A. & Gray, B., 1994, "Bargaining Power, Management Control and Performance in US-China Joint Ventures: A Comparative Case Study", Academy of Management Journal, 37(6), pp. 1478–1517.

148 Bacharach, S.B. & Lawler, J.L., 1984, "Bargaining: Power, Tactics and Outcomes" (San Francisco: Jossey-Bass).

149 Fisher, R. & Ury, W., 1981, "Getting to YES: Negotiating Agreement Without Giving In" (New York: Penguin Books).

150 Root, F. R., 1988, "Some Taxonomies of International Co-operative Agreements", in Contractor, F. J. and Lange, P. (eds) "Co-operative Strategies in International Business" (Lexington, MA: Lexington Books), pp. 69–80.

151 Yan, A. & Gray, B., 1994, "Bargaining Power, Management Control and Performance in US-China Joint Ventures: A Comparative Case Study", Academy of Management Journal, 37(6), pp. 1478–1517.

152 Killing, J. P., 1983, "Strategies for Joint Venture Success" (New York: Praeger).

153 Yan, A. & Gray, B., 1994, p. 1511.

154 Inkpen, A. C. & Beamish, P. W., 1997, "Knowledge, Bargaining Power and the Instability of International Joint Ventures", Academy of Management Review, 22(1), pp. 177–202.

155 Ibid.

156 Hamel, G., 1991, "Competition for Competence and Inter-Partner Learning within International Strategic Alliances", Strategic Management Journal, 12, pp. 83–103.

157 Young, C. & Olk, P., 1984, "Why Dissatisfied Members Stay and Satisfied Members Leave: Options Available and Embeddedness Mitigating the Performance Commitment Relationship in Strategic Alliance", Academy of Management Best Practice Papers, pp. 57–61.

158 Bacharach, S. & Lawler, E. J., 1980, "Power and Politics in Organisations" (San Francisco: Jossey-Bass).

159 Hamel, G., 1991, Competition for Competence and Inter-Partner Learning within International Strategic Alliances", Special Issue, Strategic Management Journal, 12, pp. 83–104.

160 Pfeffer, J., 1981, "Power in Organisations" (Boston, Mass.: Pitman).

161 Kogut, B., 1988, "Joint Ventures: Theoretical and Empirical Perspectives", Strategic Management Journal, 9, pp. 319–322.

162 Parkhe, A., 1991, "Interform Diversity, Organisational Learning and Longevity in Global Strategic Alliances", Journal of International Business Studies, 22, pp. 579–602.

163 Pucik, V., 1991, "Technology Transfer in Strategic Alliances. Competitive Collaboration and Organisational Learning", in Agmon, T. and Von Glinow, M. A. (eds) "Technology Transfer in International Business" (New York: Oxford University Press), pp. 121–138.

164 Dodgson, M., 1993, "Learning, Trust and Technological Collaboration", Human Relations, 46, pp. 77–95.

165 Hamel, G., 1991, "Competition for Competence and Inter-Partner Learning within International Strategic Alliances", Special Issue, Strategic Management Journal, 12, pp. 83–104.

166 Inkpen, A.C., 1995, "The Management of International Joint Ventures: An Organisational Learning Perspective" (London: Routledge).

167 Inkpen, A. C. & Crossan, M. M., 1995, "Believing is Seeing: Joint Ventures and Organisation Learning", Journal of Management Studies, 32, pp. 595–618.

168 Simonin, B. L. & Helleloid, D., 1993, "Do Organisations Learn? An Empirical Test of Organisational Learning in International Strategic Alliances", in Moore, D. (ed.) Academy of Management Best Paper Proceedings, pp. 222–226.

169 Hedlund, G., 1994, "A Model of Knowledge Management and the N-Form Corporation", Strategic Management Journal, 15, pp. 73–90.

170 Nelson, R. R. & Winter, S. G., 1982, An Evolutionary Theory of Economic Change" (Cambridge, MA: Harvard University Press).

171 Inkpen & Beamish, 1997, p. 190.

172 Hamel, G., Doz, Y. L. & Prahalad, C. K., 1989, "Collaborate with Your Competitors – and Win", Harvard Business Review, 67 (1), pp. 133–139.

173 AAR press release, March 10th, 2003, Moscow.

174 Vernon, R., 1971, "Sovereignty at Bay" (New York: Basic Books).

175 Moran, T. H., 1974, "A Model of the Relations between the Host Country and Foreign Investors: Balance of Power, National Interest and Economic Nationalism", from "Multinational Corporations and the Politics of Dependence (Princeton: Princeton University Press), pp. 153–172.

176 Smith, D. & Wells, L. T., 1975, "Changing Relationships in the Concessions Process", from "Negotiating Third World Mineral Agreements: Promises as Prologue" (Cambridge, MA: Ballinger), pp. 1–25.

177 Harrigan, K. R. & Newman, W. H., 1990, "Bases of Interorganisation Co-operation: Propensity, Power, Persistence", Journal of Management Studies, 27(4), pp. 417–434.

178 Yan, A. & Gray, B., 1994, "Bargaining Power, Management Control and Performance in US-China Joint Ventures: A Comparative Case Study", Academy of Management Journal, 37(6), pp. 1478–1517.

179 Hamel, G., 1991, Competition for Competence and Inter-Partner Learning within International Strategic Alliances", Special Issue, Strategic Management Journal, 12, pp. 83–104.

180 Inkpen, A. C. & Beamish, P. W., 1997, "Knowledge, Bargaining Power and the Instability of International Joint Ventures", Academy of Management Review, 22(1), pp. 177–202.

181 Ibid.
182 Hedlund, G., 1994, "A Model of Knowledge Management and the N-Form Corporation", Strategic Management Journal, 15, pp. 73–90.
183 Hamel, G., Doz, Y. L. & Prahalad, C. K., 1989, "Collaborate with Your Competitors – and Win", Harvard Business Review, 67(1), pp. 133–139.
184 Sturgeon, T. J., 2002, "Modular Production Networks: A New American Model of Industrial Organisation", Industrial and Corporate Change, 1(3), pp. 451–496.
185 Ibid.
186 Swann, G. M. P., 2006, "Putting Econometrics in its Place: A New Direction in Applied Economics" (Cheltenham, UK: Edward Elgar), p. 160.
187 Silverman, D., 2001, "Interpreting Qualitative Data: Methods for Analysing Talk, Text and Interaction" (London: Sage Publications).
188 Douglas, J. D., 1985, "Creative Interviewing" (Beverly Hills: Sage Publications).
189 Ibid., p. 25.
190 Foddy, W., 1993, "Constructing Questions for Interviews and Questionnaires" (Cambridge, UK: Cambridge University Press).
191 Swann, G. M. P., 2006, "Putting Econometrics in its Place: A New Direction in Applied Economics", Chapter 13 (Cheltenham, UK: Edward Elgar), pp. 100–112.
192 Swann, G. M. P., 2006, "Putting Econometrics in its Place: A New Direction in Applied Economics", Chapter 10 (Cheltenham, UK: Edward Elgar), p. 75.

Chapter 3   Joint Ventures from the 1990s

1 "Bankruptcy in Russia", Dr. Leonard Bierman, Professor, Department of Management Lowry Mays College & Graduate School of Business, Texas A&M University & Dr. Yuri Fedotov, Vice Rector for International Relations, St. Petersburg State University, January 2002, p. 4.
2 Article 17, Order No. 65 of the RF Ministry of Natural Resources allowed a company to transfer a license to a new venture in which it held at least a 50% stake.
3 Modern operations meant the application of new more expensive drilling and production equipment that resulted in much higher oil flow rates and therefore improved project economics.
4 According to the RF Law on Subsoil, license transfer was only allowed if the holder re-organized and the license was re-registered with the re-organized company, which was not the case with TMNG's license transfers.
5 Under Article 17 of the F Ministry of Natural Resources Ordinance No. 65 a license could be re-registered if the new holder was at least 50% owned by the previous one. However, under Article 17 of the RF Law on Subsoil, a license may be re-registered only if the new holder is a reorganized version of the previous one.
6 The use of the Russian bankruptcy law in this fashion is described by Gustafson (2012), pp. 420–422, with reference to the bankruptcy of Sidanco subsidiaries in 1999.
7 Bureniye is the Russian word for drilling.
8 Neft is the Russian word for oil.
9 "Kreesha" – cover or protection.
10 Dow Jones International News, "Sibir Energy: Salym Fields Production to Start", 24 November 2005.
11 Financial Times, 25 September 2013, "Russian Energy: Frozen Assets".
12 Wall Street Journal, 30 November 2010, "Shell, Gazprom to Combine Beyond Russia", London.
13 Guardian, 26 May 2009, "Gazprom Closes In on Sibir Energy Takeover", London.

Chapter 4   The Key Drivers of Foreign Partner Success – A Quantitative Analysis

1 Foddy, W., 1993, "Constructing Questions for Interviews and Questionnaires" (Cambridge, UK: Cambridge University Press).

2 Dijkstra, W. & Van der Zouwen, J., 1977, "Testing Auxiliary Hypotheses Behind The Interview", Annals of Systems Research, 6, pp. 49–63.

3 Brenner, M., 1985, "Survey Interviewing", Chapter 2 in Brenner, M., Brown, J. and Canter, D. (eds) "The Research Interview: Use and Approaches" (New York: Academic Press).

4 The details of the survey and the overview of the respondents can be found in Appendix A.

5 Foddy, W., 1993, "Constructing Questions for Interviews and Questionnaires", Chapter 11 (Cambridge University Press), pp. 153–180.

6 Although there has been significant debate about the style and extent of ranking systems used in questionnaires, with authors varying in their preference for scales ranging from 5 to 13 or more, the system used here was chosen for its simplicity and also because it was recognized that any ranking would ultimately be subjective and open to the potential criticism that the distances between scores (i.e. between 2 and 3, and between 3 and 4) would not necessarily be identical. Therefore non-parametric testing was always going to be required and it was felt, during the pre-testing of the questionnaire, that a more limited ranking would adequately cover the necessary potential responses.

7 Watson, J., 1996, "Foreign Investment in Russia: The Case of the Oil Industry", Europe-Asia Studies, 48(3) (May 1996), pp. 429–455.

8 For example Yan, A. & Gray, B., 1994, "Bargaining Power, Management Control and Performance in US-China Joint Ventures: A Comparative Case Study", Academy of Management Journal, 37(6), pp. 1478–1517.

9 Foddy, W., 1993, "Constructing Questions for Interviews and Questionnaires", Chapter 9 (Cambridge University Press), pp. 112–126.

10 Data from BP Statistical Review, June 2012.

11 James Watson, May 1996, "Foreign Investment in Russia: The Case of the Oil Industry", Europe-Asia Studies, 48(3), pp. 429–455.

12 Thomas Sauer, 1999, "FDI in the Former Soviet Union: New Insights", in David A. Dyker (ed.), Foreign Direct Investment and Technology Transfer in the FSU (Cheltenham, UK: Edward Elgar Publishing).

13 Introduction to Transnational Corporations and the Exploitation of Natural Resources, Edited by Bruce McKern, General Editor John H. Dunning (London: Routledge), 1993.

14 Respondents were permitted to nominate more than one objective for their domestic partner, hence the total of the percentages for each objective adds up to more than 100%.

15 The difference between foreign expertise in international rather than domestic issues is emphasized by a Wilcoxson Signed Rank (WSR) test comparing the responses to various related questions. The test results show that foreign participants regard themselves as bringing significantly more knowledge of export markets (mean score 3.06) than domestic markets (mean 1.97), $Z = -2.981$, $p<0.05$, $r = -0.52$, significantly more knowledge of international formal issues (mean 4.0) than domestic formal issues (mean 2.73), $Z = -3.988$, $p<0.05$, $r = -0.69$, and significantly more knowledge of informal international issues (mean 4.0) than informal domestic issues (mean 2.39), $Z=-A222$, $p<0.05$, $r = -0.73$.

16 The relative Wilcoxson Signed Rank test scores demonstrate that the contrast in scores is significant as all the relevant r scores, reflecting effect size, are above 0.5, indicating a large difference in result. Field (2005) defines effect size as "simply an objective and standardized measure of the magnitude of the observed effect". Pearson's correlation coefficient "r", which is used here, defines a score of 0.1 or less as a small effect (accounting for 1% or less of any variance, a score of 0.3 as a medium effect, accounting for 9% of any variance, and a score of 0.5 or above as a large effect, accounting for 25% of any variance). The fact that all the r scores mentioned here are above 0.5 indicates that the difference between the domestic and foreign partner contributions were large.

17 Field, A., 2005, "Discovering Statistics Using SPSS" (London: Sage Publishing), pp. 630–631 offers justification for Principle Component Analysis as a sound procedure, and is further confirmed by Guadagnoli, E. & Velicer, W., 1988, "Relation of Sample Size to the Stability of Component Patterns", Psychological Bulletin, 103, pp. 265–275. Hair, J. F., Anderson, R. E., Tatham, R. L. & Black, W. C., 1998, "Multivariate Data Analysis" (New York: Prentice Hall International), pp. 100–103, also states that component analysis is appropriate when trying to identify the minimum number of factors for the maximum portion of variance, as I am attempting to do in this analysis, while they also point out that the widely debated complications of common factor analysis, which is another technique for identifying groups or clusters of variables, have contributed to the widespread use of component analysis in preference. Overall, though, "both component analysis and common factor analysis arrive at essentially identical results if the number of variables exceeds 30".

18 The excluded variables were the foreign partner contributions of Export Market Access, Informal and Formal Domestic Knowledge, Brand and Tangible Assets.

19 The six variables produced suitable correlations with a determinant score of 0.075, a Kaiser-Meyer-Olkin (KMO) score of 0.701 and a significant Bartlett's test result. The average communality of the variables was 0.73, and the Measure of Sampling Adequacy (MSA) for each was well above the required 0.5 level. Two factors, which used five of the variables, were then extracted with eigenvalues higher than 1, and the reproduced correlations matrix showed that the level of non-redundant residuals was an acceptable 40%.

20 The reliability of the variables included in both the factors was confirmed by the Cronbach Reliability Analysis, where both new factors registered Alpha scores above 0.8, with no variable altering the result significantly due to its removal. This analysis will be used to confirm the reliability of factors created throughout the chapter.

21 The domestic partner contributions of Formal and Informal International Knowledge, technology and access to capital were excluded from the analysis. The remaining seven contributions were found to show sufficient, but not excessive correlation, with the Correlation Matrix having a determinant score of 0.061 (indicating no problem of multi-collinearity), a KMO score of 0.66 and a significant result from the Bartlett's test. Further, all the variables had MSA scores of 0.5 or higher in the Anti-Image Matrix, and the average communality score was 0.78. Three factors were then identified, which resulted in a non-redundant residuals score of 42% from the reproduced correlation matrix. The reliability of the variables included in these factors was confirmed by the Reliability Analysis, in which the Alpha score was 0.75 and none of the variables was seen to significantly improve the Alpha score by its removal.

22 Hamel, G., Doz, Y. L. & Prahalad, C. K., January–February 1989, "Collaborate with Your Competitors – and Win", *Harvard Business Review*, 67(1), pp. 133–139.

23 The standard deviations for the three types of learning were very close (1.34 for operational learning, 1.27 for management and 1.24 for technical) suggesting that the shape of the overall responses were very similar.

24 A Wilcoxson Signed Rank test showed that all the results with r scores below 0.3 were insignificant, indicating a very small effect according to Cohen's criteria.

25 In all cases the r score is > 0.5, demonstrating (through Cohen's criteria) that the difference effect is large, while the results are all significant to a level < 0.00.

26 A Wilcoxson Signed Rank test was carried out between the scores for foreign partner control over technology development and implementation with those for foreign partner contribution of new technology, control of strategic planning and finance with a management contribution and control of investment finance with a contribution of capital. In all cases the differences between the scores are not large (r < 0.3 using Cohen's criteria) and are not significant, implying that on average foreign partners had most initial control where they had made the greatest contribution.

27 A determinant score of 0.009 for the correlation matrix confirmed that there was no problem of multi-collinearity. The KMO score of 0.696 confirmed the adequacy of the sample, while the Bartlett's Test of Sphericity produced an approximate Chi-Square of 133 (df 28) with $p < 0.001$, confirming an adequate relationship between the variables for factor analysis. The anti-image matrices produced MSA scores above 0.5 for all the variables, and the average and individual communalities were all above 0.7, adequate for a sample of this small size. Three factors were then extracted, explaining more than 80% of the total variance between the variables, and the non-redundant residuals totalled 50% in the reproduced correlations table. The reliability test for the variables included in the final analysis showed a Cronbach's Alpha score of 0.85, and none of the variables increased this score through their removal, confirming the overall reliability of the analysis and the variables included within it.

28 Four of the 13 variables were removed due to low communality scores, after which the determinant score of the correlation matrix for the remaining nine variables was 0.001, while the KMO score was a high 0.75. The Bartlett's Sphericity Test showed a Chi-Square of 191.8 with a $p < 0.001$ (df 36), while the MSA scores in the anti-image matrices were above 0.5 for all the variables, further underlining the viability of factor analysis in this case. The average communality score is 0.82, with all the individual variables having scores over 0.7, and three factors were extracted that explain 81% of the variance between the variables. The Reproduced Correlations matrix showed non-redundant residuals at 44%, an acceptable level, and the oblique rotation then identified the following factors. The reliability of the variables included in the analysis is confirmed by a high Cronbach's Alpha of 0.89, and none of the variables cause any increase in the Alpha by their removal and so the inclusion of all of them is justified.

29 We use non-parametric tests that allow for the comparison of questions with different ranking systems and with ranking systems where the intervals between the scores may be seen as somewhat subjective.

30 The r score in both cases is in the 0.3–0.5 range, indicating only a medium effect according to Cohen's criteria.

31 Nine of the 13 variables had adequate communality scores and the analysis of them allowed the justifiable extraction of two factors. The determinant score for the correlation matrix in this case was $1.3 \wedge 10^{-5}$ while the MKO score was good at 0.78 and the Bartlett's Test of Sphericity was significant. Furthermore the MSA scores in the anti-image matrices were all above 0.5, all the individual communality scores were above 0.7 and the average communality score was 0.83. On this basis two factors were extracted that could explain 83% of the variance between the variables, with non-redundant residuals at an acceptable level of 41%. The reliability test was then carried out on the nine variables used in the final factor analysis, with a high Cronbach's Alpha score of 0.946 confirming the overall reliability of the test. It also confirmed that the Alpha score would not have been improved by the removal of any of the variables, thus justifying their inclusion in the analysis.

32 Confirmed by a Wilcoxson Signed Rank test showing r scores in the range 0.4–0.8, all with significance < 0.05.

33 A Wilcoxson Signed Rank test revealed that all the r scores are below 0.3, indicating that the variance between the variables in each case is small (according to Cohen's criteria), and the significance score of all the comparative tests is greater than 0.1, showing that in essence the success results cannot be differentiated.

34 A WSR test for difference shows an r score of only 0.1 at a significance of 0.5.

35 I have used a non-parametric correlation analysis, choosing the Kendall's tau coefficient as I am using a relatively small data set and a large number of tied ranks. Indeed Howell, D. C., 1997, "Statistical Methods for Psychology" (4th edition) (Belmont, CA: Duxbury), p. 293 suggests that the Kendall's tau is actually a better estimate of the correlation in the population than the Spearman coefficient (the main alternative non-parametric correlation measure), and that more accurate generalisations can be drawn from it.

36 The correlation coefficient between the two is 0.33 at a significance level of 0.01.

37 The correlation between CFPC_FAC_LOC and Foreign partner confidence (CONF_FAC_FPS) produces the statistics Kendall's tau-b = 0.30, N = 32, p < 0.05.

38 The Mann Whitney U test.

39 Field, A., 2005, "Discovering Statistics Using SPSS" (London: Sage Publications), pp. 522–535.

40 The median score for classic JVs was 14.58 compared to a median for the corporate model of 23.44, with a U score of 50.0 and p < 0.02. As a result the test demonstrates that those entities formed using the corporate model experienced significantly higher levels of foreign partner success than those using the classic JV model.

41 Kendall's tau-b = 0.46, N = 23, p < 0.01.

42 Kendall's tau-b = 0.41, N = 23, p < 0.05.

43 Our data is non-parametric, while the data for a standard OLS regression analysis should ideally be parametric. As a result, we have also run logistic and truncated regression models in an attempt to confirm our results.

44 Hair, J. F., Anderson, R. E., Tatham, R. L. & Black, W. C., 1998, "Multivariate Data Analysis" (New York: Prentice Hall International), p. 173.

45 The ANOVA tests confirm the significance of the first three models in that the regression predicted by the independent variables in each explained a significant amount of the variance in the dependent variable. For Model 1: $F(1,29) = 16.628$; $p < 0.01$, for Model 2: $F(2,28) = 14.40$; $p < 0.01$ and for Model 3: $F(3,27) = 16.413$; $p < 0.01$. It can also be seen in each case from the Mean Square calculation that the regression explains significantly more than the Residual. However, it is interesting that the ANOVA analysis also tells us that Model 4, which includes the JV Investment Model dummy variable, is also significantly better than chance at predicting foreign partner success. This would seem to imply that, although the variable JV Investment Model does not make a significant contribution to a Model including the other three variables, nevertheless a model including it is still a significant predictor of foreign partner success, and as such the impact of the JV Investment Model variable as a separate independent variable outside the current multiple regression analysis needs to be considered further.

46 The significance score for the change in the adjusted r2 is < 0.01 in the model with all three predictors included, confirming that it provides the largest significant explanation of the drivers of foreign partner success.

47 The F change is not significant (> 0.7).

48 The analysis of excluded variables confirms that this model is the best overall significant description of the variance in Foreign Partner Success. Furthermore the

Collinearity statistics show tolerance scores for all the predictors well over 0.1, indicating that the data has no problem of collinearity.

49 From the Beta scores in Table A2.2 in Appendix 2.

50 In running the model I included control variables concerning Business Group Link, Production, Type of Investor, and Size of Foreign or Domestic Partner, but none of these dummies made any significant contribution to a regression model.

51 The significance of the Beta score when the JV Investment Model variable is added to a model to describe foreign partner success confirms its explanatory power. With "0" being use of a classic JV model and "1" being use of a corporate model, it is clear that the use of a corporate model has a positive impact on Foreign Partner Success. Further confirmation that the model explains a significant amount of the variance of the dependent variable is shown by the ANOVA analysis which reveals that $F(1,30) = A759; p < 0.05$.

52 The significance of the Betas for both variables (Change in Foreign Partner Control over Local Knowledge issues and Domestic Partner Success) is confirmed, establishing their explanatory power in Model 2. Further confirmation that both models explain a significant amount of the variance of the dependent variable is shown by the ANOVA analysis which reveals that $F(1,21) = 19.841; p < 0.001$, and $F(2,20) = 16.168; p < 0.001$. Further, the Excluded Variables table confirms the significance of "Change in Foreign Partner Control – Local Knowledge" and "Domestic Partner Success" to the regression analysis and confirms the need to exclude "State Influence over Governance Issues" as not significant in this case. It also justifies the use of Model 2 as the best overall significant description of the variance in Foreign Partner Success. Furthermore the Collinearity Statistics show tolerance scores for all the predictors well over 0.1, indicating that the data has no problem of collinearity.

53 See Table A2.6 in Appendix 2.

54 A standard OLS regression model.

55 Our data is non-parametric and an OLS regression model should normally use parametric data.

56 Field, A., 2005, "Discovering Statistics Using SPSS" (London: Sage Publishing), pp. 219–221.

57 We ran the logistic regression analysis using the forced entry method (as argued by Studenmund & Cassidy, 1987). It should also be noted that the analysis only includes the JVs classified as "Other", in other words the classic JV structures rather than the Corporate ventures also identified above, of which there were 24 in total. However, in both calculations one venture has been excluded here due to missing data leaving 23 for analysis. It should also be noted that on a scale of 1–5 we denoted 1 and 2 as failure and 3, 4 and 5 as success.

58 On inclusion of the predictor variables the –2 Log likelihood was changed from 26.433 to 5.633, with the model Chi-Square of 20.80 (measuring the difference) being significant (bl 0.001) and confirming the impact of the predictors on the model. The Hosmer and Lemeshow test was insignificant, confirming the predictive ability of the model, and the classification table revealed that the model could now predict the correct outcome 91% of the time. Finally the impact of each of the predictors was confirmed by the significance of the Wald statistic for each at the < 0.1 level.

59 Dodge, Y., 2003, *The Oxford Dictionary of Statistical Terms* (Oxford University Press) states that truncated regression is appropriate where observations with values in the outcome variable below or above certain thresholds are excluded from the sample. In this case the artificial nature of the ranking process may have caused the exclusion of some scores which respondents might have used if given an unlimited ability to rank variables.

60 Model was created using the STATA programme.
61 The model predicting foreign partner success from the variables of domestic partner success (DP Success) and Change in Foreign Partner Control over Local Knowledge (CFPC Local Knowledge) is statistically significant (chi-squared = 11.88, df = 2, $p < 0.005$). The predictors (DP Success and CFPC Local Knowledge) were both significant, although at different levels. DP Success was significant at the 0.05 level while CFPC Local Knowledge was significant at the 0.1 level.

Chapter 6   Reflections on Partnership at TNK-BP

1 Browne, "Beyond Business", p. 146.
2 Speech by BP CEO Tony Hayward at Renaissance Capital conference in Moscow, July 2007.
3 Gustafson, T., 2012, p. 419.
4 The Kovyktinskoye field is located near Irkutsk in East Siberia.
5 BP Press Release, 17 November 1997, "BP Plans Initial $750 million Investment in Russia".
6 Gustafson, T., 2012, p. 420.
7 Browne, J., 2010, "Beyond Business", p. 140.
8 The Russia Journal, 14 May 2000, "Will $500 million Pump Up TNK?" sourced from http://www.russiajournal.com/node/3167 on 15 May 2013.
9 BP Press Release, 13 December 2001, "Chernogorneft Assets Returned to Sidanco".
10 BP Press Release, 16 April 2002, "BP Increases Its Shareholding in Sidanco".
11 Speech by John Browne, 16 October 2003, "TNK-BP – A Presentation to the Financial Community", London.
12 BP and TNK-BP Presentation to the Financial Community, October 16th and 17th 2003.
13 Savchik, E. & Landes, A., 2006, p. 17.
14 Production data from Interfax Market Survey, "Russia's Oil Sector in 2011", p. 20.
15 Vedomosti and other articles.
16 Gazprom press release, 22 June 2007, "Gazprom, BP and TNK-BP Enter into Agreement on Major Terms of Co-operation", Moscow.
17 Guardian, 28 November 2007, "Gazprom Targets Half of BP's Russian Oil Business", London.
18 Yenikeyeff, S., 2011, p. 11.
19 New York Times, 7 May 2007, "BP Chief Resigns Amid Battle With Tabloid", New York.
20 Gustafson, T., 2012, p. 427.
21 New York Times, 27 August 2010, "Rosneft Deal for German Refineries Could Help BP", New York.
22 BP Press Release, 14 January 2011, "BP and Rosneft Form Global and Arctic Strategic Alliance", London.
23 Moscow News, 2 February 2011, "London Court Blocks BP-Rosneft Deal", Moscow.
24 Reuters, 24 March 2011, "Arbitration Panel Thwarts BP-Rosneft Deal", Moscow.
25 Financial Times, 17 May 2011, "BP Under Fire as Rosneft Deal Collapses", London.
26 Daily Telegraph, 30 August 2011, "Blow for BP as Rosneft and ExxonMobil Sign Arctic Oil Deal", London.
27 Daily Telegraph, 1 June 2012, "BP Plans Shock Sale of TNK-BP stake", London.
28 Guardian, 21 March 2013, "Rosneft Takes Over TNK-BP in $55bn Deal", London.
29 TNK-BP Investor Presentation, May 2012.
30 TNK-BP IFRS Financial Reports for 2003 and 2012.
31 Financial Times, 21 March 2013, "Rosneft and BP Plan Arctic Projects", London.

32 BP Press Release, 21 March 2013, "BP and Rosneft Complete TNK-BP Sale and Purchase Transaction", London.
33 BP already owned a 1% stake in Rosneft, purchased during the company's IPO in 2006.
34 Asian Times, 14 April 2011.
35 Business Week, 4 June 2008.
36 Fortune, 8 November 2011.
37 Namely the inspections by the tax and environmental authorities, the problems with expat visas, and the arrest of a TNK-BP employee.
38 A general presidential mandate was announced to the effect that all government ministers should resign from any positions within state companies. Sechin, as a Deputy Prime Minister with responsibility for Energy, was forced to resign from his position at Rosneft, although a number of other government officials remained in dual roles.

Chapter 7   Conclusions on a Strategy for Foreign Partners

1 Kononenko & Moshes, 2011.
2 Mommsen, 2012.
3 Mendras, 2012.
4 Ibid.
5 Aidis & Estrin, 2006.
6 Washington Post, 3 August 2005, "Chinese Drop Bid to Buy US Oil Firm", Washington.
7 Financial Times, 24 May 2012, "Putin's Power Play", London.
8 Ledeneva, 1998.
9 In particular McKern, B., 1993. "Introduction: Transnational Corporations and the Exploitation of Natural Resources", from McKern, B. (ed.) "Transnational Corporations and the Exploitation of Natural Resources", UN Library on Transnational Corporations (London and New York: Routledge).
10 Hellman, J. S., Jones, G. & Kaufmann, D., 2000, "Seize the State, Seize the Day – State Capture, Corruption and Influence in Transition" (Washington: World Bank Working Paper No. 2444); Kock, C. J. & Guillen, M. F., 2001, "Strategy and Structure in Developing Countries: Business Groups as an Evolutionary Response to Opportunities for Unrelated Diversification", Industrial and Corporate Change, 10(1), pp. 77–113; Djankov, S., Glaeser, E., La Porta, R., Lopez-de-Silanes, F. & Schleifer, A., 2003, "The New Comparative Economics", Journal of Comparative Economics, 31(4), pp. 595–619.
11 Ledeneva, A., 2006, "How Russia Really Works" (Cornell University Press).
12 International Energy Agency, 2002, "Russia Energy Survey, 2002", p. 83.
13 Case study two in Chapter 3, pp. 124–131.
14 See Chapter 1, p. 43.
15 Koplianik, A., July 2003, "PSA Debate Not Over Yet", Petroleum Economist.
16 Cook, Caroline, 1997, "Diamonds & Rust: Exposing Value Amongst the Russian Oils" (Edinburgh: NatWest Securities Research), p. 39.
17 McKern, B., 1977, "Foreign Investment and Technology Transfer in the Australian Mining Industry", from Germidis, D. (ed.) "Transfer of Technology by Multinational Corporations" (Paris: OECD).
18 See Lane, D., 1999, "The Political Economy of Russian Oil" (Rowman and Littlefield), pp. 39–41.
19 See Case study three, Chapter 3, pp. 131–138.
20 Interview with German Khan in "Insight TNK-BP, December 2003", p. 4.

21   Radosevic, S. & Henderson, J., 2004, "Restructuring and Growth of Post-Socialist Enterprises through Alliances: LUKoil and Yukos", Chapter 14 in Radosevic, S. & Sadowski, B. M. (eds), 2004, "International Industrial Networks and Industrial Restructuring in Central and Eastern Europe" (London: Kluwer Academic Publishers).

22   Hamel, G., 1991, "Competition for Competence and Inter-Partner Learning within International Strategic Alliances", Strategic Management Journal, 12, pp. 83–103.

23   Ledeneva, A., 2006, "How Russia Really Works" (Cornell University Press).

24   Ibid., p. 2.

25   See Case study two, Chapter 3, pp. 124–131.

26   In particular we would like to thank Alexander Landia of Lambert Energy Advisory for his help with this section and his initial idea to investigate theories concerning sales techniques.

27   Miller, R. B., Heiman S. E. & Tuleja T., 2004, "The New Strategic Selling" (London: Kogan Page).

28   See Case study three in Chapter 3, pp. 131–138.

29   Ibid.

30   Rosneft press release, 11 June 2013, "Rosneft and ExxonMobil Finalise Arctic Research Centre and Technology Sharing Agreements", Moscow.

31   http://info.worldbank.org/governance/wgi/index.asp sourced on 12 June 2013.

32   http://www.doingbusiness.org/rankings sourced on 12 June 2013.

Appendix 1   Survey Questionnaire for Joint Venture Statistical Analysis

1   State corruption is defined as the provision of unofficial payments, gifts or private benefits to public officials to gain advantages in the drafting of laws, decrees or regulations and other binding government decisions that have a direct impact on the provider's business (The World Bank gives as the example of a powerful oil company bribing legislators to vote for or against PSA legislation).

2   Administrative corruption is defined as the provision of benefits to influence the implementation of the established rules (The World Bank gives the example of a shopkeeper bribing an official to overlook minor infractions of existing regulations or to avoid extra unauthorized checks on his business).

3   This question on corruption is deliberately phrased in line with the World Bank Survey entitled "Anticorruption in Transition 2 – Corruption in Enterprise-State Interactions in Europe and Central Asia 1999–2002" published in 2004.

Bibliography

Chapter 1   The Turbulent History of Foreign Involvement in the Russian Oil and Gas Sector

Alekperov, V. (2011). *Oil of Russia: Past, Present and Future*. Minneapolis: East View Press.

Alexander's Oil & Gas Connections (2002, June 27). BP causes impressive turnaround in Sidanco battle. Vol. 7, Issue 13.

Alfa Group (2001, August 3). *TNK Strikes Deal for Sidanco*. Retrieved from www.alfagroup.org.

Allan, D. (2002). Banks and the loans for shares auctions. In D. Lane, *Russian Banking* (pp. 137–160). Cheltenham: Elgar.

Allen, S. (2001). *Valuations Overstate the Risks*. Moscow: Renaissance Capital.

BP (2009). *BP Statistical Review of World Energy*. London: BP.

Browne, J. (2010). *Beyond Business. The Inside Story: Leadership and Transformation in BP*. London: Weidenfeld and Nicholson.

Centre for Energy Economics, University of Texas (2002). *Soviet Legacy on Russian Petroleum Industry*. Austin: University of Texas.

Cook, C. (1997). *Diamonds and Rust: Exposing Value amongst the Russian Oils*. Edinburgh: NatWest Securities.

EBRD (1999). *Ten Years of Transition*. Brussels: EBRD.

Economides, M. & D'Aleo, D.-M. (2008). *From Soviet to Putin and Back*. Houston: Energy Tribune Publishing.

Economist, The (1995, November 18). *Economist*.

Elf (1998, August 25). *Elf Decides Not to Pursue Its Alliance with Sibneft*. Retrieved from www.total.com

Energy Intelligence Agency (n.d.). www.eia.doe.gov/emeu/jv. Retrieved from www.eia.doe.gov

Energy Intelligence Group (2000). *Almanac of Russian Petroleum*. Moscow: EIG.

Furlow, W. (2001, October). Schlumberger, Yukos creating Moscow-based planning hub. *Offshore Magazine*.

Gaddy, C. & Ickes, B. W. (2002). *Russia's Virtual Economy*. Washington: Brookings Institution Press.

Gazprom (2003). *Annual Report*. Moscow: Gazprom.

Ghiselin, D. (2003, November). Technology and brotherhood at the new frontier. *Hart's E&P*.

Goldman, M. (1980). *The Enigma of Soviet Petroleum*. London: Allen & Unwin.

Goldman, M. I. (2008). *Oilopoly: Putin, Power and the Rise of the New Russia*. Oxford: One World.

Gorst, I. (2007). *LUKOIL: Russia's Largest Oil Company*. Houston, Texas: James Baker III Institute for Public Policy, Rice University.

Gustafson, T. (1989). *Crisis Amid Plenty*. Princeton: Princeton University Press.

Gustafson, T. (1999). *Capitalism Russian Style*. Cambridge: Cambridge University Press.

Gustafson, T. (2012). *Wheel of Fortune: The Battle for Oil and Power in Russia*. Cambridge, Massachusetts: Harvard University Press.

Hanson, P. (2009). The resistible rise of state control in the Russian oil industry. *Eurasian Geography and Economics*, 50(1), 14–27.

Hart's Petroleum Finance Week (2002, July 1). Drilling contractors, service companies are in no hurry to increase rates.

Hellman, J., Jones, G. & Kaufmann, D. (2000, September). Seize the state, seize the day: State capture, corruption and influence in transition. World Bank Policy Research Working Paper No. 2444.

Henderson, J. (2001). *Russian Oil: The Non-OPEC Alternative*. Moscow: Renaissance Capital.

IHS (2005, February 22). Is Russian oil just for Russians? *IHS Global Insight*.

Inozemtsev, V. (2009). The nature and prospects of the Putin regime. *Russian Social Science Review*, 50(1), 40–60.

International Energy Agency (2002). *Russia Energy Survey 2002*. Paris: IEA.

International Herald Tribune (2006). Shell cedes control of Sakhalin 2 to Gazprom. *International Herald Tribune*.

International Trade Reporter (1994, June 29). US-Russia business committee urges changes aimed at Russia's energy sector. *International Trade Reporter*, p. 1033.

Kommersant Daily (1995, April 5). Usloviya kredita banka predlagayut v pyatnitsu. *Kommersant Daily*.

Kononczuk, W. (2012). *Russia's Best Ally*. Warsaw: OSW Studies.

Kostanian, K. (2012). *Russia's Unconventional Future*. Moscow: Merrill Lynch.

Kryukov, V. & Moe, A. (1999). Banks and the financial sector. In D. Lane, *The Political Economy of Russian Oil* (pp. 47–74). Oxford: Rowman & Littlefield.

Landes, A. (2002). *Russian Oil & Gas Yearbook*. Moscow: Renaissance Capital.

Landes, A. (2003a). *Russia Oil & Gas Yearbook*. Moscow: Renaissance Capital.

Landes, A. (2003b). *Transneft: Oil for Pipelines*. Moscow: Renaissance Capital.

Landes, A. (2003c). *Yukos: Enjoying Growth*. Moscow: Renaissance Capital.

Landes, A. (2004). *Russia Oil & Gas Yearbook*. Moscow: Renaissance Capital.

Lane, D. & Seifulmulukov, I. (1999). Structure and ownership. In D. Lane, *The Political Economy of Russian Oil*. Oxford: Rowman & Littlefield.

Locatelli, C. (2006). The Russian oil industry between public and private governance: Obstacles to international oil companies' investment strategies. *Energy Policy*, 34, 1075–1085.

Macalister, T. (2003, February 13). Prime Minister argues case for Blair Petroleum. *Guardian*.

McPherson, C. (1996). Political reforms in the Russian oil sector. *World Bank Finance and Development Report*, 33(2).

Moser, N. (1999). *The Privatisation of the Russian Oil Industry*. M.Phil Dissertation, Oxford.

Moser, N. & Oppenheimer, P. (2001). The oil industry: Structural transformation and corporate governance. In B. Granville & P. Oppenheimer, *Russia's Post-Communist Economy* (pp. 18–40). Oxford: Oxford University Press.

Nash, R. (2002). *Foreign Direct Investment: Ready for Take-Off?* Moscow: Renaissance Capital.

Ostrovsky, A. (2006). Sakhalin 2 fell foul of zealous official. *Financial Times*.

Pirani, S. (2010). *Change in Putin's Russia: Power, Money and People*. London: Pluto Press.

Pleines, H. (1999). Corruption and crime in the Russian oil industry. In D. Lane, *The Political Economy of Russian Oil*. Oxford: Rowman & Littlefield.

Poussenkova, N. (2004). *The Energy Dimension in Russian Global Strategy – From Rags to Riches: Oilmen vs Financiers in the Russian Oil Sector.* Houston: James Baker III Institute for Public Policy, Rice University.

Russia Petroleum Investor (2003). *M&A Opportunities in the Oil & Gas Sector of Russia.* Moscow: RPI.

Sagers, M. (1993). The energy industries of the former USSR: A mid-year survey. *Post Soviet Geography,* pp. 341–418.

Sagers, M. & Nicoud, J. (1996). *Russia's Upstream Oil Industry: Derailed but Not Dead Yet.* Moscow: PlanEcon.

Sakwa, R. (2009). *The Quality of Freedom: Khodorkovsky, Putin and the Yukos Affair.* Oxford: Oxford University Press.

Schneider, E. (2012). The Russian federal security service under Putin. In S. White, *Politics and the Ruling Group in Russia.* Oxford: Palgrave Macmillan.

Shleifer, A. & Treisman, D. (2000). *Without a Map: Political Tactics and Economic Reform in Russia.* Cambridge, Mass.: MIT Press.

Stern, J. (2005). *The Future of Russian Gas and Gazprom.* Oxford: Oxford University Press.

TNK-BP (2003, December). Insight TNK-BP. Moscow.

Tompson, W. (2005). Putin and the oligarchs: A two-sided commitment problem. In A. Pravda, *Leading Russia: Putin in Perspective* (pp. 179–203). Oxford: Oxford University Press.

UBS, B. (2003). *Russian Equity Guide.* Moscow: Brunswick UBS.

Watson, J. (1996). Foreign investment in Russia. *Europe-Asia Studies,* 48(3), 429–455.

Wood Mackenzie Consultants (2002). *The Challenges of Investing in Russia.* Edinburgh: Wood Mackenzie.

Wood Mackenzie Consultants (2009, June). CAT Corporate Database.

World Bank (2002). *BEEPS Survey.* New York: World Bank.

World Bank Staff Appraisal Report, No. 11556-RU (1993). *Russian Federation: Oil Rehabilitation Project.* New York: World Bank.

Yergin, D. (1991). *The Prize.* London: Simon & Schuster.

Chapter 2   A Review of Academic Theory on Joint Ventures, Partnership and the Importance of Local Knowledge

Aidis, R. & Estrin, S. (2006). *Institutions, Networks and Entrepreneurship in Russia: An Exploration.* Bonn: IZA.

Anderson, J. & Van Wincoop, E. (2004). Trade costs. *Journal of Economic Literature,* 118, 1375–1418.

Aslund, A. (2007). *Russia's Capitalist Revolution.* Washington: Peterson Institute for International Economics.

Bacharach, S. & Lawler, E. (1980). *Power and Politics in Organisations.* San Francisco: Jossey-Bass.

Bacharach, S. B. & Lawler, J. L. (1984). *Bargaining Power, Tactics and Outcomes.* San Francisco: Jossey-Bass.

Beamish, P. & Lane, H. (1982). *Joint Venture Performance in Developing Countries.* London, Canada: University of Western Ontario.

Black, B., Kraakman, R. & Tarassova, A. (2002). Russian privatisation and corporate governance: What went wrong? *Stanford Law Review,* 52, 1731–1801.

Boone, P. & Rodionov, D. (2001). Rent seeking in Russia and the CIS. *EBRD 10th Anniversary Conference.* London: EBRD.

Boone, P. & Rodionov, D. (2002). *Sustaining Growth: Three Investment Strategies – Turnarounds, ROIC Growth and Yields.* Moscow: UBS Brunswick.

Braguinsky, S. (2007). *The Rise and Fall of Post-Communist Oligarchs: Legitimate and Illegitimate Children of Praetorian Communism.* Washington: World Bank.

Buckley, P. & Casson, M. C. (1976). A long run theory of the multinational enterprise. In P. Buckley & M. C. Casson (eds) *The Future of the Multinational Enterprise.* London: Macmillan.

Caves, R. E. (1971). International corporations: The industrial economics of foreign investment. *Economica,* 38, 1–27.

Coase, R. (1937). The nature of the firm. *Economica,* 4(16), 386–405.

Cowling, K. & Sugden, R. (1987). *Transnational Monopoly Capitalism.* Brighton: Wheatsheaf.

Devereux, M. P., Griffith, R. & Klemm, A. (2002). Corporate income tax reforms and international tax competition. *Economic Policy,* 17, 451–495.

Djankov, S., Glaeser, E., La Porta, R., Lopez-de-Silanes, F. & Schleifer, A. (2003). The new comparative economics. *Journal of Comparative Economics,* 31(4), 595–619.

Dodgson, M. (1993). Learning, trust and technological collaboration. *Human Relations,* 46, 77–95.

Douglas, J. D. (1985). *Creative Interviewing.* Beverly Hills: Sage Publications.

Dunning, J. H. (2000). The eclectic paradigm as an envelope for economic and business theories of MNE activity. *International Business Review,* 9, 163–190.

Fagre, N. & Wells, L. T. (1982). Bargaining power of multinationals and host governments. *Journal of International Business Studies,* 13(2), 9–23.

Fisher, R. & Ury, W. (1981). *Getting to YES: Negotiating Agreement Without Giving In.* New York: Penguin Books.

Foddy, W. (1993). *Constructing Questions for Interviews and Questionnaires.* Cambridge: Cambridge University Press.

Fouraker, L. E. & Siegal, S. (1963). *Bargaining Behaviour.* New York: McGraw-Hill.

Freinkman, L. (1995). Financial industrial groups in Russia: Emergence of large diversified private companies. *Communist Economies and Economic Transformation,* 7(1), 51–66.

Frobel, F., Heinricks, J. & Kreye, O. (1980). *The New International Division of Labour.* Cambridge and Paris: Cambridge University Press and Editions de la Maison des Sciences de l'Homme.

Ghemawat, P. & Khanna, T. (1998). The nature of diversified business groups: A research design and two case studies. *Journal of Industrial Economics,* XLVI, 35–61.

Gillham, B. (2000). *Case Study Research Methods.* London: Continuum.

Goldman, M. (2010). *Oilopoly: Putin, Power and the Rise of the New Russia.* Harvard: Harvard University Press.

Granovetter, M. (1995). Coase revisited: Business groups in the modern economy. *Industrial and Corporate Change,* 4(1), 93–130.

Grossman, S. & Hart, O. (1986). The costs and benefits of ownership: A theory of vertical and lateral integration. *Journal of Political Economy,* 94, 691–719.

Guillen, M. (2000). Business groups in emerging economies: A resource-based view. *Academy of Management Journal,* 43(3), 362–380.

Hambrick, D. (1981). Environment, strategy and power within top management teams. *Administrative Science Quarterly,* 26, 253–275.

Hamel, G. (1991). Competition for competence and inter-partner learning within international strategic alliances. *Strategic Management Journal,* 12, 83–103.

Hamel, G., Doz, Y. L. & Prahalad, C. K. (1989). Collaborate with your competitors – and win. *Harvard Business Review,* 67(1), 133–139.

Hanson, P. & Teague, E. (2005). Big business and the state in Russia. *Europe-Asia Studies*, pp. 657–680.

Hanson, P. & Teague, E. (2013). *Liberal Insiders and Economic Reform in Russia*. London: Chatham House.

Hanson, S. (2005). *The Uncertain Future of Russia's Weak State Authoritarianism*. Prague: Club de Madrid.

Harrigan, J. & Venables, A. (2004). *Timeliness, Trade and Agglomeration*. London: LSE.

Harrigan, K. R. & Newman, W. H. (1990). Bases of interorganisation co-operation: Propensity, power, persistence. *Journal of Management Studies*, 27(4), 417–434.

Hart, O. (1995). *Firms, Contracts and Financial Structure*. Oxford: Oxford University Press.

Hart, O. & Moore, J. (1990). Property rights and the nature of the firm. *Journal of Political Economy*, 98, 1119–1158.

Hedlund, G. (1994). A model of knowledge management and the N-form corporation. *Strategic Management Journal*, 15, 73–90.

Hellman, J. (1998). Winners take all: The politics of partial reform in postcommunist transitions. *World Politics*, 50, 203–234.

Hellman, J. S., Jones, G. & Kaufmann, D. (2000). *Seize the State, Seize the Day – State Capture, Corruption and Influence in Transition*. Washington: World Bank Working Paper No. 2444.

Hellman, J. S., Jones, G. & Kaufmann, D. (2002). *Far From Home: Do Foreign Investors Import Higher Standards of Governance in Transition Economies*. Washington: World Bank.

Henisz, W. J. & Zelner, B. A. (2003). *Legitimacy, Interest Group Pressures and Change in Emergent Institutions: The Case of Foreign Investors and Host Country Governments*. William Davidson Institute Working Paper No. 589.

Hennart, J.-F. M. A. (1986). Internationalization in practice: Foreign direct investment in Malaysian tin mining. *Journal of International Business Studies*, 17(2), 131–143.

Hines, J. (1999). Lessons from behavioural responses to international taxation. *National Tax Journal*, 52, 305–322.

Hughes, H. (1975). Economic rents, the distribution of gains from mineral exploitation and mineral development policy. *World Development*, 3, 811–825.

Hummels, D. (2000). *Time as a Trade Barrier*. Mimeo: Purdue University.

Hymer, S. (1976). *The International Operations of National Firms: A Study of Foreign Direct Investment*. Cambridge, MA: MIT Press.

Inkpen, A. C. (1995). *The Management of International Joint Ventures: An Organisational Learning Perspective*. London: Routledge.

Inkpen, A. C. & Beamish, P. W. (1997). Knowledge, bargaining power and the instability of international joint ventures. *Academy of Management Review*, 22(1), 177–202.

Inkpen, A. C. & Crossan, M. M. (1995). Believing is seeing: Joint ventures and organisational learning. *Journal of Management Studies*, 32, 595–618.

Inozemetsev, V. (2009). The nature and prospects of the Putin regime. *Russian Social Science Review*, 50(1), 40–60.

Iverson, C. (1935). *International Capital Movements*. London: Frank Cass.

Jack, A. (2004). *Inside Putin's Russia*. London: Granta Books.

Jemison, D. (1981). Organisational versus environmental sources of influence in strategic decision making. *Strategic Management Journal*, 2, 77–89.

Kay, J. (1993). *Foundations of Corporate Success*. Oxford: Oxford University Press.

Keynes, M. J. (1939). Professor Tinbergen's Method. *Economic Journal*, 49, 558–568.

Khanna, T. & Palepu, K. (1997). Why focused strategies may be wrong for emerging markets. *Harvard Business Review*, 75, 41–50.

Killing, J. P. (1983). *Strategies for Joint Venture Success.* New York: Praeger.

Killing, P. (1980). Technology acquisition: License agreements or joint ventures. *Columbia Journal of World Business,* pp. 38–46.

Kindelberger, C. P. (1969). *American Business Abroad.* New Haven CT: Yale University Press.

Kinossian, N. (2012). *Strong Presidency, Weak Institutions. The Problems of Modernisation in the Russian Federation.* Helsinki: University of Tromso.

Knickerbocker, F. T. (1973). *Oligopolistic Reaction and Multinational Enterprise.* Cambridge, MA: Harvard University.

Kock, C. J. & Guillen, M. F. (2001). Strategy and structure in developing countries: Business groups as an evolutionary response to opportunities for unrelated diversification. *Industrial and Corporate Change,* 10(1), 77–113.

Kogut, B. (1988). Joint ventures: Theoretical and empirical perspectives. *Strategic Management Journal,* pp. 319–322.

Kononenko, V. & Moshes, M. (2011). *Russia as a Network State: What Works in Russia When Institutions Do Not?* Houndmills: Palgrave Macmillan.

La Porta, R., Lopez-de-Silanes, F., Schleifer, A. & Vishny, R. W. (2000). Investor protection and corporate governance. *Journal of Financial Economics,* 58, 3–27.

Lane, D. (1999). *The Political Economy of Russian Oil.* Maryland USA: Rowman & Littlefield.

Lecraw, D. J. (1984). Bargaining power, ownership and profitability of transnational corporations in developing countries. *Journal of International Business Studies.*

Ledeneva, A. (2006). *How Russia Really Works.* New York: Cornell University Press.

Ledeneva, A. (2009). From Russia with Blat: Can informal networks help modernise Russia. *Social Research,* 76(1), 257–288.

Luxemburg, R. (1913). *The Accumulation of Capital.* London: Routledge and Kegan Paul.

Makino, S. & Delios, A. (1996). Local knowledge transfer and performance: Implications for alliance formation in Asia. *Journal of International Business Studies,* 27, 905–927.

Markusen, J. (2002). *Multinational Firms and the Theory of International Trade.* Chicago: MIT Press.

McKelvey, B. (1983). *Organisational Systematics: Taxonomy, Evolution, Classification.* Berkeley: University of California.

McKern, B. (1977). Foreign investment and technology transfer in the Australian mining industry. In D. Germidis, *Transfer of Technology by Multinational Corporations.* Paris: OECD.

McKern, B. (1993). *Transnational Corporations and the Exploitation of Natural Resources.* London and New York: Routledge.

Mendras, M. (2012). *Russian Politics: The Paradox of a Weak State.* New York: Columbia University Press.

Mommsen, M. (2012). Russia's political regime: Neo-Soviet authoritarianism and patronal presidentialism. In S. Stewart, M. Klein, A. Schmitz & H.-H. Schroder, *Presidents, Oligarchs and Bureaucrats: Forms of Rule in the Post-Soviet Space* (pp. 63–87). Farnham, UK: Ashgate Publishing.

Moran, T. H. (1974). A model of the relations between the host country and foreign investors: Balance of power, national interest and economic nationalism. In T. H. Moran, *Multinational Corporations and the Politics of Dependence* (pp. 153–172). Princeton: Princeton University Press.

Murray, R. (1972). Underdevelopment, the international firm and international division of labour. In R. Murray, *Society for International Development: Towards and New World Economy* (pp. 160–239). Rotterdam: Rotterdam University Press.

Navaretti, G. B. & Venables, A. J. (2004). *Multinational Firms in the World Economy*. Princeton: Princeton University Press.

Nelson, R. R. & Winter, S. G. (1982). *An Evolutionary Theory of Economic Change*. Cambridge, MA: Harvard University Press.

Nielsen, K., Jessop, B. & Hausner, J. (1995) Institutional change in post-socialism. In J. Hausner, B. Jessop & K. Nielsen, *Strategic Choice and Path Dependency in Post Socialism* (pp. 3–41). Aldershot, UK: Edward Elgar.

Nierenberg, G. (1968). *The Art of Negotiating; Psychological Strategies for Gaining Advantageous Bargains*. New York: Hawthorn Books.

Nurske, R. (1972). Causes and effects of global capital movements. In J. Dunning, *International Investment* (pp. 97–116). Harmondsworth: Penguin.

Parkhe, A. (1991). Interform diversity, organisational learning and longevity in global strategic alliances. *Journal of International Business Studies*, 22, 579–602.

Parkhe, A. (1993). Strategic alliance structuring: A game theoretic and transaction cost examination of interfirm co-operation. *Academy of Management Journal*, 36, 794–829.

Penrose, E. (1959). *The Theory of the Growth of the Firm*. New York: John Wiley and Sons.

Penrose, E. (1968). *The Large International Firm in Developing Countries*. London: Allen & Unwin.

Perman, R. & Scouller, J. (1999). *Business Economics*. Oxford: Oxford University Press.

Peteraf, M. (1993). The cornerstones of competitive advantage: A resource-based view. *Strategic Management Journal*, Vol. 14.

Pettigrew, A. M. (1977). Strategy formulation as a political process. *Internal Studies of Management and Organisation*, 7, 78–87.

Pfeffer, J. (1981). *Power in Organisations*. Boston, Mass: Pitman.

Pirani, S. (2010). *Change in Putin's Russia: Power, Money and People*. London: Pluto Press.

Prahalad, C. K. & Hamel, G. (1990). The core competence of the corporation. *Harvard Business Review*, pp. 79–91.

Prokop, J. E. (1995). Industrial conglomerates; risk spreading and the transition in Russia. *Communist Economies and Economic Transformation*, 7(1).

Pucik, V. (1991). Technology transfer in strategic alliances. Competitive collaboration and organisational learning. In T. Agmon & M. A. Von Glinow (eds) *Technology Transfer in International Business* (pp. 121–138). New York: Oxford University Press.

Reinert, E. (1999). The role of the state in economic growth. *Journal of Economic Studies*, 26(4/5), 268–326.

Root, F. R. (1988). Some taxonomies of international co-operative agreements. In F. J. Contractor & P. Lange (eds) *Co-operative Strategies in International Business* (pp. 69–80). Lexington, MA: Lexington Books.

Sakwa, R. (2010). *The Crisis of Russian Democracy: The Dual State, Factionalism and the Medvedev Succession*. Cambridge: Cambridge University Press.

Salanchik, G. R. (1977). Commitment and the control of organisational behaviour and belief. In B. M. Staw & G. R. Salanchik, *New Directions in Organisational Behaviour* (pp. 1–54). Chicago: St Clair Press.

Schaan, J. (1982). *Joint Ventures in Mexico*. London, Canada: University of Western Ontario.

Schneider, E. (2012). The Russian federal security service under President Putin. In S. White, *Politics and the Ruling Group in Putin's Russia* (pp. 42–62). Basingstoke: Palgrave Macmillan.

Seabright, M. A., Levinthal, D. A. & Fichman, M. (1992). Role of individual attachments in the dissolution of interorganisational relationships. *Academy of Management Journal*, pp. 122–160.

Shevtsova, L. (2001). From Yeltsin to Putin: The evolution of presidential power. In A. Brown & L. Shevtsova, *Gorbachev, Yeltsin and Putin: Political Leadership in Russia's Transition* (pp. 67–111). Washington: Carnegie Endowment for International Peace.

Shevtsova, L. (2003). *Putin's Russia*. Washington: Carnegie Endowment for World Peace.

Silverman, D. (2001). *Interpreting Qualitative Data: Methods for Analysing Talk, Text and Interaction*. London: Sage Publications.

Simonin, B. L. & Helleloid, D. (1993). Do organisations learn? An empirical test of organisational learning in international strategic alliances. In D. Moore, *Academy of Management Best Paper Proceedings* (pp. 222–226). London: Academy of Management.

Slinko, I., Yakovlev, E. & Zhuravskaya, E. (2003). *Institutional Subversion: Evidence from Russian Regions*. William Davidson Institute Working Paper No. 604.

Smarzynska, B. K. & Wei, S.-J. (2000). *Corruption and Composition of Foreign Direct Investment: Firm Level Evidence*. World Bank Working Paper No. 2360.

Smith, D. & Wells, L. T. (1975). Changing relationships in the concessions process. In D. N. Smith & L. T. Wells, *Negotiating Third World Mineral Agreements: Promises as Prologue* (pp. 1–25). Cambridge, MA: Ballinger.

Sonin, K. (2002). *Why the Rich May Favour Poor Protection of Property Rights*. Washington: World Bank Working Paper No. 544.

Sonon, K. (2002). *Why the Rich May Favour Poor Protection of Property Rights*. William Davidson Institute Working Paper No. 544.

Stalk, G., Evans, P. & Shulman, L. (1992). Competing on capabilities: The new rules of corporate strategy. *Harvard Business Review*, 70(2), 57–69.

Starodubrovskaya, I. (1995). Financial industrial groups: Illusions and reality. *Communist Economies and Economic Transformation*, 7(1).

Sturgeon, T. J. (2002). Modular production networks: A new American model of industrial organisation. *Industrial and Corporate Change*, 1(3), 451–496.

Sunkel, O. (1972). Big business and 'dependencia': A Latin American view. *Foreign Affairs*, 50, 517–531.

Sutela, P. (2012). *The Political Economy of Putin's Russia*. Abingdon: Routledge.

Swann, G. M. P. (2006). *Putting Econometrics in its Place: A New Direction in Applied Economics*. Cheltenham: Edward Elgar.

Thomas, A. B. (2004). *Research Skills for Management Studies*. London: Routledge.

Tompson, W. (2007). *Back to the Future: Thoughts on the Political Economy of Increased State Ownership in Russia*. London: Birkbeck, University of London.

Travers, M. (2001). *Qualitative Research Through Case Studies*. London: Sage.

Vernon, R. (1971). *Sovereignty at Bay*. New York: Basic Books.

Vernon, R. (1983). Organisational and institutional responses to international risk. In R. Herring, *Managing International Risk*. New York: Cambridge University Press.

Walde, T. W. (1991). Investment policies and investment promotion in the mineral industries. *Foreign Investment Law Journal*, 6, 94–113.

Williamson, O. (1981). The economics of organisation; the transaction cost approach. *American Journal of Sociology*, 87, 548–577.

Williamson, O. (1985). *The Economic Institutions of Capitalism: Firms, Markets, Relational Contracting*. New York & London: Free Press.

World Bank (2005). *From Transition to Development: A Country Economic Memorandum for the Russian Federation*. Washington: World Bank.

Yan, A. & Gray, B. (1994). Bargaining power, management control and performance in US-China joint ventures: A comparative case study. *Academy of Management Journal*, 37(6), 1478–1517.

Yin, R. K. (1994). *Case Study Research: Design and Methods*. Thousand Oaks, US: Sage.

Young, C. & Olk, P. (1984). Why dissatisfied members stay and satisfied members leave: Options available and embeddedness mitigating the performance commitment relationship in strategic alliance. *Academy of Management Best Practice Papers*, pp. 57–61.

Chapter 4   The Key Drivers of Foreign Partner Success – A Quantitative Analysis

BP (June 2012). *BP Statistical Review 2006*. London: BP.
Brenner, M. (1985). Survey interviewing. In M. Brenner, J. Brown & D. Canter (eds) *The Research Interview: Use and Approaches* (Chapter 2). New York: Academic Press.
Dijkstra, W. & Van der Zouwen, J. (1977). Testing auxiliary hypotheses behind the interview. *Annals of Systems Research*, 6, 49–63.
Dodge, Y. (2003). *The Oxford Dictionary of Statistical Terms*. Oxford: Oxford University Press.
Field, A. (2005). *Discovering Statistics Using SPSS*. London: Sage Publishing.
Foddy, W. (1993). *Constructing Questions for Interviews and Questionnaires*. Cambridge: Cambridge University Press.
Guadagnoli, E. & Velicer, W. (1988). Relation of sample size to the stability of component patterns. *Psychological Bulletin*, 103, 265–275.
Hair, J. F., Anderson, R. E., Tatham, R. L. & Black, W. C. (1998). *Multivariate Data Analysis*. New York: Prentice Hall.
Howell, D. C. (1997). *Statistical Methods for Psychology*. Belmont, CA: Duxbury.
Sauer, T. (1999). FDI in the former Soviet Union: New insights. In D. Dyker (ed.) *Foreign Direct Investment and Technology Transfer in the FSU*. Cheltenham: Edward Elgar.
Studenmund, A. H. & Cassidy, H. J. (1987). *Using Econometrics: A Practical Guide*. Boston, MA: Little, Brown.
UCLA (2007, November 3). www.ats.ucla.edu/stat/sas/notes2/. Retrieved March 12, 2010, from www.ats.ucla.edu

Chapter 6   Reflections on Partnership at TNK-BP

Browne, J. (2010). *Beyond Business: The Inside Story: Leadership and Transformation in BP*. London: Weidenfeld and Nicholson.
Savchik, E. & Landes, A. (2006). *TNK-BP Holding: Beyond Short-term Decline*. Moscow: Renaissance Capital.

Chapter 7   Conclusions on a Strategy for Foreign Partners

Aidis, R. & Estrin, S. (2006). *Institutions, Networks and Entrepreneurship in Russia: An Exploration*. Bonn: IZA.
Hamel, G. (1991). Competition for competence and inter-partner learning within international strategic alliances. *Strategic Management Journal*, 12, 83–103.
Hellman, J. S., Jones, G. & Kaufmann, D. (2000). *Seize the State, Seize the Day – State Capture, Corruption and Influence in Transition*. Washington: World Bank Working Paper No. 2444.
Kononenko, V. & Moshes, M. (2011). *Russia as a Network State: What Works in Russia When Institutions Do Not?* Houndmills: Palgrave Macmillan.
Koplianik (2003, July). PSA debate not over yet. *Petroleum Economist*.

Lane, D. (1999). *The Political Economy of Russian Oil*. Maryland USA: Rowman & Littlefield.

Ledeneva, A. V. (1998). *Russia's Economy of Favors:* Blat, *Networking and Informal Exchange*. Cambridge Russian, Soviet and Post-Soviet Studies. Cambridge University Press.

Ledeneva, A. (2006). *How Russia Really Works*. New York: Cornell University Press.

McKern, B. (1977). Foreign investment and technology transfer in the Australian mining industry. In D. Germidis, *Transfer of Technology by Multinational Corporations*. Paris: OECD.

Mendras, M. (2012). *Russian Politics: The Paradox of a Weak State*. New York: Columbia University Press.

Miller, R. B., Heiman, S. E. & Tuleia, T. (2004). *The New Strategic Selling*. London: Kogan Page.

Mommsen, M. (2012). Russia's political regime: Neo-Soviet authoritarianism and patronal presidentialism. In S. Stewart, M. Klein, A. Schmitz & H.-H. Schroder, *Presidents, Oligarchs and Bureaucrats: Forms of Rule in the Post-Soviet Space* (pp. 63–87). Farnham, UK: Ashgate Publishing.

Radosevic, S. & Henderson, J. (2004). Restructuring and growth of post-socialist enterprises through alliances: LUKOIL and Yukos. In S. Radosevic & B. M. Sadowski (eds) *International Industrial Networks and Industrial Restructuring in Central and Eastern Europe* (Chapter 14). London: Kluwer Academic Publishers.

Yan, A. & Gray, B. (1994). Bargaining power, management control and performance in US-China joint ventures: A comparative case study. *Academy of Management Journal*, pp. 1478–1517.

Index

Printed and bound by CPI Group (UK) Ltd, Croydon, CR0 4YY